The Politics of Egypt

SEVEN DAY LOAN

This book is to be returned on
or before the date stamped below

UNIVERSITY OF PLYMOUTH

PLYMOUTH LIBRARY

Tel: (01752) 232323
This book is subject to recall if required by another reader
Books may be renewed by phone
CHARGES WILL BE MADE FOR OVERDUE BOOKS

The Politics of Egypt

State–Society Relationship

Ninette S. Fahmy

RoutledgeCurzon
Taylor & Francis Group

First Published in 2002
by RoutledgeCurzon
11 New Fetter Lane, London EC4P 4EE

Simultaneously published in the USA and Canada
by RoutledgeCurzon
29 West 35th Street, New York, NY 10001

RoutledgeCurzon is an imprint of the Taylor & Francis Group

© 2002 Ninette S. Fahmy

Typeset in Janson by LaserScript Ltd, Mitcham, Surrey
Printed and bound in Great Britain by
MPG Books Ltd, Bodmin

British Library Cataloguing in Publication Data
A catalogue record of this book is available from the British Library

Library of Congress Cataloguing in Publication Data
A catalogue record for this book has been requested

ISBN 0–7007–1610–6

Contents

1 *fake democracy* v

List of Tables

List of Figures

Acknowledgements

I wish to acknowledge my thanks to many people for the completion of this work. First and foremost to Michael Rush not only for the supervision and the valuable comments he gave me on my doctoral thesis, but also for reading and re-reading all the papers I presented in conferences and the one that I managed to get published. He has been extremely patient and generous with his time and my gratitude to him is beyond any expression. Jeffrey Stanyer has always been supportive and has always been there to provide guidance. His help and support is equally appreciable. The late Peter Butler was always sympathetic and never hesitated to offer his succour when needed. Raymond Hinnebusch was kind enough to comment on parts of this book presented as papers in conferences and was always encouraging. I also owe my thanks to the Department of Politics at the University of Exeter for financially supporting most of the conferences I went to, and for providing me with the opportunity to expose and test my ideas against a wider audience. I would also like to thank Mrs Carol Bebawy who edited most of this book.

Special thanks to Adel who works in al-Menia Governorate, for escorting me during the interviews I conducted in Tihna al Gabal. Adel has dedicated a lot of his time and effort throughout the seven months I resided in the village. In an environment which is highly suspicious of outsiders, let alone a Coptic woman, he helped build the trust with the peasants which facilitated my fieldwork. Many people in Tihna have provided me with inside information, but prefer to remain anonymous, to them all I am thankful.

Finally I would like to thank my mother. Not only has she financially and morally supported me during the period of my study, but also being a professor of political geography herself has always held arguments with me on Egyptian politics and, although at times we did not agree, her comments were extremely beneficial.

Introduction

The relationship between state and society in Egypt has long been a controversial issue. The prevailing literature tends either to overestimate the strength of the Egyptian state or overestimate that of society. This books explores the nature of the Egyptian state and how it shapes society. Through the analysis of the various societal forces this study will show how society reacts towards the state and how this reaction in turn shapes the state's capabilities to penetrate society and change it.

A most influential study in developing the principal hypothesis set forward in this book is that of Robert Putnam in his book *Making Democracy Work*. Putnam's analysis was based on Italian society, seeking to explain why regions in northern Italy were developed and enjoyed a strong economy, whereas the southern regions are economically backward. Contrary to what Joel Migdal and other scholars of political development argue, when they claim that more and stronger groups mean weak government i.e. a strong society and a weak state, Putnam's study of northern Italy revealed that: "Strong society, strong economy; strong society, strong state."[1] Putnam, however, argues that societies – with their historical, social, traditional and cultural values – shape states and that this was the main reason why democracy works in north Italy where there is a civic society, while it failed to mature in the south. He thus comments,

> On the demand side, citizens in civic communities expect better government and (in part through their own efforts), they get it. They demand more effective public service, and they are prepared to act collectively to achieve their shared goals. Their counterparts in less civic regions more commonly assume the role of alienated and cynical supplicants. On the supply side, the performance of representative government is facilitated by the social infrastructure of civic communities and by the democratic values of both officials and citizens.[2]

Inverting Putnam's hypothesis, to: *strong state, strong society; strong society, strong economy*, and taking his findings as guidelines, the book analyses Egyptian society in order to explore the nature of the interactive relationship between state and society in Egypt, and the effect such interaction has on growth and development.

To achieve this two approaches are adopted in this book. The first is a broader analytical framework, analysing major societal forces in the Egyptian society, and assessing their relative weakness/strength. The analysis thus covers political parties, which play a fairly significant role in Egyptian politics. Four syndicates: the Lawyers', Journalists', Engineers' and Doctors' Syndicates were thoroughly reviewed and their role as interest groups examined. These syndicates have been chosen as case studies due to their political nature on one hand, and the confrontation they instigated with the state on the other. Examples from other syndicates are also provided as deemed essential to the discussion. Labour organisations, business associations (both indigenous and joint ventures) and agricultural co-operatives are also included in the analysis. To carry out this analysis both primary data from official reports, media coverage and, in some cases, interviews, as well as secondary sources found in earlier literature are used. Religious institutions and private voluntary ones are excluded from this study. The former is excluded because of the sensitivity of religion in a country like Egypt and the latter because of the specificity and apolitical nature of their activities.

The second approach is narrower in perspective, concentrating on peasant society and exploring the dynamic interaction between it and the state. Peasant society was chosen as a focus for the fieldwork because of the controversy and in most instances the conflicting views found in the literature on their interaction with the state. Since the village is a smaller community than the madina and markaz, a factor, which facilitates personal interaction and familiarity with the peasants and their problems, Tihna al-Gabal, a typical village in upper Egypt, is chosen as a case study. Tihna al-Gabal is chosen because of prior connections established there. The case study is based on fieldwork, which included a seven-month residency in the village. The information gathered draws on a sample of random interviews both, structured and unstructured, carried out with government officials in the village, as well as with ordinary peasants. Two general models of the state-society relationship and a third describing this relationship within the Egyptian context are developed which challenge current prevailing views. The possibilities for change are also explored and a model is suggested for the initiation of change in the Egyptian case.

The book is divided into ten chapters. Chapter one presents a literature review of the different theories, which deal with the state and society and with theories of development, change and underdevelopment. It pinpoints where such theories are relevant to a country like Egypt and where they are flawed, as the setting for major hypothesis presented in this book. Chapter Two describes the historical background of peasant society and the historical development of the Egyptian state. Chapter Three analyses the contemporary legal and constitutional system and assesses the performance of the legislative, executive, and the judicial branches. It also discusses the evolution of the multi-party system, with particular emphasis on the government ruling party. Chapter Four summarises the main laws that govern political parties, discusses the main opposition parties in Egypt and assesses their performance. Chapters Five and Six provide a detailed analysis of the various interests groups. Chapter Five concentrates on professional syndicates and assesses recent developments that have been taking place within them. Chapter Six discusses labour unions and business associations. Chapter Seven provides a detailed analysis for the evolution of the local administrative system and a summary of the various governing laws. Chapter Eight discusses the agricultural policies that have been initiated from Nasser to Mubarak, their effects on Egyptian peasants, how they react towards these policies and the effect of this reaction on the state's developmental programmes. Chapter Nine presents the case study of Tihna al-Gabal. Chapter Ten summarises the findings of the book and concludes by suggesting three models offering alternative explanation of interaction between the state and society in Egypt, and a fourth model explaining how change can be initiated in the Egyptian case.

CHAPTER ONE

Theories of State and Society

1. Introduction

The central question of the relationship between society and the state is the need for the state and, therefore, the extent of its role. Dealing with such a question, two sets of competing values have to be weighed: those promoting security, material well being, social order, risk-sharing, sociability and culture; versus those values enhancing individual equality, freedom, justice and self-esteem. Such an issue would no doubt lead to a discussion of the preference for one set of values over the other. If the first set of values were chosen, then the conclusion would be that there is a need for a stronger role of the state. If, however, choice were geared towards the second set of values, then common sense would dictate that there is a need for a lesser role of the state. Although both sets of values are competing (collectivism versus individualism), yet both are still considered components of political development, the latter could accordingly be defined as either an increase or as a decrease in the role of the state. Solving the dilemma necessitates exploring the different political theories that have dealt with the state both in an ontological and epistemological sense.[1]

2. Pluralism and the State

Pluralism evolved among political philosophers as a challenge to state monism whose famous advocate was Hobbes. Hobbes argued in *Leviathan* the necessity of vesting the government with absolute power "to avoid an anarchic 'war of all against all'".[2] Targeting Hobbes, the English philosopher, John Locke, responded in his *Second Treatise of Civil Government*, that the state should be based upon consent and that the ruling authorities should be limited in their power. The same idea prevailed in Montesquieu's *The Spirit of the Law*, where he denounced absolute monarchies and the doctrine of sovereignty and advocated instead the separation of political power between the legislature, executive and judiciary. James Madison's contribution stems from his advocacy of institutional checks, both vertical in terms of the separation of powers among the legislature, executive and judiciary and horizontal division of sovereignty through federalism and provisions for the exercise of vetos, which he deemed necessary for preventing any government from acting despotically.

Alexis De Tocqueville in his study of the American political system, argued that freedom in a democracy required 'intermediate associations' between the state and the citizenry. Hence local government and strong group organisations could act as a medium for citizens' political education and the development of a public spirit. It helped individuals to go beyond their self-interest and develop themselves as citizens.[3] Analytical pluralism, however, can be traced back to Arthur Bentley, the founding father of group theory. According to Bentley, what is real is what is measurable, and it is only the observable that is measurable. It follows then that human activity, which is measurable, constantly produces an ever-changing configuration of power, privilege and welfare. In other words, human activity leads to the formation of groups. No wonder then that he conceived the idea of the state as being fictional or not real. It is only an apparent phenomena that is always in flux. He had thus stated that,

> All phenomena of government are phenomena of groups pressing one another, forming one another and pushing out new groups and group representatives (the organs or agencies of government) to mediate the adjustments. It is only as we isolate these group activities, determine their representative values and get the whole process stated in terms of them, that we approach to a satisfactory knowledge of government.[4]

Thus at the core of Bentley's theory the state is just another group which tends to mediate or balance conflict among the various groups which exist in society. The process of continuous change is, however, an important concept in Bentley's theory since it has important implications for the sustainability and adjustability of the system. It is this 'state of flux' that determines the legitimacy of the system rather than the allocation of political values by the state among the different groups. Accordingly, democracy is the only political system that would allow such continuous change to take place.[5] The idea that society is composed of conflicting interest groups, with each group interest leading to the appearance of a countervailing interest group, became the core of analytical pluralism. Thus Bentley's theory turned out to be a major inspiration to all group theorists who tended to borrow from and add to it.

Truman, for example, one of Bentley's disciples, acknowledged the existence of unorganised latent interests which, needed no organisation, simply because the state accounted for them. He argued that:

> these notions of fair play are represented largely by unorganised or potential groups, the generality of their acceptance is such that their claims do not require organised expression except when these notions are flagrantly violated or when they are in process of alteration. In a sense one may think of the principal government leaders – legislative, executive and

judicial – as the leaders of these unorganised groups. Part of the official's task is the regular representations of these potential groups in the action of government.[6]

Bentley and Truman were criticised by various scholars from different angles. Kress and Greenstone, among contemporary political scientists, pointed to the inherent contradiction between Bentley's social flux and the methodological requirement of social sciences for fixed unchanging objects as a unit of analysis. To solve the dilemma, Greenstone tried to introduce the concept of class,[7] but, as Binder commented, "the addition of another concept or an intervening variable in the eclectic spirit of normal science, cannot reconcile fundamental conceptual and ideological differences".[8] Baskin attacked Bentley's discussion of the group as a concrete structure that exists in the physical sense rather than as an analytic unit, which reflects an intersection of activities.[9]

Olson criticised Bentley and Truman when he argued that

It follows that the analytical pluralist, the 'group theorist', have built their theory around an inconsistency. They have assumed that, if a group had some reason or incentive to organise to further its interest, the rational individuals in that group would also have a reason or an incentive to support an organisation working in their mutual interest. But this is logically fallacious, at least for large, latent groups with economic interests.[10]

On the one hand, Olson criticised Bentley for ignoring individual interests and for assuming that these naturally coincide with group or organisational interests.[11] Of course, this is not always the case since individual interests has sometimes been in conflict and may defeat organisational goals.[12] On the other hand, Olson attacked the assumption that large groups would behave in the same manner as small ones. He distinguished types of groups, the small, which he labelled privileged, intermediate groups, and large or latent groups. Such a distinction represents, however, a challenge to the pluralistic notion that states that demands of one pressure group would be counterbalanced by the demands of other groups, since

relatively small groups will frequently be able voluntarily to organise and act in support of their common interests, and since large groups normally will not be able to do so, the outcome of the political struggle among the various groups in society will not be symmetrical.[13]

Another point raised by Olson as a counter-argument to group theorism is the fact that there are many groups in society which despite their needs, are not recognised.[14] Olson's line of argument, however, seems more logical and provides more relevance to the analysis of the various societal groups that exist in a developing country, like Egypt, which does not by any means conform to the pluralistic vision. For, if all groups in society were accounted for, riots and radical movements would not have been founded in the Middle East.

3

Lowi had also attacked the analytical pluralist theorists on the ground that, through their conception of the state as another interest group, they were eliminating both the concept of legitimacy and that of administration. This was dictated by the urge to transform rather than replace capitalist ideology, which is the prevalent feature of pluralistic societies.[15] In Lowi's view this had led to the degeneration of public philosophy.[16] He argued that:

> Destruction of the principle of separate government, the coerciveness of government, the legitimacy of government, the administrative importance of government, was necessary if capitalist ideology was to be transformed rather than replaced. The fusion of capitalism and pluralism was a success, destruction of the principle of separate government was its secret.[17]

Several group theorists have sought to modify Bentley's theory and to counteract some of the criticism raised against it. Among such theorists was Robert Dahl whose attempt to discover who governed in an American city represented both a change from and yet still a continuity of group theory.

The fact that Dahl attempted to describe the city government of New Haven in the 1950s as an independently acting entity and identifying the state with individual political leaders, in other words, individualising the state was a departure from conventional analytical pluralism. However, he continued to describe New Haven in the 1950s as a micro-corporate state.[18] In his analysis of the various groups that existed in New Haven, he acknowledged that business groups, owing to the abundance of their resources, are among the most privileged ones with respect to their influence on policy making,[19]

> No one influence resource dominates all the other in all or even in most key decisions. With some exceptions, an influence resource is effective in some issue areas or in some specific decisions but not in all.[20]

Thus although some groups may have access to economic resources, which they utilise to influence policy making, other groups have different resources which can equally be successful in influencing policy making.

The same idea was emphasised by Finer when he argued that:

> The comparative strength of rich associations is an argument, which does not impress me, partly because there are such effective ways for poor associations to influence public policy and partly because the capacity of publicity to mould political attitudes is so highly problematical.[21]

Dahl attempted to expose the dilemma of pluralistic democracy. No democracy can exist without some form of plurality, i.e. the existence of autonomous or quasi-autonomous organisations, yet plurality in itself can impose certain limitations on democracy. Hence pluralist democracy embodies within it several factors that can be self-defeating.[22] Thus:

4

yet as with individuals so with organisations, independence or autonomy (I use the terms interchangeably) creates an opportunity to do harm. Organisations may use the opportunity to increase or perpetuate injustice rather than reduce it, to foster the narrow egoism of their members at the expense of concerns for a broader public good, and even to weaken or destroy democracy itself.[23]

Stabilising political inequalities, deforming civic consciousness, distorting the public agenda and alienating final control are therefore among the vices of pluralistic democracy.[24]

Lindblom is another pluralist writer who made a similar attempt to highlight the paradox inherent in pluralistic democracy. In his essay, 'The Market as Prison', Lindblom argued that business enterprises influence policy and policy reform by virtue of the 'punishment' that they are capable of inflicting on society. This 'punishment' takes the form of investment reduction that triggers a series of negative consequences to the various sectors in the economy including government officials themselves.[25] He comments,

> That result is why the market might be characterised as a prison. For a broad category of political economic affairs, it imprisons policy making, and imprisons our attempts to improve our institutions. It greatly cripples our attempts to improve the social world because it affects us with sluggish economic performance and unemployment simply because we begin to debate or undertake reform.[26]

Again, where such reform is to be applied despite the disapproval of businessmen, it has to be accompanied by new benefits to the business community. In this case, "policy is imprisoned not in the sense that it cannot break out of its confinement but in the sense that to release it we must pay ransom".[27] Thus Lindblom acknowledges the advantageous position which businessmen have over other interest groups in society, including government officials. Though, implicitly stated, he argued that business elites are thus in a superior position which enables them to influence state and society by virtue of their resources and by the means of 'punishment' through which they could inflict political and economic harm. Lindblom's theme tends thus to damage one of the important characteristics of pluralism, viz. the balance of interest groups in society, and, although different from the Marxist perception of the dominance of the bourgeoisie over the proletariat, it does not part completely from it.

So far a brief review of pluralism theory with its various critiques has been presented. What remains here is to present the liberal theory of development.

Pluralism and the Theory of Development

Group theorists were mainly pre-occupied with the analysis of group behaviour and the nature of the interactive process which occurs between them. Development, however, is connected with change and the means through which such change is introduced. What triggers change thus represents the core question for system analysis theorists.

Talcott Parson's theory of action and his social system theory had been very influential in this area. Parson's theory differs from the other theories of behaviour in that it takes into account the values, norms and motivation which control behaviour. Control of behaviour is explained in terms of a relationship between organic energy, personality, society and culture.[28] The core of Parson's theory is thus cultural pragmatism, where cultural beliefs and values affect individual choices of means and ends, and the latter determine how culture will adapt to new social conditions.

David Easton is also one of the earlier scholars to apply system analysis to political systems. Easton suggests that:

> the behaviour of every political system is to some degree imposed upon it by the kind of system it is, that is, by its own structure and internal needs. But its behaviour also reflects the strains occasioned by the specific setting within which the system operates.[29]

Accordingly, there are certain inputs into the system from the environment or the political system itself which are processed and conversed into outputs. These outputs may in turn change the environment and thus affect the total political system.[30]

Modernisation Theory and Change

From an economic point of view, Rostow identified five stages through which societies undergo change or as Rostow calls it 'growth' in their economic as well as their socio political environment. These stages are the traditional, the transitional, the take-off, the drive to maturity and the age of high consumption. In the transitional stage the pre-conditions for change start to accumulate, paving the road for the actual change which takes place in the take-off stage. The drive to maturity is the stage where change is sustained while no setbacks occurs leading to the age of high consumption. According to Rostow, the transitional stage may result either from indigenous forces (within society) as occurred in Britain or exogenous forces as in India. The drive to maturity stage may take as long as sixty years before the following stage to be reached.[31] Rostow's analysis relied highly on developed industrialised countries, and some developing countries like India and Turkey that represented the exception rather than the norm. Change and the ability of societies to sustain this change to move forward is at the core of his theory of modernisation.

6

Karl Deutch associated change with social mobilisation. He argued that any form of social mobilisation, away from what is traditional toward what is new and more advanced, will be accompanied by a series of changes which will ensue as a result,[32] and,

> Thus what can be treated for a short time span as a consequence of the modernisation process, appears over a longer period as one of its continuing aspects and as a significant cause in the well-known pattern of feedback or circular causation.[33]

Eisenstadt considers the forms and level of social mobilisation identified by Deutsch as necessary conditions of modernisation, but he argued that they are not sufficient conditions for its continuation.[34] Following Rostow he equates modernisation with the ability of the system not only to change or grow but also to sustain such change or growth. He comments that,

> The central problem of political modernisation can be seen as the ability of any system to adapt itself to these changing demands, to absorb them in terms of policy-making and to ensure its own continuity in the face of continuous new demands and new forms of political organisations. In other words, political modernisation creates in its wake problems of sustained political growth which become its central concern.[35]

Samuel Huntington differentiates between modernisation and political development. According to him political development is defined as "the institutionalisation of political organisations and procedures."[36] Only when such institutionalisation occurs, those political organisations become strong and capable of achieving political development. Without strong political institutions, modernisation with its various components: increases in education, urbanisation, mobilisation and participation, and economic growth, leads not to political development but rather to political decay, since the result might be "a revolution of rising frustrations."[37] This over-emphasis on the strength of political organisations led Huntington to describe public interest as "whatever strengthens governmental institutions" and to define it as "the interest of public institutions."[38] Huntington seems here to confuse the cause and effect. For without modernisation ie: the attainment of an adequate level of education, awareness, mobilisation and participation, it becomes increasingly difficult to build strong political organisations which are in turn needed for the implementation of developmental policies and the achievement of economic growth. Again Huntington's explanation suggests that modernisation and development can occur under all types of regimes be it totalitarian, authoritarian, or democratic, a thesis which is challenged in this work.

To sum up, the liberal theory of development is based on two theoretical components, the Bentelyan theory of motion or change and the Parsonian system theory and cultural pragmatism.[39] It assumes that political development, modernisation and democracy would occur in the long run, as long as change (increases in education, urbanisation, media exposure . . . etc.) is introduced in some parts of the system. Such change would normally be accompanied by a series of changes that would affect the various units or parts of the system leading at the end to its transformation.

Important changes have taken place in the Middle East since the fifties: more than half the Middle Eastern population now live in urban areas, more than half the adult males in most of the Middle Eastern countries are literate, the ratio of university students to total population in several large Middle Eastern countries, among which is Egypt, is similar to ratios prevailing in Europe, and their middle classes have been extensively expanding.[40] Yet, it has not resulted in modernisation. For example, the increase in the level of education in Egypt since the fifties has not triggered change neither in the economic nor in the political sphere. This would no doubt question the relevance of the liberal theory of development to a developing country like Egypt.

In western societies, where modernisation or change has been long established, it is easy to distinguish general requirements, the existence of which become crucial for triggering change and for the latter's infiltration throughout the entire system. States need to be strong enough to initiate policies, which trigger change. At the same time, societies should also be strong for that change to be sustained. When this occurs, and as a result of continuous sustained change, economic development occurs which in turn enhances and strengthens state power. Finally a state of equilibrium is reached between state and society.

3. Marxist and neo-Marxist Theories of the State

Hegel

Since Marx's theory of the state was far from being complete and coherent, but was based mainly on his critiques of Hegel, it seems logical then to start with a presentation of Hegel's theory on state and civil society.

Hegel's first conception about the state is extracted from his lecture course on Natural Law and the Science of the State from the winter term of 1818–19. It was then that the "Ethical State" appeared in Hegel's writing as the last stage of development in a series of rational social orders or ethical communities. The other two stages being the family and civil society.[41] He commented that:

> The ethical idea, is that in which [individuals] are immersed as ideal along with their natural feeling, and [also] the aims of personal singularity and particularity which tear them away from their unity and absorb them in themselves, and [in which they] only produce it as moments of this one mind, have it as their end and depend on it, is the state.[42]

Thus, as members of families and civil society, individuals, who at the same time are part of the state, have got private interests, which do not necessarily conform with the state community. But these private ends link them with the ends of the state, whose main task is to co-ordinate the various social interests. It is thus crucial that individuals realise the convergence of their private interests and that of the community.

It is only then that they would work for the preservation of the state community.[43] Thus, for Hegel the state represents the public or universal interest, which becomes the privilege of a single class, viz: the bureaucrats. These are the 'official' or 'universal' class, which is equivalent to Rousseau's *volenté générale* as opposed to *la volenté de tous*.[44] Accordingly the right (Recht) of the state is the highest law for the individual. However, in this first edition of State/Society theory, Hegel acknowledged citizens' rights of self-determination, both in the private as well as the political sphere, without which freedom cannot be real. Thus in as much as citizens have certain duties towards the state, they also have rights of political participation.[45]

Itling had summarised Hegel's earlier stand in the following statement:

> The unity of the state is thus, according to his conception, only guaranteed where the organs of the state are not independent of the particular interests of citizens, but act in public and with the consent of the citizens, and, conversely, where the citizens are not confined to the pursuit of private interests but can at the same time also act in accordance with the interests of the general community and with an eye to universal aims. If these conditions are met, then Hegel can indeed say of the citizens of a modern state that they too 'only produce it as "moments" of this one mind'. His republicanism, centred on antiquity, is thus clearly articulated into a conception of modern free and democratic legal state.[46]

However, Hegel had in fact faced a conflict between the democratic theory of the state and the restoration doctrine of the monarchic principle. This he opted to resolve in his revised version of the *Philosophy of Right* in 1820 by depriving the individual of his rights while maintaining all his duties towards the state. He thus eliminated the participation aspect of individuals, which he had earlier emphasised, in the political sphere.[47]

Despite such political accommodation with the Prussian State, Hegel's originality lies in the distinction or separation he made between state and civil society, a distinction which later on Antonio Gramsci captured and elaborated in his theorisation about the state/society relationship. As mentioned earlier, Marx's theory on the state was mainly derived from his critiques of Hegel, and it is within the boundaries of such criticism that an analysis of Marx and Engels' state theory would be presented.

Marx

To begin with, Marx repudiated Hegel's conception of the development of the state as a result of the development of human mind and consciousness and from the collectivity of men's will. He had thus criticised Hegel's notion of the eternity of the state, which transcends society and represents its collective will in an idealised form. Instead Marx had placed the state in a historical context and argued that it developed from the relations of production.[48]

In doing so, Marx had inverted the Hegelian concept of state/society relationship. Criticising Hegel, he commented,

> Hegel is not to be blamed because he describes the essence of the modern state as it is, but rather because he presents What Is as the essence of the state. Whether the rational is real [actual, existent] is manifested precisely in the contradiction of the irrational reality which everywhere is the opposite of what is predicates, and predicates the opposite of what it is.[49]

This translated into Marx's political thoughts would mean that it is not the state that shapes society as Hegel theorised but it is rather society, which shapes the state.[50] Marx, however, did not have a single view of the state but had developed several approaches as was reflected in his and Engels' writings. For example, in an earlier work and while still influenced by Hegel and the prevalent conditions in Germany in the early 1840s, he agreed with Hegel's definition of the state as representing communal interest. However, since it is only the democratic state that reflects such interests as the communal interest, the Prussian state was 'no state at all'.[51]

Although Marx agreed with Hegel on the separation made between state and civil society as two distinct spheres in modern society, he disapproved of Hegel's notion that such a separation could be resolved through the rule of a universal and neutral bureaucracy or through the election of a legislative body to govern for the common good. Instead he viewed the state bureaucracy as another interest group, which manipulated state power for the pursuance of both corporate and individual goals.[52]

The third approach, which Marx had adopted towards the state follows automatically and logically from his *critique* of the Hegelian development of the state. As has been mentioned earlier, Marx argued that the state had developed from the relations of production. This was emphasised by Engels:

> The state is a product of society at a certain stage of development, it is the admission that this society has become entangled in an insoluble contradiction with itself, that it has split into irreconcilable antagonisms which it is powerless to dispel. But in order that these antagonisms and classes with conflicting economic interests might not consume themselves and society in fruitless struggle, it became necessary to have a power seemingly standing above society that would alleviate the conflict and keep

it within the bounds of 'order', and this power, arisen out of society, but placing itself above it, and alienating itself more and more from it, is the state.[53]

If, according to Marx, the state emerged as a result of the relations of production, it therefore represents the political expression of the class structure inherent in the modes of production.

Again, since the capitalist society is a class society dominated by the bourgeoisie, it follows then that the state is the expression of the bourgeoisie's political will.[54] Thus in *The German Ideology* Marx and Engels say that the "state is the form in which the individuals of a ruling class assert their common interests" and in the *Communist Manifesto* they noted that "the executive of the modern state is but a committee for managing the common affairs of the bourgeoisie".[55] However, such an instrumental approach to the state as a class-bound institution encounters various problems. This approach does not account for the different forms of the state and does not justify Marx's solution for smashing the state in order to create the classless society, instead of simply its seizure by the proletariat.[56]

Miliband had discussed some of the problems, which are encountered in such an approach. According to him, Marx's statement, 'the common affairs of the whole bourgeoisie' acknowledges implicitly that, although the bourgeoisie are represented as a totality, this totality is made of different and hence competing and conflicting interests, a fact which would hamper the state's action as an instrument of bourgeois control. Miliband also referred to the phrase "common affairs" as implying the existence of a particular rather than a general interest. In such a case the state would act as a mediator between the various bourgeois interests and would assume a major role in its performance as an arbiter. For this to occur, however, the state has to have a certain degree of independence or autonomy from the ruling class.[57] Miliband had thus summarised his point of view when he mentioned that,

> In so far as that class is not monolithic, and it never is, it cannot act as a principal to an agent, and 'it' cannot simply use the state as 'its' instrument.[58]

Some Marxist scholars who adopt such an approach to the state defend their argument on the basis that the personnel of the state system tend to belong to the same classes that dominate civil society and hence use the state as an instrument for promoting and protecting their class interest. Donhoff, for example, argued that even when people who are recruited in the state apparatus do not belong to the bourgeoisie class through social origin, they tend to be affiliated with it by virtue of their education and connections and thus acquire the behaviour typical of that class.[59]

Miliband, on the other hand, provides several examples to counter the previous discussion by showing clearly that there were some instances where no such class correlation exists within the capitalist state. Ranging from a state dominated by landed aristocracy to one, which was led by people recruited even from the lower classes, Miliband undermines the previous thesis. Moreover, he set out to show that the bourgeois-led state tends in time of crisis and social unrest to pursue policies, which are against capitalist interests.[60]

A third argument raised by those who advocate the instrumental approach is related to the economic resources which the bourgeoisie own and their success in influencing policy through pressure politics.

Although Miliband acknowledges the strength of the economic resources which the bourgeoisie class has at its disposal, he rightfully differentiates between the latter fact, which could provide this class with a leeway for manoeuvring as a pressure group and their usage of the state as an instrument which serves their interests.[61] He thus commented that:

> Capitalist enterprise is undoubtedly the strongest 'pressure group' in capitalist society, and it is indeed able to command the attention of the state. But this is not the same as saying that the state is the 'instrument' of the capitalist class, and the pressure which business is able to apply upon the state is not in itself sufficient to explain the latter's action and policies. There are complexities in the decision-making process which the notion of business as pressure group is too rough and unwieldy to explain. There may well be cases where that pressure is decisive. But there are others where it is not. Too great an emphasis upon this aspect of the matter leaves too much out of account.[62]

Miliband's criticism of the instrumentalist approach to the state leads to the last approach which Marx and Engels adopted towards the state viz. its autonomy.

As has been mentioned earlier, Marx while still under the Hegelian influence spoke about an autonomous bureaucratic state which served its own private interests. Later on Marx wrote about the autonomy of the state under two sets of conditions. The first is the normal condition and here he follows, to a certain extent, his early notion of the bureaucratic state, acknowledging the autonomy of such a state but subordinating it to the bourgeois society and bourgeois production.[63] In other words, the relative autonomy of the state within this context means that "it simply consists in the degree of freedom which the state (normally meaning in this context the executive power) has in determining how best to serve what those who hold power conceive to be the 'national interest' of the interest of the ruling class".[64] The second is the abnormal or exceptional situation. Using as an example the Bonapartist state, Marx explained that there were exceptional periods in history when no class has enough power to rule through the state, in which case the state itself rules. This would happen as when Bonaparte took power after all social classes showed their incapacity to rule and have exhausted themselves in the attempt of trying. In this case the Bonapartist state would take the initiative to modernise the economy. As this occurred both the bourgeoisie and the proletariat would regain strength now under favourable economic circumstances due to the successful state development policy, and the state would fall again under the dominance of the bourgeoisie class. In other words, the case where the state has complete autonomy is short-lived.[65]

To sum up, Marx adopted numerous approaches towards the state, but he never really parted from the base-superstructure model, which inspired his class-theory of the state. Just as politics is reduced to economics, the state is accordingly reduced to the political will of the economic class. Marx's reductionist approach and the base-superstructure as a model for analysing state/society relationship in Egypt is rejected. Rather this work is based and borrowing Marx's term, on the 'inversion of the Marx inversion' that is: reinstating Hegel. Hence as a starting point, the main hypothesis of this work is that the state, more precisely the Egyptian State, shapes the society.

Gramsci

Gramsci's novelty lies in his rejection of economism and the reductionist approach inherent in the orthodox Marxism, of the various levels of super-structure to the position of "appearance" or "phenomenon", which in turn had developed an evolutionary determinist conception of history governed by objective laws whose revealability falls beyond human intervention.[66] Not only did economism fail to provide a valid explanation for some of Gramsci's contemporary social and political events, such as the role of Catholicism or the rise of fascism, but it had also failed in providing, apart from a limitation to the alteration of the economic structure, a comprehensive vision of the socialist future.[67] Hence Gramsci's attempt is to restore the role of ideas, consciousness and human subjectivity within the Marxist theory.[68] This was manifested in his definition of the state and civil society and in his concept of hegemony. The concept of civil society will be taken as a starting point of analysis here "because – precisely in the individuation of the nature of civil society and of its placement in the system – Gramsci's theory introduces a profound innovation with respect to the whole Marxist tradition".[69] It is important to stress here that Gramsci's civil society reflects a Hegelian heritage and not a Marxist one. This fact is manifested in the nature of civil society as conceived by Hegel, Marx and Gramsci.

As with Hegel, civil society represents the predomination of 'dissoluteness, misery and physical and ethical corruption', hence the need to be regulated and dominated by a superior order, the state. Hegel's concept of civil society, though more restricted, is at the same time a wider concept than that used by Marx and Engels. It is restricted in the sense that Hegel's trichotomic system pictures civil society as an intermediate stage between family and the state, which does not include pre-state institutions. It is, however, a wider concept because for Hegel civil society encompasses not only the economic sphere and class formation, but also the administration of justice and the organisation of the police and of corporations. Marx's civil society on the other hand, included the whole of pre-state social life as a moment in the development of economic relations. As mentioned before, according to Marx the state, which is the political order, is subordinate, whereas civil society which is the realm of economic relations is the determining element.[70]

Gramsci's conception of civil society – its placement within the system, as well as his view on the state – is best reflected in his Prison Notebooks:

> What we can do, for the moment, is to fix two major superstructural 'levels', the one that can be called 'civil society' that is the ensemble of organisms commonly called 'private', and that of 'political society', or 'the state'. These two levels correspond on the one hand to the function of 'hegemony' which the dominant group exercise throughout society and on the other hand to that of 'direct domination' or command exercised through the state and 'juridical' government.[71]

This passage reflects Gramsci's definition of civil society where he equates it with the various institutions which mould ideas and thinking in general.[72]

Gramsci, in contrast to Marx, places civil society within the superstructure level and by doing so he "transformed the problem of relating state and civil society into the problem of clarifying the relationship internal to the superstructure".[73] Gramsci's definition of civil society stems from the traditional distinction, so prevalent in the Italian political thought, between force and consent, hence Gramsi's distinction between 'domination or coercion' on the one hand, and 'intellectual and moral leadership' on the other. The latter form is what he labelled hegemony. Thus social control would include both.[74] This distinction was also reflected in his various definitions of the state. Thus he defined the state as:

> State = Political Society + Civil Society, that is hegemony armoured by coercion.

> State in the integral sense: dictatorship + hegemony.

> [The State is] the entire complex of political and theoretical activity by which the ruling classes not only justify and maintain their domination but also succeed in obtaining the active consent of the governed.[75]

Thus, whereas the moment of force is reflected in the coercive apparatus of the state, hegemony is institutionalised through a complex ideological apparatus which is imposed on the entire social structure.

It is in the sphere of civil society that so-called private organisations, such as the mass media and political parties, and in the activities of the intellectuals which is shaped by the ideology of the state itself, rather than being manipulated, that ideologies are elaborated and the masses are educated in such a way that would ensure the continuity of the hegemony of the dominant class.[76]

Gramsci's concept of the ruling hegemony, which is maintained through the diffusion of the dominant ideology throughout the various institutions of the civil society fails to account for the problem of the lack of legitimacy that is facing most Arab regimes, not least Egypt in contemporary times. It is the absence of this ability to achieve hegemonic control on behalf of the Egyptian state, which necessitates its use of coercive measures.

Despite the distinction between state and society, Gramsci sometimes speaks about the political society as "the state proper". This is mainly derived from his second definition for the concept "hegemony" which is an overcoming of the "economic-corporative".[77] Since this is the case, Gramsci's definition of the state would not be inconsistent, for as Adamson commented:

> To the extent that Gramsci was thinking of hegemony as a suppression of the economic-corporative, he was thinking of an isolated civil society, and of the state as an object to be gained by a rising class, he could thus slip easily into referring to political society as 'the state proper'. To the extent, however, that he was thinking of hegemony in contrast to domination, he had in mind how existing bourgeois state actually function, viz. as linkage of political society.[78]

According to Gramsci, revolution would take place when the proletariat developed its own hegemony in order to undermine the prevailing hegemony of the present ruling class. Although he acknowledged that a revolution could take place at the economic-corporative level he emphasised the fact that for a revolution to be complete and to bring into power a coherent class, it should take place not only at the political but also at the socio-cultural level.[79] Again, here Gramsci's revolutionary strategies are debateable.

First of all Gramsci argued that proletarian revolutions do not necessarily take place in countries where capitalism is most advanced, but where there is a weakness in the fabric of the capitalist system making it prone to an attack by the working class. Put another way, Gramsci stated implicitly that it is a particular type of weak state that provides the type of conditions for revolutionary trends to occur.[80] In order to substantiate his argument, Gramsci compared western democracies to Tsarist Russia. He argued that the complex institutions that developed in the capitalist systems of Europe and North America emphasised the role of hegemony, which acquired decisive weight in securing class domination. In contrast, the weakness of the institutions of the civil society in Tsarist Russia, combined with a weakness in the hegemony of the ruling elites and the presence of a weak repressive state had allowed the violent destruction of state power.[81]

The aim of this work is to prove otherwise. It is based on the assumption that first revolutions are likely to occur in systems with strong states rather than with those of weak states. Second, that when the institutions of civil society are strong and independent from the state apparatus, their strength represents a limitation on the hegemonic ideology and prevents its permeation throughout the entire society. Accordingly, these institutions would develop alternative ideologies challenging the hegemonic one and hence will result in the circulation or change in the ruling elite.

On the other hand, where the institutions of civil society are weak, they are usually under the complete or partial control of the state. In such a case, they fail to produce alternative ideologies to challenge the existing hegemonic one. This would secure the continuing dominance of the ruling group.

Poulantzas

A most influential Marxist political theorist, Nicos Poulantzas developed a body of work on the capitalist state, social classes and socialist strategy. Although considered by most contemporary theorists as a structuralist, mainly influenced by Althusser, Jessop considers Poulantzas as a neo-Gramscian, asserting that Gramsci's effect on his thoughts was far more influential.[82]

However, Poulantzas' work, especially that concerning the capitalist state, shows a major change between his earlier writings in *Political Power and Social Classes* (1968) and his later work *State, Power and Socialism* (1978). For, in spite of his attempts to remove the residue of structuralism that strongly marked his earlier work, his views on the capitalist state in his later work still owe a great deal to French structuralists, especially Althusser in his rejection of economism, his commitment to the concept of relative autonomy and his belief that history could not be understood in terms of a linear form of development (historicism).[83]

Binder, on the other hand finds in Poulantzas' definition of social class traces of both the Benteleyian and Parsonian influence.[84] In *Political Power and Social Classes* Poulantzas argued that the state is part of class relations in production:

> agents of production actually appear as 'individuals' only in those superstructural relations which are juridical relations, and not on relations of production in the strict sense, that the labour contract and the formal ownership of the means of production depend. The fact that this appearance of the 'individual' at the level of juridical reality is due to the separation of the direct producer from his means of production does not mean that this separation engenders 'individual-agents of production' within those same relations of production.[85]

He had thus stated that the separation of the direct producer from his means of production led to his socialisation into a capitalist bourgeois ideology and to a concentration of capital.[86]

It is at the juridico-political superstructure of the state that "individuation" of the agents of production occur. Hence economic agents experience capitalist relations as relations of competition between isolated individuals and/or fragmented groups.[87] This 'effect of isolation' ". . . produces the following effect on economic class struggle: the effect of concealing from these agents in a particular way the fact that their relations are class relations".[88] This 'isolation effect' permeates all spheres of economic relations as well as classes belonging to other modes of production, and is extended to the field of political class struggle.[89] However, this isolation by the state of workers and capitalists into individuals is coupled with a "unifying effect", where the capitalist state appears as the political unity of an economic struggle and hence is projected as representing the "general interest" of competing groups. It becomes in this sense the national-popular class state.[90] This unifying role of the capitalist state as a factor of cohesion and unity is nevertheless conditioned by the need to reproduce class domination, hence Poulantzas' argument that the capitalist state has two complementary yet contradictory functions.

On the one hand, it must prevent the formation of any political organisation that may end the economic isolation of the dominated classes, and, on the other hand, it must work continuously on the dominant classes to cancel their economic isolation, to unify their factions under the leadership of a single power block and to secure the hegemony of the power block over the dominated classes by projecting their political interest as that of the people nation.[91] In the course of achieving these functions, the capitalist state, because of its autonomy,

> can allow the satisfaction of the economic interests of certain dominated classes, even to the extent of occasionally limiting the economic power of the dominant classes, restraining, when necessary, their capacity to realise their short-term economic interests but on the one condition, which has become possible in the case of capitalist states, that their political power and the state apparatus remain intact.[92]

Thus the capitalist state offers certain short-term concessions to the dominated classes in order to secure the long-term political domination of the dominant class in what Poulantzas called an "unstable equilibrium of compromise".

In order to explain how the state accomplishes this function, Poulantzas had to resort to Gramsci's concept of hegemony and Althusser's ideological state apparatuses. According to Poulantzas' interpretation of Gramsci, hegemony represents for the latter, a world view that is imposed on a social formation and can be achieved through ideological domination before taking over political power.

Poulantzas, however, contradicted this theme and being at his most Althussurian, argued that ideology is incorporated within a certain structure from which it cannot be separated. Hence ideology cannot be separated from the dominance of a given class.[93] Thus,

> the correspondence between the dominant ideology and the politically dominant classes is not due (any more than the specific internal coherence of the ideology is) to some kind of historico genetic relation. It is due to the fact that the ideological (i.e. a given ideology) is constituted as regional instance within the unity of the structure, and this structure has the domination of a given class as its effect in the field of the class struggle.[94]

Ideology is thus part of the class struggle. Beside the values and norms of the dominant class, the dominant ideology may represent other classes' values and norms. At the same time, the dominant ideology may not be congruent with the ideology of the dominant class, but the fact that a particular class is dominant in the class struggle make the dominant ideology serve the interest of the dominant class in the political region, i.e. the state.

As Poulantzas commented,

> The political role of the dominant bourgeois ideology, dominated by the juridico-political region, is to attempt to impose upon the ensemble of society a 'way of life' through which the state can be experienced as representing society's 'general interest', and as the guardian of the universal vis-à-vis 'private individuals'. . . . One of the particular characteristics of dominant bourgeois ideology is, in fact, that it conceals class exploitation in a specific manner, to the extent that all trace of class domination is systematically absent from its language.[95]

In other words, the dominant ideology legitimises the existence and functioning of a class state. Thus the hegemonic class or faction is in charge of the state. However, what seems ambiguous in Poulantzas' formulation is his citation, for example, of the social democratic governments in France, where the faction in charge of the state may be neither hegemonic nor part of the power block.[96] In this case there seems to be a shift between the role of this class and its party representation:

> In this case the characteristic dislocation between this class and its party representation is generally found: its party plays the role of 'clerk' with a hegemonic class or faction or even for another class or faction in the power bloc. The same holds true for the class in charge of the state.[97]

However, there seems to be a contradiction here between this formulation and his earlier hypothesis of the incarnation of ideology with class structure: if his earlier assumption is followed, and in the case where a faction is in charge of the state without being at the same time hegemonic or part of the power block, then this faction would have an ideology that should be functioning parallel to that of the hegemonic class. Also the shift in role between the faction that is controlling the state and its party is not justifiable, nor is it logical that the party would function as a 'clerk' for a certain faction of the power bloc.

The Late Poulantzas

Poulantzas, in his later work *State, Power and Socialism*, embarked on expanding many of the earlier concepts which he had promoted in *Political Power and Social Classes*. In developing the concept of the ideological apparatuses and by raising the question of whether the state equals repression plus ideology he went beyond both Gramsci and Althusser in two respects.

The first was when he denounced the rigid classification of the various state apparatuses as either being ideological or repressive. Such a demarcation can be

18

only applied at a purely descriptive level. In practice, however, there tends to be an interchangeability of roles between the two categories:[98]

> But this distinction is itself highly debatable. Depending on the form of State and regime and on the phase of reproduction of capitalism, a number of apparatuses can slide from one sphere to the other and assume new functions either as additions to, or in exchange for, old ones.[99]

Accordingly the army in a military dictatorship acts as an ideological apparatus. Likewise the courts, prison and the police have an ideological role, besides being repressive apparatuses. The school, which is an ideological organisation, can act at certain times in a repressive manner.[100] Thus ideology and repression are not practically separable. Based on this theorisation, Poulantzas repudiated Gramsci's concept that an expansion of the state's ideological apparatus for maintaining and extending dominant class power is accompanied by a contraction in its usage of violence and repression. Instead, Poulantzas argued that the capitalist state does not detach law from violence nor replace mechanism of manipulation-persuasion, i.e. ideology-repression,[101] quite the opposite,

> State-monopolised physical violence permanently underlies the techniques of power and mechanisms of consent: it is inscribed in the web of disciplinary and ideological devices; and even when not directly exercised, it shapes the materiality of the social body upon which domination is brought to bear.[102]

The second aspect is that of Poulantzas' rejection of the negative notion of the state's role. Thus

> The restrictive character of its analysis of the state's role is no way changed by locating the ideological function in material practices. For according to this conception, the economic is an instant capable of self-reproduction and self-regulation, in which the state serves merely to lay down the negative rules of the economic 'game', Political power can only frame the economy, it cannot enter into it through its own positivity, since its reason for existence is to prevent through repression and ideology, any unsettling encroachment into the economy.[103]

In contrast, Poulantzas argued in *State, Power and Socialism*, that the state's role far exceeds the simple dual function of repression-ideology. He viewed the state as actively engaged in forming and preserving the relations of production and the social divisions of labour, in arranging hegemonic class unity within the power bloc, and in managing the material bases of consent among the popular masses.[104] He therefore argues, "In short, the State also acts in a positive fashion, creating, transforming and making reality."[105]

In his later work Poulantzas went beyond his first formulation about the relationship between the state and political struggle. Initially in *Political Power and Social Class*, he discussed the main function of the state in terms of organising the power bloc while at the same time disorganising or isolating the dominated classes.

In *State, Power and Socialism* Poulantzas pictured the state as a strategic field where the various factions of the dominant classes are pursuing different strategies and hence it provides the ground for the political manoeuvring of the hegemonic faction. It is within such an embodiment of the political struggle that the state is capable of organising the power block. On the other hand, the state is continuously involved in disorganising the masses in order to prevent their unification against the state. At the same time, it works to link the petit bourgeoisie to the power block in order to guarantee their support for the dominant classes and thus to block their alliances with the proletariat.

Whereas the different factions within the power block pursue different strategies with regard to the masses, the interests of the dominated classes are also represented within the state. Hence whereas the dominant classes have "centres of power" within the states, the dominated classes have "centres of resistance" which are utilised to oppose the power of the dominant classes without threatening the latter's long term interests.

Poulantzas also discussed the role of the state personnel whose internal divisions stem from their affiliation to different class factions but which are overcome and hence unified through the dominant ideology. However, through their idolatry of the estate and their protection for their economic-corporate interests, they maintain the continuity of the state apparatus during the transition to democratic socialism.[106]

Poulantzas' formulation of the autonomous state and the dual nature of his hegemonic ideology have been criticised earlier and hence there is no need for repetition here. It is worth emphasising thought that the effect of Bentley became more obvious in his last theorisation on the state as it appeared in *State, Power and Socialism* where the state became a "battlefield" or a "Strategic terrain", in which the different competing fractions, whether dominant or dominated, try to pursue their own interests, either by forming centres of powers or of resistance dependent on their class affiliation. Poulantzas is also greatly influenced by Hegel. Just as Marx inverted Hegel's structure-superstructure model, Poulantzas had transferred Hegel's notion of competition among groups within the society to the state.

Considering the Egyptian case and believing that each case has its own specificity, this thesis reinstates Hegel and contradicts Poulantzas' formulation of the state as a battlefield or a strategic terrain. Rather it is within the confinement of the society that the competition between the various interests groups as well as within the same group, takes place. The state is hence autonomous, shapes the society but in doing so, it imposes certain limitations on its autonomy and capabilities.

4. Theories of the State in Third World Countries

The Asiatic Mode of Production

Theories of the state in third world countries were triggered by Marx's and Engels' writtings on the Asiatic Mode of Production and colonialism, and hence these two topics should be the starting point for discussing the various theories which attempted to trace the phenomenon of development and underdevelopment, and tackle the problems of the latter in developing countries.

Marx's interest in studying Asian societies is dated from 1853 when he was driven by the parliamentary debates about the renewal of the East India Company's charter to study the company's history as well as the Indian social conditions. The Asiatic Mode of Production had thus started to evolve in Marx's writing in a series of journalistic articles as he worked as the regular London correspondent of the *New York Daily Tribune*.[107] According to Marx, the precolonial Indian society possessed three main characteristics, which rendered it stagnant and resistant to change from within. These were the despotic nature of the state which was necessitated by the requirement to manage large-scale irrigation for cultivation purposes by a centralised power, the absence of private property and the existence of isolated, self sufficient village communities. It was, however, the last two factors in Marx's view rather than the despotic state that were more pertinent to the static nature of the Indian society.[108] Since Asiatic societies lack the internal contradictions that lead to its destruction from within either by reproducing it on an extended scale i.e.: the introduction of capitalism or by failing to cause such reproduction on the old scale, the solution according to Marx lies in an external force which should perform the dual function of destruction (of the old system)/regeneration (of the new capitalist system) via colonialism. In the case of India it was British rule which had performed this historically positive and revolutionary role.[109] In an article titled "The Future Results of the British Rule in India" written in July 1853, Marx commented

> England has to fulfil a double mission in India: one destructive, the other regenerating – the annihilation of the old Asiatic society and the laying of the material foundations of Western society in Asia.[110]

Marx views on colonialism in Ireland, which was expressed in 1864, bear a different image than that expressed on India in the 1850's. In Ireland, Marx and Engels viewed British rule as playing one-sided, destructive role. They had thus described it as a 'crime', a record of 'oppression' and 'destructive'. Whereas the destruction of handicrafts and 'the separation of agriculture from domestic industry', viewed as positive and progressive in the Indian case, is destructive and regressive in Ireland.

Likewise, the breakage of communal property, which paved the way for the rise of private property, was viewed as a positive step towards capitalism in India, but negatively perceived in the case of Ireland and was described by Marx and

Engels as a confiscation of the land in favour of the English landlords and clan chiefs.[111]

In *Capital (Volume I)* Marx wrote:

Ireland is at present only an agriculture district of England marked off by a wide channel from the country to which it yields corn, wool, cattle, industrial and military recruits.[112]

And Engels added in May 1856,

How often have the Irish started out to achieve something and everytime they have been crushed politically and industrially. By consistent oppression they have been artificially converted into an utterly impoverished nation.[113]

Lenin had also described the Irish conditions under British rules as follows:

Britain owes her "brilliant" economic development and the "prosperity" of her industry and commerce largely to her treatment of the Irish peasantry, which recalls the misdeeds of the Russian serf-owner Saltychikha. While Britain "flourished", Ireland moved towards extinction and remained an underdeveloped, semi-barbarous, purely agrarian country, a land of poverty-stricken tenant farmers.[114]

The question which arises here, is whether Marx and Engels' views on colonialism suffered confusion and inherent contradictions. To answer this question, criticism of the concept of the Asiatic society and the Asiatic Mode of Production should be carefully exposed and thoroughly analysed. In his classical work *Oriental Despotism: A Comparative Study of Total Power*, Wittfogel criticised the concept of Asiatic Society which unlike Marx's three other forms: the ancient, feudal and modern industrial, obscures the character of the ruling class and points a single person as the major beneficiary of economic privilege.[115] Considered by Wittfogel as a step backward in Marx's analysis and expressing his surprise that such mystification would come from Marx himself, he comments:

This was a strange formulation for a man who ordinarily was eager to define social classes and who denounced as a mystifying 'reification' the use of such notions as 'commodity' and 'the state', when the underlying human (class) relations were left unexplained.[116]

In a further retrogression, Marx avoided the discussions of the managerial role of the despotic state, since it would have lead to the appearance of a ruling class, which performs certain socio-administrative control without owing the means of production.[117] In adopting such obscurity in discussing the bureaucratic managerial function of the despotic state, Marx had, according to Wittfogel committed a 'sin against science', since his intention was to hide the similarities which exist between Oriental despotism and the state of his programme and which may finally lead to the creation of the despotic rule of a privileged minority over the rest of the population.[118] That such obscurity continued in Lenin's and Stalin's writing was an attempt to hide that the existence of a ruling class which controls the means of administration without owning the means of production meant a continuity of political power from Tsarist to Stalinist Russia and hence the preservation of Asiatic despotism.

According to Aveniri, the concept of the Asiatic society has two components. The first is the Hegalian heritage represented in the unchanging, stagnant and hence ahistorical characteristic of Asiatic society and the second is Marx's further analysis of this stationary nature, which he attributed to the specified Asiatic Mode of Production. But whereas in Hegelian historical worlds the Oriental, the classical and the Germanic Christian can coexist, Marx's philosophy of history depends on the dialectical nature of the process of production which is changing and subverting the very conditions of its existence.[119]

Marx commented in a classic passage:

> No social order ever disappears before all the productive forces, for which there is room in it, have been developed and new higher relations of production never appear before the material conditions of their existence have matured in the womb of the old society.[120]

It is in this sense that Asiatic society is problematic to Marx's philosophy of history and challenges its claim to universality. For whereas the three familiar modes are dialectically related, the Asiatic Mode of Production stands apart from the others.[121] It also follows that since Asiatic Societies are static and lack the inherent forces that should change them and direct them on the roads to capitalism and, since Marx anticipated the victory of socialism following the universalisation of capitalism, "he necessarily arrives at the position of having to endorse European colonial expansion as a brutal but necessary step toward the victory of socialism. Just as the horrors of industrialisation are dialectically necessary for the triumph of communism, so the horrors of colonialism are dialectically necessary for the world revolution of the proletariat since without them the countries of Asia (and presumably also Africa) will not be able to emancipate themselves from their stagnant backwardness"[122]

Chandra's analysis of the Indian societies, both before and after British colonialism, highlights the existing deficiency in Marx's Asiatic Mode of Production. To start with Chandra criticised Marx's lack of adherence to the same strict standards of analysis that were present in his previous studies of Western societies, which he described as "more or less a residual category in his thought and treatment of social development"[123] Chandra highlights in his criticism the paradox that is found in Marx's description of the Asiatic state, both with regard to its nature and functions or role.

In 1853 Marx attributed the centralisation and despotic nature of the state to geographical and climatic factors, which necessitated the appearance of a centralised government capable of performing large-scale irrigation. This had inevitably led to the appearance of a centralised despotic Asian state. However, in an article titled "The British rule in India", Marx contradicted himself when he mentioned that India when not colonised seemed to be fragmented and dissolved into a number of independent states with conflict arising among them, thus explicitly attributing the rise of a centralised despotic state not to the needs of the economy, but to the needs of the foreign conqueror.[124] In the *Grundrisse*, Marx attributed the development or lack of development of communities in Asia and Europe to two sets of factors: the external one represented in climatic, geographical, physical and other conditions, which does not necessarily involve despotism and the second to the "special natural make-up of men" or "their tribal character". Whereas the first set of factors determine the 'appearance' or legitimacy of the government, the second determine the character of the state that is whether it is despotic or democratic. Like Wittfogel, Chandra draws the attention to Marx's failure to identify the ruling classes in India. His study of pre-colonial India discredits Marx's characteristics of the Asiatic Mode of Production since he was able to show that private property did exist in pre-colonial India and that commodity production was highly developed in the countryside, where a large part of rural production entered the market as commodity, hence disputing Marx self sufficient isolated villages.[125] Moreover, Chandra showed that India under the Mughals was full of contradictions, interest conflicts, and antagonism between the various groups of landed classes and was not 'stagnant', as Marx had described it. He has thus commented

> the British did not occupy a stagnant but a crisis-ridden society. They could not perhaps have succeeded in conquering a large society like that of India unless it was because of internal contradictions, already in the throes of a prolonged internal social crisis which had been transformed into a political crisis.[126]

Dependency Theory

The origins of dependency theory can be traced back to Marx, Engels and Lenin but it is essentially a neo-Marxist theory. An influential study of dependency theory in the fifties is that of Paul Baran who elaborated on it in his classic work *The Political Economy of Growth*. In this book Baran sought to reveal the main reasons underlying the development and more precisely the underdevelopment of a vast number of countries. Baran's theory rests on the assumption that development and underdevelopment are interrelated and intertwined in a cause-effect relationship so that a positive change in the direction of one would automatically trigger negative change in the direction of the other. Hence the development of the Western countries depended on the exploitation of the so-called underdeveloped countries in such way that caused the former to develop and modernise while retarding the same process for the third world. Thus he argues, that Western Europe left the rest of the world far behind was, however, by no means a matter of fortuitous accident or of some racial peculiarities of different people. It was actually determined by the nature of western European development itself.[127]

Hence,

> the Western European visitors rapidly determined to extract the largest possible gains from the host countries, and to take their loot home. Thus they engaged in outright plunder or in plunder thinly veiled as trade seizing and removing tremendous wealth from the places of their penetrations.[128]

After most of the colonised countries had assumed their political independence, the process of expropriation/appropriation of the economic surplus is carried indirectly by the foreign enterprises who are investing in the developing countries particularly those producing commodities for exportation. Foreign enterprises here transfer the economic surplus gained in the developing countries to their own developed countries, either through transferring their profits directly back home or through what Barran called "investment in kind", where the expansion in current business is achieved through the purchase of more equipment from the home country. In either case the surplus transferred help the markets of the developed countries to expand and accordingly accelerate their industrialisation process, while depriving the underdeveloped countries from such an opportunity. This is usually done in collaboration with a local parasitic class, which benefits from preserving the status quo in the developing countries.[129] Countries in the capitalist west are therefore opposed to the industrialisation of third world countries[130] since this would mean the deprivation of their economy from the much needed raw materials and surplus injected back to foster their own development process. Such opposition can even take the form of direct intervention in the politics of the underdeveloped countries by staging coups against nationalising regimes that may threaten foreign companies' interests.[131]

Adopting Barran's theory of surplus expropriation/appropriation, Frank, in his influential book *Capitalism and Underdevelopment in Latin America* went a step further in polarising the world's countries into a metropolitan centre, the few developed countries, and the peripheral satellites, the many underdeveloped, where

> Capitalist contradictions and the historical development of the capitalist system have generated underdevelopment in the peripheral satellites whose economic surplus was expropriated, while generating economic development in the metropolitan centres which appropriate that surplus – and, further that this process still continues.[132]

Emmanuel and Amin on the other hand, view underdevelopment as embedded in the relations of exchange. Emmanuel's theory of unequal exchange attributes the economic inequality between the nations to the idea that on the world market the poor nations are forced to sell the product of their labour cheaply. Labour in developing countries is paid less and works longer hours than their counterparts in developed countries. The fact that the labour factor does not move from one country to the other i.e. from low-wage countries to high-wage countries creates a situation in which international division of labour is advantageous to rich countries and disadvantageous to poor ones. Emmanuel has labelled this form of exploitation as "commercial exploitation."[133]

Amin argues on the same lines when he calls this kind of exploitation "onslaughter from without", which is carried out by means of trade that the capitalist mode of production imposes on pre-capitalist formations causing certain distortions. These distortions manifest themselves in terms of export activities, where the superiority of productivity at the centre forces the periphery to restrict itself to the role of supplier of products in which it enjoys a competitive advantage. As a result the periphery suffers from inadequate industrialisation, unemployment and an increase in ground rent.[134]

There are some theoretical problems inherent with dependency theory. To start with dependency theories do not provide an explanation of how surplus products are formed and appropriated in developing countries but only how they are exchanged. Secondly, dependency theories analyse the extraction of surplus in the contiguity of countries, thus ignoring the relationship between classes. Thirdly, dependency theories fail to provide a logical explanation for the appropriation and investment of profit in developed countries if the rate of profit is higher in developing countries.[135] Fourthly, dependency theories seem to be in contradiction with Marx's view since they indicate that economic development in the periphery could have been achieved without capital domination. According to Marx, capital domination should first occur at a universal level for a proletarian revolution, and hence socialism to take place. Finally dependency theories fail to provide a viable solution for countries of the periphery to break out of their dependent situation.[136]

Bureaucratic Authoritarianism

Bureaucratic authoritarianism as a concept, is ascribed to Guillermo O'Donnell as a result of his analysis of various types of Latin American states. To start with O'Donnell relates particular kinds of states to the different stages of industrialisation. The oligarchic state prevails when the economy is still in the phase of primary product exportation, whether mineral or agricultural, and the primary export elite's attempt to shape state policy around their interests. The state is neither inclusionary nor exclusionary, since the popular sectors are not yet politically active. The second kind of state is the populist, which appears during the early phases of industrialisation or what is known as the import substitution phase. This state is inclusionary and is based on a multi-class coalition of urban-industrial interests, which includes the industrial elites and the urban popular sector i.e. the masses. Finally the bureaucratic authoritarian state on the other hand, prevails with the advanced phase of industrialisation. It is based on an alliance, which includes high-level technocrats, both civilian and military outside and inside the state, working closely with foreign capital.[137] O'Donnell described the bureaucratic authoritarian state as

> first and foremost, guarantor and organiser of the domination exercised through a class structure subordinated to the upper fractions of a highly oligopolised and transnationalised bourgeoisie. In other words, the principal; social base of the BA State is this upper bourgeoisie.[138]

The bureaucratic authoritarian state is exclusionary and non-democratic both on the political as well, as on the economic level. Such exclusion not only occurs to the popular sector but is also applied to the national fraction of the bourgeoisie who like the former, suffer from the state's normalisation policy.[139] Repression and coercion is the state's tool in achieving strict control over the previously activated masses and specialists in coercion have a considerable weight in its organisation.[140] As a result, the bureaucratic authoritarian state creates a society characterised by what O'Donnell labelled 'tacit consensus' i.e.: depoliticised, apathetic, and marked by the individual's "retreat into a completely privatised daily existence".[141]

O'Donnell, however, pinpoints the inherent tensions, conflict and ambiguities, which exist within the bureaucratic authoritarian state. The conflict and ambiguities stem from the nature of the system of domination. On the one hand the bureaucratic authoritarian state, through its repressive measures and its orthodox economic policies which are geared towards privatisation, denationalises civil society.

On the other hand and like other states the bureaucratic authoritarian state claims to be national and must statise the meaning of the nation.[142] In this situation and

> when the state institutions attempt to redefine the nation in terms of exclusion and of national infirmity, the power they exercise no longer has an external basis of legitimation and cannot but appear as its own foundation. In other words, domination becomes naked and dilutes its consensual mediations, it manifests itself in the form of overt physical and economic coercion. In addition, the suppression of citizenship, together with the prohibition against invoking lo popular,[143] not merely dilutes but radically eliminates other legitimating mediations between the state and society.[144]

In other words the bureaucratic authoritarian state lacks not only legitimacy but also any chance that the system it supports will ever achieve hegemony.

Another source of tension stems from the very nature of the alliance which constitutes the state. The fact that the bureaucratic authoritarian state is based on a coalition which includes the military élites, on one hand, and the upper bourgeoisie and technocrats who have a strong relations with foreign enterprises

27

on the other, with both groups having opposing political and economic values, contributes to the conflicts that are likely to ensue within the bureaucratic authoritarian state. Whereas the upper bourgeoisie and technocrats are transnational in their orientation and view national boundaries as construing obstacles for the free movements of the factors of production, the military has the opposite orientation, since it is the more nationalistic and the least capitalistic of the alliance.[145]

Due to the tension inherent in the bureaucratic authoritarian state coupled with its lack of legitimacy that is derived from the absence of political mediations between state and civil society, the bureaucratic authoritarian state is a weak state which fears the silence of the excluded masses, who may be suddenly activated and revolt not only to destroy the bureaucratic authoritarian state, but also the entire system of social domination on which it is based.[146] The state is thus continuously faced with a dilemma. On the one hand it recognises that fear by itself is a short-lived solution and that it needs a firmer base on which it can rule society. i.e. legitimacy. On the other hand, the corporatist formula, which it attempts to introduce, fails since the latter can only serve as a control tool on associations and unions but cannot replace the absence of mediation between state and society.[147]

Hence the bureaucratic authoritarian state is in continuous search for a form of democracy that would legitimise its rule but

> at the same time maintain the exclusion of the popular sector. In particular, it would have to be one that sustains the suppression of invocations in terms of pueblo and class. Such suppression presupposes that strict control of the organisations and political movements of the popular sector are maintained as well as controls over the form of permissible discourse and rhetoric on the part of those who occupy the institutional positions which democracy would reopen. The search for this philosopher's stone is expressed in the various qualifying adjectives that customarily accompany the term 'democracy'.[148]

This creates in the bureaucratic authoritarian state what O'Donnell labelled a "nostalgia for democracy".[149]

5. Conclusion

To sum up, since the state is at the core of the analysis undertaken in this study which deals with the interactive relationship between the Egyptian state and society, this chapter reviewed the different theories of the state, in both the pluralist and the Marxist and neo-Marxist schools of thought, as well as in the writings on states in third world countries. It also reviewed theories of development (modernisation theory) and of underdevelopment(Asiatic Mode of Production and dependency theory). It pinpointed where various analysis of the role of the state and of the process of development are relevant to states in the Arab world, including Egypt and where they are flawed. Specifically, this study is set to show the similarities which exist between O'Donnell's bureaucratic authoritarian state and the Egyptian state, and hence the first hypothesis set in this research is that like O'Donnell's bureaucratic authoritarian state, the Egyptian authoritarian state is a weak state. A second hypothesis is the Hegelian notion of the state i.e. in Egypt, state shapes society. A third hypothesis set forward is that similar to the Bonpartist state, the Egyptian state is relatively autonomous. The state in Egypt is therefore weak, relatively autonomous and shapes society. It is in light of the previously mentioned assumptions that the Egyptian society will be analysed in the following chapters showing how the state shapes society and how the latter in turn reacts to and determines state's capabilities.

CHAPTER TWO

The Historical Relationship between the State and the Peasants

1. Introduction

The relationship between state and society is controversial. It entails a dynamic interaction through which societies are moulded by the state and their leaders, whose abilities to shape their societies are in turn enhanced or weakened by societal forces.

In a country as ancient as Egypt, history inevitably plays an important role in shaping socio-political conditions. It is undeniable that state-society interaction today represents the natural outcome of cumulative historical events. Wittfogel's comment is indeed true,

> No doubt there is structure and cohesion in man's personal history. All individuals base their behaviour on the conviction that the regularities of yesterday are linked to the regularities of today and tomorrow. And there is structure and cohesion in the history of mankind.[1]

History, then, plays a major role in determining the characteristics of states and societies alike. This chapter will examine, from a historical perspective, the type of governance that characterised Egypt's rulers and the effect of that rule on shaping the character, values, and attitudes of the ruled masses.

2. The Rulers and the State

Any analysis of Egypt's political history constantly encounters the persistent phenomenon of despotism. The definition of despotism that will be used as this analysis proceeds confirms with Mosca's description:

> The absolute preponderance of a single political force, the predominance of any oversimplified concept in the organisation of the state, the strictly logical application of any single principle in all public law are the essential elements in any type of despotism whether it be a despotism based upon divine right or a despotism based ostensibly on popular sovereignty.[2]

Thus the prevalence of one-man-rule, or the control by a single political organisation of the entire society (which necessitates the subordination and/or elimination of all other political societal forces and institutions that might restrict a despotic ruler or government), is an essential element in any type of despotic regime. Such autocracy has manifested itself in Egypt's rulers from its early history. From the age of the Pharaohs to the present time, Egypt's rulers exhibit a remarkable continuity in their tendency to maintain the despotic nature of their rule despite the different forms that it may take.

History, then, is a determining factor in the evolution of different forms of government. But geography is equally important in shaping the political life in Egypt; in fact, it takes precedence in setting the stage for the development of historical events.

Egypt's climate and topography gave the Nile, as an arid oasis surrounded by an extended area of desert, a leading role in the country's economic and political development. Thus Egypt's fate was and always will be linked with the Nile, that benevolent master which provides the country with life and prosperity. The ancient Egyptians realised this fact and the urgently felt need to control the Nile was the major factor in the unification of the land from the Delta to Aswan.[3]

Exploiting the Nile thus necessitated,

> Un réglement de l'irrigation, équitable et satisfaisant pour toute la vallée, et créent, enfin, une autorité supérieure à tous nomes pour en surveiller l'application, il a déterminé la subordination de tous à un maître et la monarchie absolue.[4]

Thus Egypt, owing to its "hydraulic" nature, was destined from the beginning to experience despotic rule. The Pharaoh was the sole master of Egypt. He was often called the "Perfect God" and was considered above ordinary human beings.[5]

In other contemporary civilisations such as those of Mesopotamia and Israel, the king ruled for the God.[6] In Egypt, "the Pharaoh ruled as the God who was upon earth and among mortals".[7] He was, therefore, the master of wisdom and knowledge, eloquent and with the power to heal as well as to start epidemics. In brief the Pharaoh was capable of satisfying every need.[8] Ancient Egyptians were, therefore, advised to,

> Honour the crown of Lower Egypt, worship the crown of Upper Egypt, exalt him who wears the double crown. Do this it will be beneficial to your person and you will derive benefit from it forever more.[9]

This doctrine or "dogma" of the Pharaoh's divinity, although taking various forms, had persisted throughout the different historical eras. In order to be perceived as the legitimate ruler of Egypt, Alexander – founder of the Ptolemaic dynasty – had to identify himself with the God Amon that the Egyptians worshipped at that time.[10] As one author puts it:

31

The important point in the affair is that the declaration of the king's divinity, and of his actual descent from Amon as his father, was the only formula known by which the priests could declare him [Alexander] *de jure* king of Egypt as he already was *de facto*.[11]

It was only then that he could rule Egypt with unchallenged authority. This tendency of Egypt's rulers to preserve one-man rule had been both persistent and continuous. In Roman Egypt, for example, the appointment of a governor whose power and decisions were equivalent to any of his counterparts of senatorial rank did not obscure the fact that "Caeser is the State".[12]

Arab Islamic rule came to Egypt in 639 AD during the reign of Omar Ibn al Khattab as the Caliph of the Muslims. However, this did not alter the pattern, for at the very heart of Islamic ideology, is the Caliph in whom all authority is vested is the "ruler of the world", and hence his power is absolute.[13] Again, he enjoyed absolutism because it is "God who bestows authority on the Caliph".[14] Although Egypt was not ruled directly by the Caliph, the latter appointed the Wali (or governor) of Egypt, who was directly accountable to him and was thus the supreme authority in the country. Having both executive and judicial functions, besides his leadership of the army and supervision of the police, his absolute authority was further enhanced by his position as leader of the ritual prayers.[15] Generally speaking, this concentration of power in one person remains the main characteristic of all the Muslim rulers of Egypt. With all executive, civilian, military, and judicial functions vested in him, the Sultan in the Ottoman Empire personally ruled the country, leaving but a limited area for the legislative functions outside the Qur'an and the tradition of the Prophet.[16]

Although Ottoman rule in Egypt had passed through different stages, the most significant characteristic of each was still autocratic leadership. Being the most important Muqata'a or province in the Ottoman Empire, Egypt was ruled by the Wali (who held the title of Pasha) as the representative of the Turkish Sultan. Assisting the Wali were individuals chosen from the military and non-military corps, who were given the rank of Beys and placed in positions of responsibility in all branches of the government. These Beys were usually chosen from the Mameluks, the locally-based military class.[17]

Throughout the entire period of the Ottoman Empire, the nature and extent of one-man rule varied in practice according to the character of the Wali. However, it remained no less autocratic. A strong Wali was always capable of controlling the Mameluks and of using the divisions that arose within their hierarchy in order to enhance his power. On the other hand, when the Wali tended to be weak, his authority would decline and the most powerful of the Mameluks would step in and become the actual ruler of the country.[18] This power struggle continued throughout the Ottoman rule until at the end of the eighteenth century Egypt became "*Une république aristocratique courbée sous le fer du despotism militaire*".[19]

The modern history of Egypt, which, is generally dated from the beginning of the nineteenth century, witnessed the appearance of rulers whose reigns epitomised the ideal type of absolute despotism. Muhammad Ali, who ruled Egypt from 1805–1848, and Gamal Abd al-Nasser, who ruled from 1952–1971, show remarkable historical similarities with respect to both circumstances and style of governance, although to begin with, Nasser, as the first native Egyptian to govern for centuries, had an advantage which his Albanian counterpart Muhammad Ali, lacked,[20] a fact that had always kept the latter separate in sentiment from the native people.

Muhammad Ali came to power at a time when the different Mameluk households had "fought one another for control of the rural surplus and the competition between them plunged Egypt even more deeply into political disorder".[21] Likewise Nasser came to power when a more or less similar condition prevailed in the country for,

> From one end of Egyptian society to the other, confusion reigned everywhere and the spectacle offered by daily life was that of a contradictory chaos on all levels.[22]

Both Muhammad Ali and Abd al-Nasser realised that it was the army rather than the masses that backed and protected their power. Although at the beginning Muhammad Ali sought the help of the Ulama, the leaders of public opinion, in order to gain power, he did not "forget for a moment that armed strength was the true basis of his authority".[23] This is probably the reason why Muhammad Ali, once his authority was secured, started to eliminate the major political forces in the society that might have threatened his power.

By suppressing the Ulama, who had helped him to gain official recognition from the Turkish Sultan as the *de jure* Viceroy of Egypt, and chasing the Mameluk troops all over the country, later slaughtering their leaders in the famous Citadel massacre, it was ensured that "Tout est fini, l'Egypte reste à Mehmed Ali, car personne n'osera plus la lui contester".[24]

Interestingly, as if history insists on repeating itself, Nasser behaved in the very same way. Realising that "his dictatorship was backed by the army not by a mass movement ... [and that] tanks, not talk, were the bulwarks of his regime",[25] Nasser, eliminated all existing political parties by confiscating their property and placing their leaders first under house arrest and later in prison.[26] Hence, "Gamal Abd El Nasser, President of the all powerful revolutionary command council, was to be the sole master of political power in Egypt".[27]

Like Muhammad Ali, Nasser ousted many of his military allies and distanced himself from the rest, thus sacrificing their trust.[28] Another point of similarity between them, is the justification given for the concentration of power in their hands and their dictatorial style of leadership, viz. the need for rapid development. While Muhammad Ali's interest lay mainly in the field of agriculture, irrigation and public works, Abd al-Nasser's was in industrialisation.[29]

After Nasser came Sadat with his "corrective revolution" promising the people a free life in a democratic society. He promised to build a "State of Institutions" in which the law and other legitimate institutions would restrict any despotic rule,[30] but as one author has mentioned:

> He did not achieve it [his promise] and in the end made a mockery of his own goal with mass arrests of opponents, real and imagined, that he ordered just before his death.[31]

Like his predecessor, Sadat was a Pharaoh and as Heikal describes him in *Autumn of Fury*, he was,

> the first Egyptian Pharaoh to come before his people armed with a camera, he was also the first Egyptian Pharaoh to be killed by his own people.[32]

Mubarak succeeded Sadat in 1981. To begin with, he retained the emergency laws initiated by Sadat. These laws give the president greater presidential power than he had previously enjoyed, including the right to appoint the Cabinet, without any provision for parliamentary majority, and the role of supreme commander of the armed forces, and chief policy-maker in matters of security, diplomacy and the economy.[33]

Despite the limited degree of political liberalisation that the régime tried to introduce by allowing all political parties, except the Muslim Brotherhood, to function, in an attempt to preserve continuity with as little disruption as possible, Mubarak continues to resist popular demands for such things as the abrogation of the emergency laws, changes in the constitution, and a limit to the number of times that the President can run for office.

Mubarak's refusal to appoint a vice-president, which would result in a peaceful transfer of authority, and to give up his leadership for the National Democratic Party "NDP" (the dominant government party during his term of office) goes against the people's will.[34] Resignation of his leadership of the dominant party has always been the demand of all opposition parties in order to guarantee the neutrality of the state apparatus and hence honest elections. Moreover, in sharp contrast to the limited power of parliament, whose vote of no confidence in the cabinet does not force its resignation, the President has the right in such an event to resort to a popular referendum and even to dissolve the parliament altogether. The fact that the President appoints the Assembly's speaker who is an appointed MP in any case,[35] further emphasises the subordinate position of parliament. In addition, the strict party law and Mubarak's insistence on strengthening the government party at the expense of the People's Assembly and tightening his grip on individual localities through the NDP and the security apparatus, clearly indicate that the liberalisation process remains extremely limited in scope. It is something that tends to resemble closely what Wittfogel has termed a "Beggars Democracy" which "in no way threatens the power of the commander and his guards",[36] a contributory factor in the continuation of Egypt's rule through presidential despotism.

The Nature of the Egyptian State

In short, both geography and history have played crucial roles in shaping Egypt's destiny with regard to despotic rule. However, in assessing the modern Egyptian State, care should be taken to avoid any confusion between autocracy and the strength or power of the state.

Ayubi, among others, validates the weakness of the state when he draws a valuable distinction between the "Strong State" and the "Fierce State". Whereas the former complement society and its strength can be measured by its ability to work with and through various centres of power in the society, the latter contradicts society and deals with it through force and coercion.[37] He thus differentiates between quwwat al-dawla, "The power of the State" and dawlat al-quwwa, the "State of power". A further distinction is made by Ayubi between "infrastructure" and "despotic" power. Whereas the "strong state" excels in the former through its ability to penetrate society and deal with social relations and conflict, the "fierce state" excels in the latter because of its inability to execute policies in the different social and political arenas. Hence, the "fierce state" is a despotic state that acts violently because of its weakness.[38] Based on his study of most of the Arab States including Egypt, Ayubi reached the conclusion that the

> Arab state is an authoritarian state, and that it is so averse to democracy and resistant to its pressures should not, of course, be taken as a measure of the strength of that state – indeed quite the reverse.[39]

He also adds that the "Arab state is therefore often violent because it is weak".[40] The modern Egyptian state from Nasser to Mubarak exemplifies this kind of "fierce state" with its coercive subjugation of the society. The weakness of the Egyptian state is manifested in its failure to penetrate society and transform it. Although the weakness of the Egyptian state has been also verified by other writers, the strength of the society is a debatable issue that will be thoroughly discussed in the subsequent chapters.

3. The Egyptian Personality

There is no doubt that the coercion of the despotic state has left its mark on the Egyptian personality. As mentioned earlier, geography has played an important role in shaping the country's destiny. Egypt's unique strategic location was as much a curse on the Egyptians as it was a blessing, for Egypt has suffered a multiplicity of invasions.

As Hussein Fawzy comments,

> After the Hyksos, they were suppressed by the Assyrians, the Libyans, the Ethiopians, the Romans, the Arabs of Tadmur in the Kingdom of Zanubia, the Greeks, the Arabs, the Dailem, the Farghanis, the Moroccans, the Kurds,

and every Turkish race that would be brought by the slave market to the near east. They are governed by the Ottomans, the French, the Albanians and the British. Egypt has thus tasted foreign rule under every colour that you can see on the map of Europe, Asia (and Africa) short only of the rule of Indians, Chinese and Japanese.[41]

One must then wonder how far the authentic Egyptian character and identity have been altered, or more specifically, fused with that of the conqueror. Wendell asserts the idea that the Egyptians never surrendered their distinctive character, but that it was the conquerors who were fused into theirs and became Egyptians themselves, to the extent of forgetting their own origins.[42]

Berque confirms the same idea when describing Egypt: "Her everlasting clay can be cast into any form imposed on her by others or by herself without ever surrendering her essential character".[43] Yet this does not obscure the fact that long years of coercion and exploitation by foreign ruling powers and native autocratic states are bound to have left their mark on the character of the Egyptian people and their attitudes towards the government. As Montesquieu says:

> In despotic states the nature of government requires the most passive obedience and when once the prince's will is made known, it ought infallibly to produce its effect. Here they have no limitations or restrictions, no mediums, terms, equivalents or remonstrances, no change to propose, man is a creature that blindly submits to the absolute will of the sovereign.[44]

However, this submission was not absolute. It created in them a sort of resistance and it is precisely this kind of passive resistance created in the Egyptians by autocracy and exploitation that helped them preserve their identity vis-à-vis their conquerors. Nevertheless it also had contrary repercussions on their personalities.

The various literature which has dealt with the Arab personality in general and the Egyptian in particular, has tended to attribute to it specific negative characteristics. It is difficult not to agree with Ayubi when he says that alienation, humiliation, defeatism, flattery, fatalism, apathy and precaution are among the worst features of Egyptian society.[45]

So far Egypt's rulers and their despotic tendencies, as they have persisted throughout the different historical eras, have been analysed and an attempt at understanding the characteristics of the Egyptian people and the factors that helped shape these characteristics has been made, highlighting the effect of despotic government on the personality of the governed people. In the following section special attention will be given to the Egyptian peasantry in an attempt to discover the nature of the relationship that exists between them and the state.

4. The Ruled Peasants

Peasants everywhere have been viewed differently by the various schools of thought. They are either revolutionary, according to Frantz Fanon and Mao or submissive, backward and ignorant, according to Daniel Lerner.[46] They either possess a political outlook that is reflected in what James Scott had labelled "the moral economy", which tends to embody within it values that are antithetical to élite values and which unify peasants in the face of threats, or they are, according to Popkin and Bates, rational beings who are individualistic, utility maximising and not necessarily opponents of or alien to the state.[47] Egyptian peasants, the bedrock of Egyptian society, have also been dealt with by the various authors in contradictory ways. Two principal schools of thought exist in the literature, which view them either as completely passive and submissive, or as revolutionary and active.

When referred to descriptively, the Egyptian peasant is either represented negatively as lazy, servile, stupid, ignorant, cunning, and evil,[48] or positively as hardworking, cheerful, intelligent, amenable, kind and hospitable.[49] He is viewed as either constantly attempting to cheat the government, or as being constantly cheated by the government.

From a more analytical perspective, in an attempt to trace the origin of some of these characteristics, some authors, have applied theories of basic personality types. According to the anthropologist Ralph Linton and the psychologist Abram Kardiner,

> The basic personality type for any society is that personality configuration which is shared by the bulk of the society's members as a result of the early experience which they have in common. It does not correspond to the total personality of the individual but rather to the projective systems or in different phraseology, the value-attitude systems, which are basic to the individual's personality configuration. Thus the same basic personality type may be reflected in many different total personality configurations.[50]

So Mayfield, for example, among others, attributes the submissiveness of the peasant to the authoritarian character of the Egyptian family, where the father represents the authority figure and authority includes physical punishment both of the wife and children.[51]

Corporal punishment is not confined to the family but is experienced later on, in adulthood, from the authorities. From the Pharaohs up to the latter part of the 19th century, corporal punishment was used in Egypt, mainly upon the peasants, in the establishment of public enterprise and in maintaining the courvee, creating what Wittfogel had termed "Government by flogging".[52] Again, in traditional families, elders are supposed to be blindly obeyed and children are not permitted to participate in decision-making. Submission to and fear of the family, which are deeply rooted in the subconscious in the early years, are extended later to those who hold authority. Mayfield also adds that lack of consistency and regularity in administering punishment drives children to be deceitful in order to avoid punishment,[53] and hence they become cunning later in their lives. A similar point is made by al-Menoufy when he refers to the lack of consistency in the relationship between the mother and her children, which may vary from complete attention to complete negligence depending on the former's mood, and creates in them a feeling of helplessness and lack of security which breeds suspicion and secretiveness.[54] Sanua identifies suspicion and mistrust as a "major characteristic of the fellahin",[55] while Patai, quoting Ayrout, describes them as "passive and fatalistic",[56] Sanua's findings asserts that this description is related to the widespread belief among Egyptian fellahin in the "evil eye".[57] This subjective view of the Egyptian peasant is epitomised by Ayrout:

> Following the pages of Herodotus, Diodorus Siculus, Strabo, Maqrizi, Vansleb, pere Sicard and Volney we find still the same fellah, no revolution, no evolution.[58]

However, the image of the Egyptian peasant as completely submissive is both untrue and misleading. In a fairly recent essay, Mitchell has critically surveyed what are known as the "classical studies" on the Egyptian peasant. He reviews the work of Critchfield, Ayrout and the French social psychologist Gustave Le Bon, to reveal that Critchfield depended heavily on Ayrout's work. The latter's work is a reflection of Le Bon's writing particularly *Les lois psychologiques de l'evolution des peuples* (The Psychological Rules of the Evolution of the Population) and his famous work the *Psychologie des foules* (The Psychology of the Crowd).[59] Commenting on Gibb's claim that Ayrout book "holds up a mirror to the peasantry as they are", Mitchell states:

> A mirror is the correct metaphor but, as we saw, it is a mirror reflecting not some original peasant reality but a series of other mirrors, ranging from the French Description d'Egypte and the writings of 19th-century European travellers to the exhibits in the Egyptian museum and, above all, the work of Gustave Le Bon. Such a system of mirrors produced an image of the peasantry appropriate to Ayrout's political concerns and pastoral sympathies.[60]

Even Ayrout himself tended to be self-contradictory when earlier he described the fellahin as "A receptive people, yet unyielding, patient yet resistant".[61] That the Egyptian peasants had, albeit on some limited occasions, revolted against the state is a historically well-documented fact. But before discussing the revolutionary aspect of the Egyptian peasant, the fundamental questions must be raised of why and when do peasants revolt.

The interest here is not the outcome of such revolutions per se, but rather the combination of factors that drive peasant to revolt. Skocpol identified the state as the major factor in rebellion. According to her, peasants rebel when they are faced with a state that has been weakened through internal divisions and foreign wars.[62]

Davidheiser, on the other hand, completely contradicts this view when he associates revolution with strong rather than weak states. He argues that strong states, through their successful effort to transform society, tend to destabilise socio-political life. With the inability of the "strong state" to respond to social forces, and with rising economic pressures, crisis triggers revolution.[63] Scott asserts that peasants rebel when their livelihood is threatened and their values are violated.[64]

Barrington Moore, in his classic study of peasant societies, has distinguished several conditions concomitant with peasant revolt, but identifies the fusion of peasant grievances with those of the other groups in society as a determinant factor in causing peasant revolutions. He argues that by themselves, peasants cannot act and that leadership from other classes is thus essential.[65]

It is important here to test the previous hypothesis and see its relevance within the context of the Egyptian peasant. History provides some vivid examples of peasant rebellion. At the end of the old Pharaonic kingdom of Egypt, peasants participated in a rebellion against unjust and corrupt rulers. Despite the fact that this was not a purely peasant revolution, but rather a social one, the peasants, whose conditions had severely deteriorated and who were suffering from the autocracy of the provincial princes, played a major part in the revolt. Here Barrington Moore's condition of the fusion of the peasants' grievances with those of the other classes is validated. Ptolemaic and Roman Egypt also witnessed peasant revolt under the leadership of the priesthood as a result of heavy taxation, the extensive courvee and the coercion of the local officials. Economic hardship and the violation of peasant values, in the presence of appropriate leadership from other classes, drove the Egyptian peasant to revolt. Again, as a result of the heavy burden of taxation, besides other political and religious reasons, Islamic Egypt experienced several revolts by Coptic peasants, which spread all over the country.

Under the Ottoman Mameluk rule, both peasants and bedouins participated in several revolts against the coercion of the state and its representatives.[66] However, this limited number of incidents does not prove the revolutionary nature of the Egyptian peasants. Again in 1882, a revolt – namely the 'Urabi revolt named after its leader – took place in which the role played by the peasants seemed disputable. Although some leftist writers have depicted the 'Urabi Revolt as a peasant struggle, the researcher has found evidence in the literature to refute this assumption.

A look at what the leftist historian Abd al-Azim Ramadan, has written about this period, clarifies the picture. Although he mentions that, ". . . they (the peasantry) had participated spontaneously and enthusiastically in the 'Urabi Revolt",[67] he asserts that it was the small class of the agrarian bourgeoisie represented in the 'Ummad and Sheikh who formed the basic core of the 'Urabi Revolt.[68] Being given enormous powers that tended to be absolute,[69] it was not difficult for them to force the fallahin to participate in the revolt. Ramadan, therefore, seems to defeat his own thesis about the spontaneity of the peasants' participation in the revolt. Despite the fact that al-Menoufy does not repudiate

39

this leftist argument explicitly, he does seem to share this researcher's view, when discussing the role of the peasants in the 'Urabi revolt, he only describes it as one of "sympathy"[70] and summarising the findings of his study on the 'Urabi revolt, Brown clarifies the argument:

> the evidence presented should dispel the view that the Urabi Revolt was in one way a peasant revolt. Peasants participated directly in the Revolt (by contributing their labour and crops) because they had to do so. Orders from above for recruits were zealously enforced by the notability. It is probable that peasants preferred Urabi to the Khadine and the British but there is no indication they would have acted on the preference if not ordered to do so.[71]

Although most writers agree on the active participation of the Egyptian peasants in the 1919 revolution, the spontaneity of their participation remains debatable. Al-Menoufy attributes it to the increased economic burden on the peasants during World War I, combined with the charismatic character of Saad Zaghloul, the leader of the revolution.[72]

Brown goes further in explaining that not only did British policy during World War I impose greater burdens on the peasants, but it deprived them of several economic opportunities that had arisen during the war.[73] Even so, peasants revolted only when they were given the green light to do so and when they were lead by the notability. Brown concludes that,

> because revolution was not in their repertoire, peasants in Egypt revolted only when allowed to do so – namely as dictated by the stance of the notability and by the national political situation.[74]

Here Davidheiser's thesis stands viable. Because the Egyptian state had been weak, i.e. had failed to penetrate society and transform it, and at the same time had allowed greater penetration of the state by different societal interests, revolutionary trends had always been minimal and once they occurred were easily crushed.[75] In addition, long years of autocracy and oppression had no doubt taught the peasants to evade rather than to confront. It had definitely created in them a sort of passive resistance.

In his study of the peasants' struggle against the state in the period between 1882–1952, Brown identifies three forms of passive action, which he labels atomistic actions, communal actions, and legal and institutional actions. Each of these actions will be critically reviewed at this point.

Atomistic actions are those in which the peasants individually or in very small groups "strike out at local manifestations (and perceived injustices) of the prevailing order".[76] Included within this category are rural crimes, particularly banditry, uprooting of crops, arson, cattle poisoning and attacks by individuals or small groups on officials and landlords or their representatives.

Brown tends to add a political aspect to these crimes. Despite the fact that some may have had political dimensions, in the majority of cases (owing to "al-Thaar" or vendetta, which is widely practised amongst peasants, particularly in Upper Egypt) it is extremely difficult to differentiate between crimes that represent anti-social action and those that have a political dimension. What adds to the difficulty is the peasants' 'conspiracy of silence', which Brown includes as a form of passive resistance and which consists of refusal to report crime, refusal to identify criminals, and refusal to tell the truth about crimes.[77] Although vendettas may explain such behaviour, so might fear of whoever committed the crime, in which case 'the conspiracy of silence' does not necessarily mean that it stems from collective approval of the crime committed.

The most common form of passive peasants' resistance, however, is that of ignoring or evading unfavourable policies.[78] Indeed, peasants continue to subvert major policies pursued by the state. This form of resistance is discussed in more detail in chapters eight and nine.

The second form of passive resistance is that of communal action. Brown's judgement is again questionable. Although he provides examples of collective attacks on government officials or of peasants gathering to prevent the execution of a certain order, Brown omits the fact that peasant loyalty is directed mainly towards the family. The family or "Asabiya" here represents the extended family, which is usually formed through intermarriage. So the whole village may actually consist of one big family, or two or three families related through inter-marriage. Al-Menoufy recognises the "Asabiya" and the results of his research show that peasant loyalty is arranged in a hierarchical order in which loyalty to the family comes first, followed by loyalty to the village and finally loyalty to the country or nation as a whole. He admits that peasants tend to suspect each other and are very cautious in their personal and social relations and that they show preference for private rather than public benefit.[79] In addition, al-Menoufy uses peasant proverbs to verify his conclusion that peasants felt like "Gharib al-Dar" or strangers.[80] However, if al-Menoufy identifies this lack of a sense of belonging as referring to the nation, it could also be lacking towards the immediate community represented in the village, for "al-Dar" had always meant to the peasant his small village. Brown himself asserts that peasants' suspicion and mistrust of the government extends to their social relationships and thus becomes an obstacle in facilitating co-operation among the village inhabitants. This attitude towards both the government and fellow villagers makes them reluctant even to become members of co-operatives that would promote their economic well being.

As Brown notes,

In spite of the efforts of some leaders, peasants seemed incapable of or uninterested in forming co-operatives even after the 1920s when the government undertook the promotion of co-operatives on a large scale.[81]

Thus, in contrast with some European countries, where co-operatives stemmed from the peasantry itself, in Egypt, co-operatives had to be imposed by the state on the peasants. Communal actions, which require trust and co-operation among individuals as well as a sense of communal identity, are unlikely to occur in this case.

41

The third form of action which Brown identifies is the legal and institutional. Here, he tries to discover the peasant attitude towards the political parties and voting in elections that existed during the period of his study. He found that at the beginning, the peasant attitude towards voting was characterised by fear and suspicion, which was replaced later by indifference.[82] Several factors helped shape peasants' opinions and attitudes towards elections. First, the very nature of the electoral system tended to discourage any kind of peasant participation in the political system. Until 1926 and during the 1931 elections, peasants were not allowed to elect their representatives directly but rather elected those who would later choose the peasants' representatives.

Second, rural membership in provincial councils and parliament was restricted to those who paid a minimum amount of property tax.[83] Thus, as Brown comments, "the electoral system was therefore structured to minimise any independent impact by the peasantry on national politics".[84]

Third, the different political parties were unable to build any roots in the countryside and with the peasants during this period. This was due to the fact that none of the national parties tried to raise the issue of agrarian reform in parliament or give it a priority on their political agenda. They knew very well that it was the local notability that controlled the country, as well as the peasants' votes, either through coercion or favours.

Political parties could not therefore have afforded to alienate the notability through any measures that might affect the latter's interests[85] and peasants thus came to discount the value of their votes and were willing to trade them for rewards: "when peasants displayed an interest in the outcome of an election, only the victory or loss of their patron was at issue."[86]

Perhaps petitioning was most widely used by peasants to express their grievances. Yet again, even in this case, most petitions that were not organised by the notables tended to reflect personal grievances, rather than community interest.[87] In these circumstances, political participation by peasants can be viewed as having a negative rather than a positive role for the development of the political system as a whole.

5. Conclusion

So far some features of state-society relationship in Egypt have been examined from a historical perspective. Long years of coercion and exploitation by a weak despotic state have created an alienated peasant who felt "Gharib" or alien in his own country and hence lacked a sense of belonging to his smaller community and to the nation at large. His suspicion and mistrust in the government have extended to his social relationships and thus constitute an obstacle in facilitating co-operation among the village inhabitants.

This being the case the limited number of revolts, documented in the modern history of Egypt, was not spontaneous and was never initiated by peasants.

Peasant's behaviour towards both the government and his fellow villagers make him reluctant to participate in elections and to become a member in co-operatives that would promote his economic well being. Such behaviour as social trust, co-operation and membership of organisations and associations have a significant impact on the political values and behaviour that permeate a society, as well as the type of culture that characterises it.

As Almond and Verba explain,

Thus attitudes favourable to participation within the political system play a major role in the civil culture, but so do such non-political attitudes as trust in other people and social participation in general.[88]

They also add that such activities,

do not in themselves indicate an active participation in the decision-making process of a society but they make such participation more possible. They prepare the individual for intervention in the political system and more important perhaps they create a political environment in which citizen involvement and participation are more feasible.[89]

To sum up, social participation and co-operation, including membership of organisations and associations, the active political participation of citizens which stems from their belief in their ability to play an active role in decision making, and the existence of the same on the part of the elites, are the elements that create a strong civic society.

It is precisely the lack of all these components before 1952 that led to the creation of a weak uncivic society. However, the continuing presence of a weak despotic state in contemporary Egypt is bound to reflect on post 1952 Egyptian society. The aim of the following chapters is to study post 1952 Egyptian society by examining the relative strength or weakness of the various political forces at work.

CHAPTER THREE

The Constitutional and Legal System in Egypt and the Change to a Multi-Party System

1. Introduction

The constitution and legal system of any country provide the basic institutional framework within which the political order and the various political forces in the society, including political parties, operate. It is therefore important to present a brief description of the Egyptian political system with its three branches, the executive, the legislative and the judicial, and to assess the relationship between them, as embodied in the constitution and as actually practised in order to highlight the inherent contradictions which exist in the system. A historical background for the change to a multi-party system as well as a brief assessment of the government's ruling party will also be presented in this chapter.

2. The Political System in Egypt

A) The Executive Branch

According to the Egyptian Constitution, the executive branch is composed of the Presidency and the Cabinet.

The Presidency

In an attempt to raise himself above his colleagues in the Revolutionary Command Council "RCC", Nasser created the special office of President (ra'is) which he endowed with enormous rights. Among these rights was the right to appoint and dismiss the Prime Minister, the Cabinet, the Commander-in-Chief of the armed forces and senior officers.[1]

The various constitutions[2] – and their different amendments – that have been promulgated in Egypt since the 1952 coup have all tended to emphasise the authority of the Presidency. For apart from his executive power, the President has also been given extensive legislative powers and is the arbitrator between the three branches, the executive, legislative and judicial.[3] For example, according to Articles 137 and 138 of the constitution, the President is the head of the executive authority and, together with the ministerial committee, he draws up the public policies of the state and oversees their execution.[4] He also has the right to "veto bills passed by the National Assembly, to issue emergency legislation and administrative ordinances, and to refer major issues to a National Assembly".[5] Under Sadat, the President was empowered with even more rights than before, since he acquired the power to issue laws by decree in economic matters, as well as for the purchase of arms. In addition, Sadat removed the limit on the number of times any one individual could serve as President.[6]

The President is also the head of the government party, the National Democratic Party, which dominates the parliament and by Article 150 of the constitution of 1980, the President becomes the High Commander of the Armed Forces.[7] As is obvious, the constitution embodies a group of contradictions with respect to presidential rights. These contradictions tend to:

a) Undermine the concept of the separation of powers. Since the President is not only the head of the executive branch, but also has enormous legislative powers and is the leader of the dominant party in the parliament, the separation of powers between the executive and legislative branches becomes significantly blurred.

b) Undermine the parliament as a legislative body that should act as a control on the executive branch.
The very fact that the President of the country is the leader of the dominant party in parliament and it is the President who appoints the speaker of the People's Assembly, who is an appointed MP in any case, directs the parliament's loyalty towards the President and his executive machinery. Not only does this marginalise the role of the opposition in general but it casts doubts on the legitimacy of the Egyptian parliament.

c) Strengthen the military as an elitist organisation. The fact that the President is the High Commander of the Armed Forces and in that capacity tends to favour the military to ensure its loyalty, makes the latter an elitist organisation that is placed above the people, and can be used by the President at any time against society. The use of the military forces to control the Food Riots in 1977 is a case in point. In addition the military could be used at any time in the future to suppress opposition. This not only represents a threat to civil rights, but is also inherently anti-democratic.

d) Grant power without accountability. Despite the wide range of power given to the President, no provision whatsoever appears in the constitution regarding his accountability to parliament i.e.: the possibility of the latter to check his power or to veto any of his decisions. The only provision found in the constitution is in article 85 in which, similar to the act of impeachment in

45

the American constitution, the People's Assembly can, in exceptionally grave cases of treason or criminal acts and by a majority of two thirds of its members, remove the President temporary from office pending investigation results.[8] Hence in theory as well as in practice the President has extensive power without any accountability.

As Montesquieu has commented,

When the legislative and executive powers are united in the same person or in the same body of magistrates, there can be no liberty, because apprehension may arise, lest the same monarch or senate should enact tyrannical laws, to execute them in a tyrannical manner.[9]

Thus the constitution which is supposed to protect democracy, liberty and civil rights, embodies in it elements which undermine these values and lay the ground for presidential authoritarianism.

The Cabinet

The Cabinet, headed by the Prime Minister, supervises the implementation of the public policies of the state. It is worth noting here that on the surface, the absence of any disagreement between the President and the Prime Minister and between the latter and his Cabinet members, a continuing phenomena since Sadat's time, reflects the major role of the President in policy-making in contrast to the mere implementation role of the Prime Minister and his Cabinet. Accordingly, the Cabinet becomes part of the expanding Egyptian bureaucracy which executes the decisions taken at the apex of the authority pyramid.[10]

B) The Legislative Branch

Legislative authority is vested a uni-cameral assembly with an elected membership of 444 plus up to ten members appointed by the President. Half the members of the Assembly should be workers and peasants with the same conditions applying to all local and popular councils.[11] According to Article 86 of the constitution the People's Assembly is empowered with legislative authority and must approve the public policies of the state, the economic and social development plan and the general budget.[12] Articles 124–131 of the constitution give the People's Assembly wide control over the executive branch, such as the right to question the Prime Minister or any of his cabinet ministers, which is considered to be the least important device, the right to send a formal request for further explanation on any issue to the Cabinet, the right to request the formation of investigation committees, and finally the right to present an interpellation on any specific subject. The latter is considered to be one of the most important controls, since it can result in the passing of a vote of no confidence in any minister, including the Prime Minister himself.[13]

To assess the efficiency of the People's Assembly, its legislative authority and its control function should be analysed.

The Legislative Authority of the People's Assembly

If the number of proposed laws presented by the MPs in the People's Assembly as opposed to the number of drafted bills presented by the Cabinet, are examined, it should act as an indicator of the strength or weakness of the legislative branch vis-à-vis the executive.

The following two tables summarise the legislative role of the People's Assembly

From tables 3.1a and 3.1b the weakness of the People's Assembly with regard to its function as a legislative body can be observed. This is reflected in the following facts:

1. The limited number of proposed bills by MPs as compared to the large number of draft bills presented by the Cabinet.
2. Apart from the years 1992 and 1996, the proportion of approved laws to the total number of those presented by MPs is extremely low since during the period covered by the table, never exceeding 39 per cent and falling as low as 14 per cent.
3. The low percentage of bills discussed to the total number presented. In 1993 this proportion was only 30 per cent and in 1994 it did not exceed 50 per cent. This means that most of the limited number of bills proposed by the MPs are either rejected or not discussed at all by a parliament in which the ruling party forms the majority.
4. The suspension of the proposed bills, which are presented by MPs reflects the marginalisation of the role of the legislative branch in Egypt. In 1995, 13 proposed bills were suspended and in 1996 the number increased to 16.
5. Although the increased number of proposed bills in the years 1992–1996 is a positive reflection of the MPs' legislative role in parliament, this activity is offset by the limited number of bills discussed and the large number of bills suspended when compared to the total number presented, as previously discussed.
6. Finally, it is quite obvious from the approval of the large number of draft bills presented by the Cabinet that the dominance of the ruling NDP in the parliament enables the government to use the People's Assembly as a rubber stamp for its policies.

Table 3.1a The number of Bills presented by Cabinet members and MPs in the People's Assembly (1988–1991)

Date	Draft Bills (presented by the Cabinet)	Proposed Bills (presented by MPs in the People's Assembly)
1988/1989	345 draft bills, of which 234 were discussed and all approved.	None.
1990	322 presented, of which 214 were discussed and all approved.	Seven presented. Only one was approved.
1991	564 presented, of which 451 were discussed and all approved.	Seven presented. Only one was approved.

Source: Qandil, A., *'Amaliyyat al-Tahawul al-Dimuqraty*, p. 62.

Table 3.1b The number of Bills presented by Cabinet members and MPS in the People's Assembly (1992–1996)

Date	Draft Bills (presented by the Cabinet)	Proposed Bills (presented by MPs in the People's Assembly)
1992	209 presented, of which 102 were discussed and approved.	28 presented, of which 22 were discussed and approved.
1993	247 presented, of which 178 were discussed and were all approved.	20 presented, of which six were discussed and approved.
1994	278 presented, of which 218 were discussed and approved.	22 presented, of which 11 were discussed, 8 were approved and 3 rejected.
1995	152 presented, most of which were discussed and approved.	23 presented, 9 of which were approved, 13 suspended and one rejected.
1996	231 presented, all of which were discussed and approved.	31 presented, 14 of which were added to government bills, 1 approved, and 16 were suspended.

Source: *Al-Taqrir Al-Istratiji Al-Arabi* for the years 1993–1996.

The Control Authority of the Legislative Assembly

Assessing the control role of the legislative over the executive necessitates an analysis of the former's performance in parliament. A quick review of the control tools available to MPs is the starting point for this analysis.

1. Questions: These are the weakest control device available to MPs and are usually used in an inquisitive manner.
   MPs who wish to gain more information about a public issue may direct a question concerning this particular issue either to the relevant minister or to the Prime Minister. Questions may embarrass the government but do not result in any legal action against cabinet members.
2. Formal requests: These are the second weakest control tool available. Like questions the topics discussed can be embarrassing to the government but still they do not result in any legal actions.
3. Interpellations: One of the strongest control devices, interpellations are presented by MPs against cabinet members in an accusative manner which usually involves charges of corruption and mismanagement, and can result in a vote of no confidence in the government.
4. Investigation committees: The strongest control tool, the formation of investigation committees is requested based on specific charges by MPs against the ministers which may result in law suits and criminal charges against any member of the Cabinet.

Table 3.2a The Control Tools used by MPS in the People's Assembly (1990–1993)

Control device	1990	1991	1992	1993
Questions.	139 presented, all answered.	86 presented, all answered.	53 presented, all answered.	54 presented, out of which 43 were answered.
Formal requests.	—	48 presented and discussed.	76 presented and discussed.	165 presented and discussed.
Interpellation.	9 presented, out of which 2 were discussed.	12 presented, out of which 4 were discussed and one withdrawn.	17 presented, out of which 12 were discussed and one withdrawn.	17 presented, out of which 12 were discussed.
Request for a vote of No Confidence.	—	—	—	—
Investigation Committee.	—	—	One requested and accepted.	—
Request for general discussion.	—	3 presented, out of which 2 were discussed.	10 presented, out of which 2 were discussed.	12 presented, out of which 2 were discussed.

Source: *Al-Taqrir Al-Istratiji Al-Arabi* for the years 1991–93.

49

Table 3.2b The Control Tools used by MPs in the People's Assembly
(1994–1996)

Control device	1994	1995	1996
Questions.	130 presented, all answered.	35 presented, all answered.	175 presented and answered.
Formal requests.	51 presented and discussed.	79 presented and discussed.	93 presented and discussed.
Interpellation.	24 presented, out of which 11 were discussed and one withdrawn.	40 presented, out of which only 6 were discussed.	8 presented, 4 discussed, 1 postponed, and 2 withdrawn*.
Request for a vote of No Confidence.	—	—	—
Investigation Committee.	One requested and accepted.	One requested and accepted.	2 requested and accepted.
Request for general discussion.	13 presented, out of which none were discussed.	Some were presented, only 2 were discussed.	1 requested and accepted.

Source: *Al-Taqrir Al-Istratiji Al-Arabi* for the years 1994–1996. *One of the withdrawn interpellations was presented by an NDP MP concerning mismanagement of funds and corruption in government. The interpellation was twice presented in two consecutive parliamentary sessions and were never raised since the MP chose, each time, to withdraw it. This incident proves one of two things: either the government pressured its own MP to withdraw his interpellation, or the latter managed to trade it off for some personal benefits, hence enhancing the weakness of the legislative assembly.

Tables 3.2a & b summarise the control performance of the Egyptian MPs.
From the preceding tables we can observe the following:

1. In 1990, 1991 1994 and 1996 questions, which are the weakest tool of control, were the most commonly used device by MPs in the People's Assembly.
2. Again, in 1991, 1994 and 1996 formal requests, which are still relatively weaker than the interpellation as a control device, ranked as the second most frequently used control device after questions.
3. Interpellation, which is one of the strongest control device, is the least used method by the MPs vis-à-vis the government. The same applies to requests to form investigation committees, which is the strongest control device.
4. Although in 1992 and 1993 70.5 per cent of requested interpellations were discussed, the percentage was as low as 22.2 per cent in 1990, 33.3 per cent in 1991, and 45.8 per cent in 1994 and it dropped to 15 per cent in 1995. Although this percentage increased to 50 per cent in 1996, it still reflects the limitation placed on the MPs in using interpellation as an effective control on the executive branch.

5. Throughout the seven years under study no attempt was made to pass a vote of no confidence in the Cabinet or any of its members, a phenomenon that was also obvious during both the Nasser and Sadat eras.[14]

6. Only five requests for forming investigation committees were formulated during a period of seven years despite the fact that for the year 1993 for example, most of the interpellations presented raised issues of financial and administrative corruption in the government and in local elections as well as issues related to government inefficiency in dealing with terrorism.[15] The dominance of the ruling NDP in the Peoples' Assembly prevents the formation of such committees.

7. The freedom of the MPs to raise general discussions concerning vital subjects is questionable, especially if, as is obvious from the previous table, the percentage of acceptance of such requests is low. For, apart from the year 1991 where it reached 66.6 per cent, and 1996 when the only suggested discussion was accepted, it was 20 per cent for 1992, 16.6 per cent for 1993 and reached its minimum in 1994 where none of the suggested discussions was raised. As for the year 1995, the exact number of requests for discussions that were presented by MPs cannot be traced and therefore the exact percentage of those discussed to the total cannot be accurately calculated. Again, the dominance of the ruling party in parliament, reinforced by the role played by the speaker, limits such discussions, especially if the issues raised are not welcomed by the government.

The weakness of the People's Assembly in its control function over the executive is obvious. This weakness can be largely attributed to the dominance of the ruling NDP in the parliament. The NDP MPs owe their loyalty to the government in the first place and play a prime role as a majority to hinder any interpellation, request for the formation of an investigation committee, or even raising discussions in the People's Assembly that may in any way embarrass the government or question its efficiency. Moreover the parliament's speaker, who is appointed by the President, and thus owes his loyalty to the executive branch, reinforces this parliamentary weakness and plays a pivotal role in frustrating the opposition and weakening its position.[16]

Another point that reflects the weakness of the People's Assembly as a control device and the ability of the government to avoid such checks is related to the general budget. According to the constitution the People's Assembly has to approve every item in the general budget and any change in resource allocation has also to be approved by the People's Assembly. If the parliament initiates changes in the budget, these have to be approved by the government. However, any objections raised by the opposition MPs to any item in the budget or to any of the resources allocation is overruled by the government party MPs who represent the majority in parliament. Hence in theory the People's Assembly can initiate changes in the budget but this right is never translated into practice. Similarly the constitution requires that the government should present its budget to the

People's Assembly at least two months before the beginning of the new financial year and the final statement of account within one year of the end of the financial year. However, the government usually presents its final statement of account at least a year later than the period of time allowed by the constitution. In one case the government presented the final statement of account for the fiscal year 1985/86 to the parliament in 1988, by which time, the People's Assembly had approved a hundred bills contained in the statement, a clear violation of the constitution.[17]

The weakness of the legislative assembly is also reflected in the limited role that the People's Assembly plays in approving international agreements despite the fact that Article 151 of the constitution makes parliamentary approval conditional for the acceptance and finalisation of these agreements.[18] In 1997, for example, 87 of these agreements were approved in one parliamentary meeting, 18 of which were never discussed by the members.[19]

C) The Judiciary

The Egyptian Judicial System from Nasser to Mubarak

An analysis of the status of the Egyptian judicial system further highlights the contradictions found in the constitution on one hand, and the nonconformity of what is being practised to the embodied rules on the other. The various constitutions that were initiated since 1952 accentuated judicial autonomy. For example, the constitutional declaration of 1953 had emphasised the independence of the judiciary. The 1956 constitution had, in addition, included an article which stated that "It is prohibited for any authority to interfere in court cases or in the course of justice."

The same article was preserved in the 1958, 1964, and 1971 constitutions and the amendments to the last in 1981.[20]

Despite this embodiment of judiciary independence in the various constitutions, the judiciary system has not been left unimpaired. The assault on the judiciary started as early as 1954 when Majlis-al Dawla (The State's Council) was adversely criticised and its Chief Justice, al-Sanhuri, retired from public life.

In 1955, a second assault on the Majlis al-Dawla took place bringing it more closely under executive supervision.[21] The final assault on the judiciary came in 1969 with what has been labelled as the 'Massacre of the Judges' when Nasser, in a further attempt to domesticate judges, promulgated several laws. Among these was the establishment of the Supreme Court, the reorganisation of all judicial institutions with the deposition of 189 judges, most of whom were critics of Nasser's policy, and the dissolution of the elected council of the Judges' Club and its replacement by an appointed council.[22] However, in 1975 a court rule restored the elected nature of the Judges' Club, and a law passed in the People's Assembly reinstated all judges who had been the massacre's victims.[23]

Although the 1971 permanent constitution included a whole section labelled "The Supremacy of Law" since Sadat had always called his state the "State of Law", a closer look at its articles reveals several contradictions with regard to the independence of the judiciary and the principal of the separation of powers. For example, articles 64 and 65 of the constitution state that the "supremacy of Law" is the basic rule of governance, that the state is subjected to the control of law, and that judicial independence and immunity are the guarantees of the protection of rights and freedom.[24] However, Law 43 of 1965 and Law 82 of 1972, which was initiated by Sadat through a presidential decree, subordinated judicial power to the executive.

This subordination manifests itself in various ways. To start with the Egyptian judiciary is more an executive rather than a legislative judiciary. In other words, judges execute whatever laws are legislated by the People's Assembly and do not themselves legislate laws. Owing to its ability, by virtue of parliamentary majority, to influence the legislation of laws, the executive apparatus can thus interfere in the course of justice. Second, according to articles 170 and 171 of the constitution, the people should participate in establishing justice, and since the President is the representative of the nation, he can in this capacity interfere in the course of justice. An example of such interference is the formation of exceptional courts and the appointments of members outside the judiciary to try cases in these courts.[25]

Third, the fact that judges are appointed and promoted by the President and that the Minister of Justice is their administrative superior, subordinate the judiciary further to the executive power, which contradicts the principle of judiciary independence. Again, this subordination is manifested in the abolition within the judiciary of the separation between the legal and juristic functions on one hand, and the administrative on the other so that the former have been subjugated to the same principals as govern the latter. This subjugation is based on the right of the government to dismiss or transfer members of the public prosecution service from their jobs without the investigation of a disciplinary council. Another measure undertaken to tighten executive control over the judiciary was the establishment of the Supreme Council of Judicial Institutions presided over by the President with the Minister of Justice as vice-president. This council was given broad responsibilities, among which were those assigned to the Supreme Judiciary Council.[26]

Although under Mubarak Law 35 of 1984 has reorganised the Supreme Judiciary Council to be presided over by the president of the Repeal Court, it retained the Supreme Council of Judicial Institutions under the direct control of the President. However, the interference of the executive in the course of justice continues at present through the Exceptional Courts, the Value Courts and the Supreme Value Court, and the Military Courts.

The executive apparatus established these courts and although the exceptional and military courts include some members who do not belong to the judiciary, their rulings are final and cannot be repealed by any authority. Similarly, the

Value Courts and the Supreme Value Court include among their members, public figures chosen by the Minister of Justice, who are in charge of cases of political nature such as stripping political rights of nomination to local councils, syndicates' council, board of directors of public companies, etc.[27]

Another example, which reflects the extent of executive interference in the course of justice, is the famous incident, which took place in 1984, when the security police bugged the deliberation room of the judges who were trying members of al-Jihad.[28]

Another contradiction found in the constitution lies within the liability and accountability of the Socialist Prosecutor. Whereas, the responsibility for securing the rights and safety of the society, the political system and the socialist gains lies within the power of the Socialist Prosecutor, he himself is accountable to and is under the control of the People's Assembly, i.e.: the legislative branch. This does not only contradict the principle of judicial independence but is also in stark contradiction to article166 which prohibits any power from interference in the judiciary and in the course of justice.[29]

The Supreme Constitutional Court

The degree of independence of the Supreme Constitutional Court is also among the current issues being discussed among Egyptian intellectuals, since it relates to the broader issue of the independence of the judiciary. Whereas article 4 of Law 47 of 1979, which organises the judicial system, necessitated that those who became members in courts should have the general qualifications and conditions that qualify them as judges, the Supreme Constitutional Court has among its members ex-judges and university professors who have acquired a chair for at least eight years. Moreover the President appoints members of the courts after the approval of the Supreme Council of Judicial Institutions. Only the President chooses the head of the Supreme Constitutional Court a system, which contradicts what is embodied in the constitution regarding the independence of the Supreme Constitutional Court.[30]

However, the Supreme Constitutional Court reflected a greater degree of independence from the executive apparatus, when, much to the government's dismay, it ruled against the government in several incidents. Among these occasions is the court ruling in 1983 on the unconstitutionality of Law 135 of 1981 by virtue of which Sadat dissolved the Bar Syndicate.[31] In 1986 the court ruled as unconstitutional article no 4 of Law 33 of 1978,[32] which banned from political activity those who had corrupted political life before the 1952 revolution. As a result of this ruling the political isolation imposed by Sadat on Fouad Siraj al-Din, the late leader of the New Wafd Party, and that of Ibrahim Farag, the party's secretary, came to an end, and they resumed their political activities.[33] The court also ruled as unconstitutional some articles in the political parties' law which led to the nullification of the election law by party slate and the

8 per cent threshold for winning elections and the unconstitutionality of preventing candidates from contesting elections as independents. Again in 1988, the Supreme Constitutional Court ruled as unconstitutional the condition embodied in the parties' law, which prohibits the formation of political parties that oppose Camp David and the peace agreement with Israel.[34] In 1994 the Supreme Constitutional Court ruled as unconstitutional the labour union laws, since the law embodied an article which restricted the proportion of professional members to 20 per cent. The court also acknowledged the right of workers to form more than one union for the same category of labour. However, the court's ruling was ignored by the government who completely opposed its execution. The persistence of the Supreme Constitutional Court in preserving its independence vis-à-vis the executive branch resulted in the latter's continuous attempts from 1996 to bring the Court's rule under tighter governmental control. In 1997 one such government attempt was aborted when a draft bill,[35] which gave the parliament, and consequently the government, control over the ruling of the Supreme Constitutional Court via acceptance or rejection of such rulings, was rejected.[36]

The bill may have been rejected because the reaction of the public was significant at the time it was announced, saving for the time being the powers of the Supreme Constitutional Court, the only remaining defender of civil liberty in Egypt.

The Administrative and the Supreme Emergency Court

Similarly, the Administrative Court and the Supreme Emergency Court showed the same degree of independence on several occasions. In 1987, the Administrative Court ruled for halting the Interior Ministry's Decree with regard to the announcement of election results, and the success of 17 members of the opposition whose names were replaced by members of the NDP, and the nullification of the results of 78 members who had succeeded in the elections by default. However, the Ministry of Interior refused to execute the court's ruling.[37] The same incident occurred in the 1990 and the 1995 elections, when the Court of Appeal nullified the membership of several NDP MPs whom were either ineligible for parliamentary membership or whose success in elections was attributed to fraud and violence. The Administrative Court also ruled in 1996 for the nullification of the election results in some districts. In the first case the People's Assembly refused to accept the court's ruling raising the slogan that "the assembly is the master of its own decision", and in the second case the Minister of Interior again refused to execute the court's order[38] thus making a mockery of the rule of law.

In 1987, the Supreme Security Emergency Court ruled for the acquittal of all railway workers charged in the strike. However, the executive apparatus represented in the President refused to accept the court's ruling.[39]

To sum up, the relative autonomy of the courts discussed above as reflected in the strength of their rulings vis-à-vis the executive apparatus is usually offset by their administrative subordination to the latter, and the refusal of the executive apparatus to accept and execute these rulings.

3. The Transformation from a Single-Party System to a Multi-Party System

A) Nasser's Era: The Single-Party System

One of Nasser's early acts, once he assumed power, was the abolition of all the political parties that had functioned under the old regime as a means of breaking up the old elites on the one hand and eliminating all opposition to his rule on the other. Instead Nasser created his own party, as La Palombara has commented,

> It is not a matter of historical chance that dictatorial regimes in the modern world rely heavily on the political party. . . . Thus political elites may create parties (or give the name of a party to some other political groupings) when in fact the conditions for the establishment and maintenance of political parties are absent and when what has been created is not in fact a political party.[40]

So was the case with Nasser except that he denounced the word party, which to him signified "partisanship, conflict and division within the body politic".[41] He favoured the term "Organisation" and labelled his own party system "Political Organisations". These he attempted to establish in order to fill the vacuum created by the sudden disappearance of all other parties from the political scene. Three such attempts were carried out for the main purpose of mobilising the masses, where in fact their existence coincided with the leader's need to sustain his hegemony or otherwise his policy.

The Liberation Rally (LR) the first such organisation, was formed in January 1952. Although the official announcement indicated that the purpose of the LR was the mobilisation of popular forces and the provision of training for the people to choose their representative,[42] the real objective was if anything quite the opposite. Lacouture has presented the following vivid description of one of the meetings held by the Rally, which supports this view.

> First came the speeches which were listened to with respect, and then a kind of forum was held during which citizens could voice their complaints and suggestions. They did so and were allowed to say as much as they liked about drains and schools. But as soon as the discussion turned toward political questions, they were cut short.[43]

In fact the LR helped to 'depoliticise' the society, a task that was intentionally designed for the Rally to accomplish.[44] In reality the Rally's main function was to mobilise support for Nasser himself in his power struggle against Naguib, the father figure of the revolution, and the first Egyptian President. Once Nasser had secured his hegemony over the entire country and emerged as the undisputed leader, the LR having achieved all its purposes, was allowed to die only to be replaced later on by yet another organisation namely the National Union (NU).

The NU was formally announced in the 1956 constitution but was not actually organised until 1959.[45] It was organised on the communist party model of the eastern bloc with its pyramidal shape and hierarchical order and with commands flowing from top to bottom. At the bottom level, the village, was the basic unit committee which elected members of the NU committee for the district level, whose activities were in turn supervised by a bureau of officers which included a president, a vice president, a secretary and a treasurer. The same structure was repeated at the provincial level.

In the capital, a central committee was established. This was controlled by an executive committee composed mainly of former RCC officers, with Anwar-Al-Sadat appointed as the secretary general of the Union.[46]

Since the interest of this study lies in the society at large, but more specifically in peasant society, the relationship between the NU and the local units at this point, deserve more elaboration. In addition to the previous structure of the National Union already described, the various local councils were established under a separate plan of the Ministry of Social Affairs in co-operation with the Ministry of Municipal and Rural Affairs. As a general rule members of the local councils had to be chosen from the NU membership or at least be approved by it. Accordingly, members of rural municipal districts and provincial local councils would have to be chosen from those elected to the NU at these different levels. The same rule was applicable to the head of the different local units. Thus any town mayors, quarter sheikhs or village 'Umdas not approved by the NU elections would automatically lose their offices.

As well as having responsibility for recommending candidates for the local councils, the local NU committees were also supposed to guide their societies to co-operative production, to analyse local problems, and make policy recommendations to local officials.[47] Thus, like its predecessor, the NU was used to prevent the participation of any group, party or person opposing the policies of the ruling elites. As a political organisation that should have mobilised the people and encouraged their participation in decision-making from the village upward, the NU fared no better than the Liberation Rally and ended up being inactive at all levels of government. As Harik noted,

> All policies were made by the national government under Nasser and the party shared in decision-making only to the extent that officers of the national command structure were also ministers of the state.[48]

With the collapse of the union which Egypt had forged with Syria in 1959, the National Union was dissolved and later re-organised in 1961 under the name of

57

the Arab Socialist Union (ASU). The ASU was Nasser's third and last attempt at creating a political mobilising organisation in the country.

In explaining the objective of the ASU and the nature of its membership, Nasser stated that it represented the alliance of the working forces, which he had identified as the peasants, workers, intellectuals, soldiers and native capitalists. The last category would include retail traders, contractors, manufacturers, craftsmen, farmers and service-oriented businessmen.[49] It would be misleading to presume that with this statement Nasser had acknowledged the autonomy of each of these groups for,

> Nasser's theory of the working forces was just a classification scheme of the population, not a recognition of organisational autonomy for each group.[50]

Membership of the ASU was voluntary and open to all adult citizens, who had to apply to the ASU and pay an annual fee. However, the voluntary nature of membership was a fiction since, in order for anyone to be eligible for elections to any co-operative board, local, regional or national assembly or the board of any union or professional association, he/she had to be a member of the ASU. In some cases, even the right to exercise certain professions, such as journalism, was conditional on being an ASU member.[51]

The structure of the ASU did not depart completely from that of the NU, except with regard to two innovations that distinguished it from the latter. The first of these was the reservation of 50 per cent of the seats on all committees, including the national assembly, for workers and peasants.[52] Its charter stated that,

> The popular and political organisations based on free and direct election must truly and fairly represent the powers forming the majority of the population. It follows then that the new constitution must ensure that its farmers and workmen will get half the seats in the political and popular organisations at all levels, including the House of Representatives since they form the majority of the people.[53]

Such reservation, had it been properly applied, would have guaranteed a broader and fairer type of representation for the poorer segments of the society. However, as Ayubi notes,

> The rising elites have gradually succeeded in giving the categories of 'worker' and 'peasant' a very loose definition that enabled several managers, technocrats and professionals to ease their way into the directing positions of the ASU, as it were under false pretence and thus to occupy more seats than those originally allotted for their occupational class groups.[54]

The second innovation was the introduction of basic units not only in the villages and urban quarters but also in places of work, be it factories, offices, schools, universities, banks and even in government ministries and agencies. People working in these places were expected to participate in these basic units.[55] Although such arrangements appear on the surface to conform with Nasser's slogans of 'true democracy', a closer look reveals the fact that the ASU's penetration in the different spheres of activity and work provided the central government with an efficient tool of control and regulation otherwise denied to it, over the whole Egyptian society.[56] In this respect the ASU did not differ much in its main function as a control device from its predecessors the NU and LR.

The ASU functioned through a dual system of congresses and committees which apart from existing in the workplace, would also exist in the village, district, province and then at the highest level viz. the national. The congress included all the committees of the lower units and elected a committee to carry on the work of the ASU between congress meetings. In this respect the congress was supreme, but the committee was more active politically. The highest authority was vested in the central committee that was elected by the General Congress and which in turn elected the powerful Higher Executive Committee.[57]

The relationship between the ASU and the local units was manifested in Law 124 of 1960 and its amendments, which necessitated the election of members of the local councils from the ASU membership within the relevant governorate, town or village. As for the appointed members, these should, according to Law 65 of 1964, be selected from the active members of the basic units or other levels of the ASU of the governorate within which the councils were located. In this respect the relationship between the ASU and local units became clear.[58] Recruitment to the highest echelons of the ASU was done by Nasser himself who hand-picked the national leaders to fill the posts in the Supreme Executive Committee and the secretariat. Whereas his aides and cabinet members were appointed by the Supreme Executive Committee, the secretariat was headed by a founding member of the Free Officers Junta.[59] Because it was devised as a means of control and to eliminate the regime's political opponents, "the ASU recruited politically impotent and pliable members rather than establishing a cadre of dedicated party professionals and ideologues."[60] A study by Dekemejian of 131 Egyptian officials who had held ministerial positions between 1952–1968 showed that only two had had positions in political organisations prior to achieving ministerial rank, whereas 83 had held their party position either during or after their term of office,[61] thus leading Moore to conclude that the ASU was "hardly a vanguard for recruiting top political leadership, the party was more like a rearguard for retiring it".[62]

It is worth noting here that during Nasser's era the ASU was made supreme to the National Assembly, a fact that was reflected in the party secretariat's major function of screening candidates for the National Assembly, all of whom had to be members of the ASU. Thus a candidate had to establish a position for himself within the ASU before he could run for election to the National Assembly. Although they ran for election as independents, as the party never openly backed or financed any of the candidates,[63] yet, "it was a common practice, however, for the regime to give confidential instructions to provincial governors to make sure that a number of favoured candidates were elected."[64]

Inevitably, the ASU simply reflected the tendency of the regime to control the masses rather than creating a real political organisation capable of mobilising them. Thus the cadres in the party were sacrificed for the sake of the experts and technocrats and ideological indoctrination ceased to be a sought objective.[65]

Eventually the ASU became bureaucratic and conformed to Ayubi's comment that it was an "indolent government department manned by 'routinist civil servants'"[66] and that "the whole experiment of the ASU has thus demonstrated that it is relatively easy – through 'slogans' and 'organisations' -to draw crowds, but difficult to make committed followers and living political institutions".[67]

The Effect of Nasserism on Society

In his "philosophy of the revolution" Nasser expressed his disappointment in the masses who did not move as he had expected to support his coup. To him the masses were in an anarchic state and the intellectuals were hypocrites and devoid of all creative ideas. Only the members of the revolutionary command council were capable of leading the country. Since he had such a negative view of the masses, it is difficult to believe that Nasser's desire to increase popular participation and to create a real democratic society was genuine, especially as one of his early acts was to abolish all political parties. This abolition deepened the participation crisis that Egyptian society has been suffering since the late forties and early fifties.

Nasser's legacy played a major role in shaping the development of the political system inherited by Sadat. Nasser had created an authoritarian, nationalist and populist state, where all power was concentrated in the hands of the charismatic leader, who enjoyed the status of an authoritarian president. Aided by a number of military cadets Nasser developed an entrenched authoritarian bureaucratic state, which he used to extend control through all sectors of the society and to impose a revolution from above.[68]

In fact Nasser's political organisations were used alongside the army, the police and the secret service to crush any opposition to his rule and to cripple the people's ability to think and act. What Nasser had actually succeeded in creating was a repressive "Mukhabarat State",[69] or a police state. In summing up the Nasserite experience and its effect on the Egyptians Fouad Zakariya has argued that it contained elements

> of oppression exceeding by far legal limits for the protection of the revolution against a minority opposition. Consequently, Egyptian man emerged from this experience quite different from what he was at its beginning. At first he felt he could speak, discuss and object and the country was his country, in which his opinion could be heard. But after mass arrests, fear crept into him gradually. Fear led to negativism, hypocrisy and double talk. The Egyptian lost his ability to object, reject and protest, for terror was

60

accompanied by an organised propaganda campaign aimed at there being only one opinion and one point of view in the country. This inner destruction of the Egyptian's soul, personality and mind was one of the greatest disasters of the Nasserite experience.[70]

B) Sadat's Era

The Single-Party System under Sadat

A major problem which confronted Sadat, as Nasser's successor, was the consolidation of his authority vis-à-vis Ali Sabri, the leader of the ASU. Sabri, who was one of the power centres during the Nasser era aspired to oust Sadat from power and take over the presidency.[71] The details of the power struggle between Sadat and the Sabri group is of little importance to us here except for the fact that it highlights two important political strategies which Sadat adopted from the outset and which persisted as major characteristics of his rule.

First, the shifting of power from the governmental party to the National Assembly and vice versa, by strengthening the one at the expense of the other, a strategy Sadat continued to employ throughout the period of his presidency to undermine the position of his political opponents and reduce the effectiveness of the opposition.[72]

Second: the fluctuation that characterised his relationship with the rural notables and which in turn was reflected in their representation in the National Assembly and in the different levels of local administration. It is interesting to note that Sadat accommodated and tolerated the rural elites in as much as they could serve his personal interest, but as soon as he sensed a change or a shift in their loyalty, he did not hesitate to strike them down and curtail their influence. Hence, at the beginning, when he needed social support during his power struggle, Sadat sought the help of the rural notables especially those landowners whose land had been sequestrated and who had been discredited during Nasser's era. Sadat succeeded in winning the support of all deputies from Upper Egypt and Behera, the very areas where traditional influence was concentrated.[73] In contrast, the support for his opponents was mainly derived from the urban areas and from such provinces as Sharqiya, Dumyat and the Canal cities, where the members of the factions had established kinship links.[74]

Sadat's tactics paid off and once he had consolidated his position in power, he purged the ASU of Sabri and his colleagues and imprisoned most of them.

During his first years in the presidency Sadat did not show any interest in reorganising or reviving the ASU.[75]

The few changes that he initiated as early as 1971, by replacing leftist officers with his loyal supporters and by allowing rural notables to recover their position in the local branches,[76] had only a limited effect, if any, on the organisational and

61

functional framework of the ASU, and were meant initially to serve Sadat's personal interests. Instead of depending on the ASU as a vehicle for achieving economic modernisation, Sadat advocated a market economy to develop Egypt, thus depriving the ASU of its major role.[77] In 1974, Ihsan Abdul Kudus, one of the closest journalists to Sadat, wrote in *Al Ahram,* probably reflecting Sadat's opinion,

> In reality the ASU is an official organisation, like any other governmental unit, and it could have been called the Ministry for Political and Popular Affairs.[78]

The Transfer to Controlled Diversity

Sadat's earlier act of giving the parliament supremacy over the ASU symbolised the return of Egypt to a relatively liberal political life. Moreover, the legitimacy which Sadat had acquired for his rule, especially after the 1973 October War, enabled him to move confidently in his liberalisation efforts. The July 1975 election that took place within the ASU came to manifest the regime's announced commitment to liberalisation and at the same time to designate the ASU's death rather than revival.

In its first meeting directly after the election, the National Congress approved the formation of platforms or manabir.[79] These platforms were to function within the framework of the ASU. Of the forty proposed platforms only three were approved and allowed to be formed. These were a 'liberal' right minbar, a centre minbar which was the pro-government faction and a 'left' minbar. These manabir were permitted to compete in the 1976 parliamentary election, the result of which was a victory for the government centre platform with a majority of 280 seats. The right won only 12 seats, the left 4 and 48 seats went to independents.[80]

This result was, however, not surprising taking into consideration that the elections were conducted under the protective influence of the 'government party', which has better access to financial, logistical and communication facilities than any other party.[81] The result of these elections encouraged Sadat to approve the transformation of the manabir into independent parties.

This move towards limited political liberalisation did not reflect Sadat's departure from the dominant single party system, nor should it be understood as the introduction of a multi-party system similar to that prevalent in Western societies. As Vatikiotis has commented, "What was being introduced under this controlled change was not so much an element of pluralism in Egyptian political life as one of diversity".[82] Nevertheless, this diversity could have constituted a transitional stage from the era of single party domination to a truly pluralistic system.

The question which should be asked here is why such a transformation failed to take place. Here again the conditions that necessitated the change should be examined and the degree to which Sadat was committed to political liberalism should be explored. It became obvious that one of Sadat's major aims for the 1973 War was to pressurise the United States into initiating the peace negotiations, which in turn would free him from an external threat and allow him to concentrate his efforts on internal problems.

In addition, Sadat had decided at an early stage to shift his alliance from the Soviet Union to the USA. The latter, he hoped, would provide him with the dollars needed to save the deteriorating economy in the form of both aid and investment. He had thus aimed to transfer the economic system from a centrally planned economy, in which the public sector played a major role, to a free market economy, in which the private sector would be the prime initiator of development. In order to encourage foreign investment, he initiated a series of laws that inaugurated the beginning of his famous "open door policy".

The most important of these laws were the foreign investment law No. 43 for 1974 and the private sector law No. 93 for 1974.[83] It was for this reason that Sadat introduced what he labelled "political liberalisation". It was these circumstances that persuaded Sadat to introduce diversity in the political system. Sadat's early pronouncements testify to the lack of any genuine commitment on his part to either pluralism or diversity. In his so-called October Paper, announced in April 1974, Sadat stated, "I refuse any appeal to fragment the national unity in an artificial manner through the formation of parties".[84] The same statement was repeated a year later in his October Paper announced in November 1975.[85] It is not surprising then that Sadat's diversity was accompanied by numerous measures to ensure its limitation, such as the constitutional supremacy retained by the President over all parties and his right to set the framework within which the parties could offer 'constructive alternatives'.[86]

The Formation of the Government Party

However, out of such diversity emerged the government party now named the National Democratic Party (NDP) under Sadat's leadership and representing the Centre, and two opposition parties, the Liberal Party (LP), Hizb Al-Ahrar, which emerged from the right-wing of the old ASU and the National Unionist Progressive Party (NUPP), Hizb Al-Tagammu', representing the nationalist left. Later on two new opposition parties were allowed to form, the New Wafd Party (NW), representing the liberal right opposition, and the Socialist Labour Party (SLP), representing the centre left.[87] The opposition in Egypt will be the subject of discussion in the next chapter and hence this chapter will concentrate on the government party, the "NDP". Apart from a number of changes, the structure and functioning of the NDP was similar to that of the ASU.

The political bureau of the party is headed by a president with one or more vice-presidents. A parliamentary group functions within the bureau a novelty addition dictated by the existence of opposition parties. Like its predecessor, the NDP was imposed and organised from the top down, including provincial and district committees, headed by secretaries. However, unlike the ASU, the NDP lacks any representation at the village level. It has failed just as much as the ASU in acting as a recruitment channel for political leadership. To a large extent, advancement within the party comes from above rather than from the support of constituencies below. Accordingly nominations, appointments and purges coming from the highest level are the major determinants of political leadership. Like its predecessor, the party has infiltrated the different institutions in society, such as universities, professional associations and syndicates.[88] However, the NDP under Sadat came to reflect and protect the interest of the bourgeoisie or munfatihun, those who had benefited from Sadat's open door policy and with whom Sadat came to identify.[89]

At the local level, the rich peasants, landlords and 'umad are often members of the party and to the extent that they represent the leadership status within their villages, districts and provinces, they tend to link the mass of peasants to the regime.[90] However, with its bias towards bourgeois interest, the NDP's committees, recommendations and lack of peasants' representation in parliament reflects the tendency of the party to have weak ties with the peasants. The same applies to relations with labour.

As Springborg has mentioned,

> Rural political mobilisation which occurred fitfully under the auspices of the ASU during the Nasser era, has given way entirely in the NDP to the priorities of control and demobilisation of the peasantry combined with the consolidation of power by the bourgeoisie. Erosion of the single party's base in the labour movement has also occurred as independent labour activists have deserted the NDP for opposition parties.[91]

C) Mubarak's Era

The ruling party under Mubarak's leadership reflects continuity from the Sadat era. Apart from being the government party, with its elites being those of the executive and security apparatus of the government and its programme being the official government programme, the NDP since its formation in 1978 continues to be devoid of any specific official ideology.[92]

As one author has commented,

> Failing to articulate a clear ideological line, the party comprises a hodge-podge of individuals with Nasserist leanings (Trade Union leaders, pro-public sector technocrats and bureaucrats), Sadatists (e.g. pro-infitah technocrats, private capitalists) and a legion of pure opportunists.[93]

Despite the fact that it was hoped that Mubarak, once he assumed power, would give up his leadership of the NDP to become above party affiliation and instead act as an arbitrator between all parties, all such hopes vanished when he accepted the party leadership as early as January 1982, a fact that frustrated most of the opposition and went contrary to the will of the people.[94] Similarly the class structure in Mubarak's NDP continues to be much the same as during his predecessor's leadership.

One of the few changes which Mubarak initiated in this respect was to rid the NDP of some of the strongest factions of the Sadat era, especially those whose names were linked to major corruption scandals. By pushing some of the conservative Nasserites to the fore, Mubarak succeeded in counterbalancing the strong Sadat faction and their clients in the NDP, only to replace them with his own clientele network of bourgeois apparatchiks, a job that was successfully carried out by his party's secretary general Youssef Wali.[95] Thus under Mubarak, the NDP continues to be "an enclave of bourgeois exclusivity".[96]

4. Conclusion

The inherent contradictions embodied in the constitution highlight the weakness of the Egyptian political system and accentuate the gap between theoretical ideals and practical realities. Whereas in theory the principle of the division of powers between the legislative, executive and judicial should exist, in reality this separation is completely blurred as a result of the enormous powers given to the President as chief executive, while he is at the same time the head of the government party, has the right to dissolve parliament and to legislate laws, and is the head of the Supreme Council of Judicial Institutions. Thus the executive branch is strengthened at the expense of the legislative and judicial branches. This is clearly reflected in the weakness of the People's Assembly both in its legislative function and in its control role vis-à-vis the government, and in the latter's refusal to accept and execute court orders. The parliamentary majority of the government's National Democratic Party, which acts more like a government appendage bureau than a real party, increases the weakness of the legislative branch. It is within this legal and constitutional framework that the performance of the Egyptian opposition parties is examined in the following chapter, highlighting to what extent they are affected by the various limitations imposed on them by this political system.

CHAPTER FOUR

Political Parties in Egypt

1. Introduction

A major criterion for assessing the stage of political development in any nation is the degree to which political participation by various segments in the society occurs, especially by those who do not belong to the dominant political elite. Political participation can be viewed as a psychological process that induces the involvement of the masses in the political system. In a civil society, such involvement is broad. This does not mean that in a civic culture, or in countries with established democracies the citizen is at all times constantly involved in politics and in checking elite behaviour, but rather as Almond and Verba argue, the citizen has

> the potential to act if there is need . . ., he is rarely active in political groups. But he thinks that he can mobilise his ordinary social environment if necessary for political use. He is not the active citizen. He is the potential active citizen.[1]

It is this psychological awareness of the people that develops in them a sense of identification with the nation-state as distinct from parochial groupings. But for such awareness to develop the ordinary citizen should not only believe in his ability to affect his socio-political environment but also in the existence of legitimate avenues of participation. Among such avenues are political parties. Political parties tend to affect the degree of "civicness" of the society in which they exist and hence the importance of the role attributed to them.

Through socialisation and mobilisation political parties help to institutionalise certain norms and values about the political system and seek to bring the apathetic, the alienated, the cynical and the ignorant into the system by reflecting their interests. Subsequently, through participation they create the medium whereby the expression of interest and choice of policies and leaders is opened to all[2] thus creating an active civic society. It has been argued that in the absence of political parties and institutions, such an objective becomes unattainable. It is quite true that,

Without strong political institutions, society lacks the means to define and to realise its common interests. The capacity to create political institutions is the capacity to create public interests.[3]

In chapter three, the Egyptian legal system has been discussed and a historical background for the change to a multi-party system has been presented. In this chapter a brief review of the major opposition parties in Egypt will be provided, the main constrains imposed on them will be discussed, and an attempt at assessing their performance will be made.

2. The Legal and Constitutional Constraints on Opposition Parties

The various contradictions inherent in the constitution have been pinpointed in the previous chapter. To continue this analysis the different laws which govern the formation of the political parties, and those which regulate their representation in parliament will now be discussed.

Limitations on Party Formation

Law No. 40, 1977

This was the first law introduced by Sadat after he allowed the formation of platforms within the ASU and their transformation into political parties in 1976. It should be first noted that this law, which was supposed to regulate the formation of political parties, was promulgated after and not before the transformation of platforms into parties. The law imposed numerous limitations on the freedom of party formation. Three of its articles in particular warrant further discussion, since they represent the bedrock of this control.

The first of these is item No. 2 of Article 4, which stipulates that the parties should have a specific programme distinguishable from that of other parties.[4] Based on this article the Nasserite party under Sadat, and a number of new parties under Mubarak, were denied formation and had to resort to the courts to gain official recognition. Item No. 3 of Article 4 states that no party should be allowed to form on a class, religion, geographical, or on gender, ethnic or religious basis.[5] Under this article the Muslim Brotherhood (MB) which supposedly represents a moderate religious movement, is denied recognition.

The second is Article No. 8, which gives the right of approval or refusal of the formation of political parties to the Committee of Political Parties Affairs. This committee is formed of:

The head of the consultative council;
The Minister of Justice;

The Minister of Interior Affairs;

The Minister of the People's Assembly and three ex-Judges or their deputies, who should not be affiliated to any party and are chosen by the President.[6]

As is obvious, the committee owes its loyalty to the executive and thus the formation of the parties is effectively at the discretion of the government.

The third of these articles is Article No. 17, which empowers the Committee of Political Parties Affairs to stop a party's newspaper and activities if the committee deems it necessary in the national interest.[7] Again, the executive is able to control the formation of political parties.

Law No. 33, 1978 for the protection of the home front and social peace

The most important article for this analysis is Article No. 4 of this law, which bans from political activity those who corrupted political life before the 1952 revolution, including those who held ministerial positions or who belonged to any political parties that ruled before the 1952 revolution. These individuals cannot participate in or manage political parties except in the case of the NDP.[8] This particular article was aimed at the New Wafd party, which is the heir of the famous pre-1952 Wafd party and its late leader Fouad Siraj al-Din. Sadat was much alarmed by the Wafd's strength and popularity among the people and was antagonised by the attack of the Wafdist MP on the government and on Sadat personally inside the parliament.

Sadat succeeded, however, by using this article in halting a major opposition force in the seventies when the New Wafd party was forced to disband, only to re-emerge in the1980s. However on 21st June 1986 the Supreme Constitutional Court ruled Article 4 of Law No. 33 for 1978 unconstitutional.[9]

Law No. 36, 1979

This law added several further restrictions to the previous law and was a prelude to Sadat's final crackdown on all kinds of opposition to his rule in 1981, by imposing still more restrictions on political parties. For example, according to Article 4 item 6, all those who opposed the peace agreement with Israel were denied the right to form a party.[10] Also item 2 of Article 15 made the party leader and the editor responsible for whatever was published in the party's newspaper.[11]

By virtue of this article party leaders could be sued for any criticism directed against Sadat, his policies or any member of his executive machinery. Again the 1979 law was introduced to set limitations on some of the privileges that were earlier granted to political parties in Articles 13 and 15 of the 1977 law.[12] For instance, opposition parties enjoyed certain tax exemptions and had the right to issue their own newspapers. However, Article 18 of the 1979 law made such privileges conditional on the party's representation in parliament being at least 10 members.[13]

Law No. 108, 1992

This law was directed at the rise of political Islam. The changes that were initiated in the law revolved around two points. The first was the prohibition of party activities by any group before acquiring official recognition by the Committee for Political Parties Affairs. This provision was aimed at the illegitimate party activities[14] of the Muslim Brotherhood. The second was targeted against the Labour Party, since it prohibited any party from having any foreign contacts or foreign connections without informing the Committee of Political Parties' Affairs and reporting to the latter the results of such contacts within fifteen days. This provision was intended to control the Labour Party's contacts with Islamic parties and organisations in the area, especially those in Sudan.[15]

The Electoral Laws

Law 114, 1983

The People's Assembly passed a most controversial law in 1983. Law 114 of 1983 departed from all the electoral systems that had been known in Egypt, even during the pre-1952 regime. According to this law the following rules were initiated:

First, membership of the People's Assembly was raised from 380 to 448, with the number of constituencies being reduced from 176 to 48. In thirty-one of these constituencies one seat was reserved for women and ten additional members were to be appointed by the President bringing the assembly total to 458.

Second, party slates under a proportional representation system replaced single-member constituencies and no one was allowed to stand for election as an independent.

Third, a party had to secure 8 per cent of the national vote to receive representation in the People's Assembly.

Fourth, a party had to reach a certain percentage in a constituency otherwise its votes were added to the majority party. The following example given by Najjar in his review of this law illustrates this point. Suppose there were ten seats for which the parties are competing. Each party had to win 10 per cent of the votes to secure one seat. If for example there were a party winning 19 per cent of the votes rather than the 20 per cent needed to secure two seats, it would be given one seat with the loss of the additional 9 per cent to the majority party. The principal beneficiary was of course the NDP.

Finally, each party had to nominate a number of candidate equivalent to the number of seats in each constituency and a similar number had to be placed on a reserve list from which replacements were made in case of death or resignation.[16]

It is clear from the previous discussion that law no.114 was intended to limit opposition parties severely by introducing the 8 per cent restriction. This, along with the bar on individuals running as independents, guaranteed the ruling party a monopoly over legislation.[17] The latter restriction was in violation of the constitution since it is a constraint on individual rights. Moreover, the law further discriminated against the opposition and in favour of the NDP through the system of bonus votes that were added to the majority party's tally.

As one author has commented,

> To deny a party which wins a majority of the votes in a number of districts representation and to give its votes to the winning party 'is contrary to reason, justice and logic and is at variance with all constitutional and democratic traditions, values and usages'.[18]

Subsequently, the Supreme Constitutional Court had ruled as unconstitutional the prohibition on individuals running as independents, since it violates equal rights and equality of opportunity as embodied in the constitution (Articles 8 and 40). Also the transfer of surplus votes to the majority party violated the same articles of the constitution and hence was ruled invalid. The government was able to maintain the 8 per cent requirement for presentation since the higher Constitutional Court did not find any article in the constitution to contradict such provision.[19] Accordingly, in an attempt to overcome the previous obstacles the government hastily initiated a new electoral law in December 1986.

Law No. 1988, 1986

This law combined elections through party slate with independent candidacy. According to this law the number of constituencies remained 48 and the seats reserved for women were abolished. Only one person in each constituency was to run in the elections as an independent. All other candidates had to be on a party slate.[20] An independent candidate was chosen on the basis of winning the support of at least 20 per cent of the total votes in the electoral district. Party slates were allocated seats in proportion to the valid votes won, with the remaining votes given to the slate with surplus exceeding half of the electoral average for that district, or it is given to the party slate with the majority on the national level.

The conditional 8 per cent threshold for representation in parliament remained unchanged.[21] It is obvious that this law was intended to circumvent the previous ruling of the Constitutional Court referred to above and to continue protecting the party slate system of elections. However, the Supreme Constitutional Court has again ruled in 1988 this law unconstitutional because of its bias against individuals, who were given only one seat to compete for in each constituency as opposed to the number of seats given to those nominated on party slates, which violates equal rights and opportunities as embodied in the constitution.[22] Consequently, President Mubarak issued a decree in 1990, whereby parliament was reduced to 444 members with the right of the President to appoint ten members. The electoral system was to return to independent elections, and the party slate system was abolished.

3. The Major Opposition Parties in Egypt: A Brief Introduction

The following table summarises all the political parties in Egypt, their date of formation and their source of legitimacy. However, most of these parties are marginal and play no role in the political life in Egypt. Accordingly the study will concentrate on the five major parties, since the government party, the NDP, has been analysed earlier in detail.

The previous table shows that all parties, which were formed since the early 90's have acquired legitimacy through court rulings rather than through the

Table 4.1 Political parties in Egypt and their source of legitimacy

Party's Name	Date of Formation	Base of Legitimacy
The National Democratic Party (NDP)	1978	Approval of Parties Committee.
Nationalist Unionist Progressive Party (NUPP)	1976	Approval of Parties Committee.
Liberal Socialist Party (LSP)	1976	Approval of Parties Committee.
Labour Party (SLP)	1978	Approval of Parties Committee.
New Wafd Party (NWP)	1978	Approval of Parties Committee, then a court ruling in 1983 after it dissolved itself.
Al Omma Party	1990	Court ruling.
Young Egypt	1990	Court ruling.
Green Party	1990	Court ruling.
Unionist Party	1990	Court ruling.
Unionist Democratic Party	1990	Court ruling.
People's Democratic Party	1992	Court ruling.
The Egyptian Arabic Socialist Party	1992	Court ruling.
The Democratic Arab Nasserite Party	1992	Court ruling.
The Social Equality Party	1992	Court ruling.

Source: Qandil, A., *'Amaliyyat al-Tahawul al-Dimuqraty,* p. 123.

approval of the parties committee. This in turn highlights two important facts. The first is the extent of limitations imposed by the government on the formation of opposition parties. The second is the relative autonomy and strength of some of the Egyptian courts, which ruled against the will of the executive branch and in favour of these parties.

The Liberal Party (LP) (Hizb-al-Ahrar)

Emerging from the right platform of the ASU, Al Ahrar was one of two parties created by Sadat in 1976 to act as a loyal opposition to his regime in the sense that it would legitimise his democratic pretence without imposing any limitation on his rule, and would at the same time contain the different political tendencies in society and place them under his tight control. The party's mission was therefore to contain both the secular liberal right representing the ex-Wafdists and other pre-1952 forces, and the religious right representing the Muslim Brotherhood (MB) and its successors.

Accordingly, the party tried to present itself as both the party of capital and of God,[23] but as one author has commented,

> The ideological combination of religiosity and property is a familiar stamp of conservatism elsewhere, but in Egypt, where the bourgeoisie is traditionally liberal and the religious right illiberal, the attempt to combine them was not apparently viable.[24]

This was reflected in the setback that the party had experienced in the 1979 election. Although the party had made a strong start, winning twelve parliamentary seats in 1976, and succeeded in securing nine more adherents in 1977, in 1979 only three deputies were elected from the party and its leader was defeated.

This deterioration occurred because of the party's attempt to combine ideologies. It failed to establish itself as a major right wing party, especially after the formation of the New Wafd party in 1978, when twelve Ahrar deputies and other party members defected to the new party. At the same time, the party failed to attract the religious right who approved neither of its leadership nor of its liberal ideology, nor, especially after 1977, its embracing of the Israeli connection. However, in its capacity as a loyal opposition, Al-Ahrar, served Sadat's purposes well. It supported his economic liberalisation policy and his pro-Western foreign policy, especially his peace initiatives, to the extent that the party's late leader Mourad accompanied Sadat on his trip to Jerusalem at a time when Sadat's own foreign minister declined to go.[25] The party's deputies in parliament also backed Sadat's policy on a number of other occasions, the most famous of which was the pyramid plateau project which at that time antagonised the whole nation. In addition, incidents were reported where the party's deputies had, in compliance with Sadat's government, staged interpellations exposing certain issues to cover up for others.[26] It was not surprising then that the party lost its credibility with the masses. Under Mubarak the party became more fundamentalist, with one of the extremely anti-Christian newspapers known as *Al-Nur*. Ever since its liberal leaders abandoned the party to join the New Wafd, the party had been trying to attract the Muslim Brotherhood, which culminated in a tripartite alliance with the Labour Party, and competition in the 1987 elections.[27]

Generally speaking, the party's role as an opposition is very marginal. The party used to revolve around its late leader, Moustafa Mourad, an ex-Free Officer, with an extremely vague ideology and programme. In the 1995 elections to the People's Assembly the LP succeeded in gaining one seat in parliament for the first time since the 1979 elections.[28] The same modest result was achieved in the 2000 elections, when the party again managed to win only one seat.[29] Mourad's sudden death in 1999 left the leadership position contested during the first round of nomination among eleven nominees for the presidency. The elimination process has finally restricted the competition among two main contestants, Helmy Ahmad Salem and Ragab Hamida. However, and in compliance with articles 6, 53, 54, 86 of the party's bylaw that has been submitted in 1988 to the Political Parties Committee, Helmy Ahmad Salem is considered the legitimate successor of Murad. This legitimacy stems from three conditions that, according to the previous articles, have been set for the presidency, and which Salem meets. The first being the party's first deputy, the second being the founder of the party, and the third being the oldest of the two candidates. The final result is pending on the meeting of the party's General Conference, where an election will take place to confer the presidency on either of the two candidates.[30] The acceptance or otherwise rejection of the election results by the loosing candidate will determine whether or not court suits will be filled and hence whether the party will peacefully resume its activities or whether it is going to witness a period of factionalisation and internal strife.

The Nationalist Unionist Progressive Party (NUPP)

The Nationalist Unionist Progressive Party emerged out of the left platform of the ASU. This was the second party Sadat created to act as an official opposition, in order to contain all leftist tendencies. Khaled Muhy Eddin, a former member of the Revolutionary Command Council, heads the party.

Although politically dominated – at least at the top level of the party – by Marxists, the party is an amalgam of Arab Nationalist, Nasserites, Social Democrats and Liberal Independents.[31] The party thus embraces different political tendencies, which creates an uneasy co-existence, and often calls for compromise solutions, which usually cause conflict with the militant members, who demand clear-cut leftist programmes.

The main recruits to the party are the sons of workers and peasants, together with public sector employees and government administrators, with the majority of the active members coming from the lower level civil servants "Muwazzafin".[32] In other words, the party's recruits come from "this layer of society that had constituted the popular base of the Nasser regime in the urban areas".[33]

Although it was created by Sadat to act as a loyal opposition, the party broke with the regime over the 1977 food riots, which were followed by government harassment of the party branding it as Communist and atheist. However, this marked the change of the party from a loyal to an authentic opposition and attracted to it many of the committed members who were previously sceptical about its seriousness as an opposition party created from above.[34]

The NUPP attacked Sadat policies on a number of occasions both inside and outside parliament and succeeded in embarrassing the government on several issues. As a result, by 1978 Sadat grew intolerant of the NUPP and called on the party to disband itself. The party leaders refused, but the government succeeded in closing the party's newspaper and in reducing the party's status to that of a "counter-elite 'party of pressure' on the periphery of the political arena".[35]

Under Mubarak the relaxation of restrictions on the Nasserites, from 1987 allegedly weakened the all-embracing leftist front, which the NUPP had been representing since 1976. This weakness was reflected in the failure of the NUPP to gain any seats in the 1987 elections and the decline of its proportion of votes from 4 per cent in 1984 to 2 per cent in 1987. Moreover, its leader Khaled Muhy Eddin was defeated despite being declared elected in the first round.[36] Being the only party to contest the 1990 elections, the NUPP succeeded in gaining six seats in the People's Assembly and thus came to represent the leading opposition in parliament.[37] The approval given for the formation of the Arab Democratic Nasserite Party on 19th April 1992 raised fears for the future of the NUPP. The main concern revolved around the desertion of most Nasserite members, among whom were prominent names, to join the newly formed party, a fact that could further weaken the NUPP. However, the real challenge to the party lies in its competition with another leftist party for recruits from the same social base and the same segments of society, especially since a wide range of similarities exist between the direction and tendencies of both parties.[38]

The 1995 elections did not see the realisation of these fears. Although it had lost its leadership of the opposition in the parliament to the New Wafd Party, the NUPP succeeded in acquiring five seats in parliament,[39] which was far better than its achievement in 1987. In the 2000 elections the party won six seats in parliament, representing 12.5 per cent of its total candidates who run for elections.[40]

The Socialist Labour Party (SLP)

This party was created by Sadat to replace the NUPP as a loyal opposition after he initiated his final crackdown on the latter in 1978. Sadat hoped that the SLP would embrace both the constituencies of the NUPP and those liberal and social elements that were becoming detached from the increasingly rightist government party.

Assigning its leadership to Ibrahim Shoukri, an ex member of Young Egypt,[41] Sadat wanted to ensure the party's loyalty by inserting his brother-in-law, Mahmud Abu Wafia, and his followers in the party and making the latter number two men.

There were no major ideological differences between the SLP and the NDP, since both claimed to represent the centre and reject the Marxist left and the extreme right. However, in practice the two parties were very far apart since Sadat's policies were moving to the extreme right of his party whereas most of the beliefs of the SLP's members were to the left of the NDP's programme. The party's disagreement with Sadat's policy, however, started to surface more particularly after he normalised the relationship with Israel in the absence of an overall settlement. The party's increased attacks on Sadat's policy led Abu Wafia and his followers to resign from the party, after which an aggressive attack against Sadat's liberalisation policy started. The party also exposed cases of corruption and abuse of power by important personalities. As a result of its increasingly antagonistic behaviour, the party was not spared in Sadat's 1981 crackdown, with the arrest of some of its members and closure of its newspaper al-Shaab.[42]

Under Mubarak, the SLP re-emerged with an increasingly nationalistic and religious stance.[43] However, from 1984 on the Islamic trend within the party grew and was reflected in the SLP's Islamic speeches. The appointment of Adel Hussein in 1985 as editor-in-chief of the party's newspaper Al-Shaab, and later his election to the central committee, had consolidated the religious tendency. Hussein asserted that he was "not an ally of the Islamic trend, but one of the original members within it".[44]

The culmination of this shift from a secular to a religious party was marked by the "alliance" which was performed with the Muslim Brotherhood and the Liberal Party prior to the 1987 elections. The alliance was justified by some members of the SLP, and seen by others, as a political tactic to subvert the tough electoral party list law and its 8 per cent threshold for representation.[45] As for the Muslim Brotherhood (MB), who were prevented by the constitution from forming their own party, the alliance served as a legitimate channel which would enable them to enter parliament.[46]

Interestingly enough the alliance took place without any consultation with party members, who were taken completely by surprise by their leader's decision. The same situation occurred with some of the party's leaders who were not consulted about the alliance and who opposed it, accusing their own party leadership of selling the party out to the MB.[47] Although in the short run the alliance enabled access to parliamentary representation in the 1987 elections, the long-term impact was detrimental to the unity of the party.

The unified socialist party had, after the alliance and more specifically after the SLP's conference convened in March 1989, split into two factions, one religious dominated by Shoukry, Hussein and some of the MB members, and one secular, which stood for the socialist ideology and which had the support of most party members. The speech of the party's leader at the 1989 conference reveals some of the practices that were taking place within the political parties in Egypt and hence is important to record.[48] Shoukry had, for the first time, declared openly in the conference that:

> I state in front of all of you that I stand with my full power with the Islamic faction of the party, and I do not approve of nor allow, the secular tendencies that want to remove Islam from the life of society . . . If I feel that the majority of the party does not support me in this stand, I will resign from my place . . . I have great confidence that this conference will succeed in electing a strong religious leading committee that will successfully represent our aim.[49]

Shoukry made sure[50] that the Islamic list won with the result that amid the conference "pro-and anti-Shoukry slogans, as well as physical aggression, made any observer have the feeling of being in the midst of a battlefield".[51] The behaviour of the party leader and the events that took place during the SLP's conference reflects an inherent weakness in the political parties in Egypt, who seem to attack the government on the very same grounds and practices as characterise their own leaders. Comparing the style of governance of the SLP leadership and that of the government, Hanaa Singer concluded

> The events of the conference show that the party proved to be no better than the political system it criticises, and accuses of being undemocratic. Moreover, we feel the hegemony of a small group consisting mainly of the President, Adel Hussein and few others over the decisions and policies of the party disregarding and yet manipulating the majority, creating terminologies and twisting facts to justify their stands. This strategy reminds us after all of the strategies followed by the ruling party in its dealings with the political system in Egypt.[52]

A final point has to be mentioned here with regard to the performance of the alliance. Although in the 1987 elections, which were held under the restrictive party list system, the alliance managed to gain 56 seats in parliament, of which 35 were allotted to the MB,[53] the results of the latest 1995 elections were disappointing.

All nine Labour Party candidates lost in the second round and its leader, Ibrahim Shoukry, failed in the first round. The same thing happened with the twenty-three candidates of the Muslim Brotherhood, who all failed in the second round elections.[54] Thus in the 1995 parliament the alliance was absent as an opposition force. The deterioration in the party's affair that continue to prevail clearly shows that the results of the 1995 elections were not considered, as far as the party's leader is concerned, a lesson from which to learn. The Islamists take-over of the party increased the internal fragmentation and the power struggle, which continued within the party and was particularly intensified during the few months prior to the 2000 elections. Two members namely Hamdy Ahmad, a popular party figure and another called Ahmad Idris in addition to Shoukry, were struggling for the leadership position, with accusations and counter accusations exchanged between the three men. As a result the Committee of Political Parties' Affairs has decided in May 2000 to freeze the party's activities pending the Socialist Prosecutor's investigation. The findings of the investigation revealed that the Labour party has violated the Egyptian law in several ways. Five of these violations are punishable by up to fifteen years in prison. These include the party's collaboration with Egypt's outlawed MB, allowing Al Shaab newspaper to become a mouthpiece for this movement and receiving underground financial contributions to the party.[55] Accordingly, the party did not contest the 2000 elections that was held in October.

The New Wafd Party (NWP)

Of all the parties that evolved under Sadat, the New Wafd was perhaps the only one that had a chance to build strong roots with the public. The New Wafd was the legitimate heir of the pre-1952 Wafd Party, which developed from the 1919 revolution and was thus associated with the great nationalist leaders Saad Zaghlul and Mustafa Nahas. The Wafd Party was an attempt on behalf of these leaders to institutionalise national sentiment, control mass agitation and mobilise the electorate in order to exert the pressure needed for the withdrawal of the imperialist.[56]

The party was abolished, along with all other political forces, under Nasser only to re-emerge in 1978 under Sadat. The New Wafd represents the liberal right and its late leader, Fouad Siraj al-Din, was the secretary-general of the Old Wafd Party.

From the outset, the New Wafd was not spared the animosity of the ruling party and its leaders. As soon as its leader declared in newspaper interviews the intention of establishing the party, the NDP assigned a group of its intellectuals and writers to attack him as the "former feudatory" and the "mummy that escaped the museum".[57] In a speech addressed to the Bar Association Siraj al-Din made a virulent attack on the 1952 revolution and on the loyal opposition parties created by Sadat. He declared that,

> The formation of the new Wafd scared a lot of people because they sensed that a real party was on its way, a party that had a mass base, unlike the paper parties that have no existence in people' mind and consciences.[58]

Despite the various obstacles that the government put in the way of its formation, among which was the requirement to secure the support of twenty deputies in parliament, the party succeeded in meeting the conditions.

The party's strong appearance was manifested, much to the regime's alarm, in two incidents. The first was the gathering of 40–50000 young people, who had no experience of the old Wafd, to listen to a speech delivered by Sirag El Din in Alexandria, despite bad weather. The second was the fact that, in the two months and a half following the formation of the party, 959,000 persons joined it.[59] The performance of the New Wafd Party in parliament completely staggered the government, who had not anticipated a vigorous opposition. For despite the limited number of its deputies in parliament, the New Wafd, along with the NUPP, succeeded in embarrassing Sadat's regime on several occasions and in forestalling some of its policies.

The Wafdist, Elwy Hafez, had for example called for an investigation into the negative effects of the High Dam. Another Wafdist deputy, Sheikh Ashur, had constantly criticised the government on a number of sensitive issues, including treatment of the poor in state hospitals, the abuse of public funds and the transport crisis. When denied the opportunity to speak about the quality of bread, Sheikh Ashur called the parliament "a puppet show" and shouted "Down with the President", an incident which led to his expulsion from the People's Assembly.[60]

Perhaps the major confrontation which antagonised Sadat and pushed his tolerance over the edge was the issue of the "Pyramids plateau scandal". This project had aroused public outrage at government plans to sell land around the pyramid to a Western tourist developer at nominal prices. Sadat had approved the project personally and there were widespread rumours about the involvement of his close associates and relatives.[61] The NUPP played a major role in opposing the project. It was joined by the New Wafd. As Hinnebusch has observed,

> It is uncertain whether most Wafdist actually opposed the project which in principle was compatible with the party's programme – but perhaps sensing the vulnerability of the regime in the matter, the Wafd played a major role in mobilising public opinion against it.[62]

The result was that the government was compelled to cancel the whole project. Sadat saw, for the first time, a consolidation, which he had never anticipated between the different opposition forces that went beyond the role drawn up for them to play and was starting to represent a real threat to his personal power. As one historian put it,

> The conciliation of the regime with the west after a long period of conflict necessitated an amount of 'Democratic Makeup' but it had not been for long, when the President discovered that this makeup had been transformed into constant colours which covered the new political life.[63]

This Sadat would not tolerate. In 1978, he cracked down on the New Wafd through his issuance of Law No. 33 for the protection of the internal home and social peace, which banned those who had corrupted political life before 1952 from political activity. This law targeted Sirag al-Din and other top Wafd leaders. Instead of purging its leadership, the party disbanded itself.[64]

A few Wafdist deputies still remained in parliament and continued their role as a true opposition, but, Sadat ensured that they all lost their seats in the 1979 elections,[65] the most falsified elections there had been during his presidency, leading Siraj al-Din to label the whole experience as "Sham Democracy".

The second return of the New Wafd was in December 1983, when the Higher Administrative Court gave the party's existence an official, legal stamp. The 1984 elections were the first to be contested by the New Wafd after its re-emergence under Mubarak.

In order to overcome the 8 per cent barrier in the elections, an alliance was formed between the New Wafd and the Muslim Brotherhood, despite the historical animosity between the two groups. The alliance was the result of an individual decision taken by Fouad Siraj al-Din, leader of the New Wafd, and the late Omar Al Talmesany, who was then leader of the MB, without consulting party members.[66]

The Wafd-MB succeeded in acquiring 57 seats in parliament, but the alliance had detrimental repercussions on the solidarity of the party. Historically the Wafd had always advocated secularism. After the alliance, though, and under pressure from the MB, the New Wafd modified its secular stance and set a precedent in the party's history by demanding the implementation of Islamic sharia law.

As a result, a number of its prominent secularist members, such as Ibrahim Talaat, Louis Awad, Mohamad Anis and Farag Fouda, left the party. The departure of Farag Fouda, a secular thinker, who was later assassinated by the Islamic fundamentalists, exposed the intellectual and political controversy that was taking place within the party.[67] Moreover, the Wafd had always been the champion of national unity. It had been the only party in which Copts and Muslims were represented in its leadership roughly in proportion to their numbers in Egyptian society at large. For example, in the seventies Hinnebusch found that the leadership was 88.3 per cent for Muslim and 11.7 per cent for Copts.[68] Hence the party had always attracted and depended on Coptic votes in the elections. Needless to say, the alliance had cost the Wafd its credibility among the secular and Coptic communities alike. However, the alliance was short-lived and ended directly after the 1984 elections. It is worth noting here that in the 1987 elections, and as a result of the alliance that took place between the SLP and MB, Wafd representation in parliament was reduced to 35 seats.

By 1986, the internal divisions, which had started in 1984, had seriously weakened the Wafd. The party was divided into a majority faction, the Fouadiyyin, revolving around the leader Fouad Siraj al-Din and the minority faction the Nahhasiyyin led by Saif al-Din-al Gahazali. Fouad Siraj al-Din had also turned against his own brother Yassin Sirag Al Din, as well as against the Islamist radical Shaikh Salah Abu Ismail who, after the alliance, became a Wafd member. Without going into detail, it is enough to mention that besides the two main factions, a number of smaller factions also existed within the party, though Fouad Siraj al-Din succeeded through his dictatorial style of leadership in keeping the party under his control.

He managed to overcome his opponents by freezing their membership, by expelling them, or by removing them from the parliamentary wing and placing the latter under his tight control. This led the minority faction to expose the conflict through the press and to bring it to public attention.[69] They revealed that the

Pasha, whose chief demand of the government was that it permit more democracy and who claimed that democracy was the solution to virtually all of Egypt's pressing problems, was a hypocrite. Sirag al Din's Wafd, they claimed, was no more democratic than Yusuf Wali's NDP.[70]

A second point which prevents unity of purpose within the party is the conflict which revolves around major policy issues. Both the subsidies and the public sector are at the centre of the controversy. Structural divisions provide a third point of conflict, notably between the higher committee and the parliamentary wing. The rivalry between the two leading provincial committees, those in Cairo and Alexandria, is a historic one, and further militates against party unity.[71] Thus the personal, structural and ideological conflict within the party continues to be the major challenge facing its leaders in the future.

In the 1995 elections, the New Wafd managed to win six seats in parliament and to regain its position as leader of the opposition.[72] This is, however, an extremely modest achievement when compared to the 1984 and 1987 election results. Again and despite the fact that in the 2000 elections the Wafd managed to win seven seats in parliament, a closer look reveals that, in reality, the election results reflect a poor performance for the party. Election results show that only 2.5 per cent (seven out of 272) of the party's total nominated candidates managed to win the elections.[73] Several factors have had an adverse effect on the party's performance.

The death of its long-time leader Fouad Siraj al-Din,[74] which came just one month prior to the campaigning season, is one such factor. The Wafd leadership elections, held on September 2000, resulted in the selection of No'man Gom'a, the former deputy leader as the new head of the Wafd party. The latter has, however, alienated Yassin Siraj al Din, who neither participated in choosing the parliamentary candidates, nor in drawing the Wafd's campaign prior to the elections, thus depriving the party from Siraj's long standing political experience and tactics. Perhaps because of this lack of experience that Go'ma erred in his election strategy. Among such errors was the fact that the new party leader has overestimated the capabilities of his own party when he announced that the Wafd would come out of the elections with at least hundred seats. This overestimation of capabilities has lead Go'ma to attempt to put forth enough candidates to cover all districts randomly without concentrating his efforts on the districts where the Wafd stands a good chance of success. In addition, where as the nominated party candidates should have included those most popular among their constituents in order to maximise their chances of winning, the party has maintained its belief that the Wafd's history was enough to guarantee the success of any candidate. Accordingly, younger candidates who lacked both popularity, and political experience were included on the Wafd list.[75] In a further development Go'ma and his supporters have removed Siraj by force from his position as the head of the party's Cairo committee, causing a rift among the party members.[76] The extent to which the party will manage in the futur to pull itself together under the leadership of Go'ma depends on the extent to which the latter will either concentrate on party issues or alternatively will become entangled in personal disputes with other party members.

The Muslim Brotherhood (MB): Extra-Legal Opposition:

It is crucial before analysing the performance of the MB in the current political arena to present a brief historical review on the evolution of the movement as a politico-religious opposition and to try to explore the principles that provide the guidelines for its actions. As described by Zubaida, the Muslim Brotherhood "is the movement which, in one form or another, has been the most prominent fundamentalist current in Sunni Islam since its inception in Egypt in 1928".[77] Although recently the MB has been trying to project themselves as "a moderate movement" as opposed to the more fundamentalist and terrorist groups, a quick look at the history of the MB not only testifies to the contrary, but also provides a better understanding of its performance in the political sphere.

Endowed with charisma and a prophetic zeal, Hassan al-Banna, a school teacher in Ismailya, founded the MB society in 1928 as a movement for the education and reform of heart and mind. It was not long before the movement had spread to all the cities of the canal-zone and by 1932 it had reached Cairo where the movement set up its main headquarters.[78]

The newly established branches followed in its foundation the same paths of the Ismailya headquarter where the establishment of each branch was followed by some projects: a mosque, a school, a club, or a small home industry.[79]

In 1933 and following the MB's second general conference, two official journals of the society were issued: first, a weekly magazine called Majallat al-Ikhwan al-Muslimin, and latter, another called Majallat al-Nadhir. Being in the stage of gaining as many adherents as possible to its call, the society also conducted oral lectures and preaching seminars in the society's headquarters, branches and in mosques.[80]

The MB's third and fifth conference, that convened in 1935 and 1939 respectively, were particularly important since both conferences set various rules and regulations that were considered binding to the society members as well as reflecting comprehensive ideological orientations.

The 1935 conference recommendations included two main principles: the first required that every Muslim had to believe that the MB course of action is the only true Islamic one and that any diminution of it is a diminution of the rules of Islam itself. The second necessitates that the Muslim should only maintain connections with those institutions that are in line with the MB ideology and refrain from maintaining any kind of relation with the institutions or groups which would contradict the latter's line of thought. According to al-Bishry, the danger in such principles lies in the fact that it attempts on one hand to monopolise Islam, and on the other to ensure the sole loyalty of the members to the movement.[81]

The ideology of the society as was reflected in the recommendations of the 1939 conference was based on their definition of Islam, which stems from the following rules: (1) that Islam in itself is a total system and should be the final judge in all spheres of life, (2) that Islam's teaching is based on and stems from its two primary sources, the revelation of the Qur'an and the wisdom of the Prophet in the Sunna, and (3) an Islam, which is appropriate to all times and places.[82]

Within this frame of thought, al-Banna defined his movement as "a Salafayia message, a Sunni way, a Sufi truth, a political organisation, an athletic group, a cultural-educational union, an economic company, and a social idea."[83]

Hillal while analysing the thoughts of the MB identifies three of its characteristics: totalitarianism, Islam as a system, and generality. Whereas the first two characteristics stem from the presentation of Islam as a complete system for all aspects of life and the movement as the only representative of true Islam, the third, which tends to embody the ideology of the movement creates obscurity.[84]

Commenting on the organisational framework of the Muslim Brotherhood, Ahmad confirms that "the ideological totalitarianism that characterised the movement was reflected in its organisational structure which engulfed the individual as it sought to organise his social life and his personal and familial relations. This resulted in a complete fusion between the individual and the movement. Moreover this obscurity was appropriate for the advancement of al-Banna's personality as a leader of the movement without any strong opposition from his followers. Obscurity of ideology is necessary for the advancement of personal authority, which depends on freedom of work and action, and this requires an absence of any accountability. Obscurity of goals and procedures deprives the followers of their ability to control."[85] Hence, complete obedience to the leader's orders remains the only code of behaviour for the pious Muslim.

Perhaps such obscurity of goals and procedures were mostly reflected in the classification of membership as declared by the third conference held in 1935, where beside the three categories of assistant (musa'id), related (muntasib), and active ('amil), a fourth category that of struggler (mujahid) was included and whose precise meaning was not explained or defined at that time.[86] It was from his last category of membership that the society's secret apparatus latter was formed.

The official recognition by al-Banna of the political activities of the society came in 1938, which was announced in the first issue of the weekly al-Nadhir. Latter during the 1939 conference al-Banna described the society as a 'political organisation'. The actual political involvement of the society, however, started earlier in 1936, which was then instigated by the disturbance that occurred in Palestine between Zionist, Arab nationalists and the British. This took the form of gathering aid for Palestinians, demonstrating, pamphleteering, and speech making.[87]

It is worth highlighting here two incidents, which reflect al-Banna's hypocritical pretence, a trend that continued to characterise the society and its members as will be shown latter when discussing their performance in syndicates in the eighties and nineties, and which had caused at the time the defection of some of the society's members to form an independent society namely Our Master Muhammad's Youth (jamiyat shabab sayyidna Muhammad).[88]

The first incident was the alliance, which al-Banna made with Ali Maher's government, especially during the few years prior to the second -world war. This contradicted one of the main rules which al-Banna had established for the society and had often propagated in his speeches, calling on society members to avoid all kinds of involvement with 'notables and names' and 'parties and societies'. Ali Maher, who was known to be the greatest foe for the Wafd party, even provided the society with some sort of aid. By encouraging and supporting other groups like the MB and Young Egypt (Misr al-Fatat), Maher sought to use these groups as a counterweight for the Wafd's influence.[89]

The second incident referred to here be the use of funds collected by al-Banna for helping the Palestinians. Al-Banna, however, spent these funds on strengthening some of the society's branches in other governorates, proclaiming this to be an indirect way of helping the Palestinian cause, an argument, which was far from being convincing to some of the defected members.[90]

Another contradiction between what al-Banna preached and what his deeds were can yet be spotted in the type of political system, which was chosen to govern the society. Although the MB advocated a presidential system with an elected shura (consultative) council, which in theory resembled western parliaments,[91] in reality, however, all authority was vested in al-Banna who opposed the idea of the shura being obligatory for the leader and viewed it instead as optional. It is thus the leader's right to accept the shura or reject it.[92] Moreover, and in congruence with all totalitarian systems and leaders, al Banna as has been mentioned earlier rejected political parties since these in his opinion "represent sectional and egoistic interests which divide and corrupt the body politic of the Umma."[93]

Reference has been made earlier to the secret apparatus that the movement had developed. What is left to mention here is that this apparatus was involved in the political assassination of the movement opponents, which included communists alongside government officials.[94] Among its famous victims was the Egyptian Prime Minister al Nuqrashi who was assassinated in 1948, which lead the secret police to retaliate by assassinating al-Banna in 1949.[95]

Under Nasser, after a short flirtation with the regime, the movement was completely suppressed, and in 1965, after an alleged plot to assassinate Nasser had been discovered by the police, its leaders were imprisoned, some of whom like Sayyid Qutb was executed.[96]

The MB reappeared on the political scene under Sadat when the latter used them to consolidate his power vis-à-vis his Nasserite opponents. Actually it was Sadat's accommodation of the Islamists in general and the MB movement in particular during the seventies, which had resulted in the latter's strong re-emergence during the eighties. A quick look at the new generation which ascended to leadership positions within the MB during the 1980's would reveal names as Assam al-'Aryan, Abd al-'Mun'im abu al-Fattuh, Hilmi al-Jazzar and Ibrahim al-Za'afaran.[97] Previously during the seventies these leaders had been politically active within student unions among the universities of Cairo, Ayn shams and Alexandria.[98] In fact they were the main founders of the Islamic student movement in Egypt in the seventies known as al-Gama'h al-Islamiyah, which had also established a military wing. Sadat had encouraged the proliferation of the Islamic groups among university students to counter balance the Nasserite and the Marxist groups. In 1978, when some of the leaders of the Gama'a were arrested, the MB lawyers volunteered to defend them in exchange for the former's joining the MB. Some of the Gama'a leaders rejected the MB offer because of the difference in agenda between the two groups. The MB nevertheless, succeeded in influencing some of the most prominent leaders like Muhyi al-Din Abu al'Lla Hadi from Sa'id, Asam al'Aryan, Hilmi al-Jazzar and abd al-Mun'im abu al-Futuh from Cairo, and Ahmad Umar and al-Za'farrani from Alexandria University. These members split from the Gama'a and accepted to follow the MB leaders.[99] The defected members, however, continued their political activities within the universities under the banner of the Gama'a capitulating on the latter's reputation among students. It was only after Sadat's assassination in 1981 and due to police harassment of the Gama'a that the defected members openly affiliated themselves with the MB.[100] This group of younger MB leaders (in their mid and late forties) were armed by their political training and organisational skills which they acquired from their work within the student unions. Hence, they decided to play by the rules and challenge the regime on its own ground, be it in parliament or any institution of Egypt's civil society including the professional syndicates.[101]

Seizing the opportunity to revitalise the political activities of the movement, the MB responded actively to the limited liberalisation process that was started by Sadat and continued under his successor. This was achieved by forming an alliance first with the New Wafd Party during the 1984 elections when they managed to secure eight seats in parliament, and increased the New Wafd representation from 50 to 58 seats. During the 1987 elections the MB formed an alliance with Socialist Labour Party and achieved their highest representation in parliament (thirty seats), thus increasing the representation of the Labour Party from twenty seven to fifty seven seats.[102] The MB continues their extra-legal political activities under the banner of the labour party causing the factionalisation of the latter and more recently freezing the party's activities. As a result the MB candidates had to run the 2000 elections as independents where they managed to win seventeen seats in parliament, outnumbering the total seats won by the secular opposition. Still holding their famous slogan "Islam is the solution", the MB's political agenda is void and vague when it comes to providing specific practical solutions to the increasingly pressing problems of the Egyptian society.

4. An Evaluation of the Performance of the Opposition Parties

So far a brief description of the major political parties which function within the Egyptian political system has been presented. In the remaining part of this chapter, an attempt will be made to set certain criteria for measuring the performance of the opposition, and a brief categorisation of the factors affecting such performance will be presented.

A) Performance of the Opposition outside Parliament

Electoral turnout

One indication of the degree of political participation within any political system is the electoral turnout. Whereas a high electoral turnout reveals a high degree of politically active constituents, especially in multi-party systems, a low turnout would reflect both political passivity and apathy.

Since the function of political parties is mass mobilisation and the encouragement of popular participation through interest aggregation and articulation, the first criterion applied here to assess the relative strengths or weaknesses of the Egyptian political parties is the degree of popular participation.

Although the percentages shown in the table reflect a low electoral turnout, they do not provide the real picture, since the number of those registered on the election list is much lower than the number of those citizens (all who are above eighteen years old) who are eligible to vote. Taking the 1984 elections as an example, it was found that between the period 1974–1983 the number of names registered on the election list was at its minimum in 1974, where it reached

Table 4.2 Electoral turnout in the 1976–2000 elections

Elections	% of those who actually voted to the total number of those registered on the election list.
1976	43
1984	43.7
1987	50.4
1990	40
1995	50
2000	15–40*

Sources: 1 – Qandil, A., *'Amaliyyat al-tahawul al-Dimuqraty*, p. 206. 2 – El Sayid, M., – *Intikhabat Majlis Al Sha b 1984. Dirasa Wa Tahlil*, p. 130. 3 – *Al-Taqrir al-Istratiji al-Arabi* for the year 1995. 4 – *Al-Ahali Daily Newspaper*, 22/11/2000. *According to the announcement made by the Minister of Interior, 2000 election turnout ranges somewhere between 15 to 40 per cent.

34.6 per cent of the total number of eligible citizens, and in 1983 it had reached its peak and was 43.8 per cent.

This means that the real percentage of those who actually participated in the 1984 elections to the total number of eligible citizens was only 23.62 per cent.[103] In 1990 it was 30 per cent.[104] In 1995 the number of registered voters on the election lists was 21 million, where as the total number of eligible citizens was 30 million, this makes the real percentage of electoral turnout 35 per cent.[105] This reflects the alienation of the masses and their apathy towards the whole political system. It in turn reflects the weakness of the political parties and the extent of the participation crisis in the Egyptian society.

Parliamentary Elections

Another major criterion for assessing the strength of political parties is the election results. Accordingly an analysis of the elections would act as another good indicator of the performance of the political parties and would also provide a valuable insight into the political system with its various defects at large. The following table summarises the results of the parliamentary elections.

Analysing the result of elections reveals the following facts:

1. The dominance of the ruling party in parliament with an increased marginalisation of the opposition, especially in the 1995 elections as compared to those of the 1984 and 1987. While this dominance is associated with a reduction in the party's overall popularity as reflected in the election results, it is also coupled with an increase in the party's representation in Parliament, highlighting one of the contradictions inherent in the Egyptian electoral system. The 2000 elections witnesses the lowest popularity of the NDP where only 170 of its 446 nominated candidates won the elections[106] i.e.: only 38 per cent of its nominees managed to make its way to parliament, which also reflects the party's poor performance.

2. The appearance of the Muslim Brotherhood in the 1984 and 1987 elections, was a significant factor in determining the largest number of seats an opposition party could gain in parliament. The fact that the MB was capable of shifting the balance in favour of certain secular opposition parties who had to form an alliance with it to increase their chances of winning and gaining representation in parliament in exchange for compromise on major ideological issues testifies to the latter's weakness. This weakness was highlighted in the 2000 elections when the number of MB candidates winning the elections exceeded the total number of all secular opposition candidates who won parliamentary seats.

3. The large number of candidates running for elections as independents is a phenomenon, which started in the 1990 elections after this right was granted through the ruling of the Supreme Constitutional Court.

In 1990, the independent candidates who ran for elections reached 2,134 at a time when the total number of party candidates was only 541. It is to be noted

Table 4.3 The results of the Egyptian parliamentary elections 1984–2000

Parliamentary elections	1984 No of Seats	%	1987 No of Seats	%	1990 No of Seats	%	1995 No of Seats	%	2000 No of seats	%
NDP	390 seats	85	348 seats	76	360 seats	79	417 seats	91.8	388 seats	85
Liberal Party	None		3 seats	0.65	Boycott of elections		1 seat	0.2	1 seat	0.22
NUPP	None		None		5 seats	1.1	5 seats	1.1	6 seats	1.3
The Democratic Arab Nasserite Party	None		None		None		None		2 seats	0.44
SLP alone	None		27 seats		Boycott of elections		None		None	
MB			30 seats		Boycott of elections		1 seat	0.22	17 seats	3.7
SLP/MB alliance			57 seats	12.4						
Wafd Party alone	50 seats		35 seats	7.6	Boycott of elections		6 seats	1.3	7 seats	1.5
MB	8 seats				Boycott of elections					
Wafd/MB alliance	58 seats	12.7								
Independent Opposition			5 seats	1.1	79 seats	17.4	13 seats	2.8	21 seats	4.6

Sources: 1 – Al-Taqrir Al-Istratiji Al-Arabi for the year 1995, p. 386. 2 – Al Intikbabat al-Barlamaniya fi Misr1995, p. 45. 3 – Al-Abram Weekly, 23–29/11/2000.

here that most of those who contested the elections as independents (900–1,000 candidates) did so either because their party had decided to boycott the elections,[107] or because they were not originally nominated by their party on its list. Most of the latter were members of the NDP. This would mean that the actual number of independent candidates who run for elections are 1,250, out of which 177 had won. Most of these have since defected to the NDP, leaving only 79 members acting as independents in the People's Assembly.[108]

The same phenomenon reoccurred in the 1995 elections. The total number of those who contested the elections as independents was 3100, where as the total number of all party nominees was 739, of whom 439 were ruling party candidates, leaving the opposition with no more than 300 candidates. However 1400 of those who ran in the election as independents were originally members of the NDP, which means that the number of truly independent candidates who contested the 1995 elections was 1700. The final results of the elections revealed that the candidates who ran as independents managed to gain 112 seats in parliament. However after the elections, 99 of these defected to the ruling party, leaving only 13 seats for the independents in parliament. The result of this defection was the increase in the ruling party's majority in Parliament from 70 per cent (318 seats) to 91.8 per cent (417 seats)[109] With the addition of the 10 appointed members in the Parliament, the NDP's majority reaches 94 per cent.

In the 2000 elections the total number of those who ran for elections as independents amounted to 3,076 candidate, at a time when all party nominees totalled 889, out of whom 446 nominees belonged to the NDP leaving 11opposition parties with no more than 443 nominees. The final results of the elections showed that the independents managed to win 256 seats in parliament. Again, out of these 256 winning candidates, 218 have joined the NDP leaving only 38 candidate acting as independent opposition. This in turn raised the NDP representation in parliament from 37.4 per cent (170 seats)[110] to 85.4 per cent (388 seats). With the addition of the 10 appointed members in the Parliament the NDP representation reaches 87.6 per cent.

4. The marginalisation of the Copts and women. A closer look at the 1990 and 1995 elections reveals a decline in the number of Copts nominated on all party lists as well as those contesting as independents. In 1990 only two Copts were nominated on the NDP list. Fifteen Coptic candidates ran in the elections as independents of whom only one was elected.[111]

In the 1995 elections, 57 Coptic candidates ran in the elections, either as independents or as nominees on the various party lists.[112] None of these candidates succeeded. It should be mentioned here that none of the Copts were nominated on the NDP list, an obvious appeasement on behalf of the ruling party to the Islamic tendency, which aggressively competes with it for votes. The same situation reoccurred for women for the same reason: only five women succeeded in gaining seats in the People's Assembly, leading one writer to comment that there could be "No sound Egyptian Democracy with the marginalisation of Copts and women".[113]

The same phenomenon of marginalisation of the Copts and women continues in the 2000 elections. Only three Copts were nominated on the NDP list representing 0.6 per cent of its total nominees and out of a total of twenty nine Copt running for elections, only three, including the Economy Minister Youssef Boutros Ghali, managed to win representation.[114] The same situation occurs for women, where only twenty three were nominated by the NDP representing 5 per cent of the NDP's total nominees. Of a total number of 120 women[115] contesting the 2000 elections, only seven managed to win parliamentary representation.[116]

Elections, Political Parties and Political Culture

The previously described phenomenon of independent candidates reveals some of the major defects in the political parties, the Egyptian political culture, and in the development of structures and hence it warrants special analysis.

First. The fact that the ratio between the number of candidates who run as independents to those nominated by all political parties amounted to almost 4:1 in the 1990 and 1995 elections and to 3.46:1 in the 2000 elections on the one hand, and the failure of the opposition parties to nominate candidates in all the electoral districts in the 1995 elections[117] and in the 2000 elections[118] on the other hand, reflects the weakness of political parties and their inability to prepare and recruit the necessary political cadres, as well as their failure to establish roots among the masses.

Second. The fact that a considerable number of candidates chose to contest the elections as independents, either by ignoring their party's decision to boycott the 1990 elections or as a result of not being nominated by their party, reflects weak party affiliation and loyalty. On the other hand, the fact that a significant number of these candidates succeeded in winning the election reflects a failure to institutionalise the party system among the masses and within the political culture as a whole. This is again a reflection of the weakness of the political parties.

Third. The success of most independent candidates, whether those who departured from the NDP or those MB candidates, and their lack of electoral programmes show that both kinship, patron-client relationships, and religious sentiment were determining factors for winning.[119] Again the success of this huge number of independent candidates confirms what Salah Eissa, the head of the opposition parties' coordination committee, said when commenting on the results of the 2000 elections he mentions:

> The fact that the electorate chose to vote for individuals and not parties reflects a lack of trust in all political parties. This, I believe, is due to the appalling performance of the opposition in the outgoing parliament, where it seemed to have been tamed by the government.[120]

Fourth. The same factors apply even to those candidates nominated by the various political parties. In a survey conducted by a leading political magazine in Egypt, it was found that most of those who won in the elections, were chosen by the electorate either because they were charismatic and popular in their electoral district and used to provide personal services to the people, or were backed by tribalism regardless of the party affiliation of the candidate.[121] In addition with the increase in the number of business tycoons running for the 2000 elections, the huge amount of money spent on the electoral campaigns becomes another determining factor for winning.

Finally, candidates' decisions to join a political party, mainly the ruling NDP, after their election in return for benefits (material or otherwise), which is described by some intellectuals as "political betrayal" and "political opportunism", has a negative impact on the electorate and would undoubtedly contribute to the lack of trust in the political system.[122] This is certainly reflected on the electoral turnout.

B) Performance of the Opposition in Parliament

The Legislative Performance of the Opposition

A fourth perspective from which to assess the performance of the opposition is through analysing its role in parliament. Reference has already been made in chapter 3 to the weak role played by the legislative branch vis-à-vis the executive branch inside the parliament. The following table shows the legislative role of the opposition in Parliament for the years 1991–1993.

Although the number of bills proposed by MPs is very low[123] as compared to the large number of drafted bills presented by the Cabinet, most of these proposed bills are presented by the NDP MPs and very few by the opposition, leading one author to comment that,

> However, because it tended to submit few legislative bills, the opposition reinforced parliament's general legislative weakness.[124]

The Control Performance of the Opposition

The same situation occurs with regard to the control devices used by the opposition in parliament, thus reflecting its weakness and the limited parliamentary role. The following table shows the control role of the opposition in parliament.

The above table reveals the following facts:

1. Questions, which are the least effective tool of control in parliament, are most widely used by the NDP MPs, since they do not represent any threat to the government. Although the constitution obliges government ministers to

answer these questions, in practice there have been many instances when the Prime Minister ignored questions directed to him by the MPs, with no serious repercussions. The independents rank second in using questions in parliament, with the minimum contribution coming from the opposition party.

Table 4.4 Legislative performance of the Opposition in Parliament

Year	Source of proposed bills by MPs	Number of proposed bills	%
1991	NDP (Government party)	7	87.5
	Independent MPs	1	12.5
	NUPP	–	
1992	NDP (Government party)	23	76.6
	Independent MPs	7	23
	NUPP	–	
1993	NDP (Government party)	19	79
	Independent MPs	5	20.8
	NUPP	–	–

Source: Al-Taqrir Al-Istratiji Al-Arabi for years 1991 and 1993, Source for 1992, Qandil, A., Amaliyat Al-Tahawul Al Dimoqraty, p. 243.

Table 4.5 Control performance of the Opposition in Parliament

Year	Party Affiliation	Questions	%	Formal Requests	%	Interpellations	%
1991	NDP (govt.party)	74	64	28	59.5	–	–
	Independent	21	24	19	40	11	91.6
	NUPP	1	1	–	–	1	8
1992	NDP (govt.party)	41	77	44	57.8	–	–
	Independent	10	18.8	28	36.8	15	93.7
	NUPP	2	3.7	4	5	1	6
1993	NDP (govt.party)	36	83.7	69	58.9	–	–
	Independent	6	13.9	44	37.6	14	87.5
	NUPP	1	2	4	3	2	12.5
1995	NDP (govt.party)	28	80	51	64.5	–	–
	Independent	7	20	26	32.9	5	83
	NUPP	–	–	2	2.5	1	16.6

Source: Al-Taqrir Al-Istratiji Al-Arabi 1991, 1992, 1993, 1995.

2. Formal requests, which are stronger than questions but still weaker than interpellations as control tools, are still frequently used by the NDP MPs, followed by the independents, with the lowest contribution from the opposition party.

3. Interpellations, which are one of the strongest control tool in parliament, are not used at all by the NDP MPs since they can embarrass the government and may result in a vote of no confidence. This control tool is most frequently used by the independents, again with minimum contribution from the opposition party ranging from one interpellation to two at the most.

It is obvious from this discussion that the NDP MPs are the most active members in parliament, both with regard to their legislative and control role,[125] followed by the independent members, who are quite active with respect to both roles, with the opposition parties playing a marginal role in both capacities.

5. Factors Contributing to the Weakness of Political Parties

From the previous discussion, the factors which contribute to the weakness of Egyptian political parties, can be classified under two categories.

A) External Factors

The constitutional and legal limitations on political parties

This point has been discussed in detail in chapter 3 and there is no need for repetition here. Suffice it to say that the constitution with its inherent contradictions, the extensive rights given to the President and the imbalance between the executive and legislative branch, together with the various electoral and political party laws are all crippling factors that tend to weaken political parties in Egypt.

Government control of elections and election results

This takes place through various methods. The two major means are by rewards, where the government would tempt strong shaiks, tribes and popular figures, especially in rural areas, with various rewards, and intimidation to guarantee their alliance with the NDP.[126]

The state of emergency, which has been in force since 1981, emphasises this intimidation of the opposition. For example, under the emergency law, parties are prohibited from holding open air rallies. Intimidation by the government can also be directed towards voters and party poll watchers in the districts where the opposition enjoys majority support. Journalists who support the opposition are prevented by the government from covering the meetings and rallies.[127] The case of the MB is one such example of government coercion and harassment, when, a week prior to the 1995 elections, the government cracked down on the Muslim Brotherhood, closing down the group's headquarters in central Cairo and arresting a number of its leaders in what the Financial Times described as, "The biggest blow to the Brotherhood since the purges and mass arrests by the nationalist leader President Gamal Abdul Nasser in the 1950s and 1960s".[128] The purges and arrests continued, especially during the second round of elections when the government arrested hundreds of the followers of the MB independent candidates.[129] The same round up of MB re-occurred before the 2000 elections when hundreds of MB members have been arrested in the month leading up to the elections.[130] Again supporters of the MB have been harassed at the poll stations by the police and by thugs who have been hired by the government to prevent voters from casting ballots for the MB candidates.[131] The aggression against the MB and their supporters would no doubt increase sympathy for them in the society at large, as one writer has, after the 1995 elections commented, "the MB might have officially lost the elections, but they have definitely won the sympathy of the elites, international observers and the fair media",[132] a fact that would increase the radicalisation of the society. The results of the 2000 elections in which the MB won 17 seats and evolves as the leading opposition in parliament reflects the intensity of such radicalisation that has been taking place in the Egyptian society. Again such aggression against those who allegedly represent the moderate Islamic trend, would no doubt open the door for the fundamentalists, and would provide justification for their cause and their violent behaviour. Moreover, this leaves the extremists as the only option towards which the frustrated Muslim youth can turn to.

The harassment that the Coptic candidates were exposed to during the 1995 and 2000 elections, to a large extent from the NDP and to a lesser extent from the Muslim Brotherhood, provides another example.

Ironically enough, at a time when the government claims that it is curtailing the Islamic tendency and protecting national unity, the behaviour of the NDP candidates during the 1995 elections could have led to sectarian strife. Urging the electorate not to give their votes to the Copts, the NDP candidates distributed leaflets with the headlines "No authority to Non Muslims" and another saying "No to the Magians . . . No to the Copts . . . No to the atheists".[133] Using religion against the Coptic candidates in the elections was not only unethical but is in stark violation of the constitution, which equates all citizens in rights and responsibilities. It also reflects the hypocrisy of a government that announces one thing and does another. This hypocrisy became even more obvious during the 2000 elections, when the same NDP candidate was permitted to use the same anti-Christian slogans against his Wafdist Coptic opponent.[134]

The abuse and use of violence carried by the police in the 2000 elections was also documented via a statement released by Amnesty International on November 17 accusing Egyptian plainclothes police officers of beating one of their representatives who was monitoring the third stage of parliamentary elections. The Cairo Foreign Press Association has also lodged a formal complaint with the Ministry of Interior regarding the mistreatment of journalists during the election coverage. Some of the harassed reporters worked for the Associated Press, Voice of America, and the New York Times.[135]

The third method used by the government is falsifying election results. Commenting on the widespread fraud that took place during the 1987 elections, Mustafa Amin, the dean of Egypt's journalists wrote sarcastically,

> The computer in charge of the law on election by party lists is well behaved. It speaks when we want it to speak and shuts up when we tell it to. At first it announced the election of Khaled Muhyi-al-Din, leader of the NPUP, but an official glared at it, whereupon it announced the failure of MR Muhyi al-Din after he had won. The computer remembered that it is an official of the Ministry of Interior and announced that all candidates of the National Democratic Party had won and all opposition candidates had lost. Curses poured down on the head of the poor computer, which was only obeying orders. Then it announced that the Moslem Brotherhood and the Socialist Labour Party had won 40 seats but the Wafd was finished, as it had not won a single seat. Some candidates digged (sic) the computer in the ribs whereupon the computer said 40 Wafdists had been returned, then it brought down the figure to 35.[136]

The Egyptian National Committee for Overseeing the 1995 Elections has declared that the government and the opposition candidates alike used forgery and fraud extensively.[137]

Again the case of the Copts in the 1995 elections reflects falsification of elections records: several incidents were reported of thousands of names of the Coptic electorate being deleted from the electoral lists.[138] In addition there were some incidents when after announcing the success of Coptic candidates, a sudden change in the results took place, usually after the visit of a government official to the committee where the vote counting took place.[139]

Despite the fact that the 2000 elections were held under Judiciary supervision, several incidents have been reported where the electoral lists presented to the Judges were incorrect and included names of deceased individuals[140] who will naturally appear later on to have voted for the NDP. It has been also reported by opposition candidates, observers, and journalists, that several voters, particularly those who supported the opposition (both secular and religious) were prevented by the police from entering the polling areas.[141]

The Parliament

Again, this has been referred to in an earlier chapter. Suffice it to mention that the dominance of the NDP in parliament and the role of the speaker in imposing limits on the opposition's inability to raise subjects and proposals for discussion and to present questions make the parliament, as Mustafa Amin described it, "A branch committee of the NDP".[142]

B) Internal Factors

Important as contextual factors are in the development of political parties in Egypt, the parties' internal conditions and practices have equally been recognised as a major source of weakness. These can be briefly summarised in the following points:

Leadership longevity

At a time when the major demand of all parties in Egypt is to change the constitution and limit the number of times a President can run for office, a look at the major parties reveals a continuity in their leadership since their formation in 1976 to the present time: Ibrahim Shoukry in the SLP, Siraj al-Din in the New Wafd untill his death in 2000, Khaled Muhy Eddin in the NUPP and Moustafa Mourad in the Liberal Party again until his sudden death in1999. Their internal regulations do not include any rules to limit their period of office.[143]

Lack of democracy and the dictatorial style of leadership

Again, in as much as the masses are not given a say in the different decisions and policies followed by the government, the same situation occurs within the parties where major decisions are taken by their leaders without any consultation with other senior members, let alone the grass-roots.[144] The case of the New Wafd and the SLP that were discussed earlier, are two such examples. This dictatorial style of leadership prevails in all the Egyptian political parties, making the similarity between them and the regime they attack striking.

Internal divisions and factionalisation

A major source of weakness inherent in all political parties in Egypt is their internal division and factionalisation. The New Wafd Party with its internal fragmentation and the ongoing struggles among its factions is a case in point. The Labour party, which was split into two factions, religious and secular, and the power struggle which is taking place between them provides another example. Needless to say, division within the parties increases their weaknesses and reduces their credibility among the masses. It also provides the government with the means upon which it depends to further weaken the parties. This usually occurs by allowing a certain division or faction to form its own party. Allowing the Nasserites to form their party for example was intended to weaken the Marxist-Nasserite alliance, which is the core of the NUPP. The government is also aware of the divisions between the parties and plays on them. For example, the formation of the Liberal Party, which took place with the government's support, was intended to weaken the New Wafd and attract some of its supporters. The Umma Party, which was allowed to form after the 1984 election, was intended to fragment the bourgeois Islamist constituency to which the Muslim Brotherhood appeal.[145]

The intolerance and repressive character of political parties

It is ironic that at a time when the parties accuse the government of being intolerant of the opposition and repressive towards parties, party leaders are themselves repressive towards any opposition to their rules within their parties and are intolerant of other competing parties. It is true that,

> where parties are totally suppressed the ruling military and/or bureaucratic oligarchies have created conditions of great potential political instability. This instability applies not only to volcanic pressure in the existing regimes but more important, also to the patterns of action that parties are likely to manifest once they do acquire the mantle of legitimacy. Such parties are likely to apply to their own future opponents the same standards and patterns of repression to which they were subjected.[146]

The inability of the opposition to unite in their stand against the government

Lack of trust and co-operation between the major political parties in Egypt has prevented them from uniting against the government. For example, the failure of the Egyptian Committee for Protecting Democracy, which was formed in the early eighties, to achieve any positive results was attributed to the reluctance of the New Wafd – the largest opposition force at that time to join the Committee and participate in its work. In fact, the failure of the committee also reflected in general the inability of the opposition to co-operate and co-ordinate its efforts in a way appropriate to the importance of the changes to which it was exposed.

The failure of the parties to enforce an election boycott in 1984, again because of the reluctance of the New Wafd to co-operate,[147] and later the boycott of all parties except the NUPP of the 1990 elections, reflects a fragmented and divided opposition.

The inability of the parties to produce the needed political cadres

This is obvious from the inability of all parties, except for the NDP, to provide candidates in all constituencies. In fact, most of them hardly succeed in covering half of the electoral districts.

The failure of the parties to establish communication channels with the grass roots, which has contributed to their failure to institutionalise the party system in the political culture of the masses

The abstention of the people from voting in elections, reflected by the low turnout, their apathy and negativism, is but another indication of the failure of the political parties to perform their major function, viz. to bring into the system those alienated and isolated. Tribalism and patronage play a major role in candidate selection during the election process. Thus instead of institutionalising the party system among the masses, political parties enhance, through their inadequacy and inefficiency, behaviour which has negative repercussions on the development of the political system.

The inability of political parties to develop specific ideologies and political outlooks

Political parties in Egypt are more "parties of persons", that is they revolve around the prominent personalities of their leaders rather than around a specific ideology or the embodiment of the demands and interests of various groups in the society, which also accounts for their weakness in their legislative capacity. Such weakness is reflected in the voting process, where people choose certain candidates regardless of their party affiliation.

Fraud and the use of violence

While one of the major complaints that the opposition raises against the government and its party (NDP) is the falsifying of election results and the use of violence by the NDP's candidates, the Egyptian Committee for Overseeing the 1995 Elections reported that fraud and violence were used by both government party candidate and the opposition alike.[148] Thus the political parties that should have been agents of change exhibit the same malfeasance which characterises the Egyptian political system.

6. Conclusion

Egyptian political parties have evolved from the political vacuum and repression of Nasser's era, not without long term repercussions on their performance.

Externally, factors represented in the inherent contradictions in the Egyptian political system, the various legal and constitutional limitations imposed on party formation and function, and government harassment of the opposition and their newspapers, have hindered the development of the Egyptian political parties. Internally, internal party conflicts and factionalism, their lack of tolerance and repressive character, the longevity of their leaders coupled with the latter's dictatorial style, their inability to unite against the government and their use of fraud and violence during elections, are further weaknesses. The weakness of political parties is manifested in the limited role that the opposition – both in its legislative and control capacity – plays in Parliament. As a result political parties have failed to crystallise into appropriate channels for interest aggregation and articulation, which has caused the alienation of the masses and various groups in the society and deepened the participation crisis. With the weakness of political parties and fragmentation of political participation, negative values have been institutionalised in the Egyptian political culture favouring small groups and factions, tribalism and patronage, leading to a further weakening of the society. In such circumstances, interest groups tend to compete with rather than support political parties.[149]

It is the aim of the following chapters to analyse the various interest groups which exist in Egypt, assess their relative strength/weakness and evaluate how their performance is reflected in the political system and the society at large.

CHAPTER FIVE

Egyptian Professional Associations

1. The Historical Formation of Professional Associations

Organised interest groups are not a new or modern phenomenon in Egypt. On the contrary, professional associations are deeply rooted in the Egyptian culture and their genesis goes back to the old guilds system, which existed in Ottoman Egypt until the turn of the twentieth century. A closer look at the functions of the guilds reveals a striking similarity between them and modern Egyptian associations and syndicates that developed later. The guilds were headed by Sheikhs, who controlled and supervised guild members. These Sheikhs had the official authority to issue professional permits to guild members and to ensure that government rules and orders were strictly followed. They were, however, held accountable for any misdemeanours of their guild's members, as well as being responsible for supplying labour and services to both government and private employers. In their capacity as heads of guilds, the Sheikhs acted as arbitrators in members' disputes. Their responsibilities also included the collection of taxes from guild members and they assisted the government in setting the amount of taxes to be paid by the guilds. Apart from controlling entry to the professions by restricting the number of people involved in certain trades, some guilds maintained a complete monopoly over their profession.

Although Mohammed Ali's drive for industrialisation was blamed for the decline of the guilds, historical facts show the proliferation of guilds till the 1880s which contradicts that assumption. Rather, it was the change in Egypt's commercial base, which was preceded by an influx of European goods and settlers that caused the gradual disintegration of the traditional guild system. The final blow came when this was followed by several measures stemming from both the government and the Europeans, whose effect was to strip the Sheikhs of most of their responsibilities. Most of the guilds failed to survive into the early twentieth century, and after World War I the guilds performed no function in Egyptian public life.[1] Four stages were classified by Reid in the development of the professional syndicates in modern Egypt. The first of these is the establishment of professional schools, then the publication of specialised journals, the proliferation in the number of school graduates and finally the formation of societies and syndicates.[2] Table 5-1 shows the stages identified by Reid.

Bianchi on the other hand identifies four historical eras through which the professional associations evolved in Egypt. The first of these is the era of British occupation from 1882–1922 which witnessed the remnant of the traditional form of corporation represented in the pre-modern guild system, which survived until the end of the World War I. This was preserved in the Lawyers' Syndicate established in 1912 as the first modern professional association to be founded along corporatist lines.[3] The old guild system had several similarities with the newly-founded associations. As one author has commented

> To the rising middle class of native professionals the guild system left a more subtle yet more enduring legacy – a prototype for the modern corporatist syndicate that authoritarian governments would use time and again to contain middle-class political ambitions while giving in to narrow demands for occupational recognition.[4]

This era also witnessed the birth of Egypt's first political parties, which were allowed to form during a short period of liberal colonial rule. Political parties, on the other hand, encouraged the formation of various voluntary groups among workers, farmers, merchants, as well as the religious charitable associations, both Muslim and Christian.

The second era 1923–1939 covers the period marked by the formation of the constitutional monarchy until the outbreak of the Second World War, which was termed "palace pluralism". During that time various groups were competing for representation among the lower classes in the cities and countryside, but were easily manoeuvred and used by pro-palace politicians.

Table 5.1 The formation of Professional Syndicates

Profession	Founding of School	Specialised Journals		Average yearly number of graduates from government schools 1886–1921	Formation of societies and syndicates	
		First Journal	First lasting Journal		First professional society	First official syndicate
Law	1868	1868	1886	32	1897	1912
Medicine	1827	1865	1895	18	1888	1940
Journalism	1939	–	–	–	1909	1941
Engineering	1820	1893	1920	8	1920	1946
Teaching	1880	1901	1928	9	1891	1955

Source: Reid, D., *The rise of professions and professional organisations in Egypt*, p. 28.

As a result, Egypt's dominant landholding and business interests became the only groups capable of building strong representative associations, which then joined the king to replace the popularly elected Wafdist government with aristocratic dictatorship.

The third era, 1940–1960, witnessed the emergence of modern corporatism in which wartime initiated the expansion of the state's regulatory role in managing the economy and in promoting import substitution. As the Free Officers consolidated their power after the 1952 coup, association groups were reshaped one after the other from a pluralist in to a corporatist line.

The fourth era extends from the early 1960's up to the present. Bianchi comments on this stage by saying;

> Despite its authoritarian character, the regime has (both intentionally and unwittingly) strengthened the organisational resources and political influence of a wide variety of interest groups. Egypt's rulers continue to encourage great diversity in associations' internal structures, their responsiveness to members' demands, their ability to penetrate decision-making process in the state bureaucracy and the legislature, their alliances with political parties, and their ability to undertake entrepreneurial activities in Egypt's mixed economy.[5]

In the previous passage Bianchi implies that Egypt is moving towards a more flexible form of corporatism. Before stating the argument raised here it is important at this point to explain what is meant by corporatism.

2. Corporatism in Theory and Practice

Despite the fact that corporatism as a concept was traced in the writings of several political theorists in their description of pressure groups politics, which long predated Philippe Schmitter's famous article *"Still the age of Corporatism?"* published in 1974, the concept is nevertheless ascribed to him. According to Schmitter,

> Corporatism can be defined as a system of interest representation in which the constituent units are organised into a limited number of singular, compulsory, non competitive, hierarchically ordered and functionally differentiated categories, recognised or licensed (if not created) by the state and granted a deliberate representational monopoly within their respective categories in exchange for observing certain controls on their selection of leaders and articulation of demands and supports.[6]

Schmitter's early theorisation of the concept resulted in a model of interest intermediation, which aimed at describing the various forms that the relationship between state and society can take. He creates a kind of continuum, which places pluralism at one end and corporatism at the other. Syndicalism and monism occur somewhere in between, with the former being closer to pluralism and the latter to corporatism.[7]

Building on his early work, Schmitter goes further in his analysis of corporatism by identifying two subtypes: societal corporatism and state corporatism. Whereas the former exists in democratic regimes where corporatism as a system of interest intermediation evolved from below, the latter is associated with authoritarian regimes where corporatism was imposed on societies from above.[8]

Schmitter's definition has been criticised by various scholars on the grounds that it fails to cover all aspects of corporatism. Echoing the previous criticism Lehmbruch, for example, provides the following definition for corporatism.

> Corporatism is more than a peculiar pattern of articulation of interests. Rather, it is an institutionalised pattern of policy-formation in which large interest organisations co-operate with each other and with public authorities not only in the articulation (or even "intermediation") of interests, but-in its developed forms – in the "authoritative allocation of values" and in the implementation of such policies.[9]

Whilst Schmitter's emphasis during the development of his model was upon interest organisations, that of Lembruch's was upon the type of political systems. He thus differentiates between "liberal" and "authoritarian corporatism and develops another continuum or model where liberalism occurs at one end and authoritarian corporatism at the other, with liberal corporatism in between.[10]

In an attempt to fit corporatism into Marxist theory of the state, Jessop develops yet a third model of parliamentarism, fascism and corporatism.[11] While focusing on the different economic systems that the various countries have, Winkler's ideal model of corporatism is arranged into socialism, capitalism, syndicalism and corporatism.[12]

Likewise, political theorists who attempted to conceptualise the term in view of authoritarian politics, more specifically Latin American politics, which tended to add to it various dimensions. For example, Wiarda, while exploring corporatism and development in the Iberic-Latin countries, describes it in terms of a specific political culture. He thus mentions,

> The second sense in which we use the term corporatism is broader, encompassing a far longer cultural historic tradition stretching back to the origins of the Iberic-Latin systems and embodying a dominant form of socio-political organisation that is similarly hierarchical, elitist, authoritarian, bureaucratic, Catholic, patrimonialist, and corporatist to its core.[13]

Analysing the Peruvian regime of 1968, Malloy describes corporatism as an "ideology of development",[14] and as a "specific subtype of development-oriented authoritarianism"[15]

Despite the different descriptions of corporatism identified by various authors, what remains at the centre of it is a system of interest intermediation/control where the bargaining process (and the outcome of such process) takes place between the state and the leaders of the various corporates. In the case of liberal corporatism, this process includes the participation of groups' leaders in the articulation of demands, policy making and implementation. The outcome is the meeting of some, but not all of groups demands. In return the leaders of these groups exercise certain controls over their constituencies, thus ensuring their compliance with state's policy. The state may also have say in the selection of these leaders. Compromise therefore, is the name of the game, and this benefits both the state and the various corporatised groups. The variation in the degree of corporatism from one country to another will therefore depend upon the role played by the leaders of these groups, and the extent to which the state control their selection. For example, in some countries group leaders may participate in policy making but not in implementation. Likewise, the state, in some countries, may exercise control on the selection of these leaders and in others it may not, and so on. But regardless of the extent or the degree of corporatism, its basic component remains this "social contract" between societal corporatised groups and the state where economic benefits, which accrue to *all members* of these groups, are exchanged for support of the state and its policy.

On the other hand, authoritarian or state corporatism includes the same "social contract", only with a difference in the component of the exchange process. In state corporatism, economic benefits are exchanged for political domination. In other words, the state provides the corporatised groups with certain benefits, which still accrue to *all members* of these groups, whilst preserving the right of exercising complete control on the selection of their leaders and in demands articulation both at the level of the organisations, and the political system at large. Coercion is ever present, and is frequently used by the state. The variation in the degree of state corporatism will therefore depend upon the extent to which authoritarian states exert such control over the different groups, as well as the frequency of employing coercion to subjugate them.

It follows then, that if this "social contract" which economically benefits the broader segments of these groups does not exist, then classical corporatism as described by Schmitter and others, is changing perhaps along a continuum of different forms of the same theme. In light of the previous explanation of corporatism, the aim of this and the following chapter is to contest Bianchi's assumption that the relationship between state and society under Sadat and Mubarak is moving away from the classical form of corporatism to a more flexible type of what has been labelled by some authors as 'plural corporatism'. Instead, it will be argued that classical corporatism prevailed in Nasser's Egypt, when the state was still in its expansionary phase, supported by the limited benefits that Nasser granted to the various professional groups – free education, a guaranteed job for every university graduate, and job security – Nasser's early reform policy, free education for everyone, was a major gain especially as far as those aspiring to join professional groups were concerned, thus providing them with both social mobility and economic opportunities for a better standard of living. Ayubi estimates that the growth in university graduates between 1952 and 1969 was 386 per cent of their original number, 315 per cent in arts and humanities and 381 per cent in natural and applied sciences. Out of these 80.6 per cent of all people qualified in humanities and 82.8 per cent of all people qualified in sciences graduated after the revolution. Similarly graduates of higher institutes (polytechnics) grew to 847 per cent of their original number during the same period, with 90.7 per cent of them finishing their studies after the revolution.[16]

The socialist policies initiated in the early sixties (the decree of July 1961) perpetrated the government to supplying administrative jobs to all university graduates, and manual employment to all graduates of secondary schools.[17]

It was such measures that helped Nasser to change professional associations along corporate lines.

The change in economic policy that started on a limited base shortly after Nasser's death started to take a sharp turn under Sadat, and was fully consolidated under Mubarak. The "Infitah" or Sadat's open door policy marked the advent of an epoch, which was completely different than that of Nasser's with a new orientation in almost all spheres of policies be it economic, social, political or foreign policy. The adoption of Infitah emphasised the importance of the private sector and privatisation became the slogan heralded in officials' statements, calling for a lesser role of the public sector in directing the economy. This signified that the state was moving away from its expansionary phase and entering its contractory phase.

A cost-benefit analysis of "Infitah" is beyond the scope of this chapter. Suffice it to mention here that "Infitah", which was initially initiated to attract and encourage foreign investment, both from neighbouring Arab countries as well as European and American investment, in productive and industrial sectors failed to achieve its purpose. Instead a commercial economy was created that flourished on the importation of luxurious goods and on heavy investment in building luxury resorts and apartments.[18] This process of commercialisation, which permeated all aspects of Egyptian life, without the achievement of any real economic growth had serious repercussions on the majority of people. The decline of the state's revenue from the big four, triggered the fiscal crisis of the state which had then to abandon its socialist measures. The "social contract" that was drawn between Nasser and the various classes, was breached and seized to exist under Sadat's and Mubarak's so called "economic liberalism".

This commercialisation of the society that started under Sadat and continues under Mubarak had affected the two major gains that professionals have acquired under Nasser viz: free education and secured jobs for university graduates.

Although in theory education is still free in government schools, in practice, the commercialisation of education resulted in the spread of the phenomena of expensive obligatory private tutoring by government teachers for pupils and its extension to universities.[19] Education became once again, and as was the case prior to 1952, the privilege of the well to do who can afford the price of these private tutorials, thus indirectly altering the gains that the impoverished classes had won under Nasser. Social mobility through education, once aspired to by the lower classes became restricted to the upper and upper middle classes.

With the contracting role of the state and the already inflated public bureaucracy, the government is finding it increasingly difficult to keep its previous obligation of securing jobs for every university graduate. Where as between 1952 and the end of the sixties Egypt produced some 250,000 graduates, all of whom where employed despite the overstaffed bureaucracy, between the end of the sixties and the end of the seventies Egypt produced some 565,000 graduates which is double the number of graduates ever produced and was finding difficulty employing them.[20]

Graduates now are given jobs up to ten years after their graduation. Unemployment of the educated is one of the pressing problems facing the state and professional associations alike.

Under these conditions the classical corporatist formula previously adopted by the state under Nasser to control the various interest groups in society could not be sustained. Instead a mixture of coercion and a new tighter rather than a flexible form of corporatism which is labelled here *co-integrationism* is adopted. *Co-integrationism here is defined as a system of state's control over the various interest groups in society through a strategy of co-option of top group leaders into the system and integrating their interests with that of the state using special privileges, patronage networks and institutionalised corruption.* Whereas classical corporatism benefits the broader segment of group members economically and socially, *co-integrationism, benefits only selected leaders and is achieved at the expense of the broader segment of group members.*

In addition, with regard to Bianchi's explanation that the state strengthened the political influence of a wide variety of groups, it will be argued that, on the contrary,

A. The state worked intentionally to weaken the various societal groups, through various laws and continuous intervention.

B. The state especially recently, tightened its grip on most of the professional groups and trade unions and attempted to curtail their political influence.

C. In doing so the state adopted a mixture of coercion and *co-integrationism* (privileges, patronage and institutionalised corruption) as complementary methods of control.

D. At the public policy level, when an increase in the influence of an association takes place, it is usually an outcome of a patron-client relationship established between a key figure in the association and a prominent political patron and is hence achieved on a personal and individual, rather than organisational or association level.

E. At the institutional level, when an increase in the influence of an undesired group takes place, like that of the excluded Muslim Brotherhood "MB", it is usually attributed to the internal weakness inherent within these associations, coupled with the successful manoeuvring of, for example, the MB and, hence, is far from being intentional on the part of the government(at least during the Mubarakist era).

F. The government has been selective in the number and type of groups to which it has granted an increase in political influence. These are mainly business groups which are the natural allies of the state, whose economic interest are tied to the state and hence conformed to its economic policies. Even in this case, measures have been taken to keep the business community weak and fragmented.

G. That interest groups in Egypt further enhance the fragmentation and weakness of the society and hence have a negative impact on the process of political development.

More historical data will be provided on each professional group in the course of their analysis. This chapter will concentrate on the professional syndicates, while the following chapter will deal with the labour movement and business groups, leaving the discussion of the co-operative movement to Chapter Eight.

3. Limitations on Syndicates' Work

Egypt has twenty-two professional syndicates with 3.5 million members. Perhaps out of all interest groups, professional syndicates have been most interfered with by the various regimes. The monarchy delayed their development for three decades, Nasser thought of abolishing them, and Sadat threatened to strip them of their power and reduce them to the status of private clubs.[21] The fact that they embody interests of the educated middle class has always been a source of fear for the Egyptian regime and hence from their birth, attempts have been continuously made to reform them along corporatist lines. Since most of these syndicates are manipulated by the state, concentration will be on those, which assume a political role. Although this chapter focuses on four major politicised syndicates, viz lawyers, journalists, engineers and doctors, examples will be given from other syndicates, especially when assessing their performance before and after the ascendancy of the Muslim Brotherhood.

A) Legal limitations on Syndicates

Since syndicates function within a specific political system that may affect its performance, it is crucial in any assessment of syndicate performance to review the external factors, which might negatively or positively affect their development. The tools used by the government to intervene in syndicate work will therefore be briefly presented.

Apart from law no. 100 for 1993 which is the only common syndicate law, each syndicate used to have its own bylaws that regulate its right and obligations. Most of the syndicates' bylaws reflect the extent of imposed legal control, by which they are prohibited from involvement in any political activities. Other devices are also employed to exert control on council members. For example, during Nasser's era, a law was initiated which necessitated that candidates running for elections in syndicates' councils should be members of the National Union and its successor, the Arab Socialist Union. This lasted until 1977. Under Sadat a new condition was adopted which necessitated the approval of the General Socialist Attorney for candidates running for council membership.

Law 100 for 1993 and its amendments in law 5 for 1995

The first common law to be applied to all syndicates, the issuance of law 100 for 1993, has divided public opinion into those who completely support the law and those who completely reject it. Whereas the first group views the law as democratic and fair, the second group views it as autocratic and restrictive.

The raison d'être for this law lies in the government's determination to combat the Muslim Brotherhood, whose influence in some syndicates has been rising since the late eighties. Advocates of the law have defended it on the grounds that, instead of allowing a few Muslim Brotherhood supporters to elect their candidates to the syndicates' general assembly and the council in the absence of wider participation from the apathetic majority, the law came to set some limits and conditions for the validity of the elections. Accordingly law 100 of 1993 requires the participation of at least half of the members of the general assembly eligible to vote (i.e. who have paid their annual subscription) for the election of council members and president, for an election to be legally valid. In cases where this requirement is not met, members of the general assembly are called to a second meeting at which the elections becomes valid if a third of the eligible voters take part. If the stipulated number of participants is again not met, the current council and its president continue their functions for a further three months, at the end of which the whole procedure for the election of a new council and president is repeated. Article three of the same law lays down that, if the election of the members of the council and its president fails to proceed according to the conditions specified in article 2, a temporary judicial committee is assigned to the functions of the council. Article 6 of the same law places the syndicate elections under judicial supervision.[22] Law 5 of 1995 gave the judicial committee, which is assigned to overseeing the syndicates elections, even broader responsibilities, among which is setting the dates and place of elections and supervision of vote counting.[23]

The law was attacked by some on several grounds. To begin with, the percentage of participation in voting specified by the law to render the election procedure valid was rejected. The 50 per cent required in the first round and a third required in the second was considered to be unnecessarily high and unlikely to occur in any syndicate. Moreover, these percentages are not specified for the validity of elections to the People's Assembly.

The second criticism is based on the contradiction between this law and some of the syndicates' bylaws. It is worth noting here that some of the syndicates' bylaws give the general assembly, in syndicates with ten-thousand members, the right to declare a vote of no confidence in the syndicate's council in the presence of only 300 members. The criticism also extends to the temporary committee of judges, whose responsibility is to manage syndicates in the case of failed elections, on the ground that it creates a duality in the role of the judiciary in that they are syndicate managers on the one hand and arbitrators among competing social forces, as well as between the government and the society, on the other. Whereas supporters of the law view it as in congruence with the constitution and international conventions, its opponents view it as against both.[24]

B) Government Intervention in Syndicates' Affairs

Government intervention in the affairs of syndicates has taken four major forms. These are dissolution, intervention in syndicate elections, use of coercion against syndicates, and threat of abolition.

Dissolution:

A common method that has been used by the government, both historically and more recently, to control and intervene in syndicate affairs is the dissolution of the syndicate council. Before1952, the Bar Association was dissolved in July 1934 when the lawyers rejected the Syndicate council elections of 1933 and attacked the draft law which the government had proposed in April 1934. Accordingly, the government issued law 47, of 1934 dissolving the Bar Association's council, and a committee was assigned to carry the council's functions. Similarly during Nasser's era (1952–1970) dissolution of a syndicate council took place twice, once in the Bar Syndicate in March 1954 and again in the Journalists' Syndicate in April 1954. In both cases this was in response to the stand the syndicates took during the Naguib-Nasser power struggle and their call for the army to return to the barracks and for democracy to be resumed. Again under Sadat (1970–1981) the dissolution of all syndicate councils took place in 1971, and of the Bar Syndicate in July 1981, when the latter vigorously attacked Sadat's foreign policy.

Intervention in syndicate elections

Before 1952 government intervention in syndicate elections had only taken place in the Bar Syndicate. This took the form of government objections to the candidates running in the council elections in December 1933 and the passing of law 86 of 1933, which invalidated the election of the "undesirable" candidates.

The second form of intervention in this period was the prevention of opposition lawyers from voting in Syndicate elections. This took place during the December 1938 elections, when the police prevented Wafdist lawyers from voting. The third form of intervention in syndicate elections was the extension given to a pro-government council in order to postpone elections. This took place when the government issued law 98 for 1944, which gave the Bar Association's council a two-year extension.

After 1952, government intervention in syndicate council elections took several forms. Among these was membership of the National Union, and its successor the Arab Socialist Union, being a condition for candidates to run in syndicate council elections. This condition was in force until 1977. Under Sadat, a new condition was adopted which necessitates the approval of the General Socialist Attorney for candidates running for council membership.

Secondly, government intervention took place through the official endorsement of particular candidates. This occurred in the Bar Association in November 1966 and in the Journalists' Syndicate in March 1981. A similar device is the postponement of syndicate elections beyond the official date specified by law. This happened both in the Journalists' Syndicate and the Engineers' Syndicate at the beginning and the end of the sixties. The extension of the council's term of office or its remission is another example of government intervention. Extension was enforced in the Bar Syndicate under law 65 of 1970, when the council's term was increased to four years, and in the Engineers' Syndicate, while remission occurred in the Journalists' Syndicate.

Under Sadat the dissolution of all syndicate councils took place in 1971, and of the Lawyers' Syndicate in July 1981.

Use of coercion against syndicates

The use of coercion against syndicate, is yet another form of government interference. It was used against the Bar Syndicate in October 1930 under Ismail Sidki's government, when the police broke into the Syndicate building to prevent the Syndicate's general assembly from convening in emergency session to protest against the abolition of the 1923 constitution. Both the Sadat and Mubarak regimes used the police to prevent some syndicates, especially the Bar Syndicate, from holding several symposia, which were perceived by the regime as attacking government policy. Police force was often used in the Bar Syndicate to protect government endorsed candidates against other candidates, and to assist their reinstatement.

Threat of abolition

The threat of abolition was also used by Nasser and Sadat as a warning to politically active syndicates. This happened under Nasser when he threatened to abolish all professional syndicates, and again in 1979 and 1980, when Sadat threatened to abolish the Journalists' Syndicate and reduce it to the status of a private club.[25]

4. The Politicised Syndicates

A) The Lawyers' Syndicate

Historical Background

The Lawyers' Syndicate or the Bar Association was the first to organise, originally founded to cater for the needs of national court lawyers. Three types of courts existed in Egypt at the time; the foreign (mixed courts), the modern Egyptian (national courts) and finally the traditional (sharia) courts. In 1876 the mixed courts became the first to form a Bar Association, which was fashioned after its French counterpart. The National Courts followed suit in 1912, and finally came the association of the Sharia Syndicate (1916).[26]

Although the National Court Association was modelled after the association of the Mixed Bar, it retained the guild tradition. Hence the conflict between those who view the association as a tool of government control and those who view it as a representative of members' interests, following its Western counterpart. The choice of the term "naqib" for the president and "niqabah" for the association itself are remnants of the old guild system.

The initiative for organising the association came from a young Coptic lawyer, Murqus Fahmi, in 1897. Aware that his youth was against him, Fahmi sought support from other prominent lawyers like Muhammad Farid who backed his proposal. In 1899 Fahmi drafted statutes for a society of lawyers (Jam'yat al Muhamin) and became its secretary. In 1902 a proposal was presented to the Minister of Justice, Fu'ad Ibrahim, for a French style bar-association, but this was rejected. The government no doubt preferred to deal with lawyers on an individual basis rather than having to face them collectively as a corporate body. Moreover, there was always the fear of the association being used by the nationalist movement against the government.[27] The future would prove that government's fears were not unjustified:

> At times when newspapers were suppressed, parliamentary elections rigged, the Egyptian University subjected to heavy-handed interference and public rallies banned, opposition lawyers made use of the Bar Association and political trials in the court room to articulate their views.[28]

The proposal was therefore abandoned until 1910, when Minister of Justice Saad Zaghlul reviewed it and, although he had already left office, the new Bar Association was officially formed in 1912 and held its first meeting in November of that year.

Although Donald Reid offers several reasons why the Bar Syndicate was the first to organise, the most significant is that, unlike other professionals (such as doctors, engineers and teachers who were still government employees), none of the lawyers in the new Bar Association held government post and hence the fear of provoking administrative superiors did not exist. Another reason given by Reid is that the expansion of commercial Western capital and the adoption of a Western civil code had increased the demand for lawyers with knowledge of Western law. A third reason is the tensions between lawyers and judges, which have strong roots in the history of the bar and which encouraged lawyers to form an association that would protect them from the encroachment of the judiciary.[29]

The first elected council of the Bar Association (1912) included a fifteen man governing body, which started to work on matters of professional concern. During the next forty years the association investigated lawyers' complaints against judges, published a journal, built up a library, established a lawyers' club and a pension fund. The Bar Association elections always mirrored the image of political life in Egypt. For example, in the five annual elections following that of 1912, lawyers showed little interest in their association and its election, thus reflecting the apathy that coloured political life in general at the time.[30] From 1918 onwards, the Bar Association was dominated by liberal nationalism represented in the Wafd party, and hence the elections within the association reflected the power struggle that was taking place between the Wafd, the British, and the palace. As one author has put it,

> When Wafdist governments held sway, Wafdist control of the Bar Association was assured, their flanks in the legal profession well guarded. When they fell from power the Wafdists could retreat to the halls of the association to lick their wounds, harass the government, and work for a return to power.[31]

Other political parties, like the Watani and the liberal constitutionalists, surfaced in the Association only when they joined an anti-Wafdist coalition, aimed at driving the Wafd out of government and therefore attempting to curtail the Wafd's hold on the Association.

It is crucial at this point and before proceeding further, to explore the presence of the Muslim Brotherhood among lawyers before1952, since they re-appear in the late eighties and nineties as a significant force. Historical evidence, however, shows that the Muslim Brotherhood, led by Hassan al-Banna, was not prominent among lawyers. For example, out of ten members of the Brotherhood's Guidance Council in the early 1950s only two were lawyers, and none of the forty-seven tried in the two major trials in 1949 was a lawyer. The wanted list of 1954 included only three lawyers out of 132 Brothers. Only the need for a respectable figure made the Muslim Brotherhood choose Hassan Ismail al-Hudaybi, a judge, as al-Banna's successor after the latter's assassination in 1949.[32] The politicisation of the Bar Association is also reflected in the fact that, from its inception, it served as a recruitment channel for Egypt's top politicians. The first governing council of the association included among its members one future prime minister (Hassan Sabry), and by the 1920s lawyers occupied a number of major political posts. The parliament of 1924 had forty six lawyers in the chamber of deputies, the second highest proportion after the landed notables, who had dominated the 1913–1914 assembly. The Zaghloul's government of 1924 had seven lawyers among the ten cabinet members,[33] Nahas' cabinets of 1930, 1936, and 1942 had six lawyers out of nine, seven lawyers out of eleven, and eight out of eleven respectively. Ismail Sidky's cabinet of 1930 had seven lawyers out of eight, Muhammad Mahmoud's 1937 government 12 out of 15.[34] Generally speaking, most cabinets until 1952 had more than half lawyers, leading Reid to comment that

> Government in Egypt almost became government of the lawyers by the lawyers and for the lawyers.[35]

The British high commissioner was indeed right when he commented that:

> Lawyers are in Egypt the last element a government should provoke, and a lawyers' strike if properly organised, has already proved effective to dislocate public life.[36]

The post 1952 rulers were well aware of this and hence their continued efforts to control the Bar Association, the natural sanctuary for lawyers.

The Lawyers' Syndicate from Nasser to Mubarak

The organisation of the Syndicate

Before discussing the policy of successive regimes towards lawyers and the syndicate, it is imperative to give a brief description of the organisation of the Syndicate. In Egypt the single type of Bar Association prevails. It is divided into twenty one branches called affiliated Syndicates.

However, decision-making is centralised and the affiliated branches are subordinate to the central body and are obliged to carry out its policies and decisions. The Egyptian Bar Syndicate is open to all registered lawyers. The highest authority within the Syndicate is the general conference or general assembly. The second level, and probably the most important in the authority structure, is the council of the Syndicate. The council has twenty four members and is elected for a period of four years. It is headed by a president or "Naquib Al-Mohamin" who speaks on behalf of the lawyers and takes initiatives when appropriate. The council, and more particularly the Naquib, is the real focus of leadership of the Syndicate and acts on behalf of the general conference during the intervals between its very short sessions, which sometimes last for a few days but in most cases only for one day.[37]

Government policy towards the Syndicate

The advent of the Free Officers in 1952 not only subverted the economic and social position of lawyers, but also served to restrict their role in political life. The destruction of the old political system, which helped the ascendancy of lawyers, was the first step in this direction.

The abrogation of the 1923 constitution (which the lawyers had helped to draft), the dissolution of Parliament (their main field of political activity), and the abolition of political parties (which they had led), severely undermined the role they now played. Moreover, the gradual limitation on land holding, the abolition of family Waqfs, and the nationalisation of private enterprises deprived many lawyers of their wealthy clients and limited their economic opportunities. As a result many were forced to seek employment in the public sector as government employees.

More crucially, the predominance of lawyers in the cabinet that had been the norm during the colonial period came to an end after 1952. For example, only 37per cent (7 individuals) of the cabinet of June 1953 held law degrees. In the1961 cabinet this fell to 10 per cent and it remained generally below 15 per cent until March 1968.[38] In his treatment of the syndicates Nasser's policy varied according to their strength and degree of involvement in politics. Since the Bar Association had been the arena of Wafdist political activity and had sided with Naguib and his call for a return to representative government in the Naguib-Nasser struggle, it was the least popular Syndicate among Nasser and his entourage.[39]

Holding an emergency meeting of the Bar's general assembly in March 1954, the Wafdist president, Umar Umar, called for the freeing of political prisoners, the abolition of special military courts, the dissolution of the Revolutionary Command Council and parliamentary elections.[40] Nasser responded by dissolving the Association's board of directors, appointing a new one and banning general assembly meetings for four years.[41] Such measures were not only a violation of the Syndicate bylaws, but also a violation of the Egyptian constitution.[42] The first elections held under the Nasserite regime in 1958 reflected the lawyers' insistence on preserving the autonomous character of the Bar Association. These elections resulted in Mustafa al-Baradie's first term of office (1958–1962) as the head of the Association.[43]

Al-Baradie, who was an early sympathiser of the Wafd and Sa'dists, was persistently defending judicial autonomy and parliamentary democracy. He also opposed social measures, which he perceived as threats to the quality of legal education and to the economic welfare of private practitioners. When Nasser resorted to austerity measures, such as confiscation and detentions, al-Baradie, as head of the Association called for the formation of a supreme constitutional court to rule on the constitutionality of all laws.

Nasser's attack on the syndicates was strongest after Syria's secession from the United Arab Republic in 1961–62. He accused professional syndicates of being "Bourgeois strongholds and dangerous anachronisms in a socialist society" and as "factions that split society". Baradie's response was to call for a constitutional limit on arbitrary state power, and to demand freedom of opinion, a political opposition, an independent press, and the cessation of government interference in syndicate affairs.[44] The clash that took place in 1962 between al-Baradie and Nasser marked the apex of his confrontation with the regime. Appointed as the spokesman of several professional syndicates, al-Baradie attacked the 50 per cent representation of peasants and workers in popularly-elected councils. He was therefore replaced by Abd al-Aziz Shurbaji (1962–1964), who was a close friend of Nasser and who joined a "free lawyers" group in the early days of the revolution. When al-Shurbaji quarrelled with the government, al-Baradie regained the presidency and spent his second term in office (1964–1966) conducting a fierce assault on government social policies. He was then removed from office again and was replaced by al-Khawaja, who spent his first term in office from 1966 to 1971.

Despite being a member of the pre-revolutionary Wafdist vanguard, al-Khawaja, in sharp contrast to the liberal and independent al-Baradie, had succeeded through disguising his political sympathies and reversing his political stance, in serving the goals of various regimes on several occasions. Bianchi, for example, attributes the passive stand that the Syndicate took in 1969 towards the famous "massacre of the judges"[45] to al-Khawaja's role in neutralising the Syndicate thus preventing any resistance to the regime's measures.[46] It was expected that an incident, which involves an encroachment on the autonomy of the judiciary, would incite the Bar Syndicate to initiate a vigorous attack on the government. That this did not take place cannot be attributed only to the role played by al-Khawaja, being the "government man", in placating and domesticating the lawyers. Rather, it can be partly attributed to Nasser's socialist policy of free education, which provided a large number of school graduates the opportunity, otherwise denied to them, to enrol in the faculty of law, and after the issuance of the July 1961 decree a guaranteed job in the bureaucratic apparatus. Knowing the fact that in 1968, the government had succeeded in forcing the Syndicate to accept as members this numerous but less prestigious group of lawyers employed in the public sector,[47] the stand taken by the Syndicate becomes quite clear. It is this group of public sector lawyers that the government relies on when using Syndicate elections in its containment efforts. Although, for the sake of protecting his own interest, al-Khawaja refrained from siding with either Sadat or Aly Sabry in their power struggle, he was nevertheless still purged by Sadat when the latter assumed power because of his affiliation with the ASU.[48]

From the outset Sadat was eager to preserve a peaceful relationship with the Bar Association and to placate the lawyers and judges who had been tarnished during Nasser's rule in order to guarantee their support, especially at the time when he was consolidating his power. Thus as early as 1971 he made the restoration of the "Rule of Law" the slogan of his era, publicly burning secret intelligence tapes, making a symbolic visit to the Bar Association and appointing two lawyers to his cabinet. However, analysing his memoirs reveals Sadat's attitude toward the rule of law:

114

During the first twenty years of the revolution, when the rule of law was 'suspended', there was a marked change in lawyers' fortunes. The legal business practically came to a standstill and many lawyers actually went bankrupt or were on the verge of bankruptcy. Today things are back to normal. As I restored the rule of law, lawyers today are in great demand to fight social injustices. The demand for lawyers has risen even higher with the adoption of our open-door policy as foreign businessmen need legal representation in Egypt. The legal business has thus regained its earlier vitality in every respect.[49]

Sadat's words clearly reflect his policy orientation towards the lawyers. He reminded the legal practice of the benefits, which it had regained owing to his open-door policy, hence implicitly demanding gratitude. Moreover Sadat treated the restoration of law as a personal choice, a grant which he had endowed on lawyers. No wonder then, that when his policy of containment failed, Sadat chose to withdraw his endorsement and the "rule of law" became a slogan void in meaning and in practice.

When Sadat purged al-Khawaja because of the latter's earlier links with the ASU, he reinstated al-Baradie as head of the Lawyers' Syndicate. This was in line with his strategy of discrediting Nasser's rule and removing his appointees. To accomplish this goal Sadat was willing to accommodate the entire pre-1952 agrarian bourgeoisie, politicians and syndicate leaders who had been harmed by Nasser.

Al-Baradie, however, proved that he would not be bought by the new regime. His first clash with the regime was in 1972 in the aftermath of the wide-spread students' strikes.[50] Directly after the strike the Syndicate issued a statement supporting the students and their demands, denounced all attempts at settlement, and called for an all encompassing struggle and the elimination of all the obstacles which hindered political freedom.[51] Whilst celebrating the first anniversary of Sadat's corrective revolution in the Bar Syndicate, al-Baradie defended public and civil freedom by calling for an independent free press and the reinstatement of all the judges who had been forced to retire in 1969 and warned against a political judiciary or any attempt to politicise the judges.[52] When Sadat suggested the formation of platforms within the ASU, al-Baradie rejected the idea and proclaimed that democracy had no meaning without free political parties.

In the 1975 Syndicate elections Sadat tried to replace him by encouraging several contestants to run for election, but his efforts were fruitless.[53] Al-Baradie won the 1975 elections and continued his criticism of the government. In January 1977 food riots spread all over the country as a result of the government's reduction of food subsidies. To prevent the recurrence of mass riots and strikes, the government issued law 2 of 1977 which provided for life imprisonment with hard labour for membership of clandestine armed organisations hostile to the state and for planners of and participants in damaging strikes and demonstrations

115

that endangered public security.[54] The Bar Association responded by issuing a statement supporting the civil right to peaceful strike action and attributed the responsibility for what happened during the riots to the absence of political parties, the legitimate channels of interest representation. The statement also warned the government against using the riots as an excuse for imposing more restraints on public liberty and the primacy of law and suggested that the only way for development lay in a more democratic system.[55] In his speech al-Baradie attacked the government's violation of civil liberties and gave Fu'ad Saraj Al-Din, founder of the New Wafd Party, a forum at the syndicate's headquarters for his provocative speech announcing the party's formation. Al-Baradie died in office in 1977 and was succeeded by the government-endorsed candidate al-Khawaja. Although al-Khawaja was earlier purged by Sadat because of his affiliation to the ASU, he was a better choice than his competitor, al-Shurbaji, who maintained a close relationship with the Nasserites and Leftists and because of al-Shurbajji's criticism of Sadat's trip to Jerusalem and the Camp David talks. Al-Khawaja had, however, avoided projecting himself as the government candidate, preferring instead to play the double role of "fusion candidate" and unofficial government representative. After his election to a full term as Syndicate leader, al-Khawaja found it extremely difficult to preserve his neutrality towards Sadat's policy, especially at a time when the public was enraged with Sadat's foreign policy and his Camp David accord.[56]

From that time he started criticising Sadat's policy, first mildly and then vigorously. Al-Khawaja's change of stance can be attributed mainly to his shrewdness and his way of "riding the tide", and was encouraged by the various opposition forces that existed. Three incidents had particularly irritated Sadat. The first was the alliance between the Bar Association and several opposition forces against the Pyramid Plateau Project,[57] which forced the government to cancel the project. The second was the Syndicate's continuing attack on Sadat's foreign policy, which was symbolised by raising the Palestinian flag on the syndicate building on the day the Camp David accord was signed and which was echoed by the Syndicate leader in the meeting of the Arab Federation of lawyers.[58] The third incident was the Syndicate's stand against the government's encroachment on the Journalists' Syndicate and Sadat's determination to change the latter into a club. As soon as Sadat's intention became public, the Bar Syndicate defended the constitutional rights of the Journalists' Syndicate and issued a statement denouncing all attempts at reducing it to the status of a private club, arguing that this would constitute an assault on liberty and democracy.[59]

Sadat thus became intolerant of al-Khawaja and started to plan a show-down in 1980, which culminated in 1981 with the dissolution of the Bar's elected council. The events started with a march staged by the ruling party and the secret police, in which a group of lawyers affiliated to the National Democratic Party forced their way into Syndicate headquarters and convened a meeting that declared a vote of no confidence in the Syndicate council. Sadat immediately intervened dissolving the council and appointing a new one, headed by Jamal al-Utayfi, a lawyer-politician who was a member of Sadat's inner circle. Moreover, among those who were arrested in 1981, were five members of the elected Bar council.

The first years of Mubarak's regime witnessed an internal battle between the appointed council, headed by Jamal al-Utayfi, and the elected one, headed by al-Khawaja, who organised an invasion of the Syndicate headquarters and restored the council's regular meeting. A march to the courts demanding judicial independence was also staged by the elected council. As a compromise solution, the elected council was reinstated for the full remainder of its term in exchange for its acceptance of Sadat's more restrictive syndicate law, including explicit controls over the Bar's affiliation with international organisations. The same year this law was adopted al-Khawaja was elected president of the Arab Federation of Lawyers. In 1985 a special seminar was held to organise the defence of Sulayman Khatar, a policeman who had fired on Israeli tourists in Sinai, after an Israeli raid on the PLO headquarters in Tunis. Although al-Khawaja gave a fiery speech in this seminar, he nevertheless personally avoided attacking the Camp David Accord. Instead his speech concentrated on attacking the 1974 disengagement policy between Egypt and Israel, attacked the USA and Israel, and asked the Arabs for arms to fight the latter. His attacks, however, took place at a time when Egypt's relationship with the USA and Israel had severely deteriorated. His speech was well rewarded, since he was elected to his fifth term as president receiving over 75 per cent of the votes.[60] Although Bianchi tends to describe al-Khawaja as a "long time opportunist and former regime pawn" who had been changed into "a darling of the opposition whose activities are followed closely in the Arab press", the events so far related prove that al-Khawaja continued to be the government's man and his criticism of the regime was carefully phrased to avoid any personal involvement that might lead to a second persecution. When he did criticise the regime's foreign policy, he made sure that a change of direction and in government orientation was taking place. The continuity of al-Khawaja as the head of the Bar Association backed by government support became more obvious after 1985 and was not without serious repercussions on the Syndicate's internal cohesion and on its performance in general.

These repercussions manifested themselves in the form of the internal struggles and factionalisation, which began in 1986 and occurred between the Cairo Syndicate and the general Syndicate, leading to the formation of two factions among the lawyers. The first supported the separation of the Cairo Syndicate and the second stood firmly for the unification of the Syndicate. It is worth noting here that the conflict was mostly among the Wafdist members of the Syndicate, giving outside observers the impression that it was a reflection of the divisions within the New Wafd Party itself.[61] In 1988, and before the 1989 Syndicate elections, internal divisions intensified.

These divisions were based on either public versus private sector interests or ideological conflicts between groups such as the Muslim Brotherhood, Marxists, Nasserites, and the Wafdists. Three main factions can be identified. The first was led by al-Khawaja and supported by some members of the council and the public sector lawyers. This group believed that the Syndicate's role should be primarily professional and was generally supported by the government. A second group lead by other members of the council, among whom was Mohammed Asfour, a prominent lawyer, saw the Syndicate's role as primarily national and political and were therefore calling for change and for the syndicate to resume its historical role in national politics. The third group was neutral and viewed both the professional and political role of the Syndicate as extremely narrow and limited. They criticised the provincial Syndicates as largely inactive and noticed that tribalism was still the determinant factor in governing the Syndicate's work.[62] It is this group that included the apathetic majority of Syndicate members. In 1989 the Bar Syndicate witnessed a series of dramatic events, which included lawyers taking refuge in the Syndicate building, the forced entrance of the police and the exchange of fire between the police and some lawyers, and lawsuits and conflict among lawyers concerning the legitimacy of the Syndicate council.

In short, the Syndicate represented an example of what the Egyptian political analysts had labelled the "internal explosion" of syndicates. Although on the surface, the main conflict started with regard to some professional issues, in reality it also had a political dimension since the major issue raised was the extent of Syndicate independence. A considerable number of lawyers at that time viewed al-Khawaja as a government puppet and believed that only by his resignation could the Bar Association gain any independence from the regime, an opinion which to a great extent was true.[63]

One of the major reasons that caused the conflict was, however, not reported. This was an accusation of corruption and mismanagement of the Syndicates' pension fund by al-Khawaja, who wasted more than £E20,000,000.00 of Syndicate funds as a result of bad investment decisions in the financially deteriorating Engineering Bank. The decision was taken solely by al-Khawaja and his entourage. An eye witness to the incident asserted that al-Khawaja was on the verge of being killed by the lawyers on that day, had it not been for Dr Mohammed Asfour, the leader of the anti government faction, who had to rush to the Syndicate to placate the lawyers.[64] Despite all these allegations, no investigation was undertaken and the government continued to support his reinstatement using the police and by imprisoning recalcitrant lawyers. Hence the Syndicate was used as a coercive tool against a segment of society it should have protected. Another incident of corruption that involved al-Khawaja was discovered by a journalist who hinted at the scandal in one of the official newspapers. The scandal pointed to al-Khawaja's involvement in a network of organised crime, which included other members of the Syndicate, policemen, traffic police and others. It was discovered that this network forged the power of attorney on behalf of some of those who have car accidents nation-wide to enable them to receive compensation from insurance companies. Although the journalist did not mention al-Khawaja's name, the latter insulted and threatened him in the office of the head of the newspaper's board of directors and ordered him to remain silent. Of course the government turned a blind eye to al-Khawaga's corruption, the case was never mentioned again in the newspaper, and again no investigation was undertaken.[65] The previous examples show how the government used institutionalised corruption (one of the components of co-integrationism) to tie al-Khawaja's interests to that of the state and how this was achieved at the expense of the Syndicate members.

Since most of this struggle was taking place among Wafdist members of the Syndicate, some authors commented that it was "an internal struggle among the new Wafd party but was taking place on the syndicate grounds".[66] The results of this struggle was a division in the Syndicate's general assembly, the involvement of the police, the arrest of one of the lawyers and the re-election of al-Khawaja as the Bar president on 12 June 1989.[67] The struggle continued throughout 1990, with legal disputes taking place between the elected council, headed by al-Khawaja, and the court's assigned temporary committee, headed by the Wafdist, Dr. Mohammed Asfour,[68] and in 1991 the continuing struggle caused the failure of the council to convene on several occasions.

These internal struggles again led to police intervention and the arrest of some lawyers in September 1991.[69] The results of the first election were nullified by court orders in July 1992 and new elections under judiciary supervision were scheduled. The temporary committee appealed against the court ruling, but their appeal was rejected. The results of the new elections brought to the fore a council with a majority of members belonging to the Muslim Brotherhood under the presidency of al-Khawaja.[70] This, however, did not end the internal struggle and factionalisation within the Syndicate. On the contrary the conflict between al-Khawaja and most of the council members was renewed, owing to the decision taken by the Islamist trend represented in the majority of the council members to halt the relationship with the Union of Arab Lawyers because of its opposition to the Islamist regime in Sudan.[71] In 1994 the conflict was resumed between the council members belonging to the Muslim Brotherhood and ten other members who belonged to other political groups under the leadership of al-Khawaja after a meeting held by the former in which it was decided to appoint new members to offices in the Syndicate, all of whom belonged to the Muslim Brotherhood. Immediately the secular trend, represented by the ten members, announced their rejection of the chosen candidates and threatened to appeal to both the court and the general attorney for further investigation.[72] At the same time another division took place among the members of the Muslim Brotherhood itself, which was divided into two factions, exchanging accusations of corruption and mismanagement. The conflict between the Muslim Brotherhood members and the regime intensified, and revolved around two main issues. The first was the commemoration of Abd al-Hareth Madeny, a lawyer and a Muslim Brotherhood member, who died under torture, after he was arrested on 26 April 1994. Madeny was accused of playing a major role in carrying orders from the imprisoned leaders of the terrorist groups to their rank and file. The second conflict was related to the arrest of forty-four lawyers, the majority of whom were Muslim

119

Brotherhood members and some of whom had spent between three and five years in jail without any legal justification.[73]

The ongoing events in the Bar Association, divisions, corruption and confrontation, led to a court order in January 1996 placing the Syndicate under judiciary guards assigned by the court, with the consequent complete loss of the Syndicate's autonomy.

B) The Journalists' Syndicate

Historical Background

The first attempt at establishing a professional syndicate for foreign journalists started in 1909, but was unsuccessful because journalists were few at that time and lacked a collective spirit. In 1912 Ahmad Lutfi Al Sayyid, the editor of the Ummah party's journal (Al-Jaridah) called for an Egyptian Press Syndicate (naqabah), which aroused some interest and the newly founded group included both Egyptians and Europeans. The advent of World War I however, aborted the attempt.

Following the war, and impressed by the role of the Bar Syndicate in presenting national demands to the British in 1918, several prominent journalists revived the idea and met to draft the plans for a syndicate. The events of 1919 revolution interfered with this attempt, but the group met in 1923 and managed to complete the draft. However, the events of the 1924, with Saad Zaghlul's sudden ascendancy and fall from power, diverted all such efforts, and this was further complicated by the growing feud between King Fuad and some journalists.

In 1926 a further attempt failed because the organisers extended membership to relatives and friends alongside genuine journalists. However in 1930, the Press Society (Jam'iyat al-Sihafah) brought together owners, as well as editors, of newspapers. A rival, Union of Egyptian Newspaper Editors (Ittihad Muharriru al-Suhuf al-Misri), was formed in 1938, which restricted membership to editors only. These bodies not only attracted different members but also had different political orientations. Ali Maher's government of 1936 had brought new hope for the profession, but his government's fall from power temporarily ended his efforts to establish a press syndicate. He regained his position as Prime Minister in August 1939 till June 1940, when his interest in the profession was renewed. Jabra'il Taqla owner of al-Ahram became the president of an unofficial Syndicate, but Ali Maher once again fell from power before a Press Syndicate law was finally passed in 1941 and the resulting Syndicate started functioning under the presidency of Mahmud Abu Al Fatah.[74]

The Journalists' Syndicate from Nasser to Mubarak

Until 1955, when Nasser had consolidated his power, the presidency of the Syndicate alternated between Husayn Abu Al Fatah of the Wafd and his brother Mahmud, and Fikry Abbaza of al-Hizb al-Watani. Before 1955 the presidency was held by an opposition figure whose power was balanced by a majority of weak right wing parties, which were more dependent on the goodwill of the government. After 1955 the situation was reversed and the president was a pro-government figure, although the members of the council included representative of several factions who sometimes outnumbered government supporters.[75] Although the Syndicate had supported the 1952 military coup, it nevertheless later sided with those who requested the army's return to the barracks. The first assault on the Syndicate came in March 1954, after the convention of the Syndicate council and journalists' demands for the nullification of the emergency rules and the release of all political prisoners. Nasser responded by dissolving the Syndicate council and forming a committee under the presidency of Salah Salem.[76] In Spring 1955 Nasser struck again by issuing a new press law that encroached on the independence of the Syndicate, which had previously been regulated by its own bylaws.[77] As one author has put it

> The new law was ingenious in that it manipulated the journalists syndicate into the role of censor and made it the tool for purge of journalists.[78]

Although government maintained a strong hold over the Syndicate, it was twice broken. The confrontation with the regime started when the Syndicate members succeeded in electing Hafiz Mahmoud and most of the council members from the opposition. A former member of the Liberal Constitutionalist Party, Mahmoud criticised Nasser's policy of managing the press and tried to form an alliance of professional syndicates, which also included Ibrahim Shukri of the Agronomist Syndicate and Muhi al-Din of the Doctors' Syndicate. This attempt was stopped when Ali Sabri came to know about the "Federation's" first meeting. The confrontation escalated when the Journalists' Syndicate voted against the government plan to place both the ownership and supervision of the press in the hands of the ASU. Ali Sabri retaliated by dismissing Mahmoud and adding some Marxists to the press corps, but he still could not prevent the election of a council that represented a diversity of views. From 1965 onwards the ASU started to consolidate its power over the Syndicate. Syndicate council elections were cancelled two years in a row and in 1967 new elections were held in which Ahmad Bahaa al-Din was presented as a compromise candidate acceptable to both the Syndicate and the ASU. When the Syndicate supported the 1968 student demonstrations, the ASU decided to enforce its list of candidates, headed by Kamal al-Zuhari. Like al-Khawaja, al-Zuhari was a creature of the ASU and, he too changed from being a regime pawn into being a darling of the opposition. When al-Zuhari assumed the presidency he helped to issue a new law which on the surface appeared to be a victory for the Syndicate, but in reality involved the

Syndicate council's president in party-ordered purges and prosecutions. Ironically, the "Zuhari Law" was used against its own authors. When the Syndicate again supported the students demonstrations of 1972 and 1973, over a hundred journalist including several council members, were expelled from the ASU and from then on the regime started to recruit more of its own supporters, more specifically those who were closely identified with the purges, like Yusuf al-Sib'ai, the former Minister of Culture and editor of al-Ahram, Muhammad Abd al-Jawad, the head of the state agency, and Salah Jalal of al-Tali'a. The tension between Sadat and the journalists never eased. In 1979 and 1980 Sadat and the regime's editors introduced measures which they claimed would clear the air.[79] In reality and as one author described them,

> these were poorly disguised attempts to reintroduce censorship through the back door while spreading out responsibility for enforcement among a number of bewildering institutions with overlapping powers.[80]

When Sadat knew that the Journalists' Syndicate intended to resist his measures, he threatened to change it into a private club. Mustafa Amin, known as the Dean of the Egyptian Press, sarcastically suggested changing it into a casino. When under his pretence of democracy, Sadat suggested that the Press was about to become the "fourth power of the state", Amin answered that the people would misread the word "power" (sulta) as "salad" (salata). When Sadat revealed his intention to form a government-appointed Higher Council for the press, Amin commented that it should indeed be called the "higher" council because its meeting room would be on the eleventh floor.[81] These sarcastic remarks no doubt reflected the degree to which independent writers had become alienated from their Syndicate. Sadat's measures increased this feeling and journalists started seeking different avenues for protecting their interests and freedom.

Under Sadat, newspapers were classified under three categories: State, Party and Syndicate, with privately-owned newspapers prohibited. These three types of papers were supervised by the Higher Council for the Press, a commission of fifty members presided over by the president of Majlis al-Shura. In practice these measures granted Majlis al-Shura wide responsibilities for the press at the expense of more marginalisation of the Syndicate. For example, it was Majlis al-Shura that appointed one half of the higher council of the press with the other half being ex-officio members drawn from editors and managers of state newspapers, and broadcasting bureau. Moreover, it was Majlis al-Shura that was empowered to appoint members of the managing councils of state publishing houses and to supervise the elections of the remaining members by the employees. These measures, together with Sadat's famous Law of Shame, placed the journalists at the mercy of their editors and the appointed board of directors. Under the law they could be charged with defamation. It was mainly the dissatisfaction of the journalists with all these restrictive measures that brought Zuhari again to the fore and enabled him to win the 1980 syndicate elections. This election also witnessed opposition journalists winning the majority of seats on the Syndicate's council, among them Amina Shafiq and Husayn Abd al-Raziq of the left wing Tajammu' party (NUPP). Zuhari soon became a regular participant in the Bar Syndicate seminars, attacking Sadat's press measures and discussing his book, against the Nile project Sadat intended to initiate, which would divert Nile water to Israel. Sadat retaliated by replacing Zuhari with the government candidate, Salah Jalal, in spring 1981.

After Sadat's assassination Zuhari fought Jalal in the 1984 elections with the latter winning the presidency by a margin of three votes-476 to 473. Again the elections created a council with a majority of opposition journalists. Although Jalal tried to convince the Syndicate members that he was acting as a "bridge" between the Mubarak government and the Syndicate, his opponents denounced his attempts as costly and threatening the Syndicate's independence. At the same time they resisted Jalal's attempts to change the Syndicate into an entrepreneurial one, like the Engineers' Syndicate, and insisted that, within their Syndicate, politics should assume precedence over economics, as in the Lawyers' Syndicate, and that their Syndicate should always remain the "Syndicate of opinion" (niqabat al-ra'i).

The existence of a council with a majority of opposition members, presided over by a pro-government chair, created much conflict. In the 1983 elections, the leading vote getter was Amina Shafiq of the NUPP and in 1985 a new Islamist face, Muhammad 'Abd al-Quddus, the son of the famous writer Ihsan 'Abd al-Quddus and an active member of the Muslim Brotherhood, gained a seat in the Syndicate council.[82] In 1988 a further confrontation between the regime and the Syndicate took place when the latter protested against the various coercive methods adopted by the Minister of the Interior towards journalists, and the imposition of limitations on journalists working for opposition newspapers. Several seminars were held in the syndicate discussing "The liberty of the press", which led some journalists to seek refuge in the syndicate as a form of collective protest against the coercion of the regime.[83]

The 1989 elections saw the emergence of Makram Mohamed Ahmed, the government endorsed candidate, as the Syndicate president. He managed to gain some benefits for the Syndicate, but this was, however, done on a personal basis through his relationship with the regime.[84] The 1995 elections again brought to the fore an opposition council presided over by Ibrahim Nafaa, the government endorsed candidate, with the Muslim Brotherhood gaining a second seat beside that of 'Abd al-Quddus.

In the same year Law 93 of 1995[85] imposed further restrictions on journalists, resulting in 1300 journalists protesting against the austerity measures taken by the regime. This led the Prime Minister to announce that freedom of press and opinion were valued and that there was no intention on the part of the regime to change this situation. Nevertheless, the Syndicate's general assembly denounced the law, considering it an imposition not only on journalists in particular, but also on civil rights in general. The assembly also protested against the speed with which the law was passed in the People's Assembly and the exclusion of journalists from consultation on legislation that affected them. The assembly also announced a one-day strike when the publication of all newspapers would be stopped, and the preparation of a "Black List" of the names of all those who drafted the Law, placing a prohibition on reporting news of them or showing their pictures in the newspapers. The assembly also decided to contest the constitutionality of the law.[86] Despite all the measures taken and the fact that the law was amended, it still represents a further attempt on behalf of the regime to control civil institutions. The Journalists' Syndicate had thus become a weak institution for promoting and protecting its members' interests. As one author has commented:

> Journalists have developed an even more cynical view of the syndicate's usefulness in advancing their interests and defending their freedom. Many writers seek a degree of independence by aligning themselves with a particular faction of the ruling elite and expressing critical views they know are being voiced inside the government itself. Their ability to survive and prosper depends not only on their willingness to respect the tacit limits of tolerable debate but also on the accuracy of their "inside" information about the changing balance of power within the ruling circle. Weaker and less tractable writers are more likely to view the syndicate as a valuable forum for protesting government abuses, but when push comes to shove, journalists in trouble with the law generally look elsewhere for support and protection.[87]

The recent removal of Adel Hamouda, a prominent journalist as the chief editor of Ruz al-Yusuf, one of the most respected and readable political magazines in Egypt, to a great extent validate the previous statement. Hamouda was removed from office because of the embarrassment, which he continuously caused the government over such sensitive issues as discrimination against the Coptic minority, the corruption of some government officials, but above all his continuous criticism of the Ganzoury government.

The case of the Journalists' Syndicate clearly reflects the erosion of corporatism previously established under Nasser and its replacement with a strategy of co-option of Syndicate's leaders under Sadat and Mubarak (another component of co-integrationism). The limited benefits that the journalists gain from time to time are usually based on personal relations that Syndicate's leaders establish with particular members of the ruling elites. Journalists thus learned to seek protection and personal interests by establishing networks with certain patrons within the ruling class, rather than through their own syndicate.

C) The Engineers' Syndicate:

Historical Background

In his book published in the late eighties, Bianchi commented on the Engineers' Syndicate:

> For those who believe that Egyptian corporatism, with its traditional diversity and flexibility, contains the seeds of pluralist democracy, the example of the Engineers' Syndicate is not merely an embarrassing contradiction, but a serious threat as well.[88]

Bianchi's comment was as valid in the late eighties as it was earlier. The first attempt at regulating the profession was embodied in the Royal Society of Egyptian Engineering, formed in 1920. Although some commentators tended to picture the formation of the society as being a reflection of the 1919 nationalist revolution, historical facts testify to the contrary, since its founders, as one author described them, "tended to be on the wrong side of the barricades."[89] Mahmoud Sami Bey, the founder of the society was the highest-ranking Egyptian civil servant in 1919 and continued in his position until 1924. His pro-British policy, which hardly qualifies him as a nationalist, was reflected in his attempts in 1920 to prevent technical criticism of British irrigation projects. Thus the early harbinger of an Engineers' Syndicate showed a tendency towards co-operation with the dominant political power. The society was elitist in nature. Members were required to pay an annual subscription of £E6 plus an introduction fee of £E10. Although fifteen years' professional experience was required, the stipulated educational qualifications were more lenient, since most senior engineers had none.

Four months before the society was established a liberal democrat, Abdallah Pasha Wahbi, headed a national committee against the British Nile projects. Wahbi helped to organise an Engineers' Syndicate based on that of the lawyers, and started a professional engineering journal to mobilise professionals for the national cause. Unlike the elitist society with its limited number of members, the Syndicate had a more widely based membership and a more rigorous educational requirement, a polytechnic degree or its equivalent. By supporting Wahbi's national committee and its anti-British stand, the Syndicate had cautiously echoed criticism of the government and the British project, both politically and professionally.

As a government man, Sami Bey, however, played an important role in controlling the Syndicate and the society and bringing both in line with the regime's policy. Hence he tried to divert the Syndicate's attention from political issues to more professional ones, helped to calm the nationalist zeal of his fellow-engineers in the society and almost succeeded in tempting Wahbi into becoming the society's vice president, but Wahbi died before the society was formally established. Sami then conveniently took over the editorship of "Engineering".

No wonder then, that with Sami directly in charge of the society, the King agreed to recognise it in December 1922, whereas the Syndicate was ignored.

Pressure for the establishment of a professional Syndicate was rekindled after the Second World War, triggered by inflation, which tripled the cost of living while the salaries of government engineers stagnated. In 1944 the rank and file young graduates organised a league pressing for a professional Syndicate and in 1945 they threatened to strike, demanding more pay. In a highly unstable political environment, characterised by mass agitation and student unrest, an Engineers' Syndicate represented an attempt at appeasement by the government to partly meet civil servants' demands. The Syndicate was seen as means of controlling the engineers, a role which the society could no longer perform and it was recognised by the government officially in 1946.

Although the founders of the 1946 Syndicate had various political affiliations, they were all closely identified with the regime. For example, the main initiator of the Syndicate, Osman Muharam, had in 1937 supported important concessions to the British. In addition, his participation in the corrupt and pro-British war-time government had tainted his nationalist credentials. His goals for the Syndicate did not go beyond providing the engineers with a pension and annuity. Another supporter of the Syndicate, Muhammed Shafiq Pasha, the first naqib, amid the conflict which ensued over the Nile projects, had agreed to serve as a minister of public works, hence giving the British projects an Egyptian endorsement, while claiming afterwards that he had used his position to undermine it. Ahmad abd al-Qawi, who actually secured the Syndicate's official recognition, had taken a pro-British stance on the Nile projects, and had also served in various palace-dominated governments, the most authoritarian of which was that of Prime Minister Ismail Sidqi, who abrogated the 1923 constitution to give the British de facto rule through the monarchy. Needless to say the existence of such figures managing Syndicate affairs had ensured that the Syndicate's policy at the political level was in line with that of the regime.

On the professional level the Syndicate fared no better. The introduction of varying grades for the graduates of different academic institutions and the struggle between them for more prestige and representation in the Syndicate resulted in the Syndicate's failure to define engineering activities and in its failure to persuade the government to adopt a new salary scale. Basically, the Engineers' Syndicate that existed before 1952 proved to be unsuccessful. Unlike the Bar association, the ancient regime had witnessed an immobilised Engineers' Syndicate that enjoyed limited autonomy from government control and hence was less critical of the latter's policy. As a result, it played a limited role in national struggle and in the political arena in general. At the professional level the Engineers' Syndicate failed to establish and enforce professional standards.[90] However, its position changed significantly after the 1952 coup.

The Engineers' Syndicate from Nasser to Mubarak

The first encounter between the Syndicate and the Free Officers took place in 1953 when Osman Muharam, ex-Minister of Supply, was removed from the presidency of the Syndicate. The government then established a committee under the chairmanship of the Minister of Commerce and Industry to review all the Syndicate's activities. At the same time it threatened to prevent membership of civil servants in the Syndicate, a blow which could have reduced membership by over two thirds.[91] The Syndicate, was saved, however, from a fate similar to that of the Lawyers' Syndicate by the final stand it took on the Naguib/Nasser power struggle. Despite the division that took place within the Syndicate council between the civil engineers, under the leadership of Aziz Sidky, who were backing Naguib, and the military engineers, under the leadership of Mashour Ahmed Mashour, who backed the free officers,[92] Nasser's consolidation of power settled the conflict. Subsequently, the Syndicate passed a recommendation on March 29 against "the return to party politics with all its disadvantages" and granted its support to "the continuation of the Revolutionary Command Council as the highest authority in the country".[93] Henceforth the Syndicate

> seems to sway with the whims and needs of the 'Chief Political Engineer' as a columnist of the Magalat Al-Muhandessin once wrote of Nasser.[94]

Under Nasser's rule the engineers and their Syndicate gained a prestige they had never acquired before. Two major factors, Nasser's close relationship with the Engineers Corps and his industrialisation drive, account for their ascendancy to this advantageous position. The close ties, which the Engineer Corps had enjoyed with the Free Officers, were manifested in the Syndicate's membership of both civil and military engineers, as a result of which officers' grievances were always supported by the Syndicate. On the other hand, although none of the members of the Revolutionary Command Council were military engineers, a number of engineers knew Nasser. For example, the 1953 Syndicate president, Mahmud Yunis, was Nasser's instructor at the War College. Moreover, ten of Nasser's twenty-three classmates in the advanced seminars for officers were also engineers. Similarly when Nasser subsequently taught at the War College he had wide contacts with military engineers.[95] Such contacts later led to Nasser's and Sadat's preference for military engineers, both in the various ministerial posts and in the Syndicate. Apart from Mahmud Yunis, the first military engineer to become Syndicate president in 1954–1956 and again in 1957–1958, several other military engineers took over the Syndicate presidency. Among those was Mohamed al-Sa'aid (1966–1968) and Salah al-Din Galal (1963). Moreover, the percentage of military engineers on the Syndicate's board of council increased to 20 percent of the total number of members (6 out of 32) in December 1954. In 1975 the number of military engineers on the board of council was raised to ten representing one third of the total and all the elected members of the council of 1979, except for the president and vice president, came from the military corps.[96]

The second major factor was Nasser's industrialisation drive, which needed the co-operation of the engineering profession.[97] With increased prestige and social status, they became, as one author has described them, "The vanguard of Nasser's inadvertently corporatist enterprise".[98]

In return for their praise of the regime the Syndicate gained some limited benefits for its members, but still, had no influence on any major professional issue. Hence it could only express its members "desires" and not "demands".[99] For example, a parliamentary attack in 1964 forced the Syndicate to admit graduates of higher institutes[100] as members on a provisional basis.[101] Unlike the Bar Syndicate, which must give formal approval to its members before they can practise law, in case of engineers the state agencies endorse engineers before the Syndicate can.[102] The Engineers' Syndicate under Nasser and his successors reflects a type of informal politics which resulted from a network of patron-client relationship on the one hand and the intermingling of a civil society's organisation with the state on the other. Accordingly,

> Syndicate chairmen usually relate to their rank and file more like traditional patrons to clients than like modern interest group leaders to their constituencies. After all concessions to professional interest are rarely achieved by bargaining, rather they take the form of favours granted by the authorities in return for enthusiastic support. It is not the position of chairman that confers influence, except marginally, but rather the incumbent's prior position in the network of personal relationships radiating from the presidency.[103]

A first look at the leaders of the Syndicate in the late fifties may appear to contradict this statement. Of the eight chairmen of the Syndicate during that period, two subsequently became ministers, while three had been previously appointed ministers. However, a careful analysis reveals that the rise of these figures to ministerial positions was not owed to the Syndicate but rather to their political patrons.[104] Hence the Syndicate "Seem more like parade grounds for displaying one's political virtuosity to potential patrons".[105] To sum up, Nasser weakened the Engineers' Syndicate to the extent that its control over its own members diminished and many engineers did not bother to enrol.[106]

One of the few occasions when the Engineers' Syndicate disappointed the regime was in January 1972, when its chair, Abd-al Khaliq al-Shinnawy, took a stand that opposed the regime by joining the Lawyers and Doctors syndicates' chairmen in supporting the student demonstrations.[107] Although al-Shinnawy avoided criticising Sadat personally, most of his criticism was directed towards his Prime Minister Aziz Sidky. Al Shinnawy demanded that the Syndicate be authorised to regulate native and foreign engineers and that it should acquire the right to review the government's technical projects. In April 1972 al-Shinnawy, together with other former ministers, used the debates on the government's proposed Suez-Mediterranean pipeline to embarrass Prime Minister Aziz Sidky, who was enthusiastic about the project.[108] Instead of attacking the government on the grounds of corruption, since it was rumoured that some of Sidky's entourage had accepted bribes from the foreign contractors, and in order to avoid raising the whole topic, al-Shinnawy, played on the salient political issue of the state of no war, no peace that so much agitated public opinion at that time. Al-Shinnawy linked between the government's acceptance of the project[109] and its intention to preserve the state of no war no peace.[110]

The issue did not trigger any confrontation with Sadat, not because of the latter's tolerance, but because al Shinnawy enjoyed the protection of strong patrons. As one author summarising the situation has commented:

> Ash-Shennawy could get away with staging the pipeline debates, for instance, because Sayyid Mari and other influential figures were protecting him. Once their common adversary, prime minister Aziz Sidky was removed from office, Ash-Shennawy ceased staging public debates and claimed relationships with the government were improving.[111]

The protection that al-Shinnawy enjoyed did not, however, prevent the reorganisation of the Syndicate under new leaders closely associated with Sadat's inner circle. The first step in this direction was the initiation of a new law governing the Syndicate in 1974 and its implementation under the Syndicate's new leader Mustafa Khalil, a leading figure in the National Democratic Party, who later became Prime Minister. The new law empowered the Syndicate to endorse members of the association and prohibited government agencies from employing engineers without certification. Foreign engineers were obliged to join the Syndicate and their work permits were to be reviewed annually. Technical school graduates were granted a separate Syndicate. A new Syndicate-wide committee was created, and the term of elected president and council was extended from two to four years. The Syndicate's income was enlarged to include not only dues and direct government subsidies, but also various stamp taxes and special levies on all locally-produced cement and steel. The contribution of both government and employers to the pension fund was increased and the council was granted full authority to invest in policy-making enterprises. Expenditure was authorised in other activities such as in housing cooperatives, clinics and hospitals, insurance, supermarkets, social clubs, sporting facilities and the vacation resorts.[112] In short, an entrepreneurial Syndicate was created to provide privileges for those "who were ready to fall in step with the new policies of capitalist development".[113]

Although it was Mustafa Khalil who laid the base for this entrepreneurial character of the Syndicate, things were actually expanded under the chairmanship of Osman Ahmed Osman, who became the syndicate president in 1979. What happened in the Syndicate under the leadership of Osman warrants special attention here for various reasons, the first being its corruption and the mismanagement of the Syndicate funds under his rule. This was facilitated on the one hand by the unique political connections he had as holder of various political positions and on the other by his family relationship with Sadat, whose daughter was married to Osman's son. The second is that this corruption laid the way for the gradual ascendency of the Islamists in the Syndicate, starting in the mid-eighties and culminating in their tight control over the council in the nineties.

Osman's official posts started in 1973 when he was appointed Minister of Reconstruction. He became Minister of Housing and Construction in 1974 and Minister of al-Tanmia al-Shaebiya in 1981. Moreover he was a member of the National Democratic Party, head of the committee for "Popular Growth" in the party, Member of Parliament for the constituency of Ismalia, and chairman of the parliamentary group of Ismalia province. In addition, he was the founder and president of the gigantic Arab Contractors Company. Another member of the Osman family, engineer Ismail Osman, was also the assistant secretary general of the Syndicate and held several posts in the bureaucracy. These included being head of the housing committee of Giza province, assistant secretary general of the Engineers' Syndicate, member of the German-Egyptian chamber of commerce, member of the Egyptian-American Businessmen's Council, member of the Egyptian-Japanese Businessmen's Council, and member of the Chamber of Industry for Building and Construction, besides being a member of the board of directors of the Arab Contractors Company.[114]

The Syndicate's money was invested in sixteen projects, varying from food production, banking, insurance and housing to steel production. Only three investors were involved in these projects: the Engineers' Syndicate, the Arab Contractors, and the Suez Canal Bank. Out of the sixteen projects, fourteen ran at a loss. The greatest loss, however, was that incurred by the Engineering Company for Food Production, and the Engineering Bank. The Syndicate's share of investment in these two projects was the largest. The Syndicate's contribution in the Engineering Company for Food Production was £E8.5 million, accounting for 28.5 per cent of the company's capital. Moreover, from the outset the company was in a seriously unbalanced financial position. At the same time, the Engineering Bank became the main lender for the company, providing the company with large credit facilities without the appropriate coverage and allowed the company unlimited overdraft facilities.[115]

The same procedures was repeated with some businessmen, to whom the bank made large, unsecured loans, despite the fact that their projects had nothing to do with its enterprises. One of these businessmen was Tawfiq Abd al-Hay who fled the country after using a $2 million "food security" loan to import several tons of rotten poultry.[116] No wonder the bank's financial situation severely deteriorated. What is crucial here is that the sixteen projects in which the Syndicate had invested were established between 1979–1983, that is, during Osman's first term in office as the syndicate leader, and that the decision for investment using the Syndicate's funds was taken solely by Osman without the approval of the Syndicate's council. In addition, most of those chosen to manage the company and its board of directors were hand-picked by Osman, regardless of their qualifications and capabilities. Most were ex-ministers and governors, who were

130

Osman's friends. Rashad Osman one of those involved in the famous Rayan scandal, was among Osman's appointees.[117]

In an attempt to trace some of the corrupt practices that took place in these projects the investigation committee that was established cited a number of examples.

A. The contract for buying raw material and expertise made between the National Engineering Company and Schweppes International was signed by Osman, who had no legal power to do so. In this case the only available alternative was either to draw a new contract that should be signed by an authorised person, or in case of Schweppes refusal of such measures, to declare the nullification of the contract through a court order. But since neither procedure was adopted the committee concluded that there was a deliberate intention to waste public funds.

B. The land on which the National Engineering Company was established was rented from "Al-Wafaa Wa Al-Amal", a philanthropic organisation established by Gihan al-Sadat. It was found that the rent paid far exceeded the value of the land. In the period between 1980–1988, the rent paid amounted to £E2 million pounds, at a time when the land could have been bought for less than £E1 million pounds. When faced with the accusation, it was argued that the rent was a kind of donation to help the organisation in its philanthropic activities. In addition a company running at a loss may not make donations.[118]

It is obvious that had it not been for Gihan al-Sadat, Osman would not have made such a generous gesture and would have saved the shareholders, among which is the Syndicate, at least a million pounds.

C. The committee's investigation of the Engineering Bank also discovered that the bank had been established without any serious feasibility studies, and that it had been functioning on a personal basis rather than on the basis of any banking rules. Moreover, when the bank, owing to its deteriorating financial position, had failed to secure the loans needed for professional Syndicate housing to save the National Engineering Company, Osman had personally phoned the presidents of four other large banks and asked them for an unsecured loan of £E6 million. The money was raised by the banks the following day without any feasibility studies or credit guarantee. This clearly reflects the effect of the political influence on the economic sphere on one hand, and the effect of patronage on the other, and highlights that in the absence of institutionalised formal relations, corruption becomes the name of the game.

D. Law no 35 of 1973 for the protection of public funds forbids any shareholder company from giving donations to any political party, but a large amount of money was donated to "Mayo" the official newspaper of the government NDP, disguised in the form of paid advertisements.[119]

E. The committee discovered that the ex-president of the board of directors of the National Engineering Company had distributed profits for the years 1983, 1984, 1985, to the members of the board, even though law no 159 of 1981, forbids the distribution of any profits where the company cannot meet its financial obligations.[120]

Mismanagement and corruption impose a cost at the economic and cultural level. On the economic level, these practices had exhausted the Syndicates' resources. This was reflected in the deteriorating quality of services to members. As a result engineers complained about the low profitability of the Syndicate's enterprises. In 1983, for example, it was reported that profits were ranging between 3 per cent and 8 per cent, at a time when savings accounts were earning 13 per cent. Even if these rates of profit were true, it was still argued that the Syndicate was losing several hundred thousand pounds each year which jeopardised its pension fund. Engineers also complained about the rise in cost of the services provided by the Syndicate, especially the price of apartments for young engineers, which had doubled despite the acquisition of public land at almost no cost.

Once again rumours about corruption surfaced. It was alleged that the reason behind the inflation of prices lay in the Saudi Arabian firm to which the Syndicate had awarded building contracts, despite the fact that lower bids had been submitted. It was known that Osman Ahmad Osman had an interest in this company.[121]

It might have been expected that with the presence of all this corrupt behaviour, some of which had been proven and documented by the investigation committee, that the council and its president would bear the responsibility and would either resign or be forced to resign through a vote of no confidence, but neither step took place. On the contrary, until the early 90's Osman continued to be the Syndicate chairman. Nor was the regime willing to interfere to rectify the situation. It is true that Mubarak had refused to endorse Osman as the official candidate in the 1983 election, but in a meeting that took place between Osman and Mubarak in 1988, the president agreed to interfere to save the Syndicate's enterprises[122] that were on the verge of bankruptcy. In this sense corruption had been rewarded rather than sanctioned by the regime. With the decline of Osman's political influence, especially after Sadat's death, the ability of the Syndicate to exert any influence on the country's political or economic life had declined substantially. On the cultural level, the cost involved included apathy among members, reflected in low turnout in council elections, a phenomenon which helped Osman to preserve his position as Syndicate chairman throughout the eighties and early nineties, and which helped the Muslim Brotherhood to achieve ascendancy in the Syndicate council. Their first success in the Engineers' Syndicate took place in the 1987 council election, when they managed to win 54 out of 61 seats.[123] It is worth noting here that Osman, backed by the military engineers won the presidency in spite of opposition to holding some of the elections in army barracks.[124] In 1991 al-Kafrawy, the Housing Minister, was elected as the Syndicate chairman, whereas the 6 contested seats for the council membership were all won by the Muslim Brotherhood members.[125]

In 1995, divisions within the Syndicate arose between the Syndicate's higher council, dominated by the Muslim Brotherhood, and the "National Engineers' Front" which was formed in opposition to the Muslim Brotherhood. The struggle between the two factions was taken to court through a secular group led by Dr Abd al Mohsen Hamouda. Hamouda demanded the placement of the Syndicate under judicial supervision, which took place by virtue of a court order in February 1995. In May 1995, the police forced their way into the Syndicate to enforce the court ruling. At the same time the Islamists escalated the confrontation with the regime and in May 1995 they brought a suit against the President, for police invasion of the Syndicate. In July 1995 the court ruled as illegitimate the general assembly meeting which had convened in April 1995. During this meeting, which was organised by the Muslim Brotherhood supporters, a vote of confidence was given to the Syndicate council with its Muslim Brotherhood majority, while at the same time a vote of no confidence was given to al-Kafrawy the Syndicate chairman.[126] Like its counterpart, the Lawyers' Syndicate, the Engineers' Syndicate lost its autonomy to judiciary supervision.

The case of the Engineers' Syndicate clearly shows that classical state corporatism, which was established under Nasser, gave way to a tighter form of corporatism under Sadat and Mubarak, which is co-integrationism. The latter being based on the integration of the interests of the Syndicate leader into the state system using patronage networks as in the case of al-Shinawy and Osman, and on institutionalised corruption as in the case of Osman Ahmad Osman. Again this was achieved at the expense of the broader members of the Syndicate.

D) The Doctors' Syndicate

Historical Background

The first step towards establishing a professional association for doctors took place in 1888 with the creation of the Egyptian Medical Society, which held its first meeting under Dr Salim Pasha Salim, who was then the Khedive's private doctor. At that time the society was no more than a place where members would gather to read papers and exchange ideas. It drew its patronage from Yaqub Pasha Artin, who was the deputy Minister of Education. Although not a doctor himself, Artin was an extremely active member of the society. Later the society came under the leadership of Dr Isa Pasha Hamdi, who became head of the school of medicine and the hospital attached, as well as being the private doctor for the Khedive and his family. Hamdi had ambitious goals for the society, which included the presentation of scientific papers, the publication of journals, the foundation of a free hospital for the poor and the establishment of a fund for needy doctors. However, the society only accomplished its first two objectives and was disbanded in 1901.

Efforts to start a professional association was revived during World War I by the young energetic Dr Ali Ibrahim, who tried to bring Egyptian and foreign doctors together in a professional association. His efforts bore no fruits, since foreign doctors had no incentive to co-operate as they had their own association, the International Medical Association, and they always held the senior positions in the profession. However, Ibrahim did not give up and World War I seems to have helped his cause. As British staff of the medical school left to join the forces, Egyptian doctors replaced them and after the war they not only kept their positions, but managed in the 1920s to expand it further. In the meantime Ibrahim begun publishing a scholarly medical journal (al-Majallah al-Tibbiyah al-Misriyah), which was later to become the publication of the new Egyptian Medical Association. Ibrahim served as the Association's vice president to the now ageing Isa Pasha Hamdi, and took over the presidency in 1926 until his death in 1947. King Fuad took an interest in the newly established association and through it, sponsored a number of international congresses. The association proliferated into various specialised bodies, such as the Egyptian Dental Association, which split off in 1935. Earlier in 1933 the Union of Medical Associations was established by a royal decree to include the Royal Society of Medicine, the Egyptian Medical Association, the Egyptian Hygiene Society, and the Egyptian Ophthalmological Society, and was presided over by Dr Ali Ibrahim. In 1940 Ibrahim became Minister of Health. Immediately afterwards, a law was initiated for the establishment of the medical syndicate with branches for doctors, veterinarians, dentists, and pharmacists. The syndicate started functioning in 1942 with Ibrahim being its first chairman.[127]

From what has been related it is obvious that before 1952, the doctors' efforts were mainly devoted to establishing their syndicate, and hence their associations failed to achieve major benefits, either politically or professionally. One author has described the doctors' professional associations during that time by commenting:

> The body has had its ups and downs since then, but at no time has it been as central to the medical profession as the lawyers' syndicate was to their profession; nor has the doctors syndicate played as prominent a part in the general political life of Egypt as has its legal counterpart.[128]

The Doctors' Syndicate from Nasser to Mubarak

Apart from a few incidents that took place during Nasser's era, the Doctors' Syndicate, like its counterpart the Engineers' Syndicate, was limited in role until the mid-eighties, when changes in the syndicate brought about a severe confrontation with Mubarak's regime.

Nasser's first assault on the profession came in 1955 through the issuance of a syndicate law, the purpose of which was to use the Syndicate to deprive the monopoly of some doctors over practice in private firms. This law necessitated that all ties between a doctor and a company or organisation should take place through the Syndicate and that the latter should distribute work in companies and organisations among doctors in the interest of fairness. A further assault against the independence of the Syndicate took place when Mahmud Nassar, a military doctor and confidant of several officers close to Nasser was appointed as the Syndicate's president.

Benefiting from the protection of their political patron, Dr Nur al-Din Tarraf, a former Minister of Health and Syndicate leader, and the Prime Minister, doctors had in 1959 fought for Syndicate autonomy by attempting to remove the government appointee Dr Muhammed Nassar from the chairmanship. They argued that his appointment violated Syndicate bylaws that the chairman should not act simultaneously as Minister of Health. A compromise was finally reached whereby Nassar was allowed to serve the last two months of his term, provided that he would not be re-elected. Their victory did not last long, however, since the successful candidate turned out to be Dr Rifai Muhammad Kamal, another military doctor with close ties with Nasser's inner core.[129] It is worth mentioning here that the Syndicate members are a conglomerate of doctors who work in the public sector, military doctors and other private practitioners and university professors with private clinics. During elections it is usually the first two categories that the government depends on for securing its election of endorsed candidates. The real opposition from within the Syndicate came from its only independent leader, Rashwan Fahmy. Fahmy's first confrontation with the government came in 1959, when he submitted his resignation in protest against the dismissal of some government doctors for alleged incompetence, and against the Minister of Health's attempts to prevent doctors from working for more than one organisation or having more than one clinic. However, his resignation was refused by the Syndicate's general assembly. Furthermore, with Prime Minister Tarraf as his political patron, Fahmy felt strong enough publicly to debate the issue with a ministry spokesman. The official newspaper gave the dispute wide coverage. In the general assembly it was argued that government plans to limit private practitioners would not improve, but rather worsen employment opportunities. At the end of the debate a compromise was reached whereby the government sought to open new rural clinics and increase the salaries of young doctors to solve the problem of the unemployment of young graduates, rather than by limiting private practice.[130] Thus, under Nasser both well to do private practitioner as well as young doctors who couldn't afford to open their private clinics benefited. While the former remained intact, the latter benefited from the socialist measures through their employment in public hospitals. It was such measures, which later on facilitated Fahmy's removal from the Syndicate's chairmanship, as will be shown shortly, once Nasser became irritated with the former's continuous attack on the regime.

In late 1961, Fahmy again started to disturb Nasser, when he called for constitutional limits to the President's power. Nasser's nationalisation and sequestration policies of 1962 had raised a controversy among the ruling elite. Dr Nur al-Din Tarraf, who was then serving as federal Minister of Health, opposed the nationalisation of hospitals and so he was removed from his ministerial position and replaced by his client an-Nabawi al-Muhandis, who shifted loyalty to Ali Sabri. Although Tarraf regained his ministerial rank later in 1962, he was excluded from all tasks linked to the Ministry of Health.

Fahmy also opposed the nationalisation policy, but under the protection of Tarraf and his friends, who outweighed Ali Sabri, he was not purged and managed to run successfully for chairmanship in 1965 and 1966. When Tarraf had retired from the ASU, Sabri took his revenge on Fahmy by purging him from the ASU. Subsequently, Fahmy's ten colleagues on the board signed a statement, some against their will, that he be removed from the chairmanship on the grounds that he had violated Syndicate bylaws on one hand and been expelled from the ASU[131] on the other. Not only was Fahmy removed from the Syndicate's chairmanship and the ASU, but he was also dismissed from his university post, his property was sequestrated and he was publicly humiliated by a march staged by his colleagues to the presidential palace to show their satisfaction at his dismiss.[132] While still considering coercion as an important factor, Fahmy could not have been sacked and his reputation tarnished without the eruption of any kind of resistance if Nasser was not backed by the majority of Syndicate's members.

Hereafter and until the ascendancy of the Muslim Brotherhood opposition within the Syndicate, it was largely curbed. It has to be noted here that the Doctors' Syndicate was the first syndicate in Egypt to witness the ascendancy of the Muslim Brotherhood, when they succeeded in winning the majority of the council's seats in the 1984 elections. An assessment of the performance of the Muslim Brotherhood within the Syndicate will be left to a later section. However, it is crucial here to detail the confrontation that took place between the Muslim Brotherhood members of the Syndicate and the regime. Direct confrontation with the regime took place on January 1995, when eight prominent Muslim Brotherhood members of the Syndicate council were imprisoned. Among them were Dr Assam al Arian, the assistant general secretary of the Syndicate, and Dr Ibrahim al-Zaafaran, the general secretary for the Alexandria affiliated syndicate.

The Syndicate considered this an "illegal aggression" and demanded an immediate release of the jailed doctors. On February 1995, the police surrounded the Syndicate and prevented an emergency meeting of the general assembly called to discuss the "government's desire to control the professional syndicates". On 1 September the government brought Assam al-Arian, Ibrahim al-Zaafaran, and Hilmy al-Gazar before tribunal courts in what was known as "the first tribunal persecution" against the Muslim Brotherhood, which included 49 prominent members. In October 1995, several other members of the Muslim Brotherhood appeared before tribunal courts. Again, some of these were prominent Muslim Brotherhood members of the Doctors' Syndicate council, like Dr Abd al-Monaam Abou al-Fatouh, the assistant general secretary of the "Union of the Arab Doctors", Dr Anwar Hassan Shihata the treasurer of the Union of Doctors' Syndicate, and the treasurer for the general syndicates of Doctors, and the treasurer for the Human Relief Committee, and Dr Mohamad Saad treasurer of the affiliated Giza syndicate, in addition to several other doctors. The Syndicate related this aggression on its Muslim Brotherhood members and other members of the movement to the parliamentary elections that were taking place in January 1995, particularly as some of them intended to run in the elections to the Peoples' Assembly. In April 1995, the confrontation between the Muslim Brotherhood members within the Syndicate and the regime was accelerated when the latter announced the discovery of a terrorist plan prepared by five of the Muslim Brotherhood members. Through their work on the Human Relief Committee they allegedly facilitated the training of some of their followers abroad on military missions which would enable them to commit terrorist acts on their return to Egypt. The police had therefore arrested four of these five members and ordered the arrest of the fifth member Dr Hosam al-Din Sayed Hussein, the assistant treasurer of the Syndicate, for his involvement in the plan.[133] Needless to say, the government policy of taking the Muslim Brotherhoods to tribunals instead of the normal courts cast doubts in the public mind on the seriousness of these charges and instead of discrediting them especially among the illiterate poor, it tended to glorify and make heroes out of them, a miscalculation on the part of the government.

5. The Performance of the Syndicates under Secular Forces

A) Measurements of Performance

In an attempt to measure the effectiveness of the Egyptian syndicates, three criteria have been chosen for assessment. These are the council election turnouts, participation in syndicates' activities and projects, and the number of beneficiaries from syndicates' projects. Each of these criteria will be briefly discussed here.

Council Election Turnout

A major criterion for assessing the performance of syndicates is the participation of their members in council elections. A review of turnout reveals that membership participation does not exceed 10 per cent of those who have the right to vote in most of the syndicates including, the highly politicised Bar and Journalists' Syndicates. As low as it is, this percentage does not reflect a true image of participation in syndicate elections. This is due to the fact that it is calculated as a proportion of those who vote to those who have paid their subscriptions, and hence have the right to vote, rather than as a proportion to the total number of enlisted practitioners. This reflects not only the presence of an apathetic majority, but also the lack of any sense of belonging and loyalty to the professional group.

Table 5.2 The beneficiaries of the health insurance projects in the Syndicates

The Syndicate	The percentage of beneficiaries to the total number of members
The Pharmacists' Syndicate	16.3
The Dentists' Syndicate	19.2
The Veterinarians' Syndicate	12
The Doctors' Syndicate	62

Source: Qandil A., *Al-Jama at Al-Mihaniya Wa Al-Musharaka Al-Siyasiya*, p. 26.

Participation in Syndicate Activities and Projects

Although it is difficult to establish the number of members who take part in syndicate activities, two examples are given here, the Engineers' Syndicate and the Doctors' Syndicate, to measure the percentage of participation in syndicate projects and activities. The Engineers' Syndicate, which has 192,550 members, had in 1989 23,000 participants in its health care projects[134] amounting to 12 per cent of the total number of members. The Doctors' Syndicate which has 200,000 members, had in 1988 43,960 participants in its health care projects[135] making a 22 per cent of the total number of members. These low proportions reflect the contrast between members' affiliation and their degree of commitment to syndicate work.

The Number of Beneficiaries of Syndicate Projects

The number of syndicate members who benefit from syndicate projects compared to the total number of members is a good indicator of the level of services provided by the syndicates. In 1989 the beneficiaries from the health care project in the Engineers' Syndicate amounted to only 3 per cent of the total number of members. In 1988 the corresponding figure for the Doctors' Syndicate was 9 per cent.[136] The previous table shows the percentage of the beneficiaries of the health insurance projects in some of the syndicates in 1990.

This data shows, that except for the Doctors' Syndicate, the proportion of the beneficiaries from syndicates' projects to the total number of members is extremely low, reflecting the limited extent of the services provided by the syndicates to their members

Thus far the weak performance of the Egyptian syndicates had been explored. What remains here is to provide a brief categorisation of the factors affecting this performance.

B) External Factors Affecting Syndicate Performance

The Legal Limitations on Syndicates

The legal limitation has already been discussed in detail and there is no need for repetition. Suffice it to mention here that the various laws which govern the syndicates tends to limit their involvement and their political participation and hence affect their role as pressure groups as well as limiting their effect on public policy.

Government Intervention in Syndicates

Again this point had been thoroughly discussed earlier, and to avoid repetition it is enough to mention that government intervention through dissolution, interference in syndicate elections, the use of coercion and the threat of abolition, all tend to weaken the syndicates as promoters and protectors of specific interests in the society.

The Weakness of Political Parties

The weakness of the political parties and their failure to establish roots among the mass of the population made them see the syndicates as a political space in which politics could be conducted, thus turning the latter into an arena for ideological conflict. The Bar Syndicate provides an example where the competing factions of the Wafd party transferred their conflict to the syndicate, leading some authors to comment that it was "an internal struggle among the new Wafd party but was taking place on the syndicate grounds."[137] Not only does this politicisation of professional associations to compensate for the weakness of political parties take place at the expense of protecting members' professional interests, but it also enhances the fragmentation and weakness of civil society and undermines the promotion of pluralist democracy via these groups.

C) Internal Factors Affecting Syndicate Performance

Internal Struggle and Factionalisation

A major source of weakness inherent in most syndicates in Egypt is their internal divisions and factionalisation, which further weaken them vis-à-vis the government. The Lawyers' Syndicate provides an example of an association that had once been active on both the national and the professional level, but was more recently shattered by internal struggles between different factions. The divisions in the Syndicate started in 1986 and were either professional, including the interests of public sector lawyers versus those of private practitioners, or ideological, involving groups like the Muslim Brotherhood, Marxists, Nasserites, and the Wafdists who were struggling to attain more representation on the Syndicate council.[138] The struggle within the Syndicate culminated in the dramatic events of 1989 which included lawyers taking refuge in the Syndicate, police forcing an entry into the syndicate building, exchanges of fire between the police and some lawyers, law suits in court, and a struggle among lawyers concerning the legitimacy of the current Syndicate council.[139] These conflicts had serious repercussions on the performance of the Syndicate and prevented the convening of the Syndicate's general assembly several times. This in turn set the stage for the rise of the Muslim Brotherhood to power in the 1992 Syndicate elections. The Commercial Employees' Syndicate provides another example of internal factionalisation where struggles lasted from 1983–1988. Two leadership groups each claimed its right to the Syndicate presidency. Again the struggle reached the courts, and although it was finally resolved in 1989, the expenses incurred were reflected, as measured, in terms of low Syndicate performance. The Pharmacists Syndicate provides another example of internal fragmentation, where the struggle between the newly-elected president and his predecessor incapacitated the Syndicate throughout the second half of 1988.[140]

Lack of Common Orientation among Syndicate Membership

The basis for the formation of any syndicate is a common orientation between members that should facilitate cohesion and integration among them and unite their interests and objectives. An examination of the Egyptian syndicates reveals that this feature is lacking. For example, the Bar Syndicate includes among its members two completely different segments, public sector lawyers and private sector lawyers, with each segment having different interests and problems, and different affiliations, which makes it hard for the Syndicate to cater for their demands. The same applies to the Commercial Employees' Syndicate, which includes graduates of the commerce universities, and graduates in economics and political sciences, as well as those of higher commercial schools and colleges. The Teachers' Syndicate provides a third example of lack of homogeneity in syndicate membership, since it includes teachers of elementary schools, higher schools, and colleges.[141] Similarly, the Engineers' Syndicate includes public sector engineers, military engineers, university professors and those working in the private sector. The Doctors' Syndicate includes doctors working in government hospitals, military doctors, and private practitioners and university professors working in private clinics. This social and professional composition of syndicate membership contributes much to the internal divisions and factionalisation that is taking place in the syndicates and hence is reflected negatively on the members' sense of belonging and their loyalty to the professional association.

Longevity of Leadership

At a time when the major demand of all societal groups in Egypt is to change the constitution and limit the number of times a President can run for office, a quick look at the major syndicates reveals a long continuity in their leadership. In the Bar Syndicate for example, al-Khawaja's term in office extended from 1966–1971, then from 1977–1980, and from 1982–1995. In the Engineers' Syndicate, Osman Ahmad Osman held the Syndicate leadership from 1979 until 1991 and in the Journalists' Syndicate Salah Jalal's presidency lasted from 1981–1987, providing further examples of extended leadership. A common characteristic between the syndicates and political parties in Egypt, leadership longevity reflects the failure of the various societal institutions to rid themselves of the vices of the regime they attack.

Lack of Democracy and the Dictatorial Style of Leadership

A common feature among the Egyptian syndicates is a lack of democracy and the dictatorial way in which the syndicates are managed, another inheritance from the regime. Striking examples from the Lawyers' and Engineers Syndicate can be given here as cases in point. In the Lawyers' Syndicate, al-Khawaja's decision to invest the Syndicate's pension fund was taken solely by himself and his entourage without any participation from the general assembly. The investment incurred the loss of more than twenty million pounds of Syndicate money.[142] In the Engineers' Syndicate, the decision to invest Syndicate money in various projects was taken solely by Osman Ahmad Osman, the Syndicate's president, without the approval of the Syndicate's council. The money was invested in sixteen projects, of which fourteen were running at a loss.[143]

The Intolerant and Repressive Character of Syndicates

It is ironic that at a time when various social groups accuse the government of being intolerant of and repressive towards any opposition, the events that take place within the syndicates reveal a similar lack of tolerance among the different factions and a reluctance to abide by democratic rules. This is reflected in the rejection of election results and court orders. For example, in 1988, in an attempt to resolve the conflict in the Commercial Employees' Syndicate between two rivals, for the presidency, the syndicate council decided to re-schedule elections that should be open to all candidates, and resolve the problem democratically. However, one of the candidates managed to secure a court order denying the right of the Syndicate's council to announce the re-running of elections. As a result the syndicate was left without a president, and hence most of the syndicate's functions were put on hold.

In the Pharmacists' Syndicate the election results were rejected by the candidate who lost the elections and were contested in court, not without serious repercussions on the syndicate's functions.[144] In the Bar Syndicate neither the 1989 elections results, nor the court order assigning a temporary committee to govern the syndicate, were accepted by the competing parties.[145] These examples reflect above all that democracy as a process of governing has not yet been institutionalised in the various institutions of society.

The Inability of the Syndicates to Unite against the Government

The criterion measured here is the ability of the syndicates to unite against the government, especially on national issues. In 1990, in the aftermath of the Iraqi invasion of Kuwait, the Committee for the Co-ordination of Syndicate Work issued a statement denouncing the invasion, emphasising the necessity of peaceful resolution to the conflict, and rejecting all American and Western interference in the Gulf area. Whereas the committee's statement was signed by ten syndicates out of twenty-two, the statement issued in 1991 was only signed by seven, a clear example of the lack of unity among syndicates.[146]

Corruption

Corruption is one of the major complaints that is usually brought against government officials. The example of the syndicates illustrates the failure of civil institutions to rid themselves of the very vices of the regime, which they attack. The previously mentioned cases of corruption in the Bar and the Engineers' syndicates are two striking examples.[147] The corruption and mismanagement of the Engineers' Syndicate funds under Osman Ahmad Osman, reflects another such example of corruption.

The falsification of syndicate election results is another aspect of the corrupt behaviour in Egyptian syndicates. For example, in 1989 the council of the Commercial Employees' Syndicate had to announce the nullification of the elections of the affiliated Syndicate in Alexandria, after it had been proved that the results of the elections had been falsified.[148]

Failure to Distinguish between the Syndicates' Professional and Political roles

Syndicate work should involve the protection of members' professional interests, their economic well being, and helping them to overcome their professional problems. The preoccupation of the syndicates with politics has been at the expense of more professional issues, at a time when unemployment among new university graduates, who constitute an increasing proportion of syndicate membership is on the rise, is rising at an alarming rate.

6. The Ascendancy of the Muslim Brotherhood in the Syndicates

A) Motives and Reasons

Before discussing the motives and factors underlying the rise of the Muslim Brotherhood in the syndicates a brief comment should be made at this point on the extent of their involvement and influence in the Egyptian syndicates. The ascendancy of the Muslim Brotherhood to become a controlling majority has taken place in the five most politically active syndicates: the Doctors, Engineers, Pharmacists, Scientists, and Lawyers. In addition, the Muslim Brotherhood have achieved partial success in other syndicates through their control of some of the affiliated syndicates or through the activities of the 'Liberty and Islamic Law Committee'. The following table shows the extent of the Islamic trend in the syndicates in the 1995 elections.

In an attempt to explain the motives underlying the Muslim Brotherhood's decision to transfer their political work into the syndicates, some authors have attributed it to government harassment and the imposition of various restrictions, both inside Parliament, which tends to inhibit their performance as an opposition, and outside, causing a decline in their representation in Parliament.[149] These authors have tended to assume an inverse relation between the rise of the Muslim Brotherhood in the syndicates and the decline of their representation in the People's Assembly, implying that their functioning within the syndicates was some sort of substitutive strategy. This notion, however, can be rejected on several bases. To begin with, the Muslim Brotherhood had started to achieve ascendancy in the syndicates, especially Doctors', in 1984, and yet it was in the 1987 elections that they achieved their highest representation in Parliament. Secondly, it is believed that the Muslim Brotherhood's activities within the syndicates were part of a comprehensive plan aimed at establishing roots among the masses. Through their alliance with political parties, the Muslim Brotherhood target the population at large, through syndicates they follow a strategy of market segmentation to target the educated middle class and, through their work within the Islamic Private Voluntary Organisations they strive to reach the poorer

Table 5.3 The Islamic trend in the Syndicates

The Syndicate	Total number of council members	The number of members of the Islamic list
The Doctors' Syndicate	25	20
The Engineers' Syndicate	61	45
The Pharmacists' Syndicate	25	17
The Scientists' Syndicate	25	17
The Lawyers' Syndicate	25	18

Source: Qandil, A., *Al-dawr al-siyasi li jama'at al-masalih fi misr: dirasa li-halat niqabat al-atibaa'*, Center For Political & Strategic Studies, 1995, p. 34.

sectors in the society. Hence their work within the syndicates is a complementary rather than a substitutive strategy.

In addition to these external and internal factors which have contributed to the weakness of the syndicates, there are other factors related to the movement itself which have facilitated the Muslim Brotherhood's success in dominating the syndicates. This includes the ascendancy during the eighties of a younger generation of leadership within the Muslim Brotherhood, who, through their earlier political activities within the student unions, acquired the political training and organisational skills, which resulted in their becoming prominent within the movement. Some of these, by virtue of their professions, became members of syndicates, such as Asam Al Aryan and Abd Al Monaim Abu Al Fatouh, in the Doctors' syndicate. This group of younger Muslim Brotherhood leaders accepted the regimes' rules governing the so-called "limited liberalisation process" and decided to challenge the regime on his own ground, be it in Parliament or in the institutions of civil society, including the professional syndicates.[150] The existence of an apathetic majority and a highly skilled and organised Muslim Brotherhood minority within the syndicates, facilitated the latter's successful take-over.

B. The Performance of the Muslim Brotherhood in the Syndicates

Council Elections Turnouts

A major criterion for assessing the performance of the Islamists within the syndicates is the active participation of members in councils elections. Out of the five syndicates the Muslim Brotherhood control, the Doctors' Syndicate had been chosen as an example for measuring members' participation in syndicate elections for three reasons. The first is that it was the first syndicate in which the Muslim Brotherhood had assumed ascendancy (1984), providing a period of time to make a better assessment. Secondly, the Doctors' Syndicate is usually considered by those who favour the Islamists as a "Model" to be emulated. Thirdly, the analysis of council elections turnouts provided in this chapter is different, in the sense that it considers the proportion of participants to the total number of members rather than to those who have the right to vote, as the real indicator of members' participation. Thus the results provided contradict those who intentionally and subjectively present an "Islamic version" of such results.

Table 5.4 shows the electoral turnout in the council elections of the Doctors' Syndicate, which was the first syndicate to witness the ascendancy of the Muslim Brotherhood.

An initial look at the table shows an increase in the numbers of the participants in the syndicate's council elections since 1984, which was the year that witnessed the ascendancy of the Muslim Brotherhood and their control over the council. A thorough analysis, however, reveals the following facts:

144

Table 5.4 The number of participants in the Doctors' Syndicate council elections (1982–1992)

Year	Number of Syndicate members	Number of those who have the right to vote	Number of participants in elections	Participants as a percentage of those who have the right to vote*	Participants as a percentage of the total number of members**
1982	50,000	20,000	2,000	10	4
1984	60,000	30,000	6,000	20	10
1986	75,000	40,000	11,000	27.5	14.6
1988	90,000	50,000	12,000	24	13
1990	100,000	65,000	21,000	32	21
1992	110,000	70,000	30,000	43	27

Source: *Qandil, A., *Taqyim ada' al-islamiyyin fi al-niqabat al-mihaniyya*, p. 28.
**This column had been compiled by the writer to show the real percentage of the total number of members who participated in the elections.

1. Except for the years 1990 and 1992, the proportion of participants in council elections, never exceeded 15 per cent and was sometimes as low as 10 per cent. This low syndicate election turnout confirms the existence of an apathetic majority.

2. The increase in the proportion of members participating in council elections in 1990 and 1992 to 21 per cent and 27 per cent respectively is not an indication of the success of the Muslim Brotherhood in turning part of the apathetic majority into active members, as some political analysts such as Amani Qandil, would like to suggest. Rather this increase in the proportion of those who actually voted is attributable to the efforts of the Ministry of Health in mobilising the pro-government members in the syndicate vis-à-vis the Muslim Brotherhood, and encouraging the former to vote by paying their subscription. It is worth noting that the same strategy of membership mobilisation was used by the Muslim Brotherhood in the Bar Syndicates during the 1992 elections, where, an attempt was made to persuade anti government lawyers to vote for them by offering to pay their subscriptions.[151]

3. The huge gap between the total number of those registered and the number of those who paid their annual subscription still reflects weak syndicate affiliation and a lack of any sense of belonging to professional associations.

The Degree of Fairness in Syndicate Council Elections

At a time when the Muslim Brotherhood was criticising both the government and other secular forces in the syndicates for falsifying the results of syndicate council elections, their practices during the elections reveal that they were no better than the forces they were attacking. In fact, they appeared to outperform the government in this area. In the Engineering Syndicate, for example, the government exerted a huge effort to mobilise its supporters, who numbered 18 thousand in the public sector, thirteen thousand engineer-officers (whose subscriptions were paid by the armed forces), and others working in the Ministries of Irrigation, Industry and Housing, whose subscriptions were again paid by their respective ministries. Thus the total number of government proponents who had paid their annual subscription and hence had the right to vote, totalled 60 thousand. However, the Muslim Brotherhood committee that was assigned to supervise the elections presented the Judicial committee with a register of only seventy thousand engineers out of 220 thousand who had paid their annual subscription and thus had the right to vote. Of course, the names omitted or, as the members call them, the "Lost Names" belonged to Muslim Brotherhood opponents. Several complaints were submitted to the judicial committee by those engineers who had paid their subscription but failed to find their names on the voting list. As a result, the judicial committee postponed the elections seven times. Meanwhile, the Muslim Brotherhood committee for supervising the elections stubbornly insisted that their list was correct since it was their computer which was used to prepare it, which made other members of the syndicate sarcastically respond that the computer should be expected to provide false results since it was a "bearded computer".[152] In the 1993 affiliated Lawyers Syndicate council elections for the Giza Governorate, the Syndicate council treasurer, the council's assistant secretary and a former member in the syndicate council made a complaint to the Syndicate's general council, accusing the Muslim Brotherhood of omitting from the voting lists some of the names of those who had paid their annual subscriptions for 1993, while adding to the list the names of 369 lawyers, who did not reside and work in Giza. Of course, whereas the former were their opponents, the latter were their supporters. As a result the head of the judiciary committee decided to postpone the elections.[153] In the Doctors' Syndicate, especially during the 1990 elections, it was reported that the Muslim Brotherhood tried to prevent Christian doctors from voting by refraining from issuing of voters' cards to them and by holding the elections on Good Friday.[154] In the affiliated Doctors' Syndicate in Dakahlia governorate, the same practice of removing certain names from the voters' lists by the Muslim Brotherhood, has again been reported.[155]

Rate of Leadership Circulation

It has been reported that changes in leadership take place frequently in the syndicates which are under the control of the Muslim Brotherhood. However, these changes are confined to the members of the MB[156] in a most undemocratic way.

The Degree of Unity within the Syndicates

The ascendancy of the Muslim Brotherhood in the syndicates under study, has not contributed to the replacement of the fragmentation and struggles that were taking place in these syndicates by unity and cohesion. Internal struggles and factionalisation continue within the syndicates between the Muslim Brotherhood on one side and the secular forces on the other. The formation of the Association of Egypt's Doctors and the on going struggle between the secular doctors and the Muslim Brotherhood is but an example of the factionalisation that is continuing in the Doctors' Syndicate.[157] The same kind of internal divisions have occurred in the Engineers' Syndicates. In the Bar Syndicate, internal struggles were taking place in 1994, between the Muslim Brotherhood and ten members of the council that were representing various trends including al-Khawaja, the Syndicate chairman. At the same time there was another struggle between two groups within the Muslim Brotherhood itself, the first led by Seif Al Banna, the Syndicate's secretary, and the second led by Moukhtar Nouh, the Syndicate's treasurer.[158]

The Degree of Integrity

The corruption of some syndicate leaders exposed in the late eighties and early nineties has had a negative impact on syndicate members, as well as on the performance of syndicates, leading the Muslim Brotherhood to launch their election campaign on an anti-corruption platform. "Vote for the Cleansed Hands" was the slogan they used in syndicate elections.

A look at their practices within the syndicate quickly reveals the hypocritical nature of their claims. In the Engineers' Syndicate the central auditing agency discovered the loss of £E13,000,000.00 from the budget in addition to money wasted on activities not related to syndicate work. For example, it was found that the Muslim Brotherhood had spent £E4,000,000.00 on religious conferences and foreign travel. £E2,000,000.00 were shifted from the pension fund to cover day to day work when the Syndicate suffered lack of liquidity. £E100,000.00 was disbursed as expenses to members of the Syndicate council and £E880,000.00 of Syndicate money was spent on advertisements and campaigning for council members. The result of all these transgressions was a court ruling in February 1995, placing the Engineers' Syndicate under judicial supervision.[159] In the Lawyers' Syndicate the central auditing agency reported the loss of £E3,467,000.00, which represented subscriptions paid by Syndicate members for their pilgrimage, which should have been deposited in the Syndicate's account but suddenly disappeared.[160] In the Pharmacists' Syndicate, the Muslim Brotherhood spent £E33,000.00 of Syndicate money on accommodation for their Brotherhood members and £E292,000.00 on publishing their own newspaper.[161]

These are examples, which show the corruption of the Muslim Brotherhood and prove that the "cleansed hand" has rather turned out to be "the unpurified hand"

7. Conclusion

In its relation with the various professional groups, the Nasserist state has chosen the classical type of state corporatism and coercion as a means of controlling society. The former was based on the limited benefits offered by Nasser, the most important of which was the policy of free education and secured jobs for all university graduates, in exchange for state's control over professional syndicates. With the advent of Sadat and Mubarak and the gradual erosion of these benefits, classical corporatism, as a means of controlling syndicates, has been replaced by a mixture of coercion and a tighter formula that is labelled here *co-integrationism*. Government continuous interventions in syndicate affairs, as well as syndicates own practices, have greatly weakened Egyptian professional syndicates, which have adversely affected their performance. As a result apathy and weak syndicate affiliation has prevailed among syndicate members. This, coupled with the presence of a well-organised and skilful minority of Muslim Brotherhood members within the syndicates, set the stage for the latter's ascendancy. The performance of the Muslim Brotherhood in the syndicates has exposed their inherent weaknesses and shown them to have the same vices as their predecessors. In this, they have not only shown that they are no better than the forces they used to attack, but also that "Islam is the Solution" is in practice an empty slogan. The result is an increase in the vulnerability of the syndicates vis-à-vis the government, thus giving the authoritarian state the opportunity to enhance the weakness of and tighten its grip over the institutions of civil society.

CHAPTER SIX

Labour and Business Organisations

1. The Labour Movement

A) Introduction

Several debates have surfaced among scholars who have studied the Egyptian labour movement and attempted to determine whether or not the workers have developed a class consciousness and hence acted as a distinct class whose interests contradict and are in conflict with other groups in society.

Three schools of thought prevail in the literature. The first is the traditional Marxist which anticipates a growth in labour strikes concomitant with the formation of a class consciousness that unites workers and increases their solidarity. These strikes should develop from being limited and individual to include the whole of industry and may lead to a general strike. The second school analyses workers' activism within the context of the rational choice theory which proclaims that all social phenomena are a consequence of individual behaviour which tends to be calculative, making decisions based on expected outcomes and weighing benefits against anticipated cost. In such circumstances preferences will be shaped by selfishness. The third school is the moral-economy theory, which attributes collective action by subordinated groups to a violation of norms and standards which they have become accustomed to and expect the elite to maintain.[1] Likewise, studies of the relationship between state and workers fall either within the mainstream of pluralism and corporatism, which view union organisations in light of state decisions, or within traditional Marxist, communist and revolutionary ideologies.[2]

The following section examines the labour movement from its inception analysing workers' activism and their relationship with the state and presenting a critical review of these schools.

149

B) Historical Background

Workers' activism started in Egypt as early as 1899, when the Cairo cigarette rollers initiated the first ever known strike in the history of Egyptian labour (December 1899–February 1900) led by Greek workers, demanding higher wages, shorter hours and better working conditions. The strike took the company's owners by surprise and resulted in limited gains for the workers. A second strike was organised by the Cairo cigarette rollers in 1903, but was easily broken by the employers, who managed to reverse most of the gains that the workers had previously achieved. Both Egyptian and Syrian workers refused to join, and the employers found it easy to isolate the Greek militants who spearheaded the strike. The only gain that stemmed from the workers' defeat in this strike is that it showed them the need for a strong organisation to represent their interests. A union, which remained weak for several years did emerge at the Matossian factory, but in 1908, after a brief and unsuccessful strike in Cairo, the union, now called the Ligue Internationale des Ouvriers Cigarettiers et Papiers du Caire, became the core for a broader category of workers.[3]

Several strikes, which were harshly suppressed by employers aided by the police, followed in various industries and although the early ones were initiated by foreign workers, Egyptian workers, such as the Cairo Tramway Workers, were no less militant. The repression to which the Egyptian drivers and conductors were subjected at the hands of the foreign inspectors, who were mainly Greeks and Italians, such as verbal abuse, and discrimination in promotion led them to initiate a strike in 1908, when the company refused to yield to a list of comprehensive demands presented to it by the aggrieved workers. Although it too was broken by the company with the help of the police, the strike marked the appearance of the Egyptian workers as an independent force on the industrial scene, with the event having a wide public impact. In March 1909, the Cairo trams workers and conductors established a union.[4]

Thus, whereas the first attempts for strikes and unionisation came from foreign workers,

> Egyptians employed in the large enterprises capitalist development had generated in this period were quick to follow their lead, and learn their techniques and forms of organization and struggle. The indigenous workers may have been inspired by the example of the foreigners, but the impulse to respond collectively derived from their own grievances as well as from the very structure and logic of the industrial experience itself.[5]

The historical development of the workers' movement was greatly shaped by the fact that from 1882 to 1956 Egypt was under British domination and that, until the late 1930s, almost all large-scale employers, whose economic power and interests were protected by the British, were foreigners. As a result, workers' views of themselves as a distinctive class, and hence the development of a class consciousness was greatly delayed, since their economic demands and the demands for more independence and respect in the work place were viewed more in terms of a national struggle than within the context of class antagonism. It was hence easier under these circumstances for the workers' movement to blend with the nationalist struggle and for the Wafd, the main driving force in this struggle, to emerge as the hegemonic ideological and organisational power within the labour movement.[6]

> The 1919 revolution is really divided into two stages: first, is a violent revolution that occurred in March after Sa'd Zaghlul and his three comrades were banished to Malta. This was a relatively short period of time but it was the revolution that the British military forces opposed with full vigor as it was the stage in which the peasants actively took part. A second stage followed that began in April and it was, in terms of time, a relatively long stage, during which the peasants withdrew from revolutionary action, and the revolution became limited to Cairo and the urban centers and in which the urban elements such as the students, employees, attorneys, and workers played the critical roles.[7]

From this point on, Wafdist officials started to assume prominent positions within the labour movement, which made its greatest advance.[8] A secret report sent by Abd al-Rahman Fahmi to Sa'd Zaghlul, while the latter was still in Europe, reflects both trade union proliferation and the realisation of the different contending forces in society of the importance of this class in mobilising political support:

> I will explain to you the results of the efforts made to spread unions (ta'mim al-niqabat) throughout the length and breadth of the land. These efforts have, praise to God, borne fruit: a union has been formed for every craft (hirfa), and there remains in Egypt no craft or trade(san'a) without a union. It is true that the government has not recognised these unions up to now, and it is not anticipated that it will recognize them in the present circumstances. But they are in any case very useful to the nationalist movement and a powerful weapon which should not be underestimated. In time of calamity they will respond to the call of patriotism as quickly as possible.[9]

Nationalist activists, both Wafdist and non-Wafdist, perceived the workers as a societal group whose social and economic status could only improve with the overall improvement of society, rather than viewing them as a distinctive group whose interests were antagonistic to other economic groups.[10] This view was mostly reflected in Sa'ad Zaghlul's[11] address in 1924 to a Wafdist trade union federation meeting. He identified himself with the workers, whom he called the "rabble", and praised them for being pure and revolutionary because they did not seek official positions. He had thus described them as

> the most numerous class of the nation, which has no special interest and whose principals are everlastingly firm [thabit ala al-dawam] these

principles being independence for Egypt and the Sudan. This class does not run after office or seek a place to fill nor have an interest to be gratified, but wishes only to live and keep the country honourable.[12]

Being far detached from reality, this view had nevertheless shaped the behaviour of both the Wafd and Prince Halim towards the labour movement during the interwar period, when a paternalistic, patron-client relationship with the trade unions developed. At no time did the Wafd attempt to strengthen the unions or allow them to develop an independent unified organisation. The failure of the Wafd during this period to achieve any real gains for the movement and to resist the British and the King, the repression that the movement was exposed to when the Wafd government fell from office, and the factionalisation caused by the Wafd and anti-Wafd leaders within the unions, isolated workers whose ability to develop or maintain their organisations and to struggle for improved wages and economic conditions was severely diminished.[13]

Some speeches delivered to the workers reflect the awareness of some of their leaders of the inherent problems within the unions and to their desire to create an independent movement led by the workers themselves. For example, a speech by Mahjub Thabit, president of the General Federation of Labour Unions,[14] advised workers to

> Keep away from the parties for your own good and the good of the country. Don't be tools of the [prominent] personalities, beware of leaders and would-be leaders and their exploitative agents. Don't be partisan; rather take a negative attitude toward the parties: support any party which works in your interest and your country's interest. Support whoever does well by you, and abandon whoever tries to exploit you.[15]

Another example is a letter published in al-Muqattam in June 1929, in which Ahmad Ali Badawi, leader of the printing workers' union urged the workers to rid their unions of non-worker elements:

> As a worker and a member of one of the unions and as someone in a position which allows broad contacts, I can confirm that most of these bosses [of unions, ru'asa'] know nothing of their union's affairs. They don't attend meetings except if they have selfish interest or if it touches on things that concern them personally. And if you will permit me I will note with great sorrow that splits among members of some of the unions have been caused by these bosses. They get some members of the union to support them and incite them to opposition toward those of their colleagues who already know the truth about [the boss] aims. The members of the union then split, and another union is formed.[16]

Law 85 of 1942 was the first legislation which officially recognised trade unions. Three main reasons induced the Wafd to recognise trade unions. The first was the decline of Wafd influence at the national level and its partial discredit by the 1936 treaty and hence the need to secure some popular support among the workers. Secondly, in order to retain the confidence of the British, the Wafd government had to show its ability to halt strikes that disrupted production and communication, especially during the critical war period. Finally, increasing discontent among the workers, as reflected in strikes and demonstrations, made the Wafd realise the high cost involved in non-appeasement policy. However, while implementing a certain amount of pro-labour legislation, the Wafd maintained a tight grip over the unions. Thus, whereas the law gave the workers in a single firm the right to form unions, a unified federation of unions including workers in several firms was prohibited. This measure ensured that the unions remained small and therefore organisationally and financially feeble.

Agricultural workers, personal servants and government employees were not allowed to join unions. Unions were restricted from engagement in any political or religious activities and police notification of all meetings of union executive boards and general assemblies was compulsory.[17] Moreover, unions were required to register with the Ministry of Social Affairs, whose approval was a condition for the formation of new unions. The Ministry of Social Affairs was also authorised to close down, without right of appeal, unions engaged in illegal activities.[18] The ministry also started in 1944 to grant subsidies to "qualified" trade unions. By controlling the allocation of funds, the Wafd could easily dominate the small and inexperienced trade unions.

The Wafd, however, seems to have partially subverted its own measure, (since it had always been reluctant to unite the workers in a single federation or confederation), when it encouraged government workers[19] to form a general federation called the Congress of Government Workers,[20] which marked the first attempt to create a unified national labour organisation.

The desire of the workers to establish independent unions, especially after World War II, triggered by the decline of patron-client associations and the corporatist ideology within the labour movement, provided the Communists with a chance to step in as main rivals to the Wafd among the workers and to champion the workers' struggle for equitable wages, security of employment, and a measure of control in the work place.[21] The Communists established the Congress of Egyptian Trade Unions (Mu'tamar Niqabat 'Ummal Misr) in 1946, the second attempt to create a confederation of labour.[22] Despite the partial success of the Communists to establish roots among the workers, several factors contributed to the demise of their influence. Among these was the repression and harassment to which Communist organisations were subjected, especially by the Sidki government, with the imprisonment of most of their leaders, and the struggle that took place among the two leading communist organisations, the Egyptian Movement for National Liberation (EMNL) and the New Dawn, which had major repercussions on the movement as early as in 1944. The late forties witnessed an erosion of Communist influence and a loss of political credibility caused by their emulation of the Soviet Union and their endorsement of the partition of Palestine and the establishment of the state of Israel.[23] However, even at the height of their

153

influence among the workers, the Communists had failed to establish a purely independent workers' movement, as Beinin and Lockman have noted:

> Even the political practice of the communists, who were the most consistent in insisting on the importance of asserting the independent interests of the working class, combined the advancement of these interests with active participation in a broad national front that included bourgeois forces.[24]

The Muslim Brotherhood also tried during the post war period to rival both the Wafd and the Communists, but apart from some partial local success, they were unable to establish strong and stable roots among the workers. This can be attributed to several factors. The vague vision of workers embedded in their call for a moral economy and the fact that "most of the Society's writings on labour affairs suffered from ambiguity, inconsistency, and programmatic unclarity",[25] constituted one such obstacle. The implicit rather than explicit support of the Muslim Brotherhood for the workers' strikes and their role as strike-breakers in some of the most famous strikes that occurred in Shubra al-Khayma, also accounts for their lack of credibility among the workers.[26] Finally, the Muslim Brotherhood ended up adopting the same paternalistic and corporatist behaviour that characterised the Wafd and other forces towards the movement.[27]

To sum up, the pre-1952 era witnessed several workers' uprising and protests. However, as a result of British colonisation and the dominance of foreign capitalism, workers' economic demands were fused with the political demands of the nationalist movement. Hence, in contrast with, for example, the Iraqi situation, where societal divisions along sectarian lines (Sunnis-Shiites and Kurds) among the upper and middle classes strengthened class rather than national loyalty and accelerated the development of class consciousness and solidarity among the Iraqi workers which manifested itself in demands that transcended mere economic gains to certain political demands[28] that were specific to the working class,[29] in Egypt the unity of the nationalist movement represented an obstacle to the development of a similar consciousness among Egyptian workers. This, coupled with the paternalistic behaviour that the different social forces adopted towards the workers and the presence of bourgeois elements as patrons of the movement, has retarded the formation of workers' class consciousness. In other words, "a false consciousness" in the Marxist sense of the term was created among the workers by their bourgeois patrons, placing their demands within the broader national struggle.

C) The Labour Movement from Nasser to Mubarak

State policy towards the Movement

After the crisis that faced the Egyptian regime during the forties and early fifties, the 1952 coup was welcomed by most segments of society. The Free Officers represented diverse political tendencies and both the communist DMNL and the Muslim Brotherhood claimed that the movement was "theirs", with each of these groups having hopes of sharing power.

While Nasser maintained communication with various political forces, his only commitment was to the Free Officers' organisation, refusing to commit it to permanent alliance with any sort of civilian-dominated political forces. The Free Officers nationalist appeal, their attack on the corruption of the old regime and their promise of social justice earned them from the outset workers' support. As a sign of trust in the new regime the tramway workers cancelled a previously scheduled strike.

The textile workers' strike which took place in Kafr al Dawwar less than a month after the Free Officers came to power marked the beginning of a tense relationship between them and the trade unions. The strike was harshly crushed by the regime, hundreds of workers were arrested and a military tribunal sentenced to death two of the strike' leaders, while the third was given a thirteen year sentence (later reduced to nine) and ten other workers received shorter prison sentences. Nasser thus clearly demonstrated that he would not permit any segments in the society, including the working class, to destabilise the new-born regime.

In his dealings with the workers, Nasser showed continuity with the traditional pattern, which basically characterised relations between political forces and the labour movement prior to 1952. He thus sought to reinstate the patron-client relationship with the workers in order to ensure tight control and to build support for the regime among the workers. In order to achieve control, Nasser had to isolate and consequently eliminate the Communists, who demanded an independent movement, and in order to build a support base for himself, labour legislation was reviewed and several benefits were granted to the workers.[30]

Bianchi views the Nasserist era as a complete departure from a long-standing pluralist tradition adopted towards the labour movement. However, as shown by Law 85 of 1942, a hybrid formula that combined pluralism and corporatism was already in operation before 1952.

The 1952 law initiated by the Free Officers represented a continuation of this trend. On the one hand, it encouraged the proliferation of unions and extended membership to agricultural workers, cancelled the conditional approval of the Ministry of Social Affairs for the formation of new unions, and transferred the power of union closure to the judiciary.[31] In addition, several material benefits were granted to the workers. These included increased severance compensation, longer annual vacations, free transportation to factories in remote areas, free medical care, and the right of appeal against unfair dismissal. Decree 165 of 1953 granted workers permanency in jobs by making workers' dismissal without cause a very clumsy and complicated procedure to undertake. This meant that the regime had succeeded in meeting one of the workers' most important demands of the post-war period: job security. On the other hand, a military order was issued which banned all strikes.[32] At the same time, an attempt was made to consolidate the working class into a unitary state-sponsored structure. Thus a law was passed to establish one union federation in each occupational category and a single confederation of labour representing all union federations at the national level.[33] However, Nasser was reluctant to grant his approval to the formation of a single body that would unite the workers and their demands. Instead, after an agreement with the non-communist union leaders was made, Nasser allowed the formation of a "permanent congress" (mu'tamar da'im) which could be seen to justify the postponement of establishing the unitary confederation. Even after the decisive role which the demonstrations of the transport workers, which was arranged by Major Tu'ayma,[34] had played in consolidating Nasser's position vis-à-vis Naguib in their power struggle of March 1954, Nasser was still unwilling to approve the formation of a national confederation and opted instead for an International Confederation of Arab Trade Unions, that was to augment his regional influence, especially during the 1956 Suez crisis. Egyptian workers were thus placed in the peculiar situation of having to join a pan-Arab confederation at a time when such associations did not exist in their own country. Nasser finally approved the formation of the confederation in 1957,[35] but this was followed by the passage of the so-called 'Socialist Union laws' represented by the Unified Labour Code of 1959 and the Trade Unions Law of 1964, which ensured the creation of a fully state controlled organisation.

By virtue of these two laws, provisions were made for the centralisation of unions around a small number of national federations which, in turn, was tightly supervised by the Confederation and the newly-established Ministry of Labour. Civil servants were allowed to join unions, which contributed to the increasing size of the labour movement. Federations were authorised to negotiate and sanction collective work contracts and the ban previously installed on union involvement in political, religious and entrepreneurial activities was abolished. In an attempt to win over union leaders, the regime bestowed on them generous benefits, including legal guarantees to job security, promotion, and retirement benefits. Various prohibitions, however, were introduced, including bans against instigating class antagonism, organising work stoppages, attempting to overthrow the political system and the use of coercion in recruitment of union members.[36]

Several other laws initiated in the sixties aimed at improving the living standards of workers and extended the benefits granted to them. These laws had, for example, reduced the working hours in industrial factories and firms to 42 hours per week, doubled the minimum wage, and introduced an insurance scheme. Law 114 of 1961 granted even more benefits to the workers since it provided for worker's representation on the board of management of all public sector firms, while the 1963 law increased their representation on the board of directors from two to four members out of a total number of nine members. It was estimated that during the period between 1952 and 1966, real wages increased roughly by 60 per cent and that this increase was not matched by an increase in worker's productivity.[37]

To sum up, in dealing with labour, the Nasserite regime adopted a corporatist formula whereby workers were given certain economic benefits in return for giving up their political rights and demands. This "social contract" between labour and the state started to change under Sadat and was completely abandoned under Mubarak.

Like their professional counterparts, the workers have lost most of the benefits that they have previously gained under Nasser's policy of industrial expansion, which includes full employment and social welfare. Most new modern joint ventures are capital intensive and hence are unlikely to create new jobs opportunities for workers. Moreover, many foreign enterprises are not bound by the Egyptian labour laws, and some of these, banks, for instance, have completely abandoned the principal of employees representation on their board of directors.[38] Workers still preserve, at least symbolically, their political gain of representation in the People's Assembly (50 percent representation for workers and peasants). However, the debates raised lately, some of which vigorously attacked such representation, especially with the increase of businessmen representation in parliament, cast doubts on the intention of the state to continue to preserve this right of the workers. Rapid inflation caused by "Infitah" coupled with stagnation in wages was bound to increase the burden of all "ordinary people" including workers.[39]

The gradual erosion of the benefits previously acquired under Nasser accounts for the increase in labour protests that took place under Sadat[40] and continue under Mubarak. Under these circumstances the classical corporatist formula previously adopted towards labour could not be sustained and was replaced by a tighter form, which has been labelled as *co-integrationism.*

As soon as he assumed power, Sadat took the first step in this direction by purging the confederation leadership and reducing the number of federations to sixteen. In his relationship with union leaders, Sadat created from top union leaders a "self-recruiting élite" that would increase the unions' alliance with the regime. He gave them broad consultative powers in economic policy-making, in an attempt to separate the top union leaders from the rank and file.[41]

Increasing labour unrest was the underlying motive for issuing the 1976 and 1981 union laws. By virtue of these two laws, Sadat strengthened the administrative and financial controls of the Egyptian Confederation of Labour over the federations and of the latter over their local branches,[42] creating one of the country's largest hierarchical bureaucracy.[43] A new system of indirect elections secured the tenure of top leaders with higher-rank leaders elected by the lower-rank leaders after being approved by the Socialist Prosecutor's office, hence removing leaders' accountability to their constituents. Mubarak continued his predecessor's policy and the confederation's power has been greatly extended by being given control over the new Workers' University, which is designed to centralise union leaders' training programmes, formerly run by different rival state and party agencies. The confederation has also been allowed to engage in syndical capitalism and to use available funds to create its own economic enterprises, mainly managed by the newly established Workers' Bank.[44]

157

The General Confederation of Labour: An Assessment

The Egyptian General Confederation of Labour has a membership of twenty-three general federations. The early attempt at consolidating labour organisations which started with the passage of the socialist laws of 1959, was accompanied by a change in membership proportions: the manufacturing sector, whose workers are the main instigators of strikes, has witnessed a decline in membership vis-à-vis civil servants and transport workers, which reflects not only the stagnation of the former and the inflation of the latter, but also the desire to replace militant workers with others who are more dependent on the state and hence more domesticated.[45]

According to law 35 of 1976, as amended by Law 1 of 1981, the organisation of the confederations is pyramidal, with union committees at the base, the federations in the middle and the confederation's council at the top. The confederation's general assembly includes all members who have been enlisted for at least six months and have paid their subscriptions. The union's council is elected by the general assembly from among its nominated members. The number of council members ranges from seventeen to twenty-one, depending on the size of the union and in conformity with the procedures and conditions approved by the general confederation. The federation councils are also elected by the federation general assembly. The number of members in the federation council range from eleven to twenty-one members, taking into consideration the proportional and geographical representation of each governorate or group of governorates and in conformity with the regulations established by the federation and approved by the confederation.

Table 6.1 The density of union membership by economic sectors

	1948	1958	1964	1976	1982
Union membership as percentages of					
Total population	0.7	1.2	2.8	5.4	6.2
Economically active population	1.1	4.1	8.8	20.1	23.2
Non agricultural E.A.P.	2.3	9.0	18.7	35.3	36.4
Union members as percentage of					
E.A.P. employed in Agriculture	–	0.5	–	3.0	5.4
Private services	0.4	4.9	10.2	15.0	15.1
Trade & Finances	1.6	4.3	8.9	15.3	12.0
Construction	3.3	8.0	23.8	35.1	43.6
Manufacturing	12.1	17.1	33.9	46.3	50.2
Transportation	12.9	22.9	32.5	70.0	85.2
Public Utilities	8.0	14.0	32.6	83.0	95.2

Source: Bianchi, *Unruly Corporatism*, p. 133.

The confederation general assembly elects its council either from among those nominated by the federation councils or from its own members, with each federation represented by one member on the council. In addition, local confederations, affiliated to the general confederation, have been established in all governments.[46]

In theory, the 1976 law provided the general confederation with the right to "state its opinion in the drafted laws, rules, and decisions involved in the regulation of all matters related to work and workers", thus reflecting the official recognition of the confederation as an interest group that should represent and promote labour's interests. However, in practice the reality is completely different.

Reference has been made earlier to Sadat's successful policy of separating top union leaders from the rank and file, a practice that is still in operation under Mubarak. The fact that the confederation leader had a dual role to play as the Minister of Labour obliged to promote the state's interest and the confederation leader obliged to act as the representative of workers' interests, which are usually in conflict with those of the state, rendered the confederation an inactive and inefficient tool for defending workers' views and promoting their demands.

The confederation's first two presidents, Anwar Salama (1957–1962) and Ahmad Fahim (1962–1969), refused to combine the two posts in order to avoid this duality and once appointed to the cabinet, they resigned their post as confederation leaders. It was the confederation's third leader, Abd al-Latif Bultiya (1969–1971) who accepted the post of Minister of Labour while retaining his position as the confederation's leader. This tradition continued with Bultiya's successors, Salah Gharib (1971–1976) and Sa'd Muhammad Ahmad (1976–1987), but ended in 1987 when the latter was removed from his position as Minister of Manpower and Vocational Training (formerly the Ministry of Labour). His removal was caused by his continuous opposition to Mubarak's pro-business policy of reducing public sector employment. He was then forced to resign his position as head of the confederation.[47] Henceforth, the two posts were separated in 1987, with Asem Abd al-Haqq becoming the new Minister of Manpower, and Ahmad al-Amawi winning an uncontested election to become the confederation leader.[48] When the latter was appointed Minister of Manpower, he was succeeded as confederation leader by Al-Sayyed Rashed, who also won an uncontested 1996 election.[49] The separation between the two posts was intended to limit the increasing power of the confederation. Sa'd Mohammed Ahmed triggered government fears by opposing some of its policies and attempting to adopt others favoured by opposition parties.

Continuing government intervention in union elections further emphasised the gap between the base and the summit. This usually takes place through direct endorsement of candidates affiliated to the NDP, while disqualifying others who are either affiliated to opposition parties or opposed to government policies.[50] The police, who screen the nominated candidates, and the General Socialist Prosecutor whose approval is a condition for allowing candidates to contest the elections, are the government tools for such intervention. In the 1987 trade union elections, for example, the General Socialist Prosecutor's approval of the nominees was given one day before the elections, which minimised the effectiveness of their election campaigns.[51] In the 1996 elections more than a hundred nominees who opposed privatisation were disqualified on the pretext that they had failed to complete the necessary procedures.[52] It is important to note here that the government had ignored the ruling of the Supreme Constitutional Court in 1994 that the trade unions laws were unconstitutional. The court based its ruling on the fact that the law includes an article, which restricts the representation of professionals to 20 per cent, and hence violates equality of rights. The court went further and upheld the workers' right to form more than one union within the same industry, an act, which the government also rejected.[53]

The longevity of leadership in the confederation, federation, and the unions is another factor that tends to aggravate the problem. Bianchi notes that

Since 1973 turnover in the federation and confederation leadership has fallen steadily, and was virtually nil in the union elections of 1983.[54]

Bianchi's comment was confirmed by the 1995 election results, which showed the continuation of most of the previous leaders in their positions at the different levels of the unions with fewer than 40 per cent being replaced.[55] This, coupled with the fact that most of these leaders are members of the ruling party, discredits the various labour organisations, including the confederation, as true representatives of workers' interests. The lack of common goals among the various labour organisations also weakens the role of the confederation as a pressure group. In some cases some of the federations refuse to accept and follow the recommendations of the confederation and choose to adopt an opposing stance.[56]

The diversification in the composition of union membership and the existence of conflicting interests renders a unitary organisation for the representation of workers a difficult task to accomplish. The difference between Egypt's twenty-three union federations in size and heterogeneity of both membership and employers and continuing government reclassification of the occupational categories in order to strengthen or weaken particular union leaders, further fragment the labour movement.[57]

The 2000 Draft for the Unified Labour Law

The failure of labour unions and the confederation to protect workers' rights in the new draft for the unified labour law highlight their weakness. The draft law, which is known as the Unified Law for 2000, managed to erode the few labour benefits that were remittance of the social contract of the Nasserite era. For example, article 24 of the current labour law (law 137 for 1981)was cancelled in

160

the new law. This article authorises the labour minister with the right to force some firms to hire workers according to their date of administrative registration with respect to certain vocations specified by the minister. The cancellation of this article in the new law was justified on the base "that economic liberalisation dictates that firms and business owners be given the right to choose their own workers." The law also ignored article 13 of the constitution which states that "work is a right that is guaranteed by the state", which renders the new law unconstitutional. Moreover, where as the current law made the dismissal of workers permissible only in the case of committing a grave mistake, article 69 of the new law stipulates that "it is permissible to dismiss the worker if he fails to carry out any of his basic duties." The phrase "basic duties" is a very elastic one, which can have several interpretations and can be used as a pretext for arbitrary dismissal of workers. Again, both the Egyptian constitution and articles 21 and 22 of the international convention for civil and political rights guarantee freedom of opinion and expression, and the right of peaceful meetings. However article 47 of the new law necessitates the dismissal of workers "in cases of money and donations collection, distribution of any leaflets, collection of signatures and the organisation of workers' meetings in the work place without prior permission of the work owners, whilst considering the specific articles of the law which regulate Syndicates".

The new law also makes it permissible for owners to dismiss workers in case of pressing economic problems. Since the law did not establish the conditions of these economic problems but left it flexible, this would give owners a pretext for workers dismissal even in cases where these economic problems are the outcome of poor management or corruption of the managerial board of directors. In addition, there was no mention of workers compensation in case of dismissal for the previously mentioned problems. Article 70 of the law gives the business owner the sole right to dismiss the worker whenever he wishes without resorting to any external arbitration. The new law thus will set precedence, since the current law (law 137 for 1981) necessitates the approval of a tri-member committee for the dismissal. The three members acting on the committee are: the director of the department of labour or his deputy acting as the head of the committee, the worker's representative chosen by the union or the syndicate to which the worker is affiliated, and the business owner or his representative. This committee is designated the responsibility of examining the complaint submitted by the business owner. Based on its investigation the committee should approve the dismissal (Article 62) or otherwise reject it, in which case the worker must be immediately reinstated in his job and is paid his full wages (Article 15). The provision in the previous law for the arbitration of this committee was intended to safeguard the workers against unlawful and arbitrary dismissal. Despite the fact that the new drafted law has in article 71 restored the committee's function with the addition of two members who should be from the judiciary, the committee in this case is formed after and not before the dismissal of workers.[58]

The Effect of the Weakness of the Confederation and Unions on Workers

The inefficiency of the confederation and the various labour unions in pushing for workers' demands is reflected in the apathetic and alienated behaviour of the workers. This is manifested in several ways, the first of which is the low level of membership in labour organisations. Unlike syndicates, where membership is compulsory and conditional for practice, membership in trade unions is optional. The fact that Egypt's workers number thirteen million, of whom only three million (23 per cent) have joined trade unions,[59] reflects the weakness of trade unions. Workers have thus developed a tendency to form informal groups, usually called leagues, to voice their grievances and demands and these have proved more successful than the formal organisations in promoting workers' demands and unifying their conflicting interests.[60] Workers also resort to illegal forms of protest including sit-ins and strikes, confirming their lack of trust in legal channels. Indeed, workers' occupation of the confederation building shows that workers view the confederation as an organisation that serves the state's rather than their own interests.

Posusney has thus commented,

> because of the interference of the government in union elections, the fact that most senior union officials are affiliated with the NDP, the historic conjoining of the posts of the ETUF president and minister of labour, and the frequent unresponsiveness of these union officials to wildcat protests, some workers have come to see the confederation itself as an instrument of the state, hence, the sit-in at confederation headquarters.[61]

To sum up, state-labour relation in contemporary Egypt has been moving away from the classical corporatist formula towards a tighter form namely here *co-integrationism*, whereby the interests of top union leaders have been tied to the regime and integrated into the state system. Whereas it was Sadat who started this process, Mubarak continues to build on it.

D) Workers' Struggle: An Assessment

Several scholars have attempted to provide a valid interpretation of the fluctuation in workers' discontent under the post 1952 regimes. Among these is Ellis Goldberg who provides an explanation for the decline of the workers' struggle in the 1950s and 1960s as measured by the number of strikes.

Goldberg rejects the traditional Marxist school analysis of the workers' struggle in Nasserist Egypt, since their behaviour defied Marxists expectations.[62] According to traditional Marxism, the workers' struggle should have increased rather than decreased during the Nasserite era and should have extended to the whole industrial sector. Since this did not occur, Goldberg dismisses traditional Marxism as a valid explanation for the Egyptian workers' behaviour. Instead, he

162

suggests an interpretation for the mutation of workers' struggle and the decline in union strength during this period based on the rational choice theory. Goldberg builds his argument on the benefits that the Nasserist state granted to workers, stripping the unions of their monopoly over collective goods represented in its bargaining power. This was achieved first through the state's policy of price control, rationing, and subsidies, which kept the price of basic consumer goods low and allowed real wages to grow faster than money wages, and, secondly through the state investment policy, which promoted demand for skilled labour, minimum wage policies and secured employment.[63] Accordingly,

> Workers increasingly would resent the trade union apparatus and refuse to participate in it (to the degree possible), only state power (in the form of mandatory check-off) would keep the unions alive at all.[64]

Since in this case employment becomes a public good rather than the outcome of market forces, the rational choice would be to enjoy the benefits and avoid the costs. Neglecting coercion as an integral part of the equation, Goldberg explains workers' quiescence during this period in terms of rational choice theory. He suggests that workers accepted low wages in return for a guaranteed income, job security, and a pension. In doing so they acted rationally.[65] It also follows from the same interpretation, that workers' low productivity in the public sector in Nasserist and post-Nasserist Egypt and their moonlighting, especially under Sadat's infitah,[66] are other manifestations of their rational behaviour in that tend to give the state what they consider a fair return for the low wages they obtain.

However, Goldberg's interpretation itself seems to contradict rational choice theory, in that workers' activism and protests should increase in prosperous times in order to achieve more economic gains and decline in times of economic slowdown so as to avoid increased costs. Hence workers' activities should have increased rather than decreased during the 1950s and 1960s.

Marsha Posusney rejects Goldberg's interpretation and argues that workers' activism under Nasser, Sadat and Mubarak can be better understood in terms of the moral-economy theory, which has its roots in Egypt in the patron-client relationship established by the state with the workers in the 1960s.[67] Evidence for this is manifested in the time when workers protests occur, their causes, the symbols they attack and finally the obligations, which the workers project. According to the moral-economy theory workers' activism should increase during times of economic deterioration, whereas periods of economic prosperity should witness a relatively acquiescent labour movement.[68] Reviewing labour protests during the sixties, seventies, and eighties Posusney found that, except for the protests occurring in 1982–1983, most of the findings for the period under study (1960–1987) conformed to the moral-economy model.[69] The reasons for the protests also support the moral-economy theory, in that the causes are of a restorative nature, i.e., preserving and protecting previously acquired gains rather than aiming at achieving new ones. Three causes of these protests, which Posusney labelled 'entitlement protest', were found. The first results from the loss

163

of previously earned gains, the second occurs when parity among workers, especially within the same industry, is violated, and the third is caused by unfulfilled promises made to the workers.[70] The retreat from the socialist state, which started in mid 1965, escalated under both Sadat and Mubarak. This was due to the policy of economic liberalisation. As a result most of the workers' aggression was directed towards symbols of the state, be it the Parliament building, the ruling party's headquarters, or the President's mansion, thus reflecting the workers' view of the state's responsibility for their difficulties and its obligation to elevate their hardship.[71] Posusney's interpretation confirms the assumption put forward in this book. The erosion of the traditional social contract which forms the base of classical corporatism in Sadat's and Mubarak's Egypt accounts for the increase in workers' protests.

Posusney also shows that the form which workers' protests took reflects their sense of obligation and loyalty towards their jobs. This is signified by the fact that, in most cases, protests took the form of abstaining from cashing paycheques or the eviction of management and foremen from factories while workers continued their jobs.[72] However, despite their display of such a high level of responsibility towards their job, the state's brutality in crushing labour protest, including imprisonment and torture of strikers and protesters was the hallmark of the Nasser and Sadat regimes and continues under Mubarak.[73]

Labour protest in Egypt should not therefore be interpreted as the development of class consciousness and class solidarity among workers, from which stem collective actions aimed at achieving more gains for the working class. Workers' protests in Egypt were always individual and limited and, as Posusney's study concludes,

> With the possible exception of the January 1977 riots, one could choose any given point in time over the thirty-five years covered here and observe, with accuracy, that the great majority of Egyptian workers were not engaged in any form of collective protests.[74]

Even the role of the workers in the 1977 riots is debatable. If the workers' participation in the riots was planned and deliberate, it would imply the existence of class consciousness, but uneven economic development, so characteristic of Egypt, has contributed to the fragmentation of the working class, both culturally and socially and thus:

> Those who actively participated in the collective actions of January 1977 did not share a unified understanding of the cause of their oppression or the solution to it.[75]

Therefore the 1977 riots pertain to Beinin's description that it

> fits a more common pattern in twentieth century Egyptian politics: a tumultuous upheaval that could not be sustained because of inability to forge enduring political alliances among the diverse components of Egypt's subaltern strata.[76]

2. Businessmen's Associations

A) The Chambers of Commerce

Although the formation of these chambers goes back to 1910 when they were still labelled "Syndicates" or "Co-operatives," their legalisation as formal governmental agencies took place by virtue of Law 189 for 1951. A presidential decree of 1955 allowed the formation of a General Federation of Chambers of Commerce and assigned to it the responsibility of organising co-operation between the various chambers, as well as representing them at the national level.[77] In Egypt there are twenty six chambers with a total membership of about three million. Each chamber is divided by function into several branches, 'Shu'ab', which are regulated in detail in much the same way as the chambers.[78] The two largest chambers, those of Cairo and Alexandria, each have more than twenty branches, overseeing the implementation of regulations on various services and commodities issued by the Ministries of Trade, Finance, and Economy.[79]

The autonomy of the chambers is very limited where the government enjoys major authority, both administrative and financial over the chambers. Governmental control is vested in the Ministries of Finance, Supply and Economy, to which the chambers report. Reporting includes gaining the approval of the ministries to which the chambers report, for any aid given to the chambers, their approval for the establishment of any chamber in a governorate, and their approval for any change in the duties of the chambers.[80] The fact that government subsidies constitute a major source of funds available to the chambers further ties them to the state and enhances the latter's control.[81]

The method of election of the board of directors of both the chambers and the federation of chambers ensures tight state control and complete compliance with whatever policy the government initiates. Since 1969 half the twenty-four directors have been appointed by the government and the other half are elected. The federation's leader is appointed by presidential decree and its board of directors includes eleven members appointed by a ministerial decree. In addition to these members, each chamber is represented by the head of its board of directors except for its Cairo and Alexandria Chambers, which are represented by two members each, the head of their board of directors and another member elected by the board. This dual nature of selection and election continues to be the main characteristic of the chambers despite the changes that took place in their governing regulations in 1978.[82] It should also be noted that apart from the appointment of a specific number of members to the chambers' board of directors by the Ministry of Supply, the Ministry has the right to judge the validity of the elections of members to the board of directors and to dissolve branches if the latter become involved in activities outside their specialisation.[83] This policy of tight control is also reinforced by a policy of co-opting top leaders to ensure their loyalty to the regime. As one author, whose research concentrated mainly on the

Cairo Chamber of Commerce, but whose findings are applicable to all chambers and to the federation, has commented:

> Perhaps, through the co-optation and special privileges bestowed on the leadership of the Chamber(s)[84] and the Federation of Chambers of Commerce in Egypt, the government has been able to check and balance through them the business community.[85]

Apart from gathering and distributing information and statistics related to commerce and industry to businessmen, the chambers may, in theory, be consulted by government.[86] In reality such advice is hardly sought. In fact, the chambers' participation in policy-making affecting the business community takes place after policies are initiated and decreed.[87] For example, in 1972 the Minister of Supply issued a decree prohibiting the private sector from selling imported goods and restricting such rights to the public sector. The decree, was issued without the consultation or participation of the chamber, which rejected it and sought its nullification by the administrative court. In 1973 the court ruled in favour of chambers and the Minister's decree was nullified. The same situation occurred again in 1977, when the Minister of Supply issued a decree placing a ceiling on the profit margin for imported goods. As a result a large number of merchants gathered around the Cairo Chamber, which was headed at that time by Moustafa Kamel Mourad, rejecting the Minister's decree and demanding that the chamber intervene on their behalf. Accordingly, the board of directors of the Cairo Chamber of Commerce issued a statement rejecting the Minister's decree and arguing the impossibility of its execution. As a result, the Minister issued a decree, by which a temporary board of directors was formed for both the federation and the Cairo and Alexandria Chambers, based on the pretext that the present boards had completed their terms in office and that the new elections were postponed until a new law for the chambers was issued. Moustafa Mourad was then replaced by Mohammed al-Balidi as head of the Cairo Chamber of Commerce. Mourad appealed to the administrative court against his removal from the leadership of the Cairo Chamber. In 1978, the court annulled the Minister's decree concerning the formation of temporary boards for the chambers and the postponement of the election of new boards, since these procedures fell outside the Minister's responsibilities. Finally the execution of the decree was postponed.[88]

Moreover, the chambers are divided among themselves and there is a recurring conflict between the federation and the chambers, which increases their weakness and their ability to serve those they represent. For example, in 1977 the Cairo and Alexandria Chambers of Commerce accepted membership in the Egyptian American Commercial and Industrial Chambers at a time when the federation's president had rejected the formation of the latter as independent chambers and insisted that they should only be branches affiliated to and under the umbrella of the federation.[89] The same conflict occurred between the federation's board and that of the Cairo and Alexandria Chambers concerning ministerial decree no 119 for 1978. Whereas, as noted above, the board of directors of Cairo and Alexandria Chambers rejected the Minister's decree, the head of the federation had accepted it and issued a statement supporting the Minister of Supply.[90] This last example not only highlights the conflict that takes place between the chambers and the federation, but also the duality in the formation of both. Whereas the federation's board is completely under the control of the government and most of its members are public sector appointees, the chambers whose boards include 50 per cent elected members, are more representative of private sector interests.[91]

Perhaps the weakness of the chambers and the federation is best illustrated by their inability to push for a law (the draft of which was completed only in 1991) which would guarantee the latter's autonomy. In 1976, discussions started on the updating of the 1966 chamber law. Two factors surfaced in the discussion. The first was a liberal view demanding that the new law grant the chambers autonomy to enable them, in the new economic liberalisation era, to be more representative and to engage more fully in policy-making, whereas the second point of view supported the continuation of the chambers as part of the state apparatus. The law that was initiated in 1978 reflected the second point of view.[92] Since then, the chambers have tried to push for another law that would provide them with the necessary autonomy, but their attempts were usually aborted by the Minister of Supply. Finally in 1991 a draft bill was completed. The bill mainly emphasises the autonomy of the chambers, and the confederation from the Ministry of Supply. The bill also provides for a separate budget for the chambers, prohibits the renewal of membership of the boards for more than two terms,[93] and provides for the formation of a general assembly for each chamber that should include all registered members in the different branches.[94]

The failure of the chambers and the federation to promote and protect the interest of its members is reflected in the level of affiliation and the degree of members' participation in the chambers' affairs. For example, whereas member-ship in these chambers is compulsory, in the sense that all business firms of whatever size are obliged to register in the chamber to which they are designated prior to the opening of their business, it is not uncommon to find many business firms actually functioning without being registered with the chambers, while others may register long after they start their businesses.[95] Although fines are levied on these members, they are not enormous.

The low level of participation in the elections of the chambers' boards of directors also reflects the degree of apathy and alienation of the members. In 1987, for example, electoral turnout in the strongest chambers of Cairo, Alexandria and Giza governorate did not exceed 10, 7, and 8 per cent respectively.[96]

Another reflection of members' lack of belief in the chambers' ability to reflect their demands and protect their interests is the separation of some branches from the main chamber and their formation of an independent separate organisation. The Egyptian Co-operative for Construction and Building Contractors formed in

1987 as a result of the separation of the contractors who felt that the chamber did not protect their interests, is one such example. There have also been discussions about the formation of an alternative federation for producers and another for the merchants, especially since these groups do not feel that their interests are protected by the federation of the chambers because of the chambers' weakness and lack of unity.[97]

B) The Federation of Egyptian Industries

The Federation of Egyptian Industries was formed in 1922 with the aim of protecting the interests of native industry and assisting the government in planning industrial policy. The Federation played an active role in protecting the interests of Egyptian industrialists against foreign competition and in demanding legislation for the development of industry, and also agrarian reform before 1952. It continued to represent the interests of the industrial bourgeoisie until Nasser's nationalisation policies of 1961.[98] The structure of the federation was in continuous flux with the different policies initiated by the regime. Under Nasser's nationalisation policy the Federation changed from being a committee which guided the business of the wealthy bourgeoisie into an agency of the Ministry of Industry. After nationalisation, the federation was re-organised around fewer chambers, whose number were reduced to twenty in 1958, thirteen in 1967, and finally twelve in 1972. Under Nasser, a mixed system of appointment and election was adopted to balance public and private sector interests. However, all the Federation's presidents have been from the public sector, while two have been former Ministers of Industry, and one was promoted to the ministerial post while serving as the Federation's president.

Since 1972, with Sadat's policy shifting towards privatisation, the private sector has been given prominent representation on the Federation's board. The board of directors now consists of twenty members, of which thirteen are elected and seven members, including the president, are appointed. Five of the appointed members are public officials, including the Deputy Ministers of Trade and Industry and the head of the Industrial Development Bank. Two of the appointed members also represent the private sector including one industrialist, beside the president of the federation. Of the elected members, only two represent the public sector, the heads of the steel and the petroleum chambers. Eleven members represent affiliated chambers with equal votes, despite the variation in contribution of the various sectors to overall employment and production. Each chamber is also represented by a private businessman.

In dealing with the private sector, the Federation has developed a dualistic attitude towards business industrialists. Whereas it emerged as the vigorous advocate of major industrialists, defending their right to a larger market share along with state and foreign enterprises, as well as their access to guaranteed and subsidised inputs, it adopted a more regulatory role towards smaller labour intensive businesses and workshops,[99] helping the government to expand its list of essential commodities which are subject to price and quality control.[100]

The federation is also pushing to the fore proposals that tend to erode what is left of the Nasserist socialist policies provided to support workers. It strives for the abolition of workers' participation in management and profit-sharing and has sought to undermine job security.[101]

In siding with large industrialists vis-à-vis small business and workers, the Federation has

> provided the business community with a ready-made mixed commission for reshaping industrial policy in close consultation with the state's key bankers, planners, and economic ministers. The federation's system of proportional representation aided (large)[102] private manufacturers not only in recapturing their original associations but also in penetrating government agencies that had become indifferent or hostile to their interests.[103]

The Federation has also been useful to Mubarak's regime in acting as a buffer between government and various other interests and in relieving conflicts between private, public and foreign businesses. The slow, step-by-step measures taken by the Federation to promote the interests of large industrialists are annoying to many businessmen, especially those who have access to foreign capital and technology and more ambitious plans, hence their attempts to create their own specialised and autonomous associations.[104]

C) The Autonomous Businessmen Associations

The changes in economic policy orientation in the mid seventies and the shift from socialism to capitalism and from nationalism to pluralism gave important signals to various business groups, who were eager to seize the new opportunities and reap the benefits of the new era.

The weakness of the Chambers of Commerce and the Egyptian Federation of Industries led some businessmen to form independent associations for the promotion and protection of their interests. These can be divided into two groups: the first includes those associations that are purely indigenous, such as: the Egyptian Businessmen's Association, and the Alexandria Businessmen's Association, also known as the Alexandria Economic Committee for Businessmen. The second includes joint Egyptian-American associations, like the Egyptian-American Businessmen's Association, the American Chamber of Commerce, and the Egyptian-American Presidential Council.

The Indigenous Businessmen Association

The Egyptian Businessmen's Association

Founded in 1982, after a meeting between Mubarak and the Egyptian American Businessmen's Committee, the Egyptian Businessmen's Association started with a loan provided by the binational Egyptian-American businessmen's committee with whom it shared the same headquarters. Gradually, the Association started to develop its own staff and branches dealing with government agencies and foreign investors.[105] By January 2000 the Association had four hundred and fifty members,[106] who were also considered Egypt's top businessmen in terms of economic wealth and political connections. While full membership in the association is limited solely to businesses in the private sector, associate membership is permitted for high level executives in the public sector. Among the associate members there are a number of previous and current government officials. Each member pays an annual membership fee. In addition, certain fees are collected by the Association from the foreign committees with which it operates.

The economic activities of the members are distributed among the different sectors as follows: 28 per cent in foreign trade (mainly importation of consumer goods), 17 per cent in food processing, textile manufacturing, furniture and cosmetics, and the remaining 55 per cent in the construction, consultation and advertising sectors as well as in tourism and transport.[107] These percentages clearly reflect that most of the investments of Egyptian businessmen are in consumer rather than productive sectors of the economy.

The Association has on several occasions played a vital role in turning economic policies to its own advantage. Two such incidents can be cited here. The first occurred in 1983/84 when, during a meeting with the Minister of Energy, the Businessmen's committee was able to extract exemption from a 20 per cent annual rise in electricity prices for three types of private industry: firms that produced for export, firms that produced for the local market while having potential for export, and firms that produced only for local markets but had a special permission from the Ministry of finance to be exempted from the rise in electricity prices.[108] The Association also played a leading role in 1985 in defeating decrees issued by Mustafa al-Said, the Minister of Economy. These decrees aimed at combating the black economy. This was done by giving the central bank full control over foreign exchange through its ability to determine exchange rates and the cancellation of the existing system of importation while substituting it with an importation system using local currency. The decrees[109] were, however, opposed by top governmental figures, leading members in the NDP,[110] the Wafd Party and the business community, who wanted a currency exchange rate determined by market forces. A fierce campaign started against the Minister and his family, who were alleged to have had dealings with black marketeers. The campaign ended only with the resignation of the Minister and the cancellation of the decrees.

The advent of Ali Lotfy's government signified a closer understanding between the government and businessmen. This was epitomised by the Prime Minister's formation of a joint committee between the government and the business community.[111] The committee included two vice-prime ministers, five ministers and fourteen businessmen. The formation of this committee, however, led to criticism of the Businessmen's Association, which was represented by eleven out of the fourteen members in the committee, against only three members representing the larger number of small and medium businesses. Conflict thus intensified between the Association and the chambers of commerce and of industry, which protested to the Prime Minister, asking for a review of the committee members and its restriction to the legal organisations that represented the majority of businessmen. At the same time, another conflict started between the Businessmen's Association and the trade unions, who were alarmed by the formation of this joint government-businessmen committee. Amid all the accusations directed towards the committee, the government embarked on defending both the committee and the Egyptian Businessmen's Association,[112] reflecting the state's intention to strengthen its ties with a privileged minority at the expense of the majority. The government strategy of co-operation with top businessmen continues at present time to generate

> resentment among business groups that continue to feel neglected by the government or that are threatened by its concessions to their more favoured rivals.[113]

In creating such conflict and rivalry among the business community and in tying the interests of their elite with its own, the state ensures the fragmentation of the business community and keeps the power of the wealthiest among them within check, thus preventing their evolution into a strong autonomous pressure group.

The Alexandria Businessmen Association
(The Alexandria Economic Committee for Businessmen)

The Alexandria Businessmen Association was formed in 1983, emerging from under the wing of the Alexandria Chamber of Commerce. In order to avoid any conflict with the chamber, the Association continues to affiliate itself with it and to emphasise that it is one of the committees of the Alexandria Chamber[114] and hence the name "The Alexandria Economic Committee for Businessmen".

The Association included up till January 2000 340 members of the top businessmen in Alexandria.[115] The economic activities of most of the members are in the foreign trade sector. The Association shares the same objectives with the Egyptian Businessmen's Association and the other business groups. Like their counterparts in Cairo, the Alexandria Businessmen depended on their personal contact with the decision makers and in this connection they have organised several meetings and conferences to which various ministers and the Prime Minister have been invited.

The Political Activities and Culture of the
Indigenous Businessmen and their Associations

The political activities of both associations were, however, completely different, as reflected by their participation in the 1987 elections. Whereas the Egyptian Businessmen's Association rejected affiliation to any political party and announced their desire to keep out of politics, the Alexandria Businessmen had among their members seventeen belonging to the NDP. No doubt the presence of these members strengthens relations and facilitates communications with the executive apparatus.

Moreover, the fact that in the 1987 elections, eight out of these seventeen were nominated on the NDP list and they all won, thus gaining seats in Parliament, strengthen the Association's tie with the legislature.[116] The 1995 elections witnessed an increase in the number of businessmen nominees, when fifty of Egypt's top businessmen contested the elections. Eighteen of these were nominated on the NDP list, ten on the Wafd party list, one on the Liberal party list and twenty-one contested the elections as independents.

The following table shows the distribution of the businessmen nominees among the different governorates.

The 1995 Parliament also witnessed an increase in the representation of businessmen, where of those fifty contesting the elections, thirty-six won. With one appointed by the President, their total number in Parliament reached thirty-seven out of 454 members representing 8.15 per cent of the total.[117] In the 2000 elections 25 business tycoon have managed to win seats in Parliament, a figure that exceeded the total number of the winning candidates of all opposition parties.[118] Yet despite this considerable representation, it has been noticeable that businessmen have failed to form a lobby independent of the government.

A series of recent studies conducted by the sociology department in Cairo University found out that 98.5 of Egyptian Businessmen prefer not to have their own party and that 70 per cent prefer to stay out of politics. It was also found that even those who do contest elections still retain the habit of maintaining close relations with the state and are reluctant to take any independent initiative.[119] Tahsin Bashir's comment on the Egyptian Business community was indeed true when he remarked,

> I don't think private business has yet crystallised a concept which will make a bigger role possible. All they want is more tax holidays. They have not developed a political culture on their own.[120]

Besides the previously mentioned indigenous businessmen's associations a number of joint associations involving Egyptian and American, Japanese and

Table 6.2 The distribution of businessmen nominees in the 1995 elections among the governorates

Governorate	Number of Nominees
Cairo	13
Al Sharqiya	6
Port Said	6
Al Qaliubiya	5
Al Dakahliya	4
Al Monoufia	4
Alexandria	3
Souhag	3
Kafr al Sheik	2
Al Suez	2
Al Gharbiya	2
Total	50

Source: *Al-Intikhabat al-Barlamaniya Fi Misr 1995*, Centre for Political & Strategic Studies, p. 86.

more recently British businessmen have been set up. Perhaps the most important of these, are the joint Egyptian-American businessmen's associations, due to the prominent role played by the USA as Egypt's main provider of loans and the party whose approval is vital for the IMF's rescheduling of debts, both in economic as well as foreign policy orientation. Among these associations are the Egyptian-American Businessmen's Association, the American Chamber of Commerce, and the Egyptian-American Presidential Council.

The Joint Businessmen Associations

The Egyptian-American Businessmen's Association

The Egyptian-American Businessmen's Association was established in 1975 following an agreement between Sadat and Nixon, and its main objective was to encourage investment in Egypt and support economic co-operation between Egypt and the USA.[121]

The American Chamber of Commerce

The Chamber received approval from Sadat for its formation during his visit to Washington in 1981. It was, however, officially formed in 1982 under Mubarak, who gave it his blessing.[122]

The Chamber had 950 members up till January 2000,[123] some of whom are also members in the Egyptian Businessmen's Association and the Egyptian-American Businessmen's Association. In 1986, the chamber extended membership to public sector companies.[124] The importance of the American Chamber of Commerce lies in the role it plays as the official representative of private sector during the negotiations over aid provided to Egypt, which is the main reason for the repeated visits and meetings between the chamber and Congressmen.[125]

The Egyptian-American Presidential Council

The Egyptian-American Presidential Council was officially formed in 1995 on the initiative of Mubarak and Vice-President Gore. The Council consists of thirty businessmen, fifteen American and fifteen Egyptian. Of the fifteen Egyptian businessmen, six are in prominent positions. Among these six, some famous names appear like that of the millionaire Ibrahim Kamel president of a company, Shafiq Gabr the president of the Egyptian-American Chamber of Commerce, Muhammad Farid Khamis, the president of another company and the head of the Egyptian Federation of Industry,[126] and Gamal Mubarak, son of president Mubarak and the executive manager of a group of investment companies. The Council's main objective is "To give advice to the Egyptian President and the American Vice-President concerning the necessary procedures to improve investment and trade between both countries"

The Council, however, works on two dimensions the first in conducting feasibility studies for investment projects, and second in providing recommendations on public policies. It is this capacity of the Presidential Council that has caused concern, since most of these recommendations concentrate on the elimination of the remaining subsidies,[127] a measure which keeps increasing the economic burden on the already suffering masses, and on the privatisation of all sectors in Egypt. The majority of businessmen themselves are not happy with the Council since they do not enjoy the same wealth and proximity to the President. A leading political magazine has accused the Council of using Mubarak's name to sanction several projects and to gain unconditional access to economic resources, and has raised the question of whether these fifteen men are the actual hidden government.[128]

D) Business and the Business Community: An overview

Reference was made earlier to the privileged treatment that a small segment of the business community receives from the government in order to tie their interests to the state and to fragment the business community through the ensuing conflict among businessmen. The by-product of this strategy is the creation of market conditions, which ignore the government's economic

174

development plans. For example, instead of a free economy based on competition and market forces, which is the main aim of economic reform, what actually exists in Egypt is either monopoly or oligopoly protected by top governmental officials. Ten to fifteen businessmen in Egypt dominate the whole economy including foreign aid. They form a kind of a "key club" to which the entrance of other businessmen is prohibited, much to the frustration and dismay of the less wealthy and less connected businessmen.[129] Once the economy is divided and it becomes known how many will be controlling a certain activity within a particular sector, a sort of cartel is formed to prevent competition and limit entrance to the market. Small businessmen who are granted access to these markets have to abide by the rules set by these cartels otherwise they face what a caricature in a prominent political magazine has called "economic assassination".[130] The protection of these is attributed to alleged corruption by senior governmental officials "including the sons of the President – who insinuate themselves into business deals merely to collect huge commissions."[131] In short Sadat's and Mubarak's liberalisation policy has created a politico-economic system which can be labelled "crony capitalism". As explained by Sadowsky,

> In such a system businessmen and bureaucrats ally in cabals to seek mutual benefit by influencing the pattern of state intervention in the economy. They do not peg the allocation of state-created rents to the performance or productivity of recipient enterprises, so the system augments personal profits and private power without promoting national economic development.[132]

3. Conclusion

Historical events, the failure of the communist movement to strike roots with the workers, the weakness of labour unions and the paternalistic policies that different regimes have adopted towards labour, have created a fragmented state-dependent labour movement, resulting in a lack of class consciousness and collective action among Egyptian workers. As such, conflict in interests between workers and other segments in the society, especially that of businessmen, does not manifest itself within the context of class antagonism, but rather in antagonism towards the authoritarian state, and hence workers' protests directed towards state symbols. In its course of domesticating workers, the state has replaced the classical corporatist formula previously adopted under Nasser with a mixture of coercion and a tighter type of corporatism, which has been labelled here as *co-integrationism*, whereby interests of top union leaders are integrated into the system through special privileges granted to them in return for supporting the regime and its oppressive policies. Such policy fragments the labour movement through the separation of rank and file and through rendering official labour organisations unrepresentative. The same policy is applied to businessmen, where

175

a narrow segment of the business community is integrated, in the same way, into the system. State's policy towards the business community creates dissent and factionalisation among businessmen, prevents their unity, and the development of an alternative political culture or ideology to challenge state hegemony. The fragmentation of both labour and businessmen results in low labour productivity and the creation of market conditions, which ignore the government's developmental plans. Thus in weakening the society, the Egyptian state places limitations on its own power.

CHAPTER SEVEN

The Local System in Egypt
A Blocked Avenue for Participation and Representation

1. Introduction

The local system of government found in any country is but a reflection of the general political indoctrination and practices of the government at the national level. To the extent that the latter is representative and tends to share power democratically, political decentralisation would naturally occur at the local level.

Having examined the national political system in chapter 3, this chapter analyses the local government system in Egypt and places it within the context of national politics.

Since the terms 'local administration' and 'local government' had been constantly appearing and disappearing within the various laws that have tended to regulate the Egyptian local system, it is crucial at this point to differentiate between them. Local administration had been defined by some authors as one form of deconcentration,

> in which all subordinate levels of government within a country are agents of central authority, usually the executive branch. Regions, provinces, districts, municipalities and other units of government are headed by leaders who are either appointed by or are responsible directly to a central government agency, usually a Ministry of the Interior or Local Government. Local functions are performed under the technical supervision and control of central ministries and the heads of the local administrations serve at the pleasure of the nation's chief executive.[1]

A system of local government, on the other hand, is a form of devolution and it tends to acquire specific characteristics. Hill provides us with a simple definition when he sates that, "Local government is about the provision of services to local people in the locality through an elected council served by a staff or professional".[2] Stanyer emphasises this aspect of election when he differentiates between directly and indirectly elected local authorities in what he terms primary and secondary local government.[3] Hicks emphasises three aspects of local government viz: localisation, efficiency, and democracy.

177

I use these words because they seem to me to contain the kernel of the whole matter; local because the system of government must be close to the common people and their problems, efficient because it must be capable of managing the local services in a way which will help to raise the standard of living and democratic because it must not only find a place for the growing class of educated men but at the same time command the respect and support of the mass of the people.[4]

Thus local government encompasses such concepts as political decentralisation, local autonomy, democracy and popular participation.

The need for creating a representative, autonomous local government stems from the fact that,

there is a need in society for civic consciousness and for political maturity if programmes for both the locality and the state are going to be carried through adequately with enthusiasm, and in fact, in some cases, without outbreaks of violence. This spread of political maturity should bring with it, through popular participation a responsive government which translates needs into policies, which can harness local energies because it is a popular government and which is accountable by periodically having to show results for its activities.[5]

It is within the boundaries of this differentiation between local administration and local government that the local system in Egypt should be analysed.

2. Historical Background

It is no wonder in a hydraulic country like Egypt, with a long history of foreign occupation, that centralisation and concentration of power have been a deep rooted tradition, whereas the devolution of power is still young and weak.

Such is the case; political considerations have always played a prime role in shaping the local system and defining the central-local relationship and they will continue to do so. The emergence of local administration goes back to the French invasion in 1798. Although the French occupation did not last more than three years, it exposed the Egyptians for the first time to western civilisation, and the admiration they developed for the French culture drove some to complete their education in France.

The infiltration of French culture into Egypt was clearly manifested in the organisation of society on the lines of the French administration with its hierarchical arrangements of the prefect, sub-prefect, cantonal officer and the mayor. In 1826, Egypt was subdivided into a four-tier hierarchical system of departments (mudiriyah), arrondissments (markez), cantons (quism) and communes (villages).[6] This administrative reform was introduced by Mohamed Ali, who wanted a clear hierarchy of power leading directly to him. He thus made the village directly linked to the governors, who in turn reported directly to him. The sole aim of the system of local administration was to increase agricultural production and facilitate the collection of taxes to finance his industrialisation drive.[7]

Shortly after the British occupation in 1882, and upon the advice of the Dufferin Report, provincial councils were established. They consisted of twenty indirectly elected members headed by the prefect. The councils, however, had very limited consultative power and were subordinated to the central administration.[8]

The provinces were headed by a governor or a director under the supervision of the Ministry of the Interior at the centre. However, although the governor was charged with the supervision and direction of government activities in his area of jurisdiction, most of the decisions were made by the central ministries. Employees for the different provinces were centrally appointed and the main function of provincial government headed by the governors, remained as basic as the maintenance of peace and order and the collection of taxes.[9] At the village level, Wickwar notes that,

> no efforts were made to ensure the educative supervision of village chiefs in any but functional fields, nor would this have been easy in view of the downgrading of the perfectoral system. No steps were taken towards making village chiefs answerable to any organs of village-life level democracy. Nor was there any easily available system of administrative justice for ensuring that the rule of the law should accompany a necessary deconcentration and decentralisation of power.[10]

This policy, however, enabled the British to tighten their grip on the country as a whole and they were reluctant to devolve any substantial amount of power to the localities, for fear of creating contending power centres that might challenge or jeopardise their very existence. The concentration of power is thus a logical outcome. As Baer comments, "In Egypt the British occupation did away with the large autonomy which rural notables had enjoyed in time of Ismail."[11]

In the first half of the twentieth century, Egypt was divided into fourteen provinces, each headed by a high-ranking police officer known as a Mudir (Governor). The provinces in turn were subdivided into several districts, each headed by another police officer with the rank of colonel. Each district was composed of fifty to seventy villages, each of which had a mayor ('Umda) appointed for life by the central government at the suggestion of the governor. The main task of the Mudir, district head or the 'Umda was simply the maintenance of law and order and the execution of the central government orders.[12]

The idea of regional decentralisation had started around 1910, but it was again dictated by political considerations rather than any genuine interest by the authorities in developing and encouraging popular participation. It is important here to describe the general political atmosphere prevalent throughout the country, which triggered this interest in providing the provinces with a degree of decentralisation and representation.

In 1881, the first revolt in the modern history of Egypt took place under Colonel Urabi, marking the beginning of Egyptian nationalism. From that time on and until the Saad Zaghloul revolution in 1919, Egyptian nationalist feeling increased and there was increasing resentment against both the British and the Palace. Thus, in an attempt to "win over an emergent indigenous rural middle class of land owning notables 'al-a'yan'",[13] the principle of representation by local councils came to the fore and was officially included in the electoral bill for these local councils in 1913.[14] This principle was embodied in the 1923 constitution which laid down the basis of a modern system of local government, since it included the establishment of provinces, cities and villages as local government units with separate identities.

The organisation of the provincial and municipal councils was defined by Article 133 of the 1923 constitution, according to which, provincial and municipal councils were to be elected bodies and local policies formulated and executed after prior approval by the central authorities. Their budgets and final accounts were to be published and they were to hold sessions open to the public. However, the legislative and executive branch of the central government held the right to veto a council's actions and decisions, if they were found to endanger national interest.[15]

Despite the limitations imposed on the sovereignty of the councils, at that time these measures were a positive step towards the creation of a more representative system of local government. However, the results were disappointing. On the one hand, it took ten years for the necessary legislation to be promulgated and on the other, the few existing village councils were bound by fiscal and legal limitations. As one author has commented,

> In the meantime, throughout the countryside, the Umda and the Sheikh El Balad, the mayor and the village headman, the traditional representatives of the localities at their lowest echelons, the 'grass-roots', continued to exercise their influence as the agents of the capital and as its executive organs in their constituencies.[16]

The 1934 Law

The 1934 law provided for the establishment of Mudiriyah councils (provincial councils) which included both ex-officio and elected members. The former represented the Ministries of Finance, Agriculture, Public Health, Public Works, Education and Communications. In total these numbered seven appointed members.

Each council had between five and thirty-two elected members. Electoral districts were each represented by two members, so that elected members numbered between ten and sixty-four. An elected member, however, had to meet certain criteria, including being an Egyptian citizen, at least thirty years of age, and literate. He had also to be a resident of the electoral district and own agricultural land within the province on which he paid tax of at least 30£E, except in the case of Aswan province.[17] If the candidate had a college or high school certificate, the tax requirement was reduced to one third or 10£E. The law also prevented members being dual representatives by prohibiting a member of the provincial council from simultaneously being a member of a municipal council, nor could membership of a council be combined with any position in civil service.

Members of the council were not paid salaries, but the government was responsible for covering their expenses. Membership was for a five year fixed term and members were eligible for re-election. The council could be dissolved only by a royal decree, which had to state the reasons for the dissolution. In such cases another council was to be appointed by the Ministry of the Interior.

The law also determined the authority of the council. Originally the council was authorised to collect taxes on land not exceeding 8 percent of state tax, two-thirds of which was to be assigned to education, twenty per cent to health, and the rest to general expenditure. The approval of the central government was, however, required in certain circumstances, including exceeding the 8 per cent tax limit on land, establishing any other tax in addition to a state tax, dispensing with any of the council's rights, in money or property, establishing or administering any public utility, and contracting a loan or undertaking any commitment that would be charged to a succeeding budget or budgets. The budget was subject to the approval of the Ministry of the Interior, which also gave approval to accounts and to the acceptance of donations.[18] It is quite obvious that the 1934 law was designed to ensure substantial central government control over local councils. The main function of the council – like that of the governor prior to this legislation – was the collection of taxes and the provision of public services. Decision-making by the councils remained greatly restricted and was subject to central approval.

The execution of central policies continued in the long-established tradition and this was strengthened by the foreign occupation. Although this tendency on the part of the central government can be explained, especially in the light of the historical, traditional and political conditions that had prevailed in Egypt for centuries, the reluctance of the local notables to obtain more autonomy from the centre seems paradoxical. As one author notes,

> Parliamentary debates on the 1934 legislation illustrate the paradox where local magnates actually argued in favour of perpetuating a pattern of dependency on the central government, at a moment when the latter was willing in face of financial pressures to relinquish a part of its control.[19]

Abu Fadl explained this reluctance on the part of the local notables to accept more power and autonomy from the centre as being due to their fear of increased responsibility and accountability. However, this explanation is not wholly convincing. A more logical interpretation would attribute their reluctance not so much to their fear of increased responsibility and accountability, but to a wish to protect their economic well-being. Bearing in mind that their cotton trade depended to a large extent on the central government and the British, their behaviour could be explained in terms of protecting their economic interests.

The 1944 Law

In 1944 a new law was passed dealing with all municipal and village councils, except those of Cairo and Alexandria. Under this law all existing councils were to be considered municipal councils and the areas they covered as municipalities, unless the Minister of Public Health should state otherwise. The population in towns and villages where municipal councils were to be established had to be 15,000 or more. Nevertheless, the Minister of Public Health could, at his discretion, allow the establishment of such councils in areas with a lower population. Membership of these councils again combined elected and appointed candidates. The number of the elected members was decided by the Minister of Public Health and usually ranged between ten and eighteen members. The appointed members were ex-officio representing the Ministries of Public Health, Public Works, Social Affairs and Finance. The council was headed by a president, who was the Mudir or the Muhafez in the province, or the Ma'mur, who was the chief police officer in the town. Members of the council elected a vice-president and, in some councils, an administrator could be appointed either to one council or to a group of councils.

Candidates for membership had to be at least 25 years of age, literate and owners of a house or place of business which should have a rental value of not less than 2£E per year or be subject to an annual built-up property tax of at least 2£E. Members of the council could not be members of other councils and their term of office was four years, subject to renewal. Members were not paid salaries, although they were paid expenses, and the council operated through various committees for public health, public works, social affairs, transportation, and finance.

The law also laid down criteria for the electorate who, according to Article 3, had to possess minimum financial qualifications, including ownership of a dwelling in the town or village, or residence in a building there for at least one year prior to the election time.

The functions of the Municipal Council

The functions of a municipal council included some which were of a compulsory nature and others, which were voluntary. In the first category fell such tasks as the construction, maintenance, lighting and clearing of roads, water supply, removal of refuse, fire fighting, and the establishment and operation of slaughter houses. The second category includes such duties as the provision of gas and electricity, drainage and sewers, provision for orphanages, hospitals, public baths, public washing places, markets, the regulation of sale of food, exhibitions, libraries, theatres, clubs and local transport.

The council also enforced the laws and regulations concerning buildings, open land, etc. within its area of jurisdiction. In addition, and with the approval of the Minister of Public Health, the council could assume other responsibilities. For example, Articles 21 and 23 of the law granted the council the right to levy taxes on stores, vehicles, theatres, markets, animals such as dogs, fishing boats and the use of the seashore. It could also impose fees for the use of public utilities and for building licences. The council could also be given a share of the taxes collected by the government within its area of jurisdiction. However, there were certain circumstances specified by law in which the approval of the Minister of Public Health was required before the council could make any decision. These included any important change to the water system or the supply of electricity.

The minister's approval was also required for any project that cost more than 500£E, even if the project was included in the budget. In such cases, if a decision was not made by the minister within two months, the council could consider it as approved. The council had to submit a draft of its budget to the Minister of Public Health, who in turn referred it to an advisory committee, which included the Under-secretary of State for Public Health as the chairman, the Director General of Municipalities, the Director of Municipal and Village Health Departments and representatives of the Ministries of Interior, Social Affairs, Education, Communications, Public Works and Finance. Although the responsibility of this committee was to review the draft budget, the final approval of the budget was made by the Minister of Public Health. The Cabinet in the central government could, at the request of the Minister of Public Health, dissolve the council, in which case new elections had to take place within three months.

In 1950 a Ministry of Municipal and Rural Affairs was established and took over all the responsibilities and authority of the Ministry of Public Health. At the same time the role assigned to the Municipal Council in education was transferred to the Ministry of Education, along with that of the total tax revenue assigned to education.[20]

Most of the council functions were greatly constrained and subject to central government approval and usually municipalities depended for their finance on an allocation from the centre. It can thus be concluded that until 1952, representation and popular participation at the local level was never very high on the government's agenda and in practice local government was largely subordinate to central government.

3. The Local System under Nasser

Following the 1952 coup, more efforts were directed towards the provinces in an attempt to establish a new system of local administration. Out of political necessity, the Junta had from the outset expressed a special interest in the countryside, triggered first by their desire to destroy the power of the large landowners who represented a political threat to their rule, and second by the need to gain support among the rural masses to legitimise the new regime. Accordingly, an agrarian reform law and several other measures were introduced. For example, in 1954 local councils were granted 1.2 million pounds from the state's income from taxation by the central government. In 1955, Law No. 66 specified yet another additional tax resource for local authorities, the result of which was the increase of local revenues to a yearly average of 5 million pounds between 1952 and 1957, which improved the quality of services provided in the rural areas. It facilitated, for example, the installation of water and electricity supplies, implementation of housing and health projects and other local services.[21]

At the same time a study group was set up to discuss such issues as popular participation within the boundaries of the regime's commitment to national development planning. The recommendations of this group were largely embodied in the new constitution of 1956 (the junta having earlier suspended the 1923 constitution), which sought to strike a balance of power between central and local authorities. Significantly, this constitution also included articles discussing local administration.[22] Articles 157–166 of the constitution established local authorities and defined their powers, composition, and functions. Article 157 of the constitution divided the republic into administrative units. Article 158 provided each unit with an elected council,[23] although it retained the appointed members.[24] Article 159 gave the councils broad powers for the establishment and management of local services and public utilities.[25] Article 161 specified the nature of local revenues, which should initially be derived from local taxes and duties. Article 162 assigned to central government the responsibility of providing the local units with the necessary administrative, technical and financial assistance. Article 163 facilitated joint administrative responsibilities between different units with independent jurisdictions. Article 164 specified the borders within which decision-making became the ultimate prerogative of local councils, and alternatively the circumstances in which the approval of the central minister is required. Article 165 dictated that the work of the local councils was to be supervised according to the rules and regulations embodied in the law. Article 166 preserved the right of the President of the Republic both to dissolve the councils and to establish temporary ones.[26]

The 1956 constitution clearly highlights the contradictory trends, which it established. Whereas it emphasised local administration, it strengthened the grip of the central government on the local units to such an extent that it made little provision for local autonomy or even initiative. A closer look at the articles of the constitution reveals the extent of subordination of the local units to the central authorities. First of all, the appointed elements in the local councils inhibited freedom of expression and discussion of sensitive policy issues by the elected members, thus undermining the concept of the independence of local councils. Nasser wanted to ensure the subordination of the nation at all levels to his single political organisation, and the effect of these appointed officials on decision-making within the councils was to turn the latter into a rubber stamp for the executive's decisions. Moreover, as Dr. Sayid Ghanim has commented, "One of the most important facts about this system is that it had been organically related with the National Union which was to dominate local councils", with the different committees of the NU represented from village to national level reflecting the regime's tendency towards centralist control.[27] Second, the dependence of the local units on the central government for financial and technical assistance further increased their subordination to the central authorities. Third, the conditional, semi-autonomous nature of the delegation of decision-making to local councils represented another impediment that prevented the councils from playing a leading role in policy-making and implementation.

Instead, major decisions were usually undertaken by the ministry at the centre. Fourth, the rules and regulations governing the work of local councils represented another limitation on the abilities of these councils to perform their function and bred in the members of the council fear of assuming responsibilities, which turned the local councils into passive bodies. Finally, the absolute right to dissolve these councils, which was the prerogative of the President of the Republic, eliminated any sovereign right the councils might enjoy through being elected and to a limited extent representative, and turned them into puppets that the President could toy with and eliminate at his discretion.

It can therefore be safely concluded that the 1956 constitution did not add much to the pre-1952 system of local administration. As Abu-El Fadl mentions in her comparison between the local councils that existed in the colonial period and those which originated after the 1956 constitution,

> Just as the organisation of local councils and local units had originally been conceived in a spirit of self-enlightened colonial interest, now their reorganisation in the republican era of revolution and independence was taking place at the initiative of an administrative-conscious reforming central authority. It could consequently afford to grant and withhold whatever powers it deemed adequate in the light of its conception of the national interest by way of law or policy. The grounds for negotiation and compromise did not seem to hold and any real contention for a power balance or for 'power-sharing' seemed illusory in this context.[28]

Law No. 124 of 1960

In 1960 the local administration system was reorganised by Law No. 124 of 1960, which was amended in1961 and 1964. By this law and its subsequent amendments, the United Arab Republic was divided into administrative units, namely governorates, towns and villages, each of which had a separate identity. Each of these units had an elected council empowered with broad authority and administrative responsibilities.[29] The number of administrative units created was 26 governorates, 134 cities and 4,000 villages. Three types of membership existed in the local councils: elected, selected, and ex-officio. The number of each of these categories varied with the size of the local unit: a governorate could have 4–6 elected members for every district and up to 10 appointed and 9 ex-officio, a city or town could have 20 elected members, up to 5 appointed and 6 ex-officio, and a village could have 12 elected and appointed members.[30] The elected members, however, were those members elected to the committee of the Arab Socialist Union "A.S.U." within the local unit, the appointed members were those active members of the ASU selected by the central authority, and the ex-officio members were representative of the different ministries in the local unit.[31] Thus both elected and selected members of the local councils were strictly tied to Nasser's political organisation and their presence was more a control on the localities rather than a local representation.

This central control was enhanced by the creation of a new central Ministry for Local Administration for the supervision of local units, assuming most of the pre-1960 responsibilities of both the Ministry of the Interior and the Ministry of Provincial Affairs. Whereas the former appointed the director of the directorate and was responsible for police and organisation administration, the latter was responsible for housing within the directorate and shared within the directorate and the central ministries the supervision of their field representatives. With the creation of the new Local Administration Ministry, the authority of the Ministry of the Interior was restricted to the maintenance of security – law and order – and the Ministry of Provincial Affairs became the Ministry of Housing.[32]

A closer look at the different administrative levels reveals the various authorities and responsibilities assigned to them.

The Governor

Appointed and removed by the President, the governor was the chief administrative officer and head of the governorate council. He had the status of a deputy minister with regard to salary and related personnel matters and of an under-secretary of state in administration.

He was accountable to the Minister of the Interior for security matters and reported to the Minister of Local Administration on issues related to local government. Representing the executive authority of the state, the governor was in control of all administrative personnel in the governorate, apart from judges. Accordingly, he had the right to appoint all personnel within the governorate who were up to the seventh grade. He supervised the work of the town and rural councils, and in some cases had to approve the decisions taken by them.[33] His responsibilities included the supervision of all public policy plans and all activities related to manpower including, planning, training, the development of popular political participation, and the preservation of socio-political security.[34] In his dual function as the representative of the central authority and the chief executive of the governorate and its local units, the governor resembled a French prefect.[35] Governors were recruited from a reservoir of military and police personnel and normally enjoyed a long period of office.[36] Perhaps the best description of the governor functioning under this system has been given by Heaphey, who portrays him as "an organisation man who serves as a point of communication between the central government and the local level. He is not seen as an instrumentality for political transactions, the specific outcomes of which cannot be controlled by a central government."[37]

The Governorate Council

Members of the Governorate Council were subject to the rules for the different types of membership mentioned earlier. In addition to this and in accordance with the National Charter of 1962, half of the members in the council had to be farmers and workers. This was achieved through the rules generated by the ASU.

The Governorate Council dominated both the town and the village councils and supervised their work, creating an apparent duality of subordination of town and village councils to the authority of the governor and that of the Governorate Council. The lack of any clear demarcation between these authorities was a source of potential conflict.[38]

This subordination of town and villages to the supervision and control of the governorate is described by Heaphey: "What happened formally was that a highly centralised administrative system operating through the ministries in Cairo was reorganised into a 'Governorate-Centred' system."[39]

This system was further strengthened by providing the Governorate Council with the power to take over the administration of towns and villages whose local authorities had proved deficient. Here again the similarity with the French system is striking. Although in theory the powers granted to the Governorate Councils were all-encompassing, including provision of all economic and social needs, in practice their power was tightly restricted by budget limitations and central government approvals and control. Again, it should be emphasised here that although the appointed governors controlled local authorities, the authority of the former was restricted by and subject to the central ministries' approval.

The English practice of local government also left its mark on the Egyptian local administration. This was reflected in the way the "all purpose" power of the governorate was generally expressed and seemed partly to coincide with that of the town and village councils, which was also "all purpose".[40]

The Town and Village Councils

The membership of these councils again conforms with the previously described pattern. Like the Governorate Council, both the town and village councils had in theory broad authority, but in practice they were subject to the control of the Governorate Councils, the governor and the various national ministries.[41]

The Resources of Local Councils

These were very limited and were derived from taxes collected within the local units' jurisdiction, though all locally collected taxes were handed to the central government, which allocated grants to the different units.[42]

It is obvious that the 1960 law contained many inherent weaknesses, which caused hindrances to the development of local government. However, the law has to be seen within the context of the regime's nationalist and ideological position because what takes place at the local level is simply a reflection of the policies and practices carried at the national level. First, the 1960s were the years of Nasser's drive towards nationalisation and his commitment to central planning. Since autocracy and bureaucratic centralism were the hallmark of his era, it was unlikely that it would give birth to any autonomous system of local government. As one author has commented,

> the political ideology of a given regime is bound to reflect on the concept and bearing of local government. To the extent that the government is authoritarian in outlook and conduct, or to the extent that it adopts central planning in conceiving of its developmental goals, local autonomy is likely to be affected.[43]

This tendency towards centralism was most clearly reflected in the wide authority given to the governorate over both the towns and villages, making it a kind of state in miniature.

Second, as noted in chapter 3, Nasser had an aversion for politics and politicians. To him politics and political parties implied diversity of opinion, which conflicted with his vision of a unified undifferentiated society. Accordingly his approach to government was that it should be organisational rather than participatory. His single party system was an attempt to govern and control society through tightly structured organisations. This organisational relationship towards society was reflected in the 1960 local administration law as it concerned the role of the governor. Broad responsibilities were assigned to him, but he was not given the authority necessary to build an effective relationship with both his subordinates and his superiors. Thus, the governor was in a position where he was unable to co-ordinate the diverse interests within his governorate and at the same time extract more benefits from his superiors for the people.[44] Describing this view of the Egyptian society Heaphey comments,

> With an aversion to politics and certainly with no notion of politics as functional, the doctrine can hardly entertain structural requisites of a political model. Rather than build a system in which Governors can accumulate power without violating community political norms, the Egyptian vision looks for a non-existent powerless leadership. [45]

Third, the dual role played by the governor as the head of the executive staff in the governorate (i.e. representative of the central government/and chairman of the governorate council), not only created conflict in decision-making but also tended to undermine the position of the governor and his council as representatives of the people. Furthermore, the fact that governors were appointed by the President and not elected, confirmed the view that they were the central government's men appointed to oversee localities. Owing his position and indeed his whole career to the central authority, the governor was inclined to protect national interest at the expense of local interest.

Fourth, a duality existed on the issue of representation with regard to both the ASU's committees and the local councils. For example, the elected committees of the ASU at the different levels of local units were supposed to represent the people and their needs. At the same time, the local councils in villages, towns and provinces were also supposed to reflect people's needs and their participation in local affairs. This lack of demarcation of the functions of the ASU's committees and the local councils led to confusion and conflict.[46]

Summarising Nasser's attempts to create a system of local administration more receptive to popular participation and pinpointing the reasons for their failure Auda states,

> The intent was to synchronise the strategy of functional decentralisation of services with territorial prefectoral structure and with the strategy of political cooptation of the locals through bureaucracy and the ASU. The three strategies did not mix together and produced contradictions which bred inertia into the whole system of local administration. Tensions over the boundaries of authorities, resource allocations and specification of functions ensued.[47]

These conflicts also surfaced in the state central ministries and central political decision-making process

4. The Local System under Sadat

From the outset of his presidency, Sadat gave the provinces special attention. There were two reasons for this interest.

First: Sadat was shrewd enough to recognise from the beginning the strength of the provincial elites, including the agrarian bourgeoisie, whose help he sought to oust his rivals and consolidate his power.

Second: In an attempt to redirect the economy and change it from a socialist welfare state to a liberal free-market economy, it was necessary for Sadat not only to destroy Nasser's legacy but also to discredit it. The agrarian bourgeoisie, who had suffered under Nasser, provided him with the perfect opportunity to do so. Highlighting the injustices they had suffered, including the sequestration of their land and their imprisonment and torture in jail, was a useful tool for achieving his purpose. Realising that they were potential allies, Sadat thus attempted to give these notables a share of power through the introduction of relatively more decentralised localities.

His first step was to abolish the Ministry of Local Government in 1971. Moreover, the employees in the service sectors of education, health, housing, foodstuffs and social affairs were transferred to the governorate authority. At the same time, the central public sector companies in the governorate were categorised as local and the governorate became a partner in managing the state.[48] In order to match his liberalisation policies, Sadat shifted the emphasis from transferring powers away from Cairo, to highlighting such issues as the democratisation of local structures and curbing their bureaucratic appendages. He thus replaced the title "Local Administration" in the 1960 law with "Local Government".

The permanent Constitution of 1971 reflected this trend. It called for the division of the country into administrative units that would be appropriate to these required developmental activities. In addition to the ongoing division of the local units into governorates, towns and cities, each recognised as a legal entity, the constitution provided for the possible creation of other administrative units wherever it was deemed to be in the public interest. Concerning the degree of representation of local councils, the constitution opted for the creation of directly elected popular councils and for their gradual introduction and dispersion.[49]

Law No. 57 of 1971

This new law provided for the creation of two kinds of councils in each governorate working parallel to each other. The first was to be elected and was called the people's council and the second was the executive council, working under the leadership of the governor. Whereas the former was vested with limited authority that included the supervision of certain services, the latter's power was comprehensive including the supervision o f public services as well as proposing local policies.[50]

Despite constitutional backing for the provision of the freely-elected local councils, the popular councils created by Law No. 57 of 1971 were filled with ASU officials.[51] Ayubi, accurately summarises their position:

Egypt remained up to the early seventies (and including Law No. 57 for 1971) basically administrative in nature, initiated as they were by the governmental authorities. Indeed until then, the concept of local government – as distinct from local administration – had not really been fully accepted either by the traditional rural leadership or by the central and local bureaucrats.[52]

Law No. 52 of 1975

A serious attempt towards establishing local government was accomplished through the passage of Law No. 52 of 1975. This law provided for the parallel existence of elected local councils and local executive commissions. Elected councils and executive commissions were to be found at the different levels of local units, viz.

- *Muhafaza*: which is a governorate or province.
- The *Markaz*: which is a county or a central town with a number of related villages. This unit was first introduced in 1975.
- *Madina*: which is an urban district, quarter or neighbourhood and was also introduced in 1975.
- *Qaria*: which is a village.[53]

As for the elected local councils, their members were directly elected and the chairman and deputy chairmen were to be elected by the council from among its members.

A comparison of membership qualifications laid down in Law No. 57 of 1971 and Law No. 52 of 1975 reveals a new practice in the latter which removed an important restriction on the eligibility of a candidate for the membership of the local councils as specified in the former. For example, under Article 5 of Law No. 57 of 1971 the governorate people's council was to be composed of:

- Members of the ASU governorate committee;
- Secretaries of the *Markaz* and *Quism* of ASU;
- Two representatives of the ASU youth organisation;
- Two representatives of ASU women's activities;
- Less than five members chosen at the national or local congress of ASU.

Article 75 of Law No. 52 of 1975, on the other hand, laid down the following conditions for members of local councils:

- To be an Egyptian;
- To be more than 25 years old on the election day;
- To be registered on the voters' list at a specific local unit;
- To be able to read and write well;

  – To have finished compulsory military service or to have been exempted from it.

Thus, for the first time since Nasser started experimenting with the one-party organisation, local councils were no longer dominated as they had been by first, the National Union and later the ASU. Active membership of the ASU as a requirement for the candidature of the local councils was dropped.[54] Another change introduced by the 1975 law is highlighted by Ayubi:

> Members of the local council were for the first time, given a certain element of 'immunity' that covered their statements and discussions in the councils or committees. The councils themselves could not be dissolved except in cases of extreme necessity or of grave malfunctioning and could be disbanded only through a decree from the Prime Minister, initiated by the Minister responsible for Local Government and the Ministerial Committee for Local Government.[55]

However, despite these positive innovations, some aspects of the law had negative effects on local autonomy and representation. For example, the governor retained a dominant role. Under Article 28 of the law he represented the President in his governorate and was responsible for the supervision and implementation of public policy. He also had responsibility for "Security and public morals" in conjunction with the Minister for the Interior. As head of all local organisations in the province, he supervised the activities of the different ministries and was also responsible for increasing the agricultural and industrial production within his governorate.[56] Another inherent weakness in the law was to be found in the broad role that the appointed executive council played. The fact that the governor and the head of the local units had the right to veto the decisions taken by the elected local councils represented a limitation on the ability of the latter to participate effectively in policy-making, hence lack of popular participation in decision-making. The control of the central government over local councils remained more obvious in the right of the former to authorise in advance any activities that the latter sought to undertake.[57]

Law No. 43 of 1979

Despite all its limitations and drawbacks, Law No. 52 of 1975 was a positive step towards the development of a more representative system of local government. The passing of Law No. 43 of 1979 was concomitant with Sadat's introduction of the so called "liberalisation process". Hence, it was expected to introduce an extension of the decentralisation and democratisation process that Sadat was calling for. However, the new law passed in 1979 in fact represented a severe blow to the hope of creating a more representative system of local government.

It is important here to review the various events that took place at the national level in the period 1976–78 since they are directly relevant to the passage of the 1979 law. As noted in chapter 3, Sadat had in 1976 approved the formation of political parties. The 1976 elections were contested by the three official parties created by the government.[58]

Since the New Wafd and the Muslim Brotherhood had been denied recognition, supporters of these parties had to run as independents in the elections. Despite the fact that the government party won 82 per cent of the seats, the total number of independent candidates exceeded the total number of party candidates.[59]

The fact that a large number of independent deputies managed to win seats in the People's Assembly was embarrassing to the government. These independent deputies, among whom were Nasserites, Marxists, Wafdists, and Ikhwan members, became increasingly critical of government policy and succeeded in embarrassing the government on several occasions.

It was because of the disruption caused by these independent deputies and their pressure on the government that two years later, Sadat approved the formation of the New Wafd party,[60] showing effect of a genuine opposition to government policy in the People's Assembly as early as 1976, a fact, which irritated Sadat.

The January 1977 widespread "Food Riots" added to government fears and represented yet another sign of mass discontent with its policies.

The riots took place as a result of the government decision, in compliance with IMF conditions, to eliminate subsidies on basic food items. What happened as a result was that, for the first time since the 1919 uprising, Egypt witnessed a mass upheaval that not only took place in urban areas, but spread throughout the country from Alexandria to Aswan. Popular unrest was so active and widespread that the government used the armed forces, for the first time internally since the military coup that overthrew the monarchy in 1952, to control it.[61] At the same time the Islamic Jama'at, who had been encouraged by Sadat at the beginning of his rule, were gaining support and began to resort to illegal methods. In 1977 one of these fundamentalist groups, Al-Takfir-wal-Hijra, kidnapped the minister of Awqaf and murdered him. Most of the members of these groups come from the rural areas where they maintain roots,[62] and, in addition, the sectarian conflict that they initiated between the Coptic minority and the Muslim majority was most serious in provincial cities, notably Asyut,[63] which are characterised by a concentration of the Coptic community.

Both the food riots and the violence created by the Islamic Jama'at represented a challenge to government authority in the rural areas, a fact that the regime was aware of and sought to combat through a tighter grip on the provinces. The emergence of the New Wafd as one of the strongest opposition parties and its popularity among the masses had an unsettling effect on the government and its growing support among the rural elites threatened the government's traditional support base.

Despite the fact that the New Wafd disbanded itself in 1978 because of the continuous government harassment, the whole experiment had shaken Sadat and his ruling elites. It was not surprising then that in 1979 Sadat sought to achieve two goals:

First, to secure the complete victory of the National Democratic Party in the election, he reduced the number of members of the rural elites on the candidacy list, thus curtailing their representation in the People's Assembly and increasing that of government officials and syndicate leaders.[64]

Second, to secure a tighter control on the provinces Sadat took important steps in adopting a new method of appointing governors. The first step was taken in 1978. Early in 1977, and after a long debate on whether provinces should have partisan or politically neutral governors, the government preference for having governors who should be 'politicians in the party, officials in the governorate' had won. Since this had been the choice, it was logical that the second issue of debate would revolve around whether the governor should be democratically elected or appointed. Not surprisingly, the latter point of view was the one adopted by the government. Thus early in 1978, a new practice for appointing "Indigenous Governors" from among the people was passed. Since all these governors were members of the National Democratic Party and were in 1979 to be given ministerial status and some of the powers endowed to the Prime Minister, the extent of central government control became obvious.[65]

The second step was Law No. 43 of 1979. Being promulgated by presidential decree, and just before the convening of the People's Assembly, the law ensured that ". . . in the name of decentralisation-governors (and to a lesser extent other leading officials) have been given quite extensive authorities while the local elected councils have been deprived of some of their previously held rights".[66]

Being the representative of the President in the province, the governor was responsible for the management of all public utilities within his governorate and could create new ones. He was also responsible for public security, food security and increasing the agricultural and industrial productivity within his governorate. In addition he was authorised to decide on issues concerning public land for constructions and that for agriculture and to set the rules governing land reclamation and its distribution.[67] With such broad authority vested in the governor, the new law truly "makes of the governor a dictator in his province".[68]

Membership for the local councils continued to have a 50 per cent representation of peasants and workers, with the new law also specifying a quota of seats for women. However under the new law, these councils experienced great curtailment of their powers.

First, the new law deprived the heads of committees within the elected councils of the right to participate as they had previously in the executive councils, since these heads were only to provide expertise without political dimensions.

Second, their right to "question" or investigate the governors and heads of public departments was cancelled. They can only "ask, enquire or seek information" from these officials.

Third, the governor was given the right to veto the decisions of the councils if he thought that they did not conform with the law.

Fourth, the policy-making bodies at the national level included only appointed officials, and the heads of local councils were excluded.[69] One further point to be mentioned here is that some elements of continuity from the 1960s can be clearly detected in the law, such as vesting the local head of public security with the authority to direct the executive local organs in the absence of the governor.

Sadat's liberalisation and decentralisation policy ended up with even more autocracy and centralisation. As one author has commented,

> Ironically, it seems that the more intent the central authorities appear to be in divesting themselves of their charge and in asserting the coming of age of their ward, the more effectively the reins are drawn in.[70]

5. The Local System under Mubarak

Assuming power after Sadat's assassination by the Jama'at in 1981, Mubarak started his presidency in the midst of a national political crisis caused by the failure of Sadat's economic and political liberalisation.

In order to consolidate his power, Mubarak had to act in two parallel directions. The first was, to accommodate the different political and interest groups in society, particularly the Islamic fundamentalists, whose strength was increasing and who had managed to establish solid support among the masses in general and the rural poor in particular, and the second was to ensure that these different groups were completely under the control of the state and its executive apparatus. The local administration Law No. 145 of 1988 reflected the regime's strategy to block completely all avenues of popular participation at the local level.

Law No. 145 of 1988

This law embodied most of the articles included in Law No. 43 of 1979, but with some significant alterations that reflected the regime's political manoeuvre. To begin with the law replaced the title "Local Government", which had been earlier introduced by Sadat, with the title "Local Administration".

As for the governor, this law made him the representative of the highest executive authority in his governorate, instead of being the President's representative. And since the title "Local Administration" was re-introduced, the local popular councils were, by the passing of this law, to be considered an integral part of the executive apparatus and their right to question the governor or his deputies or any of the heads of the executive councils or governmental departments was abolished.

Consequently, since these councils were to be considered part of the state apparatus, and since the governor was the highest executive authority in his governorate, this law ensured that local popular councils came under the complete control of the governor, i.e. the state machinery.[71]

Although the supreme constitutional court had, as early as 19 May 1990, ruled as unconstitutional the party list system for elections to the People's Assembly,[72] so that the government was forced to abolish this system at the national level, it was retained at the local level to strengthen the control of the government party over the local councils.

The November 1992 local council elections used the party list system, not only highlighting the contradictory nature of the elections at the national and local level, but also reflecting the evasive behaviour of the government and its contempt for both the constitution and the rule of law. In contrast, the court had also, based on the principle of equality and equal opportunities as embodied in the constitution, ruled as unconstitutional the reservation of a certain number of seats for women in the local councils, and so this article was cancelled in the 1988 law.[73]

The 1992 local council elections revealed the weaknesses of the political parties and reflected the degree of popular participation. To begin with, the competition between the political parties took place in 42 out of 2769 constituencies representing only 15 per cent of the local number of constituencies. This means that the NDP won uncontested elections in 85 per cent of constituencies.

These results exposed the weakness of the political parties and their inability to provide candidates for all the local areas. If the approximate proportions of the total vote in all contested and uncontested constituencies are calculated, it will be found that the total share of the opposition did not exceed 5 per cent, 3.5 per cent went to the Labour Party and the remaining 1.5 per cent shared between the Wafd party, the Nasserites, and the Green party. This means that the NDP won 95 per cent of the total list throughout the country. As for the independent seats, 30 per cent went to the opposition, and 70 per cent were acquired by the NDP representatives.[74]

Electoral participation in the forty-two constituencies where the political parties contested the elections was, (as the national level) extremely low, ranging from 5 per cent to 20 per cent. This apathy was attributed by political analysts to the party list system, doubts about the honesty of the election, and mistrust of candidates' integrity.[75]

However, in February 1996, the supreme constitutional court ruled the 1992 local council elections unconstitutional, leading the government to consider dissolving the councils and calling for fresh elections.[76] The result of the recent April 1997 elections, reflected a continuity in the regime's policy towards the provinces and the governing NDP won 93 per cent of the seats.[77]

The 'Ummad Law of 1994

Earlier, in March 1994, a final blow to democracy, and indeed to any hope for popular participation and representativeness at the local level, was dealt when the People's Assembly, dominated by the NDP approved the new "'Umad and Sheikh" law or what can be called, "the Mayors law", which the government had proposed in November 1993.

Under this law, the 'Umda and Sheikh who are influential both as formal and informal leaders at the village level were to be appointed instead of being elected. Ironically, the reason given by the government for the introduction of this law was "to maintain more democracy and security".[78] Thus, in the name of democracy, centralised bureaucratic autocracy is maintained and seems to be the only strategy pursued by Mubarak's regime.

6. Conclusion

In a country like Egypt, where autocratic rule, the dominant party system and the lack of avenues for popular participation continue to be features of its post 1952 rulers, it is unlikely that a representative democratic system of local government will come into existence in the foreseeable future.

What actually exists in Egypt is a system of administrative centralism which manifests itself in various ways. It includes the broad role given to the governor and his appointed executive councils, at all local levels, vis-à-vis the limited functions of the elected local councils, the latter being subordinated to the former. The tight control, which the central government exerts on provincial budgets and on decision-making at the local level makes the provinces an appendage of the central government rather than autonomous representative units. This in turn is reflected in a low local electoral turnout and hence deepens the participation crisis and contributes to the uncivicness of the society. As Tocqueville has commented,

> administrative centralisation serves to enervate the people that submit to it, because it constantly tends to diminish their civic spirit. . . . So it can contribute wonderfully to the ephemeral greatness of one man but not the permanent prosperity of a people.[79]

Thus administrative centralisation, which is one of the control tools of weak autocratic state, tends to exacerbate the weakness of the Egyptian society. With the weakness of the various political forces in the society and with avenues for participation both at the local and national level blocked, policy-making tends to become the outcome of patronage and the interplay of interest groups at the expense of the poorer segments in the society.

It is the aim of the following chapter to analyse the various policies within the agricultural sector and to explore their exploitative effects on peasants' behaviour towards the weak authoritarian state.

CHAPTER EIGHT

The State, Peasant Politics and Development

The Inherent Dilemma

1. Introduction

Development is a term that has been frequently used by many authors to describe the process of change in third world developing countries. Some of them like Spengler defines it in a general way as "when an index of what is deemed desirable increases in magnitude."[1] Others have broken down the term into different phases as economic or political development, with each phase having its own characteristic.[2] Some researchers associate development with economic growth, thus disregarding the socio-political and cultural context within which the economy functions and measuring a country's development from a quantitative perspective.

Development is an all-encompassing term. Just as a country's economic sub-system cannot be isolated from its social or political sub-systems, since they all act and interact, affect and are affected by each other, so it is with changes that may take place in any of these sub-systems. Economic change cannot be achieved in isolation, change must feed through into the whole system. Development is thus an integrated process, that entails a quantitative aspect measured by the increase in GNP or per capita income, and a qualitative aspect measured by changes in attitudes, values and behavioural norms and hence

> It should no longer be necessary to speak of economic and social development, since development as distinct from growth-should auto- matically include both. Development is growth plus change, change in turn is social and cultural as well as economic, and qualitative as well as quantitative.[3]

It is within the parameters of this definition of development that the agrarian reform and the agricultural policies of the Egyptian authoritarian state will be analysed, highlighting how such policies affect the economic welfare of the peasants, and how the latter respond to such policies. This in turn will reflect the extent to which the government succeed or otherwise fails in achieving its developmental goals.

2. The Agricultural Crisis

A) The Importance of Agriculture

Owing to its "hydraulic" nature, Egypt's economy has been and will continue to be predominantly agricultural, with all the other various aspects of economic activity, including services, transport, commerce and government still linked to agriculture. The fact that agriculture accounts for some 45–47 per cent of total employment, 30 per cent of GDP and more than 50 per cent of exports, and that more than 50 per cent of Egypt's industry consists of agricultural based activities,[4] illustrates Alan Richards' view that "if agriculture flags, Egypt falls".[5]

B) The Economic Reality of the Problem

Egypt has an area of 386.000 square miles, of which only 2.5 per cent is cultivable. In 1897 the cultivated area was 7 million feddans[6] with a population of only 10 million. The per capita share of harvested land was thus seven tenths of one feddan. In 1970, however, and although the cultivated area had increased to 10 million feddans, an increase in population of over 200 per cent caused the per capita share to drop to less than three tenths of one feddan.[7]

With such a rapid increase in population, roughly a million people every nine months, the economic problem that faces Egypt stems from the fact that the national food production fails to meet the demand of the population.[8]

The fact that Egypt's population is now 65 million, and is expected to exceed 75 million in the year 2000, serves only to aggravate the problem. Egypt has thus become one of the most food dependent countries in the world. In 1988 Egypt produced only 22 per cent of its food needs. The remaining 78 per cent was imported, including 32 per cent of the country's sugar consumption, 78 per cent of its wheat, 79 per cent of its cooking oil, and all of its tea.

Translated into per capita figures, the degree of dependency looks even more dramatic. For example, for each of its citizens Egypt imported 180 kilograms of wheat, surpassed only by Japan, which imports 223 kilograms per person, but lacking, of course, Japan's wide industrial base and large trade surplus.[9] In 1985 Egypt's food imports amounted to £E2.1 billion, which exceeded Egypt's earning from petroleum exports (£E1.8 billion) and was more than four times the total value of its agricultural exports (£E475 million).[10] Despite the crucial role that agriculture plays in the Egyptian economy, it has been neglected in favour of industry, most notably at the end of the sixties and during the seventies, with agriculture's share of the total investment declining from 20 per cent in the mid sixties to 8 per cent in 1976.[11] The failure to increase the cultivable area through land reclamation, coupled with the loss in agricultural land to urban growth estimated to be 40,000 acres a year, represents another obstacle that adds to the economic problem of agriculture in Egypt.[12] A closer examination of the growth performance of Egyptian agriculture may however, highlight the ominous nature of the picture.

Yields of all major crops, as well as per capita resources in food grains have stagnated since the middle 60s.[13] Measuring the output per capita between 1960 and 1974, Radwan concludes that

after a modest increase in the index of output per capita during the 1960's a slow but steady decline began by the early 1970.[14]

This reflects the effect of a slow growth of total output of 2 per cent per year combined with a population growth rate of 2.5 per annum. Thus agriculture expansion, which was needed to introduce a sort of balance in the economy for the acceleration of development, was not achieved.[15] It is not surprising that Egypt has developed such a heavy dependency on food importation. As Weinbaum has noted,

Egypt, which purchased abroad 7 per cent of its foodstuff in 1961, saw its imports increase to one-fifth of national requirement a decade latter. Though as late as 1974, the country maintained a favourable net agricultural balance, by 1981–1982 shipments of agricultural products from all foreign sources accounted for one-half of the total domestic food consumption.[16]

The first five year plan starting in 1960, aimed at increasing the country's exports, which depended mainly on cotton. However, this was not achieved, due to the cotton weevil, on one hand, and fierce competition from other cotton exporting countries (such as Sudan) on the other. Accordingly, Egypt's cotton exports – the main source of foreign currency – failed to increase from 1960–1972, and produced a severe deficit in the balance of payments,[17] which has continued to increase. In 1983, for example Egypt's imports amounted to £E6750 million, while its exports were only £E3788 million, with the traditional exports of cotton and textiles occupying only fifth position among sources of foreign exchange. Egypt's agricultural exports, including cotton, did not earn more than $600 million for the same year.[18]

3. Agrarian Policy from Nasser to Mubarak

A thorough analysis of the various agrarian policies is needed in order to explore the different factors, which have caused the agricultural crisis in Egypt. Three particular aspects of agrarian policies will be reviewed here: land reform, co-operativisation, and price and output regulations.

A) Land Reform

Historical Background

Before Nasser's coup of 1952, rural Egypt was characterised by severe inequalities in terms of land distribution and income. These inequalities, deeply rooted in Egypt's history, manifested themselves in the existence of a very few large land owners while the majority owned small pieces of land. The situation was worsened by further fragmentation of the latter's limited land, which worsened rural conditions. Maldistribution of land and growing poverty among the rural peasants have been distinctive features dominating the rural scene since the beginning of the nineteenth century.

Although a large part of Egypt's agricultural land was confiscated by the state during Mohammed Ali's reign in 1814, some remained in private hands with certain restrictions on the full right of ownership. A part of the confiscated land was registered in the names of the villages, who had to pay the taxes directly to the state. During that time the fellah was given full rights to the land during his lifetime but could not pass it to his heirs. After 1829 Mohammed Ali's policy witnessed some changes that marked the beginning of a new era of private ownership. Mohammed Ali started granting sizeable areas of uncultivated land, "Ib' adiyat", to clients and high officials and to members of his family "Jiflik". His main objective was to encourage investment in land reclamation in order to increase the area of cultivable land. From that time on private ownership had started to evolve gradually. In 1838 Ib' adiyat became heritable and, in 1858, Said, Mohammed Ali's successor, issued a land law which gave the holders of Ib' adiyat full ownership rights. The same rights, although with some restrictions, were given to fellahin who had cultivated plots and paid taxes for five consecutive years. In 1891 and 1893 all remaining restrictions were abolished and all owners enjoyed full property rights.

The presence of both Ib' adiyat and Jiflik, together with a tax farming system, resulted in the existence of large properties. Although Muslim inheritance law usually leads to the fragmentation of properties,[19] Mabro notes that

> although inheritance laws affected all groups in the same manner medium and large properties seem to have escaped fragmentation.[20]

Small properties were most affected by inheritance laws. The continuous fragmentation of small properties, combined with the preservation of medium and large ones, had by 1952 created a peculiar situation in the Egyptian countryside.

At one end of the continuum, large landlords who owned over 50 feddans numbered less than 1 per cent and held 35 per cent of the land, whereas small farmers, owning less than 1 feddan represented 72 per cent of total landowners and were holding only 13 per cent of the land.[21] It is no wonder that Egypt was described at that time as the "half per cent society".[22]

Sequestration Policy under Nasser

Agrarian reform, to achieve social justice and emancipate the oppressed peasants, thus ranked high among the goals of the free officers. The first step in the reform was to redistribute the land held by large individual landowners. This was carried out in three stages, first by reducing the ceiling on individual land ownership to 200 feddans in 1952, then to 100 feddans in 1961, and finally to fifty feddans in 1969.[23] It is true that over 300,000 poor peasant families benefited as direct recipients of land, but the law did not solve the problem of landlines. In 1950, 44 per cent of agricultural families were landless. In 1972, due to the increase in population, this reached 45 per cent.[24]

Another unique consequence of the land reform law was the increase both in the numbers and acreage of medium sized properties, especially those of 20–50 feddans. As Abdel Fadil commented

> these medium landowners owned almost one third of Egypt's cultivated land in 1965, while they made up only 5.2 per cent of the total numbers of land owners.[25]

Hence the actual benefit from the redistribution of land remained limited and did little to enhance equality in terms of land ownership and distribution.

De-Sequestration Policy under Sadat and Mubarak

The limited benefits which were obtained by the peasants as a result of Nasser's land distribution policy has been altered by Sadat's re-traditionalisation policies, whose first step was spelled out in the October paper issued by Sadat in 1974. Although Ansari believes that through the October paper "Sadat was eager to stamp out any memory of Nasser, but not of the system he had imposed on his People"[26] and that "the October paper recognised the legitimacy of the 1952 revolution, the agrarian reforms, and the socialist charter"[27] it is widely believed that the paper was meant to discredit Nasser and his policies. This interpretation is congruent, first with the fact that it was the agrarian bourgeoisie who helped Sadat to consolidate his power in the Sabri-Sadat struggle, and hence he increased their representation in the People's Assembly and set out to restore their property and prestige, and second was the fact that Nasser's socialist policies were not in line with Sadat's intention to change foreign policy orientation and initiate a capitalist open door policy. Indeed by declaring the supremacy of law, Sadat gave the agrarian bourgeois the green light to resort to the courts in order to restore their sequestrated property, and this was the first stage in the desequestration policy.

Meanwhile, the draft for a new law was being discussed in the People's Assembly whereby those individuals who came under sequestration between 1961 and 1964 were distinguished because of their dependent relationships to individuals who were the main subjects of sequestration. Another distinction was made between the acquired properties that remained under state control and those which had been divided into small parcels and given to small farmers with ownership rights. Accordingly, Law no 69 of 1974, the second step in the desequestration policy, was enacted. Article 1 of the law provided for the revocation of all sequestration which took place between 1961 and 1964 and for the payment of compensation up to £E30,000. Article 2 provided for the restoration of all sequestrated land to dependants, provided that the land was acquired by means other than inheritance from sequestrated principals. In cases where the sequestrated land had been sold to small farmers, the dependants would be entitled to the full face value of the sale contract. As for property sequestrated from principals, the law decreed the restoration of property in kind up to £E30,000 per dependant, but not exceeding a total of £E100,000 per family. The value of the sequestrated property was to be determined on the basis of 70 times the land tax or 160 times the rates imposed on urban property. In addition article 7 of the same law ordered the restoration to its former owners of land that had been taken over by agreements between the Department of Sequestration and the Ministry of Agrarian Reform, as long as it was not claimed by a third party.

In 1981, when more legislation was discussed in the People's Assembly to further benefit the agrarian elite, it was announced that the total value of property compensation, including agricultural lands and urban properties, was £E36 million, based on taxes imposed in 1949 for agricultural properties and taxes imposed in 1960 for real estate.[28] It was noted that the numbers of the elite who had had portions of their sequestrated land restored had increased dramatically in 1974, following Sadat's official adoption of the open door policy. For example, in August 1974 it was announced that 22000 feddans under sequestration were to be returned to their owners in November. In September, it was announced that 1700 feddans in Sharqiya were to be handed back to eighty-six citizens, among whom were members of the family of Siraj Al Din, leader of the pre- and post-1952 Wafd party.

The final step in the de-sequestration policy was accomplished through the enactment of Law no 141 of 1981. By virtue of this law all socialist measures taken under emergency Law no 162 of 1958 were declared illegal. This meant the restoration of all sequestrated land to its former owners. As for properties to which a third party had made a claim, generous compensation was paid to the former owners, who were provided with a 50 per cent increase over the earlier compensation of 70 times the tax rate for agricultural property. For urban property, a 50 per cent increase over its sale price in the amount of compensation, was given. In both cases a 7 per cent return on investment was added from the time law 69 of 1974 was enacted. As a result of this new legislation, 147000 feddans, which the Ministry of Agrarian Reforms had previously contracted to small farmers, were restored to their former owners, and the land for which compensation had been made by the government amounted to 17000 feddans.[29]

B) Tenancy Laws

Tenancy Laws under Nasser

The second step in the agrarian reform law was an attempt to adjust the relationship between landowners and tenants so as to prevent abuse of and provide security for tenants. Before the revolution, landowners used to lease their land either under a system of share-cropping or cash rent. Usually, when high crop prices were anticipated, the landowner would prefer the former system, whereas when crop prices fell, the latter was chosen. In addition, tenancy agreements were orally arranged, leases were granted for only one year and sometimes for a one-crop period, that is a period of four to six month, and finally landowners could terminate the lease at any time and for any reason they chose.[30] Thus tenants were left completely at the landowners' mercy, with no legal protection.

In order to illustrate the impoverished conditions, under which the tenants used to live, it is useful to consider in more detail the leasing system that was functioning at that time. As mentioned earlier, two methods were used. The first is the share-cropping system. Under this system, tenant farmers were obliged to give landowners the entire cotton crop and half of their wheat as payment for the use of land. In addition to retaining the rest of the wheat, they also kept the maize and the berseem (clover), to sell in the village market. This was a very low income for the tenant farmers, while the large landowners, providing seeds and fertilisers, guaranteed for themselves a sizeable cotton crop each year with no labour cost at all.[31] Under the second system, cash payments in the form of rent were paid by the tenants in exchange for land use. However, rents were excessive, leading Issawi to note that

> the rents charged were in some cases higher than the net output from the land operated by the owner. This shows that tenants in Egypt are little better off than agricultural labourers.[32]

Reaching the same conclusion Ghonemy, using the department of Agriculture data, found that the average net revenue per feddan of owner-operated land was £E16 in 1946–1947 and £E19 in 1947–1948, while the average cash rent per feddan was £E22 and £E23 respectively for the same periods.[33]

In order to rectify this situation, the land reform law attempted to protect tenant rights and improve their conditions. Accordingly, tenancy regulations were passed requiring that leases be in writing and for a minimum of 3 years. The law also settled the cash rent at a rate not to exceed seven times the basic land tax. In case of the share-cropping system, crops and costs had to be equally divided between landowners and tenants.[34]

Although many writers including Mayfield, Radwan, Issawi, Gadalla and others agree that the regulations for landlord-tenant relationships had benefited far more people than had the initial redistribution of land, they all pinpoint the

204

fact that evasion of the law, and especially of rent limitation was, not uncommon. Given the high rate of illiteracy among the rural peasants and their increasing demand for cultivable land, such evasion was not difficult to maintain.[35] In a further attempt to evade the law landowners also resorted to the use of wage-labour workers. The percentage of cultivated area which was leased thus declined from 60 per cent to 50 per cent after the enactment of the law.[36]

The attempt to secure tenants' rights culminated in the issuance of Law 52 of 1966, which had extended tenancy rights and prevented eviction except for non-payment of rent.[37]

Tenancy Laws under Sadat and Mubarak

Under Sadat, tenancy laws were constantly altered in favour of owners. In 1975–1976, rents determined for agricultural land since 1952 were increased, and the committees that acted as arbitrators in the disputes between owners and tenants were abolished (much to the relief of the former). Provisions to evict tenants and to facilitate sharecropping were changed to the benefit of owners, and agrarian reform co-operatives whose boards of directors were elected by the peasants and which acted politically on their behalf, were stripped of their authority, and their financial activities transferred to the village banks that answered directly to the government.[38]

Although rents had been increased twice under Sadat, the Mubarak regime considered further changes for the benefit of owners. The basic argument of the regime was the growing gap between rents and land values. In 1985, the rent was less than £E80 per feddan at a time when the market value of an isolated piece of land had reached £E20000. Profits from agricultural production, especially horticulture and livestock, had dramatically increased, much to the benefit of the tenants. Eviction of tenants could therefore benefit owners on both accounts.[39] Accordingly, the Agriculture Committee of the NDP had in 1985 suggested several modifications to the law. These included increasing the rents to fifteen instead of seven times the land tax, preventing the inheritance of rental contracts except to those heirs working the land themselves, with a compensation of an amount equivalent to 150 times the amount of land tax to be paid to the disinherited. The owners would be provided with the right to sell their land in two instalments within a period of five years with the priority to purchase given to tenants who held rental contracts, with the alternative of compensation to be paid to the tenants by land owners which should amount to 150 times the land tax.

Since land tax amounted to £E10 per feddan, tenants would receive a compensation of £E1500 per feddan. This would replace the former arrangements where informal agreements between owners and tenants resulted in the latter receiving half the land sale price.[40] The reason given by the government for the issuance of the law appears in the Peoples' Assembly report of 1986 which states that, the necessity of reviewing the law which organises relations between owners and tenants of agricultural land so that one does not dominate the other.[41]

The debate concerning the new legislation continued between the pro and anti camps from 1985 until 1992, when finally the new law was passed by the People's Assembly. At its heart is the increase of the rent to five times the current land tax, reassessment of the conditions of rent and changing it to be based on share cropping, limiting the inheritance of the rent contracts to those of the tenants' children whose major job is farming, and making contracts for a limited time period with the right reserved to the owner to sell his land whenever he deemed it necessary.[42] The state even interfered on behalf of some of the agrarian bourgeois to force the peasants into returning the land leased to them to its former owners. A report in an opposition newspaper revealed that police raided Kamshish village in al-Monoufia governorate to force peasants who have received land after the agrarian reform law into surrendering their land to its former owners. This took place despite the fact that some of these tenants had leasing contracts with the landowners for a period of five years, which started in 1997 and should have ended in the year 2001. In addition to this a current case is being held in court to settle the dispute between the tenant peasants and the landowners, in which no court verdict had been reached yet.[43] Thus the limited benefit which the peasants enjoyed under Nasser from the tenancy laws was gradually undermined under Sadat and Mubarak.

Even Nasser's land reform law, with its two complementary constituents, land distribution and tenancy regulations, ignored a considerable segment of the rural population, the rural labourers, who remained landless with no security whatsoever after the enactment of the law. Landless rural labourers in Egypt fall into two categories. Permanent rural labourers who are employed all the year, and known as the "Tamaliya", represent the first of these categories. Although they are paid minimal wages, they establish a kind of informal network in the village and enjoy a rather stable and secure relationship with their employers. The employers, whether land owners or tenants, are in a sense responsible for their permanent labourers and are expected to protect and help them, especially at times of financial crises, such as death, illness and marriage.

The second, less fortunate category of rural labourers, who constitute the majority of landless peasants in Egypt, are the casual labourers known as the "Tarahil". These are usually employed during a specific season for a particular agricultural task or for other rural public works. Leaving their home village and living in work camps, they work for minimal wages.[44] As one author puts it "Tarahil workers were (and are) the poorest of the poor in rural Egypt."[45] Since casual labourers represent 40 per cent of the agricultural population,[46] it is crucial to analyse the effect of the agrarian reform law on their status. Prior to the enactment of the law, the minimum wage for an eight hour day work was 10–15 piasters[47] for men and 6–7 piasters for women. For the same number of daily working hours, the law set a minimum wage of 18 piasters for men and 10 piasters for women.[48] The law also allowed the formation of agricultural trade unions to protect the rights of this group, but "labour unions eventually became instruments of the regime and declared all strikes to be illegal."[49] Ironically instead of improving the conditions of this large segment of the agricultural population, both the rise in prices and the reduction in the demand for hired labour following the break-up of estates, contributed to a deterioration in their conditions.[50]

Although Professor Warriner admits that the land reform law did not benefit the casual labourers, she quickly and (enthusiastically) states that this "is a result, not of weakness in reform policy, but of population pressure."[51] However, the fact that the rapid increase in population contributed to the creation of rural unemployment does not in any way negate the fact that the law had an adverse effect on casual labourers, simply and ironically because policy makers at that time, either intentionally or unintentionally, did not include them in their plans, although a central slogan of the revolution was to improve the conditions of these landless labourers. As el-Messiri mentions:

> it was only ten years after 1952 that some attention began to be directed to them and they became part of the rhetoric of the sixties.[52]

4. The Co-operative Movement

A) Historical Background

Although co-operativization has been linked in one way or another to Nasser's regime, the co-operative movement in Egypt goes back to the beginning of the twentieth century. As early as 1908, Omar Lutfy, a private philanthropist, sought to introduce "Agricultural Syndicates" to help the farmers meet their supply and marketing needs. Despite the refusal of the government to act upon the recommendations presented by a committee of agricultural specialists for the creation of a special bank providing credit for farmers, and for the enactment of a law that allows the formation of co-operatives, the movement swiftly started. By 1911, seventeen agricultural co-operatives, along with a General Central Syndicate co-ordinating their efforts, were already functioning. Legal status was conferred on these co-operatives by the enactment of Law 27/1923 that allowed any ten farmers to form an agricultural co-operative company to be managed by a board of directors and a supervisory committee, with both bodies elected by the general assembly of co-operative members. A department of co-operation was established in the Ministry of Agriculture and by 1925, the co-operatives numbered 135 and their main task at that time was the provision of credit, supplies and marketing.[53]

Although the 1923 law had restricted membership to those "small owners" of no more than thirty feddans, the Agricultural Banks' continuous raising of this ceiling had by 1937 resulted in there being members with as much as two hundred feddans.[54] Later, due to the increasing role that these co-operatives had assumed, especially during the interwar years, it was agreed that a part of their profit should be utilised in providing social services. Accordingly in 1939, supervision of co-operatives was shifted from the Ministry of Agriculture to the Ministry of Social Affairs.

Membership in these co-operatives was voluntary. Although prior to 1944, the value of co-operative shares was high enough to prevent those with low incomes from participating, Law 58/1944 allowed payment in instalments of capital shares, thus opening membership to less prosperous farmers. It was, however, the same law that increased government control and supervision over co-operative societies.[55] This law, initiated by the Wafd party just before it fell from power, linked the Department of Co-operatives and local societies through a Supreme Advisory Council in the capital that supervised regional advisory councils in each province. Representation in both councils, the Supreme Advisory Council and local co-operative boards, included elected and appointed members, but the former were always outnumbered two to one by bureaucrats, bank officials, technical advisors and politicians chosen by the Minister of Social Affairs or the provincial governor.[56] Accordingly, registration with the Ministry of Social Affairs became obligatory, the co-operatives' accounts were subject to official review, and ministerial decree could cancel decisions taken by their elected boards. This bureaucratic assault on the co-operatives' autonomy led a resident foreigner and a defender of co-operatives to note that "privately, the spirit of the co-operators was healthy, [but] officially, the picture was not satisfactory."[57]

The conversion of the Egyptian Agricultural Credit Bank in 1949 into the Agriculture Co-operative Bank with the co-operative societies represented on its board of directors, was an important step for the peasants since credit became cheaper, thus motivating more farmers to join in. By 1952 co-operatives numbered 2,103 with a membership of 746,836.[58]

B) The Co-operative Movement from Nasser to Mubarak

Adopting the co-operative movement as Nasser's own achievement, and in order to counterbalance the disruptive effect on agricultural productivity resulting from the breaking down of large estates into small parcels, on one hand, and responding to the growing need to provide the beneficiaries with cultivation facilities, on the other, the land reform law had, as early as 1953, necessitated the establishment of the land reform co-operatives, which all recipients of land were compelled to join. Membership was thus obligatory, not voluntary, and served only those who received land as a result of the redistribution of large estates.

These co-operatives were completely different from the free co-operatives that existed during the pre-revolution period. In 1960, however, the system of the traditional free co-operatives was abolished and replaced by a second type of reform co-operatives, in which all cultivators in Egypt became members. The only difference that existed between the land reform co-operatives of 1953 and the more inclusive reform co-operatives of 1960's, is that in the former the security for credit advanced to members was the land, whereas in the latter it was the produce.[59]

The Politicisation and De-politicisation of Co-operatives

Apart from being used as a tool for economic control, as will be discussed later, the co-operatives were intended to mobilise political support for the regime. However, Nasser never intended to strengthen the co-operative movement for fear of creating an independent force in the countryside that might threaten the local power of the rural middle class.[60] He was thus reluctant to create a more unified co-operative organisation, and only in the final days of his life did he approve the foundation of the Egyptian Confederation of Agricultural Co-operatives.

Nevertheless, two steps were taken earlier to counterbalance any future threat that might ensue from the confederation. The first step was the issuance in 1969 of a new co-operative law which severely reduced the representation of small peasants on village co-operative boards. Before this law, the majority of seats were reserved for peasants owning less than five feddans. After the introduction of the law the ceiling was raised to ten feddans and literacy became conditional for membership. The second step, which was taken in the same year, was the prevention of the Arab Socialist Union (A.S.U.) from controlling elections to parliament. Nasser thus increased the representation of rural notables in parliament and in many local party branches as well.[61] By the time the confederation was formed

the most radical advocates of agrarian reform had been seriously weakened and co-operatives throughout the country were being torn apart by renewed power struggles between agents of the A.S.U., newly participant peasants, and larger landholders, who were beginning to re-establish their dominance over local polities. Thus the first tentative efforts to consolidate the cooperative movement at the national level coincided with an increasing fragmentation of its base in the province.[62]

When Sadat assumed power and directly following his corrective revolution, he appointed one of his protégés, Ahmad Yunis, to the leadership of the confederation. Yunis, however, tried to change the confederation into the very national power base whose formation Nasser had attempted to prevent. He started to create a strong autonomous organisation which would not only fall outside the domain of state control, but which would challenge the government and demand a say in state policy making, especially that related to agriculture.

To achieve this, Yunis enhanced the organisation's internal structure, establishing eighteen provincial branches with over 4000 employees. Moreover, the confederation published a newspaper with wide circulation in the countryside and contributed financially to other international co-operative groups in Europe and the Arab world. Yunis also managed to become the chairman of a 160-member inter-ministerial committee on agriculture and irrigation, which included several former cabinet members as well as other prospective confederation appointees. He also succeeded in building a network of clients within the People's Assembly by placing deputies on the confederation's payroll as consultants. Through this bloc of parliamentary supporters, rural middle-class opposition was organised and succeeded in defeating proposals for direct taxation on agricultural land.

In 1976, Yunis refused the Prime Minister's demand that the confederation support the government party in the elections. Although he declared that the confederation should remain non-partisan, it was obvious that he was endorsing Wafdist candidates who were running in the elections as independents. Organising a mass rally in Feb 1976, which was attended by over 7000 members of co-operatives, Yunis announced what he termed a "spontaneous declaration of independence". At the rally, Yunis called for an end to "administrative interference" in confederation affairs, and for a new draft proposal that would give the confederation total control over all co-operative societies, including the land reform co-operatives. Yunis challenged the government notion of co-operative debts mentioning that the total amount owed was only half the official figure and that a lot of peasants were entitled to refunds of excess payment. He called on the government to cancel the system of compulsory delivery and administered prices for crops and freedom to build "democratic links" with labour unions and professional syndicates. The rally was, however, a prelude to the return of Wafdist influence to the provinces.[63] This Sadat could not tolerate. As one author comments

> Sadat had encouraged Yunis to use the co-operatives to strengthen the hand of the rural middle class in many ways – by increasing the representation of larger landowners on co-operative boards, by helping to return sequestered lands to their original owners, by transferring the settlement of village disputes from the co-operative to the courts and by easing the legal limits on agricultural rents. But all these economic concessions were intended to secure the gratitude or at least the acquiescence of rural notables, not to whet their appetite for a return to power.[64]

Accordingly Sadat started to stage Yunis's downfall and the death of the confederation. A publicity campaign had thus started against Yunis charging him with mismanagement and embezzlement, and demanding his removal from the confederation presidency. Two months before the 1976 elections, the findings of a bi-national committee of Egyptian and American experts revealing evidence of widespread "corruption and anarchy" in the agricultural co-operative was published, immediately after which the confederation was abolished and the local co-operatives were stripped of their functions which were transferred to the newly established village banks. The village banks now lent money directly to individuals instead of to co-operatives and demanded land and crops as collateral. Co-operative leaders were not represented in the banks' boards.

By shifting the economic development of the provinces from the co-operatives to the village banks, the Organisation for the Rehabilitation and Development of Egyptian Villages (O.R.D.E.V.), and local administration,[65]

> Sadat ended any possibility that the co-operatives would be used to mobilise a mass opposition and he managed to divert much of the rural middle class into entrepreneurial associations controlled by the state. However, his emasculation of the co-operative movement also eliminated the only symbol of representation that could be identified with the principal victims of rural poverty and depopulation.[66]

Pressures from European co-operative leaders and the refusal of several European countries to renew international co-operative agreements with the Egyptian government were the main reasons for Sadat's and later on Mubarak's attempt to re-establish a new confederation. In 1980, just before his assassination, Sadat initiated a new co-operative law, which he amended in 1981. The implementation of the law was however, postponed until 1983. Unlike the old confederation, the newly established had no controlling power over the regional federations and the local branches. Instead, both the Ministry of Agriculture and the provincial governors were vested with broad authority to appoint co-operative leaders, veto the decisions of elected councils, supervise their accounts and close co-operatives by administrative orders. Similar powers over the confederation were granted to the president who also has the power to suspend or abolish the confederation by a special decree. Confederation meetings were to be supervised by government observers who should be informed about the date of the meeting at least ten days in advance. Elections at the various levels of the co-operatives were to be held once every five years under the supervision of a committee of officials representing the Ministries of Interior, Justice, and Agriculture.[67] The first elections to the confederation council took place in 1983 and all the seats were won by the government NDP, making of it what Bianchi described as a "paper confederation".[68]

The assault that has taken place on the co-operative movement supports the argument raised earlier in chapters five and six that the Egyptian State deliberately weakens all societal forces that might threaten its power. It may attempt, in order to achieve certain political ends, to strengthen certain groups like the agrarian bourgeoisie, but these attempts are usually short-lived, lest these groups challenge the state's authority. Similarly, although there is a sort of alliance between the state and a certain segment of the business community, the state is relatively autonomous and defies Sadowsky's claim that

> over the last twenty years the formulation and execution of government policy have increasingly been shaped by businessmen.[69]

Sadowsky's statement obviously overestimates the power of societal forces in Egypt. An example that supports the view that state has the final say, is the debate, over owner-tenant relations, which was discussed earlier. This debate lasted for almost ten years before the law was issued, which led Springborg to assert

> the fact that the state continues to be relatively autonomous from some of the most powerful forces. . . . If it were not so, the tenants would have been evicted from their plots years ago.[70]

Co-operatives as a Tool for Government Intervention

Since 1952 expansion in the co-operatives took place not only in their numbers, but also in the wide range of tasks allocated to them. Supplying farmers with different kinds of loans, seeds, fertilisers, livestock, agricultural machinery, organisation of production and marketing of crops, co-operatives controlled both the agricultural input and output.[71] Comparing the system of agricultural co-operatives to the pre-revolutionary system of large estates known as "'izab", Alan Richards pinpoints some striking similarities that are worth mentioning here. Although the land reform law aimed at redistributing the land in these "'izab" to landless peasants, the beneficiaries were more like tenants than owners, since the agrarian reform co-operatives that were established enjoyed the same rights that the previous landowners, the Pashas, had. Just as the Pasha could terminate his labourers' or tenants' leases, if they disobeyed instructions, Law 554 of 1955 gave the co-operatives' supervisory staff the right to evict recipients of land for mismanagement of their holdings. In addition to this the co-operatives assumed all the managerial functions that were previously handled by the Pasha or his estate manager the "Nazir", and the same staff who had been the landowner's employees, became government employees. Thus the co-operative system was nothing but an extension of the "'izbah" system, or putting it more specifically became "government 'izab".[72] Comparing the position of farmers before and after the revolution, one author has noted,

> As tenants, they had formerly paid rent on a share-cropping basis, under which the landowner took all the cotton and half of wheat, leaving the tenant half the wheat for sale, the maize for his consumption and the berseem for the buffalo. . . . Under the new law . . . they deliver the whole of the cotton crop to the co-operatives for sale, as they formerly delivered it to the estate managers, and the proceeds of the sale meet the cost of the fertilisers and seed and administrative expenses. The farmers retain their maize and berseem as before. The chief difference in their position is that the whole income from the wheat crop is their property instead of half.[73]

This statement reflects that, on the surface, the benefits that accrued to the peasants were minor. In fact, an in depth analysis would reveal that the whole system was designed for the exploitation of the peasants, adding a new chapter to their historical oppression.

A major drive underlying the creation of the co-operatives was the strong belief of Nasser's regime in the necessity of the rapid industrialisation of Egypt and hence the urge to squeeze agriculture and use its surplus to finance huge industrial projects. Heavy taxation of the agricultural sector required the government to strengthen its grip on all agricultural output which in turn necessitated its control on the input as well. Commenting on this policy Sadowsky mentions that,

> Heavy taxation of the peasantry, the poorest element of the population, seemed to make a mockery of Nasser's claim to champion the common man.[74]

In an attempt to analyse the different policies initiated by the government through these co-operatives and how these affected agricultural production, policies which affect the input side, like area allotment, subsidised fertilisers, pesticides and seeds and finally the credit policy will be discussed.

Area Allotment

The government used the co-operatives to allocate certain areas for specific crops. By doing so, it aimed at preventing excessive production of some export crops, such as cotton and rice in order to protect the soil's fertility, while at the same time ensuring the production of the required quantities for the generation of the needed foreign currency.[75]

Equally important was the prevention of inflation, which might have an adverse effect on industrialisation and the government's ability to provide the urban population with cheap food in order to maintain the country's political stability.[76] The latter factor, which is known as an urban bias in government policies, has been debated by Sadowsky, who saw in the agricultural policies of the Egyptian state, even under Nasser, an element of class bias. He thus comments,

> This exploitation resembled urban bias but it was always combined with an element of class bias. Rich peasants and the agrarian elite worked the system so that they escaped its exactions and tapped its benefits. This trend would accelerate in the 1970's as the power of the agrarian elite grew.[77]

Farmers, however, tended to deviate from the allotted crop area if they could earn a higher income from another. Accordingly a gap always existed between the actual area for crops and the planned one.[78] The effect of this deviation on the output side will be clarified when the government policy of controlled output prices is discussed.

Subsidised Input

As mentioned earlier, the co-operatives assumed most of the functions of the old landowners and became the only supplier of key inputs in the agricultural sector.

It was hoped then that this policy would enable the government to promote new inputs and techniques which would accelerate the development of agriculture in Egypt. This took place through the provision of farmers with seeds, pesticides and fertilisers.[79] The expansion in the usage of chemical fertilisers during the fifties was, however, a unique feature of the Egyptian Agriculture.

Using its monopoly of fertiliser importation, production and distribution, the government had guaranteed strong control over what was cultivated. Establishing the amount of fertilisers to be used for each crop and knowing each farmer's area of land and the crop rotation that he had to follow, co-operatives were able to set a specific quota that each farmer could purchase on credit. Within a certain limit, farmers could acquire more than their quota, provided that they paid cash. In an attempt to promote its use, from 1956 the government kept down the price of fertiliser.

However, during the 1960's this policy was partly reversed and farmers were paying 87 per cent more than international prices. Being insulated from international market prices, Egyptian farmers did not benefit from the decline in the price of fertilisers in the international market from 1967 to 1971. Nevertheless, they were protected against the prices explosion of the mid 1970's when they were paying only some 40 to 60 per cent of international prices.

Heavy use of subsidised pesticides was also introduced, especially after the 1961 crisis, when one third of the cotton crop was lost to pests. In 1967, Egypt was using nearly four times as many tonnes of pesticides per cultivated area as the United States.[80]

Not surprisingly these inconsistencies in policy-making generated negative results, not only for agriculture but for the economy in general. For example during the 1960's due to the high prices of fertilisers, their use, which the co-operatives were supposed to promote and encourage, was greatly reduced.[81] The policy of subsidised inputs encouraged the creation of a black market, which was developed partly by the farmers themselves and partly by the co-operative bureaucrats.[82] However, the major beneficiaries from trade in the black market were again the rich farmers, who used to buy these fertilisers, which they were not entitled to acquire, and use them profitably on their own land.[83]

Finally, subsidisation created price distortion which led to inefficient allocation of resources.[84]

The Credit Policy

Among the services that the co-operatives provided for the farmers were credit facilities. Granted the permission to borrow money from the central bank, the

Agricultural Credit Bank issued bonds worth 30 million Egyptian pounds to finance its operations. After 1956 a rapid increase in agricultural credit occurred. In 1961 interest on co-operative loans was abolished, but it was, however, re-imposed in 1967, after the Arab-Israeli war, at a rate of 4.5 per cent,[85] which was far below that of the commercial banks. However, these agricultural credit facilities have benefited large more than small landholders. It is true that over 80 per cent of the co-operative borrowers owned less than five feddans, but they received less than half of the total number of loans. This means that 20 per cent of the borrowers, who held land between five and twenty-five feddans, received more than half of the total loans. In 1966, it was found that fifteen per cent of the loans were being given to landowners with more than twenty-five feddans.[86]

To conclude, the government's input and credit policies did not help the poor peasants, who were supposed to be the main beneficiaries, but rather the rich ones. Sadowsky sums up the whole situation when he says,

> But rich peasants were not the only beneficiaries of the inequitable distribution of input and credit. Corruption in the cooperatives and black market resale of state-subsidised inputs augmented the fortunes of village notables, the rural gentry, and agrarian capitalists. As a group, these wealthy strata controlled more than twice as much land as rich peasants and probably consumed a proportional share of agricultural resources. Thus, inequitable distribution of farm inputs benefited the productive rich peasants, but it also squandered resources on their richer but less efficient neighbours.[87]

Output Price Control and Procurement Policy

As mentioned earlier, farmers were compelled to deliver certain crops to the co-operatives in accordance with a specific quota system. This included all their cotton, 27 per cent of the wheat, 66 per cent of the rice, and 57 per cent of the onion crop, and subsequently the list of compulsory delivery was broadened to include sesame, groundnuts, broad beans and lentils. The co-operatives set the prices of these crops and, as a state agency, monopolised their purchase. Crops other than these, together with the quantity that exceeded the predetermined quota, were left to the farmer to sell at a price he could set himself.

This led to the creation of two markets for agricultural crops in rural Egypt. The free village market, in which prices were determined by supply and demand, and the co-operative marketing system, with controlled prices set by the state bank. The difference between the two markets in terms of agricultural prices was enormous. In the 1960's for example, the compulsory prices in the co-operative system were 50–20 per cent below those of the free market. In addition to this, free market prices were rising at a faster rate over time.[88]

5. Peasants' Political Behaviour

A) Peasants' Behaviour towards Unfavourable State Policies

Not only did this policy of controlled prices result in price distortion and the isolation of farmers from domestic and international market forces,[89] but, combined with the policy of area allotment, it caused suboptimal land allocation. In order to clarify this point the producer prices for cotton, the most important export crop may be taken as an example, and compared to that of berseem, which is not subject to government control and which is cotton's main competitor. Analysing the producer prices for cotton, it was found that it had risen at an average rate of 1.7 per cent a year. Since 1950 this rise has accelerated and in the period 1965–1975 reached 3.7 per cent a year. However, in the same period the prices of purchased inputs rose 5.8 per cent a year, resulting in a net loss in return of 2.1 per cent. In contrast the estimated increase in berseem's output prices of 11 per cent a year, associated with an increase in input prices of 5 per cent, would leave producers with a net increase in return of 6 per cent.[90] Accordingly, in an attempt to increase their net-return, producers tended to maximise the area under non-controlled crops at the expense of cotton, rice and beans. This is reflected in the fact that between 1978 and 1981 the area under berseem reached 25 per cent of the total cultivated area, and that under maize, lentils and beans, constituted a further 15 per cent.[91] Another way of circumventing the law was by delaying the plantation of the required crop, as in case of cotton for example, in order to take an extra cut from the berseem crop. This would normally result in a severe drop in cotton yields, since the optimum plantation period was lost, and this is reflected in the overall production of cotton.[92]

Analysing the result on the welfare of the economy of the losses incurred from such land misallocation, Hansen and Nashashibi conclude

> These losses are big enough to cause serious concern for a poor country. On the national level, the equivalent of the loss, invested wisely, could have increased the growth rate of per capita income by 1 or 2 per cent or at a given growth rate could have served to make Egypt self-financing during the sixties-free from those foreign exchange and balance of payments problems, that to some extent, were the very excuse for introducing the controls.[93]

Although compelled by law to abide by the rules concerning the allotment of certain areas for cash crops, peasants tend to resist successfully unfavourable government policies, and in doing so hinder the regime's developmental plans. It is this form of resistance that is labelled here *active passivity*. Through their passivity, the peasants actively defeat the authoritarian regime's policies and its developmental objectives.

B) Peasants, the State, and Political Parties: Coercion and Exclusion

Ironically enough, the same measures of force and coercion used against the peasants in the past were still operable under Sadat and Mubarak. The following scene described by one author is most illustrative:

> In May 1982, the Egyptian Government began to stage pre-dawn raids on villages in the Nile Delta. Police troops, helmeted and heavily armed, roused villagers from their homes. Masked informants identified suspects from the resulting line ups. In Daqahiliyya Province alone fourteen thousands peasants were dragged before the courts. When the police could not find the suspects they were hunting for, they sometimes took members of their families hostage – a standard technique used to intimidate the political opposition. But the villagers arrested in these raids were not members of the political opposition. They were merely peasants who had failed to grow the government-mandated quota of rice.[94]

Beside being oppressed economically, the Egyptian peasant, as has been shown earlier, is excluded from the political system at large both locally and nationally. At the local level, the exclusion is manifested in a tightly controlled system of local administration where the NDP dominates the majority of the governorate, markaz, and local village councils, usually winning more than 90 per cent of the seats of these councils. At the national level, the 50 per cent representation of peasants and workers in all elected councils which is mandatory, was more theoretical than real even under Nasser. However peasant representation was still better than at present. Under Mubarak peasant participation in the People's Assembly has drastically declined. In March 1986 one close observer declared that "since the 1984 elections there have been no peasant members at all."[95]

Again the failure of the opposition to embrace peasant demands, as shown in the debate over landowner-tenant relationships, reflects another continuity from the past and conform to Brown's findings referred to earlier in chapter 2.

The Liberal Party's stand on the whole issue, for example, was more conservative than that of the government itself, since its leader went as far as demanding the abolition of both tenancy laws and the ceilings on land ownership.

The Socialist Liberal Party "SLP" whose main constituency stemmed from the urban middle class and which had to compromise on its socialist ideology, especially after its alliance with the Muslim Brotherhood, which is dominated by wealthy Islamists, was not inclined to side with tenants against owners and chose to ignore the whole issue, as is reflected in the party's platform for the 1987 elections. The New Wafd Party "NWP" took a similar stand to that of the SLP, and only touched on the issue when it wanted to embarrass the government. The National Unionist Progressive Party "NUPP" was the only party to run a debate on the issue in the party's newspaper al-Ahali, along side Sawt al-Arab, which is a Nasserite newspaper.[96] Commenting on the way both government and opposition media handled the debate Springborg states,

217

The government media simply promoted presidential directives, while the opposition performed its ritualistic task of opposing, despite the fact that it was essentially in agreement with the government. In such a context, the opposition is irrelevant to policy formulation, but its presence justifies the government's claim that it supports freedom of speech and democracy. The fact that the many millions of peasants who would be affected by the proposals were precluded from voicing their views indicates that the roots of government and of opposition political organization scarcely tapped into civil society.[97]

The only linkages that the opposition parties have with the peasantry take the form of occasional tours that party leaders undertake in rural areas, which are usually heralded in the party's newspapers. Even the NUPP's rural arm, the Peasant Union, exists only on paper, as reflected in the al-Ahali practice of referring to it as "taht al-ta'sis" (under construction).[98]

C) Peasants' Behaviour towards the Electoral System

How does this exclusion affect the political behaviour of the peasants?

In order to study the political participation of the Egyptian peasant in contemporary Egypt, the criterion used here will be electoral turnout. The results of two elections (1984 and 1995) will be analysed, since precise data are not available for the 1987 and 1990 elections.

The following table reflects the share of each of Egypt's provinces in the 1984 and 1995 elections.

Table 8.1 The share of each of Egypt's provinces in the 1984 & 1995 elections

Province	% of those who actually voted to the total number of those registered on the election list		Average % of urbanization*
	1984 elections	1995 elections	
Lower Egypt	48.482	65.00	26.00
Upper Egypt	44.872	50.00	25.57
Canal & border governorate	39.195	45.00	69.00
Cairo	23.932	13.00	100.00

Sources: 1 – *Intikhabat Majlis Al Shaab 1984: Dirasa Wa Tahlil* (The 1984 People's Assembly election: Study and Analysis) 1986, pp. 225, 233.

2 – *Al Intikhabat Al Barlamaniya Fi Misr 1995* (The 1995 Parliamentary Elections in Egypt), Centre for Political & Strategic Studies, 1997 p. 41.

*This column had been compiled by adding the percentage of urbanisation of all Lower Egypt governorates and calculating the average. The same has been done with respect to Upper Egypt governorates. The average percentage of urbanisation has been calculated for the canal governorates and then added to the average percentage of the border governorates to find the percentage of urbanisation for the total. The level of urbanisation has been taken as a constant variable for the years 1984 & 1995.

From the previous table the following facts can be observed:

1. There is an inverse proportion between the degree of urbanisation and the percentage of electoral turnout. The lower the degree of urbanisation, the higher is the proportion of voters.

2. This means that there is a direct relation between the degree of ruralisation and the percentage of electoral turnout. The higher the degree of ruralisation, the higher is the proportion of voters. In other words, the political participation of the Egyptian peasant tends to be higher than his urban counterpart.

3. Comparing the results of the 1984 and 1995 elections, it can be noticed that whereas the tendency of peasant political participation is on the rise, as exemplified by Lower and Upper Egypt, where the electoral turnout increased from 48.4 to 65 per cent and from 44.8 to 50 per cent respectively, urban political participation is experiencing a sharp decline as reflected in the drop in electoral turnout in Cairo from 23.9 to 13 per cent.

So, can the Egyptian peasant still be labelled as passive? Certainly not, but investigating the motives behind the relatively high peasant electoral turnout reveals an astounding historical continuity and conforms to Brown's study referred to earlier.

Analysing the results of the 1990 elections, in which the Egyptian President commented on the low electoral turnout in the cities, especially Cairo, as compared to rural areas, it was found that both kinship and patron-client relationship appeared as determinant factors in the success of most independent candidates, especially in rural Egypt, since most of them lack any electoral programmes.[99] Asabia, i.e. family affiliation also continues to be a determinant factor in peasant voting preference.

The same factors apply, even to those candidates nominated by the different political parties. In a reportage conducted by a leading political magazine in Egypt, it was found that most of those who won the elections, especially in rural areas, were chosen by the electorate either because they were charismatic and popular in their electorate district and used to provide personal services to the people, or as a result of tribalism regardless of the party to which candidate was affiliated.[100] Of course the government party candidates, which dominates the provinces would have the lion's share of "services rendered" due to their affiliation with the executive apparatus, the main source of patronage. It is exactly this lack of patronage that makes the opposition parties' linkages with the peasantry even weaker than that of the government.[101]

Again in a study analysing the increase in the rural electoral turnout in the 1995 elections, it was asserted that personal loyalties and tribalism are the determinant factors for this phenomenon.[102]

The Egyptian peasant is therefore in a sense more active than his urban counterpart, but his activity is based on personal and traditional rather than communal or national affiliation. His activity tends therefore to have a negative impact on the political system at large and helps preserve the continuity of the autocratic regime. Hence it is labelled *passive activity.*

6. Conclusion

Throughout the years and up to the present time, Egyptian peasants have been economically exploited and politically oppressed. The limited benefits that a small segment of peasants gained from Nasser's agrarian reform law, to an extent from tenancy law and to a lesser extent from land distribution, have been altered under his successors who continue to issue policies that are both urban and class biased against the majority of peasants. Even agricultural co-operatives that once emerged as the sole champion of peasants' interests and voiced their demands have been weakened and stripped of their functions. Lacking the appropriate channels of representation at all level of local administration and having their interests ignored by both the government and opposition parties alike, Egyptian peasants have developed their own strategy of resistance, labelled here as *active passivity,* which defeat state's reform policy. Exploitation and oppression by the authorities have created among peasants a culture which promotes lack of trust, deceit, clientalism and tribalism. Patronage, thus becomes the only avenue through which peasants can pursue individual rather than communal interests, and although this situation and through peasants behaviour that has been labelled here as *passive activity,* the continuity of the authoritarian regime is preserved, its developmental objectives are obstructed. This places the government in a dilemma, since due to peasants' continuous evasion of law, it fails to enforce various reform programmes. Hence as the weak autocratic state tends to undermine and fragment the peasants and their organisations, so the latter in their turn enhance the weakness of the state

CHAPTER NINE

Tihna al-Gabal

A Case Study of a Village in Upper Egypt

1. Introduction

A) Al-Menia Governorate

Tihna al-Gabal is a village situated in al-Menia governorate, which lies in middle Egypt, bounded by Beni Suef governorate from the north, Asyut governorate from the south, and by desert from the east and west. Its capital is al-Menia city on the western side of the Nile, 245 kilometres south of Cairo. The population of al-Menia governorate was 3,248,063 in the last census in 1993.[1] The governorate has an area of 2,262 square kilometers, equivalent to 543,176 feddans, which amounts to 7 per cent of the country. The governorate is divided into nine administrative centres (Markaz) arranged from north to south as follows: al-Aidwa, Maghagha, Beni Mazar, Matay, Samalot, al-Menia, Abou Qorqas, Malawy and Dir Mawas. These administrative centres include 346 village and 1,102 'izab and Nagu'.[2] There are fifty seven local council village councils in al-Menia Governorate.

Agriculture is the major economic activity in the governorate, and its agricultural productivity represent 11 per cent of that of the country. The few industrial activities found in al-Menia are mostly dependent on the different agricultural crops, especially cotton. Al-Menia governorate is distinguished by the presence of many Pharoanic, Roman, Coptic and Islamic antiquities and is therefore one of the areas which attracts tourists.[3]

B) Markaz al-Menia

The area of Markaz al-Menia is 340.39 square kilometres[4] and its population was 604,374 in 1994.[5] Markaz al-Menia consists of forty-one villages and 182 'izab, distributed among seven local units named: Mohammed Beni Sultan, Damshur, al-Bergaya, Nazlet Hussein, Saft al-Khomar, Tella, and Toukh al-Kheil. In other words, each local unit has a number of villages and 'izab connected to it and together they form the local village unit. Each village unit has an executive local council and an elected popular council serving the whole unit at village level.

C) Nazlet Hussein: The Local Village Unit
(Al-wihda al-mahalliyya al-qurawiyya)

Affiliated to the local village unit of Nazlet Hussein are eight main (horizontal) villages: Zawyet Sultan, Sawada, Nazlet Hussein, al-Dawadia, Nazlet Faragalla, al-Hawarta, Nazlet Ebeid and Tihna al-Gabal. Connected to some of these main villages are smaller villages or 'izab (vertical) and these amount to thirteen. Thus the total number of villages in the local village unit of Nazlet Hussein is twenty-one villages.[6] However, it is the eight main (horizontal) villages that are usually referred to as distinctive villages.

The total area of the local village unit of Nazlet Hussein amounts to 5964 feddan and 14 qirrats, with a total population of 43,593 in 1994.[7] Being centred in a mid location among the eight villages, Nazlet Hussein was chosen as the resident village for the executive and popular councils.

The eight appointed members of the executive local council are: the head of the social unit, a school headmaster, the local chief of police, the local bank manager, the head of the health unit, and the council's secretary. They are headed by the chairman known as "chief of the local Unit". The executive council is the highest authority at the village level and their membership on it is by virtue of their administrative positions within the bureaucratic hierarchy.

In addition to the executive local council, there is an elected council of the village unit "Al-Wihda al Mahalliyya al-qarawaya". The twenty elected members of the popular council represent the eight main villages affiliated to al-wihda al-mahallia in Nazlet Hussein. However, the distribution of the twenty members of the popular council among the eight villages, that is the eight main populated areas, is not proportional. For example, Nazlet Sultan and Nazlet Ebeid the two most populated villages among the eight, are represented by one and two members respectively, whereas Nazlet Hussein and Sawada, which are less populous, have five and four members respectively. Again whereas it should follow that the more remote and isolated villages should be represented by more members than the nearer, and more accessible villages, Nazlet Ebeid and Tihna al-Gabal the furthest villages are represented by two members each, whereas Nazlet Hussein and Sawada as previously mentioned are represented by five and four members respectively.

The availability of the NDP members in each village seems to be the sole determinant for the number of members representing each village in the local popular council.

The main responsibilities of the popular council are to oversee the various services provided by the different governmental organisations in the village and to ensure that they are rendering these services efficiently. They also press the executive council to increase and improve the quantity and quality of services where they are either lacking or inadequate. The council is also responsible for monitoring government employees working in the local organisation in order to prevent corruption and abuse of power. In this capacity they should examine individual complaints and deal with them whenever necessary.

The popular council convenes once a month. The chairman of the local executive council is normally expected to attend meetings to answer questions or alternatively, to call on any of the relevant executive members to do so. If the popular council at the village level passes a resolution, which the executive council refuses to execute, it can submit a complaint to its counterpart at the Markaz level, which in turn asks the Markaz executive council to carry out the resolution. If the latter refuses, the same procedure is repeated at the governorate level. The governorate executive council is, however, the final arbitrator and its decision is final.

2. Tihna al-Gabal

A) Situation and Site

Tihna al-Gabal is situated between Nazlet Ebeid in the south and Gabal al-Tir in the north and is the last village affiliated to the local village unit of Nazlet Hussein. The distance between Tihna al-Gabal and the nearest village in Nazlet Ebeid is one kilometre and between the former and both Nazlet Hussein and al-Menia city is six and eleven kilometres respectively. The total area of Tihna al-Gabal is 651 feddan and 11 qirrats.[8] The total population was 5,263 on 1/1/1994.[9]

Agriculture is the main source of income for most of the people in the village, whether they cultivate their own land or are the landless peasants who work as agricultural labourers. Some peasants who own few qirrats, which is barely enough to keep their families at a subsistence level, also work as agricultural labourers for others in order to augment their income. Animal husbandry comes second and is mostly carried out by women. Women also help men in cultivation and grain storage and participate in marketing and selling produce in the near-by markets where they are usually shrewder than men in obtaining the highest possible price for their products.

B) The Social Aspects

Considered a typical Egyptian village, the social aspects of Tihna al-Gabal are similar to the rest of the villages of upper Egypt. The usual size of the family ranges from five to eight members and intermarriage between members of the same family is still the prevailing rule.

223

Intermarriage is considered an important factor in strengthening family ties especially since both tribalism and the extended family still dominate life in the village. At the same time the stringent economic conditions favour this kind of marriage. Although the law specifies the minimum marriage age for both sexes, at sixteen for women and eighteen for men, the law is usually ignored with the marriage actually taking place at the age of thirteen for women and sixteen for men. Usually such violation of the law takes place either through fraud, in which case full co-operation is guaranteed, or through the use of coercion against the village's physician, the mosque's Sheikh or the church's priest. Most are arranged marriages. Polygamy also still exists, but because of economic conditions, it is less common than in the past, albeit it is more common among well-to-do peasants.

The culture of Vendetta persists, and vengeance feud may continue between families for a number of years and reach a serious stage in which the whole village may be literally isolated with no one able to leave his/her home, let alone leave or enter the village.

C) Culture and Education

Two important factors have affected the cultural development of the Egyptian peasant. First provision of electricity to the village helped the spread of televisions, which are now found in most of the houses in the village. The television and, to a lesser extent now, the radio are almost the only link between the peasant and the outside world, that is the world falling beyond the domain of his own village or markaz, or governorate. Second, the internal migration of the peasants to work in the cities, or external migration, especially that which accompanied Sadat's open door policy with its encouragement for the migration of tremendous numbers of peasants to work in the oil rich Arab countries, exposed the Egyptian peasants, especially the better educated ones, to an array of new ideas. Some of these ideas, however, have had a negative impact on Egyptian culture since they stem from radical Islamic ideologies which prevails in some of the receiving countries, a factor which has contributed to the re-traditionalisation of the society and an upsurge of terrorist groups during the last twenty years. However, the overall result of the previously mentioned factors is that the Egyptian peasant, as noticed in Tihna, has been exposed to wider cultural influences, but these do not appear to have had a major impact on peasant traditions and customs.

There are two schools in Tihna, a primary school, which serves the 6–12 year-olds, and a preparatory, which serves 13–16 year-olds. The total number of pupils in both schools is 576 pupils among whom 438 are boys and 138 girls. Thus boys outnumbered girls to almost four to one in the academic year 1993/1994. This may be related to the common belief that education for Woman is "'ayb" or shameful. In addition girls are expected to have been long married by the age of

224

fifteen or sixteen,[10] a tradition which drives even the few enlightened men in the village, including the school's headmaster, to prevent any schooling for their daughters after this age. Only three girls in the whole village have been permitted to continue their education to the university level. As far as boys are concerned, there is a growing trend among the parents in the village to provide their sons with a proper education that may even extend to university. However, this development is slowed down by various factors such as, limited family resources making it difficult to meet the various additional expenses of education,[11] the need for the sons to work to obtain extra income for the family, and the pressure for early marriage.

D) Infrastructure

Transportation is available from al-Menia city to Tihna al-Gabal by privately-owned and run mini buses, since no public transport exists. The road from al-Menia city as far as Nazlet Hussein is paved, but from Nazlet Hussein to Tihna al Gabal, a distance of six kilometres it is unpaved and particularly dangerous at night because of the narrowness of the road and the fact that it is unlit.

The extension of water pipes into the village and the availability of clean tap water in most houses has played a significant role in improving the general health and sanitary conditions in the village.

The role of the police in the village is to control crime and any violation of the law that may cause instability in the village. It is noticed, however, that the 'Umda[12] plays a major role in solving many of the disputes that occur and it is only when the 'Umda fails that things proceed further to the police.

Besides a church and a mosque, there is an agricultural co-operative, a health centre, a youth club, a post office and two schools. The village is served by the executive village council of the village local unit in Nazlet Hussein, a village bank and a social unit, both of which are situated in Nazlet Hussein. Two members of the village represent it in the popular local council. Their task is to represent the people's interest and carry their grievances to the executive council.

In the following section the interaction between the state and the peasants will be explored through an assessment of the role of the various organisations that represent peasant interests and the services provided to the peasant society. The information provided in this section is based on primary sources, obtained through field trips and a seven month residency in the village, using both structured and unstructured interviews as well as personal observation to gather the data.

3. Tihna's Organisations and Representatives

A) Tihna's Representatives in the Popular Local Council of the Village Unit "Al-Wihda al-Mahaliyya al-Qurawiyya"

Two members, who will be given the fictitious names of Samir and Mohsen represent Tihna al-Gabal on the village's popular council. They are both members of the National Democratic Party, and were both nominated to the party's election list for membership and appointed in an uncontested election. Samir is about seventy years old, a shrewd politician who is highly knowledgeable and cultured, despite the fact that he received only primary education. Before his retirement he worked in the local village bank. A typical "yes man", Samir is a Nasserite, a Sadatist and a Mubarakist. He started his political life with Nasser's Liberation Rally when he was appointed to represent Tihna among the twenty members of the Committee of the Liberation Rally at the village level. At that time his main role was to spread the revolution's principles among the people. When the Liberation Rally was replaced by the National Union, elections officially replaced appointment, but according to Samir these elections were fictitious. What used to happen was that orders were sent either to the police commissioner at the Markaz level or to the police director at the governorate level to ensure the election of certain people whose loyalty to the revolution was trusted by the government; among them was Samir. He said that during that period his main task was to keep an eye on the "'Umad" in the surrounding villages, 90 per cent of whom were the remnant of the pre-revolutionary landlords, and who the government feared might conduct a counter-coup.

When the ASU succeeded the NU, Samir continued to represent Tihna as the "government man" and no change occurred in his role. When Sadat came to power and he started his attempt to reform the ASU by creating platforms (manabir), Samir's political career ceased for a while. According to him, this happened because he did not like the "manabir" and so chose not to join any of them. This was, however, far from the truth.

Corruption of an NDP Representative on the Popular Local Council

What really happened, as was told by most of the people in the village, is that Samir, who used to work as a clerk in the Agricultural Co-operative[13] before being transferred to the village bank, was charged, together with a member of his family, with embezzlement of the co-operative's money. He was also charged with fraud since he used to forge fictitious possessions, using imaginary peasant's names, to acquire their quota of seeds and fertilisers, which he then sold on the black market. When he was discovered or, to put it more accurately, when the government chose to expose him, he was sentenced in court and should have been imprisoned. However, since the government wanted only to teach him a lesson

226

but did not intend to get rid of him, a settlement was reached whereby he sold his land and paid back what he owed to the co-operative.

However, since, according to the constitution, a person who has been found guilty of any felony or crime cannot resume his political career and is ineligible for membership of all kind of local councils, Samir appealed against the court verdict and was surprisingly found innocent.[14] Nevertheless, he was transferred to the tightly-supervised village bank. Most people in the village failed to explain how this happened, although they all knew that he was guilty as charged.

When the peasants were asked why none of them had tried to expose Samir earlier to the authorities if they were so sure of his crimes, they answered that no one dared stand against Samir. "He is the government's man and representative and has high connections. Beside what happened when he was exposed?"

After his successful appeal, Samir became once again Tihna's representative on the popular local council of the village unit, first in Sadat's Misr Party which was later changed to the National Democratic Party, and currently in Mubarak's NDP. This means that except for a short period of time during the mid-seventies, Samir has been for almost thirty years the only member representing Tihna on the village unit popular council.

Only recently Mohsen, a school teacher, was presented by the NDP to the village council. The nomination of another member to the village local council has not been welcomed at all by Samir, who feels that it is an intrusion on his own domain. According to him Mohsen, who is in his late thirties, is but just "a foolish child who is politically immature and understands nothing about the rules of the game". Samir even tried to convince this researcher not to interview Mohsen for "this would be a real waste of her time."

What have been discovered is that almost all the members of the popular council of the village unit – apart from Mohsen – are either from the same age group or have a long history in common. Although being an equal member, Mohsen, who represents an injection of new blood into the village local council, is completely rejected by the other elderly members and they tend to treat him more like an outsider or an enemy than as one representing the same common interests.

When Samir was first interviewed and asked about the services provided by the different governmental organisations, he insisted that all the institutions were functioning efficiently and providing the peasants with all the needed services.

In a second interview, when he was confronted with the peasants' complaints and their dissatisfaction with the various services provided by these organisations, especially those provided by the agricultural co-operative and the health centre, Samir was extremely angry and blamed the ungrateful and ignorant peasants who in the past i.e.: before the 1952 revolution would not dare open their mouths with any complaint, despite their deteriorating conditions. For three hours he kept talking about the government and its achievements and condemning the peasants, whose lack of awareness prevented their appreciation of what the government was doing for them. When he was pressed with direct questions about the agricultural co-operative, as the interview was being taped, Samir asked for the tape recorder

227

to be turned off so that he could answer the questions. However, even when giving his personal opinion, he spoke in a general way refusing to provide any specific examples. According to Samir, the co-operative system is a failure and instead of strengthening it as the government had recently started to do, it should be abolished completely. Riddled with corruption, the co-operative harmed rather than benefited the fellahin.[15]

When asked about the reason for his insistence that the tape be switched off before he would give his opinion, and whether such behaviour was not in contradiction to what he had been describing as a healthy democratic atmosphere, he answered that the government, and more specifically Youssef Wali, the Minister of Agriculture, was the leading figure behind all the recent attempts to revive the co-operative movement. At the same time Youssef Wali was the Secretary-General of the NDP, which made Wali his superior in the party. Accordingly he would not dare state an opinion contradictory to Wali's policy, for fear it would be considered as a personal offence against him, which could end Samir's political career.

Samir's shrewdness prevented the eliciting of more information about the performance of the various institutions. The case of Samir shows that the government is ready to tolerate and even protect corruption, insofar as it serves its own purposes. In such a case corruption is not only used to control particular figures, but is also institutionalised, so that honesty becomes the exception rather than the rule, an outcome of the practices of the weak authoritarian state and a characteristic of the weak society.

Mohsen, the second member in the village council, was also interviewed. Still in his mid thirties, Mohsen started his political life in 1984 as the village youth supervisor in the NDP. He was then appointed as an assistant to the president of the activity committee in the party. He attended several conferences held by the NDP and was nominated to various committees within the party. In the local council elections held in 1991, he was nominated by the youth committee for membership on the village popular council. Young and enthusiastic, Mohsen spoke more openly and critically than his counterpart about the different services provided to the peasants.

Attacking the government for weakening the agricultural co-operatives, Mohsen said that it was the peasants who were victimised by this policy. His first complaint was about the village health clinic. The clinic was built on a large piece of land, donated by one of the pre-revolutionary élites for the purpose of building a large health centre, which would serve not only Tihna al-Gabal, but also the surrounding villages. However, instead of the health centre a small building, which has deteriorated over time, has been erected, with a huge amount of wasteland surrounding it. Mohsen said that he had tried more than once to ask the executive council to press the governorate to build the health centre, but all his efforts were in vain. Moreover he had sent an official note to the Minister of Health and another to the Prime Minister, asking them both to intervene first to prevent the deterioration of the building which affects the quality of health service provided, and second to use the land and build the health centre for which it was originally donated. However, he had received no respond from any of the authorities.

His second complaint concerned one of the primary schools, whose building had been damaged in the earthquake in 1992. He said that they were promised that the school would be repaired within six months, but up till then i.e. after more than a year and half, nothing had happened.

Generally speaking, as the peasants' representative, Mohsen is a promising young man. His success or failure in performing his task depends on two factors. The first is the extent to which the government party will allow members of the local popular council more freedom of opinion and more power to express the people's will, which is highly unlikely, and the second factor is the extent to which Mohsen himself will be able to resist all kind of pressures, oppositions and temptations that will come from Samir and the other fellow members.

B) The 'Umda: The Traditional Village Leader

What follows is based on an interview with the 'Umda of the village. The position of the 'Umda had been in his family since its inception. His great grandfather was the first 'Umda in the village in 1928 and he has been the 'Umda since 1969. The system as it used to exist in the village before the 1952 coup is that big families used to have a sheikh who was responsible for that particular family and for solving its problems. When the sheikh failed in his efforts, then the 'Umda, who used to be the head of the village, intervened and his ruling used to be binding on all parties concerned. In most cases the 'Umda was successful in solving the villagers' problems because he was given enough freedom to do so. Since 1952 the 'Umda's power has been greatly curtailed. The 'Umda says he does not interfere or try to solve any of the villagers' problems. When asked why, he said that now the police and the district attorney compete with the 'Umda in the village. He says that nowadays, when the 'Umad try to interfere and solve problems, the district secretaries attempt to humiliate and belittle them in front of the villagers to show the people that it is they who have the greatest authority, even over the 'Umad themselves. As a result, Tihna's 'Umda does not interfere in any of the villagers' problems in order to save himself any humiliation that may come from "someone who is as young as my youngest son". Thus the abuse of power by the police and the district attorney has forced the traditional village leaders to adopt a passive attitude towards their communities. When asked about his opinion on the new law which made the position of the 'Umda by appointment rather than by election, he denounced the law as being dangerous, since it may create more friction and problems, especially among the big rich families if these appointments showed preferences for any of them or for the least popular in the village. The 'Umda could not understand why the government should choose to pass such a law. When told that it might be an attempt to impose certain government men on the villages, he answered that the government ensures through the elections that all the 'Umad are affiliated to the NDP. Those who are not, are never elected. Hence changing the elected status of the 'Umad brings the government no additional benefit.

C) Political Awareness and Participation of Tihna's Peasants

In an attempt to establish the degree of political participation and awareness that the peasants have, several random interviews were conducted in which almost thirty villagers were asked about the various political parties. The majority of those interviewed showed no knowledge or awareness whatsoever of the existing opposition parties. Some of the interviewees, especially the older age group, were familiar with the name of the Wafd but still identified Sa'ad Zaghloul as its leader. One of the peasants identified the Wafd as the "Present ruling Party i.e.: the government". The Labour Socialist Party was also identified, but when asked about its leader, none of the interviewees knew him and some mentioned Mubarak as the Labour Party's leader.

When asked whether they participated in the elections, most of the interviewees gave an affirmative answer. During the 1990 elections, the NDP gave each peasant 10£E to vote. "I just put a mark on a piece of paper. It only took me one second and I earned a 10£E note. Not bad at all", was the answer of one of the peasants. "Besides did you know what happened to those who did not care to vote?" A group of peasants who were not happy with the deterioration of the services in the village decided not to vote. They were individually called to the police station without being given any reason. There they were all locked up in a room and were informed that they were not going to leave, no matter how long it took, before they voted for the government; they all ended up voting for the NDP. Wondering how the police came to know about these individuals, it was found out that the peasants have discussed it in the village cafe, and there must have been a police informant. Usually these informants are villagers who spy for the police in return for material and other benefits.

The case of Tihna clearly reflects the failure of the various opposition parties to put down roots among the peasants, and the same applies to the ruling party, which has to adopt a mixture of coercion and bribery to force peasants to vote and to compensate for its own weakness. Again the first group of interviewees shows that peasants through their *passive activity* preserve the continuation of the autocratic regime.

D) Political Activists in Tihna

Two of the political activists in the village, and one at the markaz level were also interviewed. The first was a member of the Wafd Party. His affiliation to the Wafd

230

seems to be hereditary, since his family was one of the pre-revolutionary bourgeois who were affiliated to the old Wafd Party. He spoke about the party with much nostalgia and seemed to be completely detached from the New Wafd. Nevertheless he showed a high degree of political awareness and criticised the Nasser and Sadat era. When he was asked about his opinion of the current political regime in general and about peasant conditions in particular, he however, refused to discuss the topic. It is interesting to observe that he discussed the Nasserite era and praised Nasser's accomplishment for the peasants despite the historical animosity between his class and Nasser, an attitude which is generally lacking among the most educated Wafd members in Cairo.

The second member ran in the local council elections in 1992 as an independent. Although he insisted in the interview that he was an independent political activist, some of the educated villagers said that he is a member of the Labour Socialist Party, and belonged more specifically to the Muslim Brotherhood wing. The refusal to reveal his political affiliation may be attributed to government harassment of the MB before the elections and particularly during the time when the research was being conducted, since it was at the height of the Islamic terrorist attacks, amid accusations that the MB supported and encouraged these groups. The member was reluctant to provide any information, although he insisted that the 1992 local council election results were forged by the government. When he was asked why none of the independents or the opposition candidates contested the election results in court, he answered by saying "And what happened when the results of the election for the People's Assembly were contested and the court ruled on the illegitimacy of many NDP winners?" referring to the fact that the government refused to execute the court order.[16]

Although the main focus of the research was the village of Tihna al-Gabal, the fact that the NDP member of the popular council at the markaz level, especially in a place like Upper Egypt, is a woman was a compelling reason to interview her. Extremely outspoken, Fayza al-Tahnawy started the interview by attacking the abolition of the allocation of women's seats on the local councils. She said that neither the NDP nor any of the opposition parties would in these circumstances nominate women to their party list, especially in places like Upper Egypt, with the excuse that women in local areas were not likely to be elected.[17]

Fayza started her career working in social services, where she was involved in several projects providing care for the elderly, health education for women in the villages, and training and development for village women. Through her social work, Fayza became popular with the local people and was able to build a good reputation for herself. She moved from there to pursue her political career and joined the NDP and was nominated to its list for the local council elections at the markaz level. Fayza admitted that it is not easy for a woman to become a politician especially in Upper Egypt. She said that she was backed by her rich and influential family, a support, which is not available to the average woman. Strong, vigorous, and somewhat aggressive, Fayza was critical of the government's bureaucratic procedures in dealing with the people's problems and demands. She spoke with great admiration about the National Unionist Progressive Party and, when asked why she chose to join the NDP instead of any other party, she replied that she wanted to change things, solve problems, and help the people, and that the only way she could do this was through the government party.

E) The Health Unit "Clinic"

The health unit was built in 1943. The land which amount to three feddans was donated by one of the pre-revolutionary élites, and the buildings by another. As noted earlier, their main purpose was to build a large health centre to serve all the villages on the eastern side of the Nile. The health unit is set on a small piece of land, with the rest of the land unused, covered with garbage and with a lot of sheep and chickens running everywhere. As well as a physician, who is at the same time the head of the health unit, and two dentists working alternately at the unit, there are a number of nurses and assistant midwives who care for pregnant women and provide the children with different types of vaccination.

There is also a clerk who is responsible for recording births and deaths. He is also responsible for the storeroom and prepares the employees' payroll each month. Two health inspectors also work there. One is responsible for the vaccination programme and the other for environmental and nutritional health.[18] Two laboratory assistants, whose sole qualification is a preparatory school certificate and a six-month training in laboratory work, also work at the health unit. The only tests they conduct are the urine and excreta tests to identify bilharzia, the most common illness among the Egyptian peasants, and according to Dr Ahmed, the head of the health unit, they are capable of carrying out these tests, despite the fact that their education is not related to any medical training. Dr Ahmed said that the lack of the financial resources is the most important obstacle hindering the health unit from providing a good quality service to the peasants. According to him the money allocated by the government to each health unit for the purpose of buying medicines is 2500 Egyptian pounds[19] which is, on the average, equivalent to £500 per annum. Thus the budget for medication for each person in Tihna is 48 piasters, or 9.5 pence, per year.

Dr Ahmed was asked about the means by which any patient in the village would obtain a specific medicine not available in the health unit for budgetary reasons. He answered that if the patient could afford it, he could buy it from the pharmacy. On the other hand, if he cannot afford it, he could either try the general hospital or al-Menia University hospital. Dr Ahmed then added that even there, the patient might not find the required medicine, in which case, "only God could be the healer".[20] Dr Ahmed was then asked if he had ever tried to press the health department in al-Menia governorate for more money for his unit. He answered that he never tried to do so simply because he knew that after a long, bureaucratic procedure, his demand would be rejected. This would not come as a surprise to him, since the allocation for the health service in the current budget at the national level is 1.6 per cent. This amount had to cover the building of new hospitals, renovation of old ones, the purchase of various medical equipment and supplies, and the cost of medicine and vaccination provisions. Finally, Dr Ahmed said that the village unit was not equipped even for the simplest operations and that, no matter how urgently a patient needed an operation, he had to be transferred to one of al-Menia city's hospitals. The problem was that this could take some time and sometimes time is the only thing that the patient cannot afford.

As mentioned earlier, two dentists work in Tihna's health unit. The first is Dr Fouad, who is in his mid -forties or early fifties and who has been working there for fourteen years. Although several attempts to interview him were made, they were unsuccessful.

The Health Unit: A Case of Institutionalised Corruption

The second dentist, Dr Hany, is in his mid-thirties and had been working in Tihna for only two years. Although this is a relatively short time, the information he provided about the Tihna health unit and another unit in which he worked previously,[21] was very illuminating. Coming from a wealthy Coptic family and the son of one of al-Menia's most famous physicians, Dr Hany, alongside his work in Tihna's health unit, has a private clinic in al-Menia city and has managed to build a wide reputation as a successful and efficient dentist. When asked about his previous work, Dr Hany revealed that he had asked to be transferred from the previous unit because he had been unable to combat or live with the corruption there.

According to him, the corruption ranged from stealing the vitamins and the anaesthetics to charging the patients fees higher than the official rate for their medical examinations. This was done by the employees with the approval of the doctors working there. After warning several times that he would expose this corruption, Dr Hany submitted an official complaint to the health department in al-Menia City. There he was advised to withdraw his complain and to live and let live. When he refused and insisted that his complaint pass through the official channels, the head of the health department himself had torn up the complaint and asked him to be more reasonable in his demands. The only solution left to Dr Hany was to submit an official request to be transferred to another health unit.

In Tihna Dr Hany is exposed to all kinds of discriminatory practices from Dr Ahmed, the head of the village health unit, as a sort of punishment for his boldness in exposing the corruption in the previous unit. He said that Dr Ahmed is behaving according to special orders given to him from the head of the health department in Markaz al Menia.

As for Tihna's health unit, the corruption there is directly carried by the doctors themselves. This will be labelled here as "*technical corruption*" to distinguish it from other forms of corruption. Dr Hany said that this kind of corruption is wide-spread among the health units in Egypt's villages to the extent that it is becoming a normal practice. What happens is that patients who pay only the official fees for a check-up see the physician in a group of nine or ten. The doctor asks each of them about the symptoms of his illness and prescribes the medicine without any real medical examination. Only those who are willing to pay the doctor his private fees are allowed to wait until the other patients leave and are then thoroughly examined and the free medicine is provided for them from the health unit.

The case of Tihna's health unit reflects the quality of the service provided to the majority of the peasants. Such poor quality can be attributed to several factors, the most important of which is the poor financial resources which the government allocates for such an important service as that of health. The prevailing corruption can also be attributed to a number of factors. First, the country's deteriorating economic condition especially the enormous increase in prices, which is not matched by a similar increase in salaries. One has only to know that a general practitioner who has spent seven years in the school of medicine, would, after accepting government recruitment, receive a starting monthly salary of £E45, equivalent to £9. Only a small segment of medical school graduates can afford to open private clinics. These usually come from rich families with one or sometimes both parents working as doctors. Thus the majority of newly graduated doctors are bound to accept government recruitment. Second, the problem is aggravated by the large number of graduates, who are too many to be absorbed either by the domestic market or by foreign markets which have a shortage of medical practitioners. Third, the reluctance of most government recruited doctors to work in rural areas and the lack of government control means that most of them are just names on the payroll, never actually visiting the rural health units, where they are supposed to be working.

The case of Tihna clearly reflects that corruption remains the only way of survival for most doctors. It also shows that instead of trying to solve the doctors' problems by increasing their salaries and working out a policy to limit the number of doctors entering the labour force by restricting entry to medical schools for a while, the government chooses to appease this segment of society by turning a blind eye and a deaf ear to deviant behaviour. Corruption here becomes an indispensable tool for controlling a discontented group in society. Thus work ethics deteriorate, and honesty is punished, but corruption is rewarded.

F) Tihna's Agricultural Co-operative

The agricultural co-operative is a small building that opens to the peasants for a couple of hours every day, although as a governmental organisation it should function from 8:30 am till 2 pm. The employees in the co-operative include the manager, the head of the agricultural unit in Tihna, who is also a member of the village executive council, four agricultural supervisors, a clerk and a mechanic.

The co-operative manager is in charge of three co-operatives: Tihna, al-Hawarta, and Nazlet Ebeid where he is situated. A board of directors representing the peasants' interests and elected by them oversees the services of the co-operative. In an interview with the manager, the head of the agricultural unit in Tihna, and one of the agricultural supervisors, the following information was provided. The co-operative manager started the interview by listing the various services that the co-operative provides for the peasants.[22] The co-operative supervises the cultivation of the various crops and treats any epidemics that occur. Together with the village bank, it provides the peasants with the needed seeds and fertilisers. The co-operative also receives the peasants' crops, the most important of which are wheat, maize and soya beans. However, since optional marketing and delivery has replaced the forced delivery of the past, the peasant has to pay cash for whatever production input he buys from the co-operative. Previously, he used to buy all his seeds and fertilisers by credit and on delivery of his crops to the co-operative the latter would reduce the amount of money due and give him the balance.

The Behaviour of Tihna's Peasants towards Unfavourable State Policy

When asked about the cotton, and the reasons for its disappearance from the village, the head of the agricultural unit mentioned that the soil in Tihna al Gabal and the surrounding villages is one of the best for the growth of cotton which was cultivated until 1978. However, because peasants grow cotton at no profit at all, and sometimes at a loss, they continued to evade the law, forcing the Ministry of Agriculture to issue a decree relieving the whole area of its cultivation. When asked about the methods by which the peasants evaded the law, he cited the case of delaying cotton cultivation for at least two months beyond the cultivation date in order to take an extra cut on their previous crops which were usually either maize or berseem.[23] The delay in cotton cultivation would normally result in a weak cotton yield.

The manager blamed the government policy of forced delivery and keeping cotton prices low for the behaviour of the peasants. In order to illustrate his point he gave the following example. Comparing the costs and price of cotton and maize in 1978 and given the rent of land for both crops is fixed at £E24 per feddan, the cost of growing one feddan of cotton is £E100, and produce four qintars. The government used to purchase each qintar for £E25 which means that the peasants were cultivating cotton at a loss, since the price covers only the production cost without covering the rent. On the other hand, one feddan of maize cultivation would cost £E40 in production cost and would produce 10 qintars sold at £E100 per qintar. After paying his rent the peasant is still making a profit. Knowing that cotton cultivation takes seven months compared with four months for maize, the peasants would take two cuts of maize as compared with one of cotton during more or less the same period of time. In addition, cotton cultivation needs a lot of effort and manual labour. Usually school pupils and agricultural workers gather the crop. However, because of the existence of the 'mountain' in Tihna, a marble quarry has succeeded in attracting all the surplus labour in the village, especially when the daily income of the worker in the quarry amounts to £E10 as compared to £E4 in the cotton fields. Faced with all these difficulties and material loss, peasants in Tihna, through their active passivity, succeeded in forcing the government to eliminate the cultivation of cotton from the whole area.

Another example provided by the co-operative's manager of the peasants' evasion of law is the deliberate sabotage of agricultural land. This took place either by selling the fertile soil per cubic metre for the manufacture of red bricks or by neglecting the land and withholding irrigation until it could be classified as uncultivable in which case it could either be sold to building contractors or used by the peasants for building. The latter practice is now widespread in Tihna. The government was again blamed for forcing the peasants to adopt such behaviour. The manager mentioned that the construction of the High Dam made things worse for the peasants. He explained that the peasants used to cultivate cotton and wheat successively. Both crops, however, exhaust the soil, as they absorbs most of its nutrients. Before the construction of the Aswan Dam, the silt and sediment carried by the Nile was nourishing the soil and renewing it. The dam withholds these nutrients and prevents them from reaching the land. As a result the peasants now have to buy these at extra cost. Moreover, the inundation which used to take place from mid-August till the end of October, provided the soil with the necessary irrigation and washed it of the accumulated salt. Although the inundation used to destroy some crops, the benefits outweighed the costs. After the dam, the peasants have to irrigate the land several times which again incurs more costs. The peasants have thus found it more profitable to build on agricultural land where they can sell the new flats with a return on investment which far exceeds their profitability from cultivation and needs less labour.

The manager was then asked about the procedures taken to protect the agricultural land from erosion, and the role of the co-operative in this respect. He answered that in the past the co-operative used to take the peasants who deliberately sabotaged their land to court, which would force them to pay a fine. With the increase in population, the agricultural supervisor is now being charged with such a responsibility. Dealing with construction on agricultural land, however, takes a different route. The agricultural supervisor first takes the peasants to court. The court would then commission on its behalf an expert whose responsibility was to inspect the land and verify whether the construction had taken place on agricultural or residential land. If proven guilty, the peasants would be fined and could serve a sentence in prison. However, this is a lengthy procedure (especially since it usually takes the expert a minimum period of three years to inspect the land) and before its conclusion several more peasants would have constructed additional buildings thus transforming the whole area into a residential one. In this case, when the expert finally arrives he is bound to classify

Table 9.1 An estimation of the distribution of land ownership in Tihna al-Gabal

Those who do not own agricultural land	50 per cent
Owners of less than one feddan	30 per cent
Owners of one to less than five feddan	6 per cent
Owners of five to twelve feddans	12 per cent

Source: *An interview with the manager of the agricultural co-operative.*

the area as non-agricultural and accordingly the charges against the peasants would be dismissed. An example was cited about a case taken to court in 1990:an expert was assigned to investigate in 1991, and two years and six months later, the expert had not appeared. Thus the government's lengthy and bureaucratic procedures aggravate the problem. According to the manager, if the government did not find an immediate solution to the problem, within the next ten years, agricultural land could be reduced by half.

The gradual reduction of the agricultural land supply also provides landowners with ample opportunity for the exploitation of tenants. In 1990 the rent of one feddan was £E500, in 1993 the rent jumped to £E1500 per feddan provided that full payment was made. If payment was made by instalments, the rent would normally rise to £E2000 per feddan. For one cut of berseem the tenants would pay £E1300 for rent, which is an extreme exploitation of tenants by the landowners. Generally speaking, peasants need to own or cultivate at least five feddans in order to be able to live above subsistence level. An estimate of the distribution of ownership in the village is shown in the table above.

Only two families in the village own more than 12 feddan. These are the 'Umda's family who own 13 feddans, and another family who own 30 feddans. Reviewing the previously mentioned estimates, it is clear that the majority of peasants live below subsistence level.

The 50 per cent who do not own agricultural land consist of three categories: non-peasants, tenants, and agricultural labourers. Some of the tenants, most of whom rent less than five feddans and in most cases only a few qirrats, also work for others as agricultural labourers in order to augment their income or to cover their rents. The agricultural labourers are among the poorest of the poor in Tihna. Their daily wages have been set at 6£E for several years without any increase to match inflation. This is attributed to the reduction in the size of the agricultural land which reduces the demand for their labour, coupled with an increase in their numbers, causing a stabilisation in their wages. Another factor, which contributes to the low level of wages for agricultural labourers, is the fact that the prices of the crops where their labour is needed do not increase at the same rate as the increase in rent and the other agricultural expenses.

The co-operative's Board of Directors

This board is an independent body elected by the peasants. Its function is to oversee the various services provided by the co-operative and to represent the peasants' interests. The board comprises a president, a general secretary, a treasurer, and five members. Neither the president nor the treasurer were willing to be interviewed despite considerable efforts. Three of the other members were interviewed, however, and they were able to shed light on the function of the co-operative. According to these members the agricultural co-operative in Tihna al Gabal has no function whatsoever. In the past, and before Sadat launched his campaign to weaken the co-operatives, they were mainly financed by the village bank. The co-operative would then buy the various agricultural inputs (i.e.: seeds and fertilisers) and supply them to the peasants, either for cash or on credit, each according to the amount of land he owns. When the peasant delivered the crops to the co-operative, the latter retained their share, and paid the bank back its loan. However, since the government stripped the co-operatives of all their functions and gave them to the village bank, the latter stopped financing the co-operative. Although attempts have been made to revive co-operatives, these attempts, as shown by the example of Tihna's co-operative, has not been successful. This is attributed to the bank's resistance and their continuous efforts to kill the co-operative. The members of the board of directors said that the warehouse of Tihna's co-operative has been completely empty for two years. Since the co-operative does not function, the board of directors has no role to play.

Comparing the services that were previously provided by the co-operative to those provided by the bank, the members made clear that the former were better. According to them the bank tended to exploit the peasants. One of the members said that he had a £E250 loan from the bank to buy some agricultural inputs. After a year he had to repay £E400. The agricultural co-operative on the other hand used not to charge any interests for its credit provisions to the peasants. According to the board members, the cash loans provided by the bank harm rather than benefit the peasants. The main objective of these loans is to provide the peasants with the cash they need to buy the agricultural inputs. However, in most cases peasants spend most of the loan on consumer needs leaving a minimal amount to be invested in their land. Thus it is not surprising that the co-operative, by supplying the peasants with agricultural inputs rather than cash was far better.

Again, because the bank charges high interest, more peasants are turning to rich merchants for loans, whether in cash or in the form agricultural inputs, in exchange for their crops. This means that the merchant would buy the peasant's crop in advance i.e.: before it is even cultivated, and would then pay the peasant the difference after subtracting what he owes him. In this case the peasants have to accept whatever price the merchant sets for their crops, a case that renders them vulnerable to his manipulation. It is interesting to note here, that the members of the co-operative board mentioned that in the case of some crops,[24] a government policy of forced delivery was far better for the peasants than the current situation, since it protected them from the exploitation of merchants.

What became clear from later interviews conducted with the peasants, is that prices for the various crops are not determined by the market forces of supply and demand, but rather by a number of merchants who monopolise the market. In the case of Tihna al-Gabal, these merchants are known to the peasants and were introduced to the villagers by the agricultural supervisors. The latter ensure that no other merchants from the surrounding areas bid for the village crops. The supervisors are of course remunerated for their services. Peasants are faced with the option of either selling to those merchants or not selling at all. Putting it differently, the policy of forced delivery to the government which was adopted in the past has been replaced by a policy of forced delivery to certain merchants who monopolise the market in Tihna and set the prices of the crops, with the least profitability to the peasants, thus representing a continuation in the tradition of exploitation of these peasants.

G) The Village Bank

In an attempt to explore the type of relationship which exist between the village bank and the co-operative and to investigate peasants' complaints about the bank, an interview was conducted with the manager of the village bank to which Tihna al Gabal is affiliated.

The hierarchical structure of these banks originates from the Development and Agricultural Credit Bank situated in Cairo, which is the central agricultural bank. This bank has several branches at the governorate level. The present study refers to the Development and Agricultural Credit Bank in al-Mania governorate. Affiliated to the governorate bank are several branches at the markaz level, which in turn have village banks that provide services to a number of villages. Each village bank has a warehouse and representatives in each of the villages it covers. Village banks function through a plan which they prepare according to the needs of the affiliated villages. This plan is then presented to the markaz branch which draws up a plan for all the village banks affiliated to it and presents it to the governorate bank. The governorate bank draws up a plan encompassing the needs of all its markaz banks and present it to the central bank for approval. In other words the plan is drawn from down-up. The plan includes the proportion of money that should be allocated for loans in the different projects.

The village bank to which Tihna al-Gabal is affiliated is situated in Nazlet Hussein, and serves all the villages affiliated to Nazlet Hussein local village unit. In the interview conducted with the bank's manager, he identified three stages in the bank's relation to the co-operative. The first stage was under Nasser's rule, when the village banks used to operate through and were affiliated to the co-operatives. The second stage was under Sadat's rule, when law 117 was passed which proclaimed the independence of the village banks and transferred to them most of the functions of the co-operatives. At this stage the bank used to sell all the agricultural inputs and receive crop delivery from the peasants. In the third stage under Mubarak, attempts were made to revive co-operatives by giving them back their previous functions. The agricultural inputs are now sold in an open competitive market by the co-operative and private individual merchants. The bank has stopped selling these inputs. The only case in which the bank interferes is when merchants establish a monopoly and start pushing prices up. The bank then starts selling a limited amount of agricultural inputs in order to pull the prices down and stabilise the market.

The manager was then asked about the high interest rates which the bank charges the peasants. Here the manager blamed the central bank, which has left the interest rate on loans open. Accordingly, most banks were charging high rates for their loans. Since the village bank itself is financed by other commercial banks, which lend to village banks and charge them high interest rates, the latter have to charge their customers, who are mainly peasants, a high interest rate. However, in the previous year the situation had improved, since the Central Bank had placed a ceiling on investment loans at 17 per cent and on agricultural loans at 15 per cent. Whereas the former encompass all investment projects, including animal breeding and the purchase of tilling machinery, the latter cover loans made for the purchase of agricultural inputs, the amount of which is determined according to the type of cultivated crop and the amount of the land.

Although he admitted that the functions of the co-operative in Tihna al-Gabal had completely come to a halt, the manager could not explain this situation and defended the bank against peasants' accusations that it had caused the collapse of the co-operative's activities. He said that if Tihna's co-operative would ask the bank for a loan, the bank would normally provide it, because in this case the loan would be secured by the central co-operative. Thus lack of financial resources does not represent an obstacle for the co-operative. It became clear later that the co-operative does receive some agricultural inputs, which are sold secretly on the black market by the co-operative employees, who claim that the warehouse is empty. None of the informants was willing to report what was going on to the police and the interviewees were not willing to be taped.

4. Conclusion

Tihna al Gabal is but a narrow reflection of the interaction which takes place between the Egyptian state and society at large. It clearly shows how corruption is institutionalised and rewarded by the weak autocratic state in order to domesticate and hence weaken civil society. The case of the corrupted NDP representative on the village council who was allowed to pursue his political career after embezzlement charges of co-operative money, and the corruption that is taking place in the village's health unit to which the government chooses to protect, are two such indicative examples. Coercion, which is the complementary strategy used by the weak state against society, is reflected in the arrests made by the local police of a group of peasants who were forced to vote for the government party. The case of Tihna also shows how the government uses its own party to control the localities and to marginalise the role of the opposition. The weakness of the society, on the other hand, is reflected in the failure of primary associations, notably political parties, to strike roots among the peasants, to function as a channel of interest aggregation and representation, and to control and supervise the quality of services provided to the peasants. Tihna-al Gabal reflects the virtual absence of opposition parties' activities in the village, which is negatively reflected on the political participation of the peasants and their political culture and behaviour. Likewise the failure of secondary associations i.e. the co-operatives to defend and represent peasant interests against the aggression of the state and other exploiters, has contributed to the creation of a fragmented peasant society in which private rather than public good prevails. As a result, peasants actively defy government development policies and in turn increase the weakness of the state.

CHAPTER TEN

Conclusion

In this work the nature of the Egyptian State and society has been explored and the dynamic interactive relationship between them analysed. In this chapter using the analysis of state-society relationship examined in this book, a model, which rejects previous scholarly interpretations about state and society in Egypt, is presented. Since the Hegelian concept of state shaping society is a major hypothesis of the proposed model, the nature of the Egyptian State will be the starting point of reiteration.

1. The Nature of the Egyptian State

The Egyptian State shares several of the characteristics of O'Donnell's bureaucratic authoritarianism. It shares with the bureaucratic authoritarian regime the fact that it is based on an alliance between the state, the military, and selected segments of the bourgeoisie who have established direct links with foreign business interests. The fact that Egypt's three presidents since 1952 came from the military enhances the interrelated interest between the executive and the military and makes the latter an elitist organisation which backs presidential rule vis-à-vis society. The use of the military to suppress the food riots in 1977 and the security police upheaval in 1986 reflect such alliance. The third side of the alliance triangle, as reflected in Chapter Six, is top businessmen who maintain a close relationship with foreign interests and corporations through the various joint Egyptian-foreign businessmen associations, the most prominent of which are Egyptian-American reflecting the interdependent relationship between the two countries. Evidence of the alliance between the state and top businessmen is manifested in the latter's increased representation in Parliament, their increasing role in shaping public policy, and their proximity to the President.

However, despite this alliance, the Egyptian State enjoys relative autonomy, exemplifying Marx's Bonapartist state. For as far as the military is concerned, and despite its expanding economic activities which include the manufacture of armaments and a wide range of industrial products and public utilities, there has been a tendency on behalf of both Sadat and Mubarak regimes towards

> Civilianisation of cabinets and of other political and administrative organisations combined with increased emphasis on professionalism within the armed forces and growing efforts aimed at depoliticising the military in addition to the enforcement of civilian control over the army.[1]

Although Ayubi suggests a future scenario in which the growing and expanding economic power of the military institution could finally lead to direct military intervention,[2] while Springborg suggests that the military will replace the state in the alliance formula with the upper bourgeoisie,[3] there is evidence to repudiate both scholars' suggestions. The first evidence is the ease with which the military institution complies with the change in the ideological orientation of the rulers, thus reflecting its subordination to the latter. As Ayubi himself notes.

> It is indeed ironical that the Egyptian army which was sent to the Congo in 1960 to support the revolutionary Patrice Lumumba was sent in 1977 to the same country (now Zaire) to help the pro-Western regime of Mobutu. And it is equally ironical that the Egyptian army, which was fighting Arabian 'reactionism' and supporting the revolution in Yemen from 1963 to 1967 was declared by Sadat in the seventies to be ready to defend the Gulf monarchs and princes against any revolutionary influences. Another important shift that took place, especially following the Camp David Accords, could be seen in the way the perceived source of military threat was transferred from the East (Israel) to the west (Libya).[4]

The second evidence being the ease with which Field-Marshal Abu Ghazala, a most influential figure at the national level and extremely popular within the army was removed from office by Mubarak in 1989 without the eruption of any dissent among army officers or an attempt at coup d'etat. This evidence clearly shows that as long as the military officers continue to benefit from the privileges granted to them by the regime and by its economic policies, they will continue to be subservient to the regime, and to protect rather than challenge it.

On the other hand, and as revealed in Chapter Six, the segment of the bourgeoisie with which the state forged an alliance is narrow, lacks a political culture of their own, and has failed to form a lobby independent of the state. Top businessmen who rise to power remain there at the discretion of the president and his sons. The case of the famous businessman Muhammad Farid Khamis who has fallen out of favour with Mubarak and been removed as a result from both the Presidential Council and from his position as head of the Egyptian Federation of Industries, is a case in point. The relative autonomy of the Egyptian State is thus indisputable. Another example that reflects the extent of independence of the Egyptian State is manifested by the inability of the agrarian bourgeoisie to employ the state to serve their interests. As indicated in Chapter Eight, it took several years of continuous efforts to pass a tenancy law that would evict tenant peasants.

Like the bureaucratic authoritarian regime, the Egyptian regime organises the relations of power in favour of the executive. As shown in Chapter Three, the legislative branch is subordinated to the executive. This is clearly reflected in the inherent contradictions embodied in the constitution which grant the President enormous powers, including the promulgation of laws, without effective accountability to Parliament, in the dominance of the ruling NDP, headed by the president, and its occupation of the majority of seats in the People's Assembly, and in the role of the Parliament's speaker in halting the performance of the opposition both in its legislative and scrutiny capacity. Chapter Seven shows how the same policy is applied at the local level, where the various laws of local administration centralise all powers in the governors and their executive councils at the expense of the elected popular councils, whose representative and control role are severely undermined. Again, and in congruence with the characteristics of the bureaucratic authoritarian regime, the Egyptian judicial system is more independent in theory than in practice. Court rulings are not respected, often ignored by the executive and in many cases justice is perverted. This is carried on either through coercion, where judges are forced to pass a particular rule, or through corruption, where judges are bribed by the executive apparatus. As the examples provided in Chapter Three show, the rulings of the Supreme Constitutional Court on the validity of membership of certain MPs, who belong to the NDP, in Parliament are completely ignored by the government. The case mentioned in Chapter Nine of the NDP's representative on Tihna al-Gabal's popular village council who, after the embezzlement charges and his dismissal from the agricultural co-operative was acquitted in court and resumed his membership in the council, is one example of the subversion of justice carried on at the executive will.

Another shared characteristic between the bureaucratic authoritarian regime and the Egyptian regime is the fact that the latter is also exclusionary and eliminates the normal mediators i.e. political parties between the state and civil society. Chapter Three summarises the various laws that are promulgated by the Egyptian state in its attempt to weaken political parties by restricting the formation and function of the opposition both outside and inside Parliament. A complementary strategy for the legal and institutional repression is the harassment to which the various opposition parties, whether secular or religious, are subjected. Chapter Four shows how the government prior to the 1995 elections has harassed and imprisoned several of its opponents.

Chapters Five and Six indicate that the same repressive policies are applied to professional syndicates and labour unions, coupled with a policy of co-option of top leaders, who are separated from their constituencies, either through turning a blind eye on their corruption or through bestowing special privileges on them. This, however, highlights one of the mistaken hypotheses that some Middle Eastern specialists like Bianchi, Al-Sayyid and some others present when they predict that Egypt's corporatist politics is evolving into a form of 'plural corporatism.' Ayubi agrees with Bianchi and, drawing heavily on the latter's opinion, distinguishes between two phases: the expansionary phase of the state and its contracting phase. According to Ayubi the expansionary phase is characterised by the direct intervention of the state in the economy, the enlargement of the public sector, and the state's expanding welfare role or what he labelled etatism. In the contracting phase, on the other hand, there is a drive towards a reduction in the role of the state in the economy accompanied by a denationalisation of the public sector and a gradual elimination of its welfare obligations.[5] Whereas he associates the former phase with populist and socialist authoritarian regimes, the latter is associated with bureaucratic authoritarian regimes. He has thus mentioned:

> Thus one can see that in the expansionary phase, the state used to take political rights away in exchange for granting socio-economic ones, in the 'contractory' phase the state concedes political rights for groups and individuals in return for being relieved from some of its financial and welfarist commitments.[6]

Accordingly,

> In general, the Egyptian State has been striving to trade the expansion of certain political freedoms for the moderation of certain economic demands. In Egypt, and in similar regimes, the state-centred variety of corporatism which was more typical of earlier stages may be giving way to a more variegated and flexible form of corporatism that will perhaps allow more play both to modern-type organised social interests – such as those of the professional and the business associations – as well as to the more 'traditional' community-centred groups that are formed around familial, factional or local nuclei.[7]

The previous scholars' views are contested here. It will be argued here that classical corporatism, as a strategy for controlling society existed in Egypt during the Nasserite era, when the state was still in the expansionary phase. It could then afford to trade political liberalism for the economic benefits bestowed on the various groups which manifests itself in the welfarist obligations of the state. As the fiscal crises of the state tightens, under Sadat and Mubarak, the contraction phase starts, and the state becomes unable to carry on with its welfarists commitments. Accordingly, the "social contract" on which classical corporatism was based has eroded and hence has been replaced by a tighter form of corporatism, which has been labelled here as *co-integrationism.* The latter is a strategy adopted by the state to control society through a mixture of co-option, integration and fusion of private individual interests (that of the leaders of various associations and organisations), with that of the state, whilst establishing tight control through coercion, over the broader segments of society. The integration of trade union leaders into the state system through granting them special privileges as indicated in Chapter Six, is but one illustrative example. Again granting a small segment of the business community certain privileges otherwise denied to the majority of businessmen as reflected in Chapter Six is another such example. Using corruption as a tool for the integration of private interests is a strategy that has been adopted by the Egyptian regime, to control syndicate leaders. As shown in Chapter Five, this type of corruption, which has been labelled by Waterbury as 'planned corruption'[8] takes place either by turning a blind eye on syndicate leaders' corruption, (as in the case of the Lawyers' Syndicate under Mubarak) or by the creation of a clientele network (as in the case of the Doctors' Syndicates under Nasser) or by adopting both methods (as in the case of the Engineers' Syndicate under Sadat). Chapter Nine shows how corruption has also been covered up by the Egyptian state in order to protect the government party's representative in Tihna al-Gabal's popular local council. It also highlights that the state institutionalised corruption among doctors as a means of controlling this uncontended segment of society. Egypt thus experiences similar characteristics of authoritarian regimes in Latin America, as described by Fernando Cardoso

> But the state does not adopt a corporative form. It does not try to stimulate class organisation, to promote a doctrine of organic harmony among social groups, or to establish corporative links among them that could form a base for political domination. Rather, the links between civil society and the bureaucratic-authoritarian regime are achieved through the co-optation of individuals and private interests into the system.[9]

Accordingly, contrary to what Bianchi and Ayubi predicted with respect to the evolution of 'associative democracy', it is argued here that it is more likely for associative democracy, which is a more flexible form of corporatism, to flourish under populist and socialist regimes. This being a better alternative for these regimes, than a multi party-democratic system. In this case 'associative democracy' would still be complemented by the exchange of the economic benefits granted by the state. On the other hand, under bureaucratic authoritarian regimes (whose states are in the contraction phase and hence are unable to continue offering these economic benefits), associative democracy would be a luxury that the state could not afford without risking a disruption of the social order.[10]

Chapters Five, Six, and Eight of this work show the tendency of the Egyptian authoritarian regime furthermore to weaken, marginalise, and consequently tighten its control over all associations, syndicates, labour unions, agricultural co-operatives and business associations

The Egyptian regime also lacks what Gramsci described as an hegemonic ideology i.e. the moral and intellectual leadership, which enables it to rule, by consent. As Ayubi explains

> Developmentalism is too vague a concept to be considered as such and in most cases it remains confined to the technocratic and 'intellectual' fractions. There may, however, be bursts of nationalistic fervour, charismatic arousal or populist jubilation-but this is hardly ideology.[11]

246

Based on coercion and repression and in the absence of an appropriate ideology of its own, the Egyptian regime lacks both legitimacy and hegemonic control over society.

2. Strong State or Strong Society: the Current Debate

If, as already argued, lack of hegemonic control over society is a major characteristic of the Egyptian regime, how did the myth of the strength of the state in Egypt and, indeed, in the rest of the Middle East arise? The answer to this question lies mainly in the debate among those scholars who, in Ayubi's succinct phrase, tend to 'overstate the Arab state'.

This group of scholars, usually referred to as 'classical orientalists' trace the origin of despotism in Islam[12] only to conclude that

> Islam was not just a religion but a total way of life. The totalistic character of the faith seemed to imply that only a totalitarian state could put its dogmas into practice.[13]

In such a state the ruler acquires a divine nature and obeying him becomes both a political and a religious obligation. Dissent is thus not only a crime but also a sin. Accordingly, orthodox Islam promoted political quietism, which was characterised by the absence of representative institutions that could act as a mediator between the ruler and the ruled. In this case no self-local government is allowed to form and professional associations represented by the guilds and craft associations could not be left untampered lest they gain enough strength to impose limitations on the state's control over its subjects.[14] The suppression of various groups in the society results "in a despotic regime in which 'the state is stronger than society.'"[15] It could be well argued here that Egypt represents a case where the orientalist thesis is flawed since the country had known despotic rule long before Islam. It was the mode of production as described by Marx's Asiatic Mode of Production (presence of large scale agriculture) coupled with the presence of a ruling class which imposes a degree of socio-administrative control (control and regulation of the Nile for irrigation purposes) without owning the means of production, as described by Wittfogel's Oriental despotism that shaped and necessitated the type of despotic state that had previously existed in Egypt. Islam might have emphasised this despotic nature of the Egyptian state but it certainly did not create it.

Among contemporary writers, Hinnebusch embraced the strong state theme when, mistakenly, he described the state during Nasser's era as being stronger and more autonomous than that of his successors.[16] According to him, Nasser had stood above and balanced off the elites and had often relied on popular support to curtail their power.[17] He was able to achieve such balance because of the legitimacy that was endowed on his rule by the society, which was based mainly on his charisma.[18] It would appear that Hinnebusch confused Nasser's brinkmanship and his ability to rule a divided elite with the strength of the state.

Although, until recently, the existence of strong, dominant Middle Eastern States which subjugate societies, was the prevailing idea among Western scholars, a growing, albeit, limited number of scholars have started to contest this thesis. The Iranian revolution, however, represented a turning point, with more Western and non-western Middle Eastern specialists started to revise their earlier views, not only about the Iranian State and society, but also about states and societies in the Middle East generally. Three factors have triggered this revisionism. The first is the growth of the Islamic movements in several Middle Eastern countries and the challenges they pose to the ruling regimes; the second, the decline in oil prices which highlighted the fiscal crisis of the state, making it obvious that those states that were once described as strong are not that strong after all (if not quite the opposite); and, finally, the growing literature on societal forces that were previously neglected such as the mob, interest groups, networks, and classes which act as equivalents to "civil society" in the region.[19]

This revisionist approach of 'Weak States-Strong Societies' came to dominate the literature dealing with the analysis of state-society relationship in the Middle East in general and in Egypt in particular. For example, in his assessment of the land reform law that had been initiated by Nasser's regime and was considered as its landmark, Migdal asserted that the state was weak because it had failed to concentrate social control in its agencies and to combat the power of the strongmen, especially at the village level,[20] with the result that the outcome of the policies and the reform undertaken turned out to be far from what originally had been planned and anticipated by the state's leaders.[21] Migdal thus concluded that in such a case the society had succeeded in transforming the state, rather than being transformed by it;[22] that is, it was a case of weak state, strong society.

Similarly in his analysis for the factors underlying failure of reform in the Egyptian agricultural sector, Sadowsky discovered that businessmen and local bureaucrats allied together and managed to subvert reform policy. He has thus concluded

> The weakness of the state and the strength of social forces, contrary to the expectations of the development community, played an important role in retarding economic growth in Egypt.[23]

He also adds

> Too often people assume that because a country has a flag and an army, it must have an effective state. They infer that, because a government is not restrained by a democratic constitution or a representative assembly, state power must be autocratic and unlimited. Westerners in particular tend to see Middle Eastern dictatorships like those of Nasser and Sadat as modernised versions of "Oriental despotism". They presume that in Egypt the state is strong and society is weak. The reality is almost exactly the opposite.[24]

Arguing along the same line of thought Springborg's work on clientele network in Egypt acknowledges the strength of these informal societal relations, and a similar revised approach was adopted by Moore and Waterbury.[25]

In a study she conducted on the political behaviour of the popular sector "sha'b" in four urban quarters in Cairo, Diana Singerman argues along essentially the same lines:

> The sha'b have turned exploiting the government into a fine art. People in the community who had a particular talent for dealing with bureaucrats, or a wide range of connections to elite politicians and officials, were sought after and valued. Individuals repeatedly stated that the government was something to "take from", an outside, external force to be patronised and exploited.[26]

This behaviour is manifested in the formation of informal networks including what is known as the informal economy. Although this informal networking provides for the wealth and upward mobility of the sha'ab, it deprives the state of a significant source of income and weaken its control over the larger political economy of the nation.[27] Although implicitly stated, Singerman argues in her study that Egypt represents a case of weak state strong society, but went on a step further in acknowledging the limitations that informal networking also imposes on the popular sector itself. She concluded her study by commenting

> The ability of the state to monopolise power and authority in Egypt remains highly contested, and informal networks keep alive alternative visions of politics and alternative strategies to achieve shared goals, despite the constraints the state's political and economic structures place on these communities.[28]

Analysing the failure of economic reform initiated in Egypt in the eighties, Alan Richards again singles out powerful societal forces, facing a weak and ineffective state, as a major reason underlying such failure. He points out,

> Economic reform in Egypt has been blocked both by the existence of powerful vested interests and by the government's fear of inchoate popular wrath over declining living standards.[29]

Although Ayubi correctly distinguished between the strong and the fierce state,[30] concluding that the Arab state including the Egyptian, is a fierce state precisely because it is weak, he did not part from the previous version of viewing Egypt as a case of weak state-strong society. Earlier his views concerning the existence of associative pluralism has been debated and there is no need here for any repetition. However, Ayubi seemed contradictory, when following Singerman's belief about the strength of what he labels street politics, he mentions at first

> One manifestation of growing dynamism and pluralism is manifested by what one may call 'street politics.' A familiar pattern of street politics in

Egypt and in Turkey used to show itself in the series of strikes/ demonstrations/riots that would be initiated by the workers and/or students and that would then spill over into the streets, engaging other social classes and fractions.[31]

But then he adds,

However, unless street politics are a spill-over of other organised (e.g. political party or trade union) politics, they are usually 'praetorian' and unmediated, and they often, as noted by O'Donnell, set the state dancing to the beat of civil society (thus, for example, the usually hurried, panicky withdrawal of price and subsidy reforms.). They are usually more protests-centred than demand-based, and are often easy to quell after a few days. They may reflect a yearning for participation, but they are often used by authoritarian regimes as an excuse to clamp down on liberties and to slow down any existing democratisation processes.[32]

Thus Ayubi acknowledges the strength of street politics on one hand, but at the same time admits to their weakness since they can be easily crushed. How can such a contradiction be explained? The following section intends to answer this question, suggesting a model which explains the relationship between state and society in Egypt.

3. State-Society Relationship: Proposed Models

This section starts with the proposition of two analytical models to shed light on the relationship between state and society in Egypt and pinpoint where previous scholars' interpretation has been flawed.

A) Model 1: The Strong State Model

The proposed model starts with inverting Putnam's hypothesis. A strong state cannot but create a strong civic society. It is crucial at this point to define what is meant by states' strength and weakness. Nordlinger talks of state's strength or power as synonymous to its autonomy[33] and presents a typology of states based on its two dimensional variables viz.; autonomy and societal control. He defines a state's autonomy in terms of its ability to enact public policies based on its own preference, whether such preference converge or diverge with societal demands.[34] Nordlinger develops a model of state-society relationship, which divides states into four types: strong, independent, responsive, and weak states.

According to Nordlinger strong states enjoy high autonomy and societal support, independent states rank high in autonomy but low in societal support, responsive states are described as being low in autonomy but high in societal

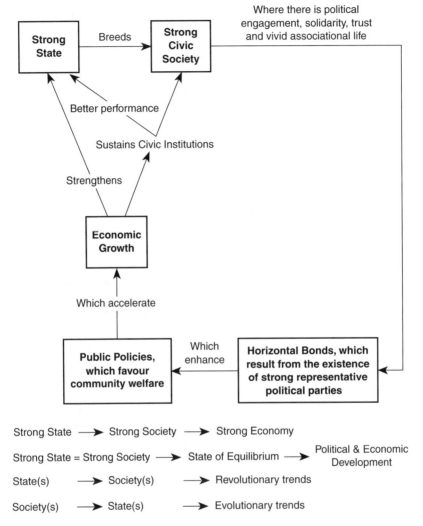

Figure 10.1 Model 1: The Strong State Model

support and finally weak states are characterised by being low in autonomy and low in societal support.[35] Certainly this convergent between the strength or weakness of states and their relative autonomy seems problematic. It would have been more valid to differentiate between the autonomy of states on one hand, and their relative strength or weakness on the other. Some weak states, for example may actually enjoy relative autonomy, Egypt being here a case in point. As shown earlier the Egyptian state had resisted for a long time to comply with the demands expressed by the landed class. Hence the autonomy of the state can be measured by the extent to which societal forces succeed or otherwise fail to penetrate the state apparatus for the purpose of extracting specific benefits from the state, where as a state's strength is measured by the extent to which the state itself succeed or otherwise fails in penetrating society and transforming it. Such dichotomy would verify the existence of states who are strong enough to penetrate society but at the same time are penetrated at least by some if not all societal forces during certain periods of time.

Accordingly, the strength of the state as measured here conforms to that of Migdal's, who defines it in terms of state's capacity to "penetrate society, regulate social relationships, extract resources, and appropriate or use resources in determined ways."[36] Thus strong states are those with high capabilities to perform such tasks. In accomplishing such a task, the performance of the state apparatus, whether at the political or the economic level is high and the accrued benefits to society is satisfactory. In such a case a feeling of citizenship, which results in political engagement, solidarity and trust prevails among the members of society. Horizontal societal bonds represented in strong political parties that are capable of interest aggregation and representation exist together with strong pressure groups that complement and enhance the former's work and produce public policies which promote community, as opposed to individual, welfare at large. In short a strong society is created. This strong society will help the strong state in achieving its task and, once change occurs society, will help to sustain it. Hence there is mutual co-operation between strong states and their societies, which can only exist when such values as democracy and liberty prevail. In a sense a strong society is both a product of and a pre-requisite for a strong state. Measured in economic terms, this mutual co-operation will accelerate economic growth, which will in turn strengthen both the state and society. The existence of a strong state and a strong society facilitates economic growth, even under severe economic conditions where resources are scarce and investments inefficient. It is precisely under these deteriorating economic conditions that strong states and strong societies are needed if any economic growth is to be achieved. Since change is self-enhancing, once it occurs the whole process will be repeated again and again and the system will be finally sustained in a state of equilibrium, where the strength of the state is matched with the strength of society. The result of such situation is both political and socio-economic development. The following figure illustrates this model. In addition, it is argued here that both revolution and evolution are related to strong states and societies. Following Davidheiser's hypothesis, mentioned in Chapter Two, which associates revolution with strong rather than weak states, this work goes a step further to argue that if the state is relatively stronger than society, (but society is still strong) revolution occurs, since the strong state will not respond to social forces, and with rising economic pressures, crisis triggers revolution. Society here has still to be strong enjoying a high level of political awareness and citizenship to develop revolutionary trends. This work also argues that evolution is also associated with strong states and societies. Evolution here refers to positive change as advocated by liberal and modernisation theories of development. The state has to be strong enough (relatively less stronger than society) to initiate change. Society is relatively stronger than the state, (but still the state is strong) in order to pressurise the state into change and to sustain it once it occurs leading to what is known as evolutionary trends. This will in turn strengthen the economy, and eventually will strengthen the state. Finally equilibrium is achieved between state and society and is restored in the long run.

B) Model 2: The Weak State Model

Following the previous logic, this model starts with the fact that a weak state cannot but produce a weak, uncivic society. The weakness of the state is defined following again Migdal's measurement in terms of its low capacity to penetrate society, regulate social relationships, extract resources and appropriate or use resources in determined ways. Because of the inability and incapacity of the state to achieve these tasks, state's performance both on the political and economic level is low and the benefits and services rendered to society is of low quality. In most situations the state has to adopt repressive measures to extract resources from society, and will not tolerate opposition to its oppressive and discriminatory policies. Accordingly, the state deliberately weakens institutions and associations that might aggregate and represent mass interests, be it primary institutions like political parties, or different kinds of secondary associations. In this case, a society is created in which suspicion and lack of trust in the state and in fellow members prevails, obstructing solidarity, co-operation among community members, and collective work. As a result values that favour personal and individual interests takes precedence over those favouring communal interests, the outcome of which is the creation of vertical "informal" bonds of clientele networks, patronage, exploitation and corruption. In short a weak society is created. This weak society will work against the state thus obstructing its policies. In a sense the weak society is a product of and at the same time the cause for the weakness of the state. As a result a situation is created whereby policies that strengthen the bargaining power of personal rather than public interests are produced. This in turn will hinder economic development and produces a weak economy, which will further the weakness of the state. The whole process is constantly repeated and the system is sustained in a state of equilibrium where the weakness of the state is matched with the weakness of society, the result of which is political and socio-economic stagnation. Needless to say, in countries with scarce economic resources, and low level of economic development, the situation is worsened. The following figure illustrates this model.

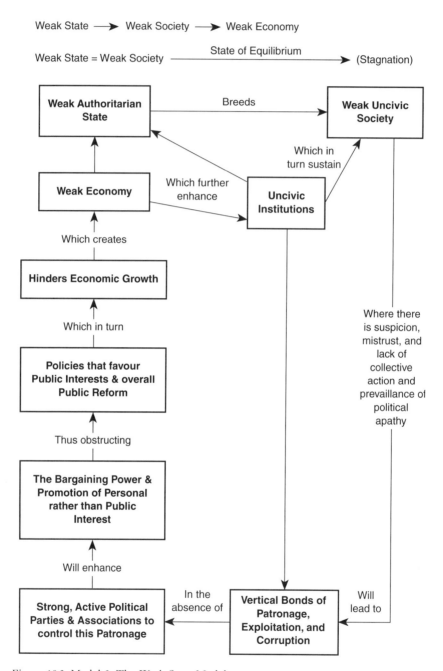

Figure 10.2 Model 2: The Weak State Model

C) Model 3: State-Society in Egypt

The two models illustrated above are a generalisation to the process of interaction that exist between states and their societies. It is hoped that by applying the analysis previously employed in the two models, to the Egyptian case, that a model, which reflects the interactive relationship between state and society in Egypt, is produced. There is no doubt that the Egyptian State is characterised by low capability in terms of both its penetration capacity into the society and its resource extraction capabilities. Repression, thus, becomes the only means by which the state can carry out its policies, on one hand, and guarantee the regime's survival on the other. The Egyptian authoritarian state thus weakened and continues to weaken societal forces by a mixture of coercion, bribery and corruption. The outcome of such policy was the existence of weak political parties whose internal behaviour, conflicts and struggles showed that they have inherited the same vices of the authoritarian state: i.e. lack of democracy and corruption. This has contributed to the alienation of the already apathetic masses. Moreover, the politicisation of professional syndicates, who fared no better than the parties in their performance and who showed the same signs of internal weakness, seriously reduced their ability to represent their members' interests. Again professional syndicates witness a lack of affiliation and apathy among their members as reflected by syndicate elections turnout. The same situation exists in trade unions, agricultural co-operatives and business associations. With all avenues of participation and of influencing public policies, both at the national and local level, blocked, and with the failure of political parties and associations to represent and promote their interests, the exploited Egyptians whether peasants, or urbanites, develop their own strategies and use the same system that the state had created and institutionalised to control society, in order to defeat state policies, reform and developmental goals. Clientele networks, corruption and patronage prevail and supplant normal channels of mediation between state and society. Accordingly, peasant behaviour in Tihna al-Gabal, when they intentionally sabotage their agricultural land, or the behaviour of civil servants who moonlight, food sellers and accountants who do not report their income to the authorities, and women who manage informal savings associations in urban communities as identified by Singerman, are not signs of a strong society defeating its weak state. Quite the contrary, these are symptoms of a weak society which further enhance the weakness of an already feeble but fierce authoritarian state. This interpretation would also solve the contradiction found in Ayubi's description of street politics. It is precisely because Egyptian society is weak that riots and demonstrations are easily crushed and do not develop into revolutionary trends. The strength of some of the Egyptian courts represent the exception rather than the norm.

Again and whereas those scholars who adopted a revisionist approach to the analysis of state society in the Middle East, including Ayubi, find in the revival of some Islamic groups and their open challenge to the regime, healthy signs of a

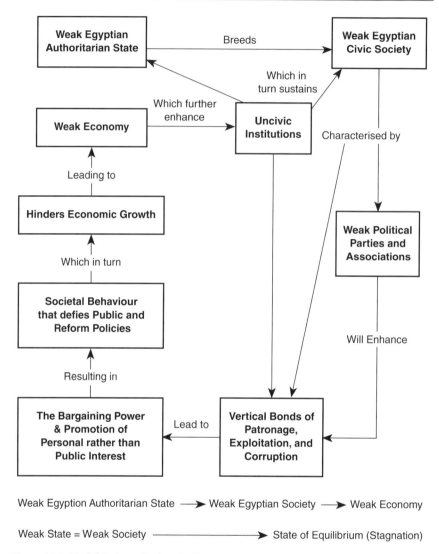

Figure 10.3 Model 3: State-Society in Egypt

strong society, this work argues still that these are signs of a weak fragmented society. As exemplified in Chapter Five, the Muslim Brotherhood took over syndicates not because of their strength and increasing popularity, but because of the syndicates' weakness caused by both external and internal factors. This has resulted in the presence of an apathetic majority of members, coupled with the presence of an organised minority of MB members facilitated the Muslim Brotherhood's ascendancy in syndicates. However, the performance of the Muslim brotherhood within the syndicates, which clearly reflected their weakness, fragmentation and corruption, proved that they exhibited the same vices of the regime and of the secular forces that they were attacking. Thus, like other societal forces, the Muslim Brotherhood are weak. A study conducted by Springborg on other Islamic but more radical and terrorist groups, such as the Takfir wa al-Hijra and al-Jihad revealed that conflict among these groups prevent any co-operation and unity among them. It also highlighted internal conflicts which weakens them.[37] This further proves the weakness of the Islamic groups in Egypt.

The failures of economic reform are the outcome of such relationship between state's weakness and societal weakness. Because state and society in Egypt are both weak, neither revolutionary nor evolutionary trends are developed. Rather the state's weakness is equalled with societal weakness and the system is preserved in a state of equilibrium, the outcome of which is economic stagnation.

The previous figure (Fig. 10.3) illustrates state-society relationship in Egypt. Although the model shows the weakness of the society it does not imply in any way that state-society relationship in Egypt is a static process. Quite the contrary, some groups or societal forces may gain strength from time to time but these again represent the exception rather than the norm and are continuously suppressed by the state.

The Suggested Models: Final Comment

The previously suggested models do not in any ways imply rigidity. Quite the contrary, the models acknowledge the fact that states' strength or weaknesses may change from time to time. Accordingly, not only can states' strength or weakness made comparable by placing them alongside a continuum where it can be argued for example that state x is relatively stronger/weaker than state y, but that the very same state has exhibited various degrees of strength/weaknesses over different periods of times whether under the same or under different regime. It is precisely by acknowledging these changes and by setting the general characteristics for the interactive relations between state and society that it is hoped that future work of comparative politics scholars will prove the generalisation of these models for comparative purposes.

4. Can Egypt Change?

Reference has been made earlier to future scenarios as predicted by Bianchi and Ayubi when they anticipated the evolution within the Egyptian society of a more relaxed form of corporatism or what they labelled "associative democracy", which would present an element of pluralism in the society. The role played by the Islamists in secondary associations was considered as yet another indication for this gradual, but slow change of the society along pluralist lines.

257

These point of views were based on the assumption that the Egyptian state is willing to allow some sort of diversity within society in order to reduce the effect of the economic hardship resulting from abolishing its socialist and welfarist obligations on one hand, and the execution of its so called "economic liberalism" on the other. This implicitly states that the Egyptian society was heading towards an evolutionary phase, which will eventually strengthen it and in turn strengthen the state. In other words a transformation of both state and society in Egypt, through adoption of more politically liberal measures will take place.

This book contests the previously mentioned views since it proved the mistaken assumption on which they were based. As the findings of this work show, the fierce authoritarian Egyptian state has adopted a tighter (rather than a more relaxed) grip on societal forces. This was achieved through its frequent use of coercion against society. Through the institutionalisation of privileges, corruption, and patronage networks the weak state further enhances the weakness of an already feeble society. Evolutionary trends are not likely to appear and that change from within is not likely in this case to occur.

The following proposed model suggests an alternative scenario, which explains how change can be initiated within the Egyptian case.

D) Model 4: Changing the Egyptian State and Society

This model explains the way change can be introduced in order to break out of this circle of weak state-society-economy situation. The Egyptian economy has been suffering lately from a reduction of its major income from the big four i.e.; tourism, Suez canal revenues, workers' remittance and oil. Since Egypt is a dependent country whose economy is sustained through loans and aid from international donors, this model suggests that change will only be initiated by the Egyptian state if it falls under pressure from international organisations like the World Bank, the International Monetary Fund (IMF) and the U.S. Agency for International Development (AID). Again this point of view has been widely debated by two different groups of scholars. The first group view pressure from international organisations on the states of developing countries as necessary and desirable for achieving economic development. These scholars were mainly influenced in the 1970s by a group of neo-classical economists who viewed government economic policy as the key to development. Government subsidies and its continuous market intervention create market distortions, which encourage inefficiency and stifle entrepreneurialship. The solution therefore lies mainly in limiting the economic role of the state through liberalisation measures, the most famous example of which is privatisation. Economic liberalisation would ultimately lead to development, which in the long run will strengthen the state.[38] A revised approach, which started to prevail in mid-80s and continued throughout the 90s, was adopted by a second group of scholars who view pressure from international organisations as detrimental to the development process, since it tends to make the "soft state" softer. Among those scholars is Sadowsky who sums up this point of view when he mentions

> Certainly many of the specific policy reforms that the Washington development community has urged on Egypt could be quite helpful. But it does not follow that a general assault on the state budget, on the powers of public officials, on the morale of the bureaucrats, is a good way to bring about these changes.[39]

He also adds:

> The irony is that the economic pressure that foreign aid agencies have laid on the Egyptian state has undermined the power of those officials whom they hope to use as instruments for reform.[40]

The proposed model contradicts Sadowsky's views. Pressure on the Egyptian state from the Washington community will in the long run strengthen the state, provided that this pressure is directed towards the achievement of liberalisation in both the political and the economic spheres. What Sadowsky identifies as the result of such international pressure-increase in deterioration of work ethics, corruption, and the imbalance in favour of the interests of businessmen (only a particular segment and not all businessmen, as shown in Chapter Six) and the other groups in the society – are actually symptoms of a weak society which is incapable of sustaining and supporting change. Whereas economic liberalisation and economic policy reform will reduce the financial burden and the fiscal crisis facing the Egyptian state, and hence contribute to the creation of a stronger state, political liberalisation will strengthen the society in the long run, by creating strong civic institutions which will help rather than obstruct the state's developmental efforts. Only when reform in both spheres, the political and the economic, goes hand in hand will change actually occur. Finally, a strong economy can be the product of the strong state-society formula. Fig. 10.4 explains how this change can take place. However, as shown in the model, the possibility of introducing change lies heavily on the willingness of the Washington community to press the Egyptian state for a more democratic and representative political system. The important question that arises here is whether the Washington community, is willing to do so. In a lecture titled "The Changing International Oil Market and the Future of United States Hegemony in the Gulf", Simon Bromley asserts that the erosion of the American hegemony in the Gulf, leaves the United States with one option, that of supporting oppressive authoritarian states.[41] Bromley's assertion can be generalised to other Arab states including Egypt. The former U.S. Secretary of Defence and CIA chief, James Schlesinger, makes the point when he poses the question;

> Whether we seriously desire to prescribe democracy as the proper form of government for other societies. Perhaps the issue is most clearly posed in

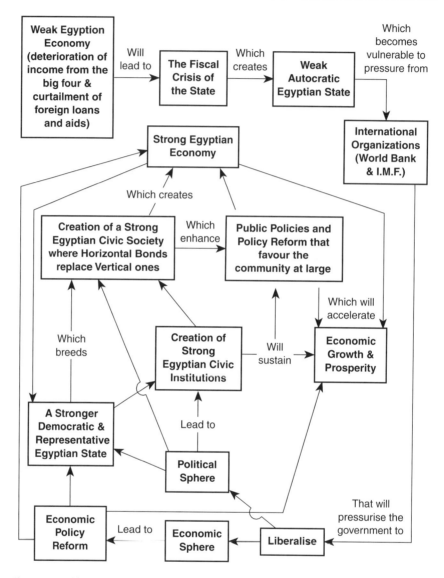

Figure 10.4 Change initiated in the Egyptian case

the Islamic world. Do we seriously want to change the institutions in Saudi Arabia? The brief answer is no: over the years we have sought to preserve those institutions, sometimes in preference to more democratic forces coursing throughout the region.[42]

The role played by Egypt in the Gulf War and the fundamentalist attacks that began and escalated in the 90s accentuated the unwillingness of the United States to press the Egyptian state for any liberalisation in the political sphere. On the contrary the United States, in its attempt to sustain the Egyptian regime, had rescheduled some of Egypt's debts and cancelled some others, while simultaneously was pressing the European debtors known as the "Paris Club" to forgo some of the country's debts. With this continuous support of the Egyptian authoritarian regime, change is unlikely to be achieved in the foreseeable future. Thus the weak Egyptian authoritarian state will continue to weaken society and the latter will continue to further enhances the state's weakness.

Notes

Notes to Introduction

1 Putnam, R., *Making Democracy Work, Civic Traditions in Modern Italy*, Princeton University Press, USA, 1993, p. 176.
2 Ibid., p. 182.

Notes to Chapter 1

1 Binder, L., *Islamic Liberalism, A Critique of Development Ideologies*, The University of Chicago Press, 1988, p. 26.
2 Quoted in Dunleavy, P. and O'Leary, B., *Theories of the State, the Politics of Liberal Democracy*, Macmillan Education Ltd., 1987, p. 13.
3 Dunleavy, P. and O'Leary, B., *Theories of the State*, pp. 13–16.
4 Bentley, A., *The Process of Government: A Study of Social Pressure*, The Principia Press of Illinois, (1908) 1935, p. 269.
5 Binder, *Islamic Liberalism, A Critique of Development Ideologies*, p. 28.
6 Truman, D., *The Governmental Process, Political Interests and Public Opinion*, Alfred Aknof, New York, 1951, pp. 448–449.
7 Binder, *Islamic Liberalism, A Critique of Development Ideologies.*, pp. 28–29.
8 Ibid., p. 29.
9 Baskin, D., *American Pluralist Democracy: A critique*, Van Nostrand Reinhold Company, USA, 1971, p. 89.
10 Olson, M., *The Logic of Collective Action*, Harvard University Press, USA, 1975, p. 127.
11 Ibid., p. 127.
12 This fact had been frequently argued by both human behaviour and organisational behaviour theorists.
13 Olson, *The Logic of Collective Action*, p. 127.
14 Ibid., p. 132.
15 Lowi, T., *The End of Liberalism: The Second Republic of the United States*, W.W. Norton & Company, 1979, p. 40.
16 Ibid., p. 41.
17 Ibid., p. 40.
18 McFarland, A., "Interest Groups and Theories of Power in America", *British Journal of Political Science*, Vol. 17, April 1987, p. 137.
19 Dahl, R., *Who Governs? Democracy and Power in an American City*, Yale University Press, New Haven & London, 1961, p. 76.

NOTES

20 Ibid., p. 228.
21 Quoted in Smith M., "Pluralism" in March, D. & Stoker, G. (eds.) *Theory and Methods in Political Science*, Macmillan Press, 1995, p. 212.
22 Dahl, R., *Dilemmas of Pluralist Democracy vs. Control*, Yale University Press, 1982, pp. 1–30.
23 Ibid., p. 1.
24 Ibid., pp. 40–53.
25 Lindblom, C., "The Market as Prison", *The Journal of Politics*, Vol. 44, No. 1, 1982, pp. 328, 329.
26 Ibid., p. 329.
27 Ibid., p. 330.
28 Lackey, P., *Invitation to Talcott Parson's Theory*, Cap and Gown Press, USA, 1987, p. 17.
29 Easton, D., "An Approach to the Analysis of Political System", *World Politics*, No. 3, April 1957, p. 386.
30 Almond, A. and Powell, A., *Comparative Politics, A Developmental Approach*, Little, Brown & Company 1966, pp. 25–27.
31 Rostow, W., *The Stages of Economic Growth: A Non-Communist Manifesto*, Cambridge University Press, 1960, pp. 4–11.
32 Deutsch, K., "Social Mobilisation and Political Development", *The American Political Science Review*, Vol. 55, No. 3, September 1961, p. 494.
33 Ibid., p. 493.
34 Eisenstadt, S., "Modernisation and Conditions for Sustained Growth", *World Politics*, No. 4, July 1964, p. 583.
35 Ibid., p. 578.
36 Huntington, S., "Political Development and Political Decay", *World Politics*, No. 3, April, 1965, p. 393.
37 Ibid., pp. 402–406.
38 Ibid., p. 412.
39 Binder, *Islamic Liberalism*, p. 34.
40 Waterbury, J., "Democracy without Democrats?: the potential for political liberalisation in the Middle East" in Salamé, G., *Democracy without Democrats? The Renewal of Politics in the Muslim World*, I.B. Tauris, 1994, p. 24.
41 Itling, K., "Hegel's Concept of the State and Marx's early Critique", in Pelorynski, Z. (ed.) *The State and Civil Society: Studies in Hegel's Political Philosophy*, Cambridge University Press, UK, 1984, p. 94.
42 Ibid., p. 94.
43 Ibid., p. 94.
44 Perez-Diaz, V., *State, Bureaucracy and Civil Society: A Critical Discussion of the Political Theory of Karl Marx*, Macmillan Press Ltd., London, 1978, p. 11.
45 Itling, "Hegel's Concept of the State and Marx's early Critique", p. 96.
46 Ibid., p. 96.
47 Ibid., pp. 100–104.
48 Carnoy, M., *The State and Political Theory*, Princeton University Press, 1984, pp. 46, 47.
49 Quoted in Draper, Hal, "Karl Marx's Theory of Revolution", Vol. 1: *State and Bureaucracy*, Monthly Review Press, 1977, p. 78.
50 Ibid., p. 79.
51 Carnoy, *The State and Political Theory*, pp. 47.
52 Jessop, B., *The Capitalist State: Marxist Theories and Methods*, Martin Robertson & Company Ltd., 1982, pp. 4, 5.
53 Quoted in: Callinicoz, A., *The Revolutionary Ideas of Marx*, Bookmarks, 1983, p. 100.
54 Jessop, B., *The Capitalist State*, p. 12.
55 Ibid., p. 12.

56 Ibid., p. 15.
57 Miliband, R., *Marxism and Politics*, Oxford University Press, 1977, pp. 67–68.
58 Ibid., p. 68.
59 Carnoy, *The State and Political Theory*, p. 52.
60 Miliband, *Marxism and Politics*, pp. 70–71.
61 Ibid., p. 72.
62 Ibid., p. 72.
63 Carnoy, *The State and Political Theory*, p. 54.
64 Miliband, *Marxism and Politic*, p. 83.
65 Carnoy, *The State and Political Theory*, p. 54.
66 Merrington, J., "Theory and Practice in Gramsci's Marxism", in Western Marxism, *New Left Review*, 1977, p. 142.
67 Ibid., p. 141.
68 Taylor, G., "Marxism" in March, D. & Stoker, G. (eds.) *Theory and Methods in Political Science*, Macmillan Press, 1995 p. 252.
69 Bobbio, N., "Gramsci and the Conception of Civil Society" in Mouffe, C. (ed.) *Gramsci and Marxist Theory*, Routledge and Kegan Paul Ltd., 1979, p. 30.
70 Ibid., pp. 28, 29.
71 Gramsci, A., *Selections from the Prison Notebooks*, Hoare, Q. and Smith G. (eds.), Lawrence & Wishard, London 1971, p. 12.
72 Femia, J., *Gramsci's Political Thought*, Clarendon Press, Oxford 1981, p. 26.
73 Adamson, W., *Hegemony and Revolution: A Study of Antonio Gramsci's Political and Cultural Theory*, California Press, 1980, p. 216.
74 Femia, *Gramsci's Political Thought*, p. 24.
75 Ibid., p. 28.
76 Jessop, B., *The Capitalist State*, p. 149.
77 Adamson, *Hegemony and Revolution*, p. 171.
78 Ibid., p. 217.
79 Ibid., p. 171.
80 Jessop, *The Capitalist State*, p. 145.
81 Ibid., p. 149.
82 Ibid., p. 154.
83 Taylor, "Marxism", p. 255.
84 Binder, *Islamic Liberalism*, p. 54.
85 Poulantzas, N., *Political Power and Social Classes*, NLB 1975, p. 128.
86 Carnoy, *The State and Political Theory*, p. 98.
87 Jessop, B., *Nicos Poulantzas: Marxist Theory and Political Strategy*, Macmillan Publishers, UK, 1985, p. 65.
88 Poulantzas, *Political Power and Social Classes*, p. 130.
89 Jessop, B., *Nicos Poulantzas*, p. 63.
90 Carnoy, *The State and Political Theory*, p. 100.
91 Jessop, *Poulantzas*, p. 64.
92 Poulantzas, N., *Political Power*, pp. 191, 192.
93 Carnoy, *The State and Political Theory*, p. 101.
94 Poulantzas, N., *Political Power*, p. 209.
95 Ibid., p. 214.
96 Carnoy, *The State and Political Theory*, p. 102.
97 Quoted in Ibid., p. 102.
98 Poulantzas, N., *State, Power and Socialism*, NLB 1978, p. 33.
99 Ibid., p. 33.
100 Ibid., p. 31.
101 Carnoy, *The State and Political Theory*, p. 117.

102 Poulantzas, *State, Power, and Socialism*, p. 81.
103 Ibid., p. 30.
104 Jessop, B., *Nicos Poulantzas*, p. 117.
105 Poulantzas, N., *State, Power, and Socialism*, p. 30.
106 Jessop, B., *Nicos Poulantzas*, pp. 124–126.
107 Aveniri, S., *Karl Marx on Colonialism & Modernisation*, Anchor books 1968, USA, p. 7.
108 Carnoy, *The State and Political Theory*, p. 174.
109 Chandra, B., "Karl Marx, his theories of Asian Societies and colonial rule" in *Sociological Theories: Race and Colonialism*, UNESCO publication, 1980, pp. 398.
110 Quoted in Chandra, B., "Karl Marx, his theories of Asian Societies", p. 397.
111 Ibid., pp. 406, 407.
112 Ibid., p. 407.
113 Ibid., p. 408.
114 Ibid., p. 408.
115 Wittfogel, K., *Oriental Despotism*, p. 380.
116 Ibid., p. 380.
117 Ibid., p. 382.
118 Ibid., p. 387.
119 Aveniri, *Karl Marx on revolution*, p. 12.
120 Quoted in Aveniri, *Karl Marx on revolution*, p. 4.
121 Ibid., p. 5.
122 Ibid., p. 13.
123 Chandra, "Karl Marx: his theories of Asian Societies", p. 386.
124 Ibid., p. 387.
125 Ibid., pp. 420–422.
126 Ibid., p. 422.
127 Baran, P., *The Political Economy of Growth*, Monthly Review Press, New York 1957, p. 141.
128 Ibid., p. 142.
129 Ibid., pp. 163–184.
130 Ibid., p. 12.
131 Ibid., pp. 211–213.
132 Frank, A.G., *Capitalism and underdevelopment in Latin America, Historical Studies of Chile and Brazil,* Monthly Review press, New York, 1967, p. 3.
133 Emmanuel, A., *Unequal exchange: A Study of the Imperialism of Trade*, Monthly Review Press, 1972, p. 275.
134 Amin, S., *Unequal development, An Essay on the Social Formations of the Peripheral Capitalism*, The Harvester Press Limited, 1973, pp. 201, 202.
135 Dore, E., "Dependency Theory" in Bottomore, T., Kieman, V. & Miliband, R., (eds.) *A Dictionary of Marxisist Thought*, Basil Blackwell Publisher Limited, 1983, pp. 115, 116.
136 Rush, M., *Politics and Society: An Introduction to Political Sociology*, Prentice Hall, 1992, pp. 228, 229.
137 Collier, D., "Overview of the Bureaucratic-Authoritarian Model", in Collier (ed.) *The New Authoritarianism in Latin America*, Princeton University Press, USA, 1979, pp. 23–25.
138 O'Donnell G., "Tensions in the Bureaucratic-Authoritarian State and the Question of Democracy" in Collier, D. (ed.) *The New Authoritarianism in Latin America*, p. 292.
139 Ibid., p. 294.
140 Ibid., p. 292.
141 Ibid., p. 296.
142 Ibid., pp. 294, 295.

143 According to O'Donnell, *lo popular* is one of the political mediations between civil society and the state. He provides the following explanation: "*Pueblo* and *lo popular* involve a 'we' that is a carrier of demands for substantive justice which form the basis for the obligations of the state towards the less favoured segments of the population".

144 O'Donnell G., "Tensions in the Bureaucratic-Authoritarian State and the Question of Democracy", p. 295.

145 Ibid., pp. 300, 301.

146 Ibid., p. 316.

147 Ibid., pp. 312, 313.

148 Ibid., p. 314.

149 Ibid., p. 314.

Notes to Chapter 2

1 Wittfogel, K., *Oriental Despotism*, Yale University Press, 1957, p. 7.

2 Mosca, G., *The Ruling Class*, McGraw-Hill Book Company Inc., USA, 1939, p. 124.

3 Drower, M., "The Political Approach to the Classical World", in Glanville, S. (ed.) *The Legacy of Egypt*, Oxford University Press, UK, 1942, p. 24.

4 Quoted in Ayubi, N., *Bureaucracy and Politics in Contemporary Egypt*, Ithaca Press, London, 1980, p. 97.

5 Montet, P., *Eternal Egypt*, Weidenfeld and Nicholson, London, 1969, p. 32.

6 Wilson, J., *The Burden of Egypt, an Interpretation of Ancient Egyptian Culture*, University of Chicago Press, USA, 1951, p. 45.

7 Ibid., p. 45.

8 Montet, P., *Eternal Egypt*, pp. 59, 60.

9 Ibid., p. 59.

10 Mahaffy, J., *A History of Egypt under the Ptolemaic Dynasty*, Methuen & Co., London 1899, pp. 15, 16.

11 Ibid., p. 16.

12 Bowman, A., *Egypt after the Pharoahs: 332 BC–AD 642: From Alexander to the Arab Conquest*, British Muslim Publications, London 1986, p. 38.

13 Safran, N., *Egypt in Search of Political Community, an analysis of the intellectual and political evolution of Egypt 1804–1952*, Harvard University Press, USA, 1961, p. 18.

14 Ibid., p. 19.

15 Ayubi, N., *Bureaucracy and Politics in Contemporary Egypt*, p. 98.

16 Ibid., p. 99.

17 Shaw, S., *The Financial and Administrative Organisation and Development of Ottoman Egypt 1517–1798*, Princeton University Press 1962, pp. 4–6.

18 Ibid., pp. 5, 6.

19 Ghorbal, S., *The Beginnings of the Egyptian Question and the Rise of Mehemet Ali*, George Routledge & Sons Ltd., London 1928, p. 228.

20 Macdermott, A., *Egypt from Nasser to Mubarak, a Flawed Revolution*, Groom Helm, 1988, p. 23.

21 Hunter, F.R., *Egypt under the Khedives 1805–1879, From Household Government to Modern Bureaucracy*, University of Pittsburg Press 1984, p. 12.

22 Abdel Malek, A., *Egypt, Military Society, the Army Regime, the Left and Social Change under Nasser*, Random House, New York 1962, pp. 43, 44.

23 Holt, P., *Egypt and the Fertile Crescent 1516–1922*, Longman Green and Co. Ltd., UK, 1966, p. 177.

24 Ghorbal, S., The Beginnings of the Egyptian Question, p. 232.

25 Joesten, J., *Nasser, the Rise to Power*, Odhams Press Ltd., London 1960, p. 171.
26 Abdel Malek, A., *Egypt, Military Society*, p. 92.
27 Ibid., pp. 96, 97.
28 Gordon, J., *Nasser's Blessed Movement: Egypt's free officers and the July revolution*, Oxford University Press, USA, 1992, p. 126.
29 Vatikiotis, P.J., "Some Political Consequences of the 1952 Revolution in Egypt", in Holt, P.M. (ed.) *Political and Social Change in Modern Egypt*, Oxford University Press, London 1968, p. 369.
30 Lippman, T., *Egypt after Nasser: Sadat, Peace and the Mirage of Prosperity*, Paragon House, USA, 1989, p. 7.
31 Ibid., p. 7.
32 Ibid., p. 6.
33 Ayubi, N., "Domestic Politics", in Harris, L. (ed.) *Egypt: Internal Challenges and Regional Stability*, Routledge & Kegan Paul, London 1988, p. 54.
34 *Sabah El Kheir Weekly Magazine*, No. 1973, October 1993, p. 40.
35 Ayubi, N., "Government and the State in Egypt Today", in Trip, C. and Owen, R. (eds.) *Egypt under Mubarak*, Routledge, UK, 1989, p. 18.
36 Wittfogel, K., *Oriental Despotism*, p. 126.
37 Ayubi, N., *Over-stating the Arab State: Politics and Society in the Middle East*, I.B. Taurius Publications, London 1995, pp. 449, 450.
38 Ibid., p. 450.
39 Ibid., p. 447.
40 Ibid., p. 450.
41 Quoted in Ayubi, N., *Bureaucracy and Politics in Contemporary Egypt*, p. 130.
42 Wendell, C., *The Evolution of the Egyptian National Image: from the Origins to Ahmad Lutfi El-Sayyed*, University of California Press, USA, 1972, p. 188.
43 Berque, J., *Egypt: Imperialism and Revolution*, Faber & Faber, London 1972, p. 41.
44 Montesquieu, *The Spirit of the Laws*, Hafner Publishing Company, USA, 1949. p. 151.
45 Ayubi, N., *Bureaucracy and Politics in Contemporary Egypt*, p. 131.
46 Brown, N., *Peasant Politics in Modern Egypt, The Struggle Against the State*, Yale University Press, New Haven & London 1990, p. 2.
47 Ibid., pp. 16–20.
48 Patai, R., *The Arab Mind*, Charles Scribner's Sons, New York, 1973, p. 23.
49 Blackman, W., *The Fallahin of Upper Egypt*, 1968, p. 23.
50 Patai, *The Arab Mind*, p. 17.
51 Mayfield, James, *Rural Politics in Nasser's Egypt, A Quest for Legitimacy*, University of Texas Press 1971, p. 61.
52 Wittfogel, *Oriental Despotism*, p. 143.
53 Mayfield, *Rural Politics in Nasser's Egypt*, p. 61.
54 Al-Menoufy, K., *Al Thaqafa Al Siyasiyya Lel falahin al-Masriyin* or (*The Political Culture of the Egyptian Peasants*), Ph.D. thesis, Faculty of Economics and Political Science, Cairo University 1978, p. 94.
55 Moughrabi, F., "The Arab Basic Personality: ACritical Survey of the Literature", *International Journal of Middle East Studies*, Vol. 9, 1978, p. 103.
56 Patai, R., *The Arab Mind*, p. 106.
57 Moughrabi, F., "The Arab Basic Personality", p. 105.
58 Ayrout, H., *The Egyptian Peasant*, Beacon Press, Boston 1963, p. 2.
59 Mitchell T., "The Invention and Reinvention of the Egyptian Peasant", *International Journal of Middle East Studies*. Vol. 22, 1990, p. 134.
60 Ibid., p. 137.
61 Ayrout., *The Egyptian Peasant*, p. 1.
62 Brown, N., *Peasant Politics in Modern Egypt*, p. 15.

63 Davidheiser, E., "Strong State, Weak States, the role of the state in Revolution", *Comparative Politics*, Vol. 24, No. 4, July 1992, p. 463.
64 Brown, N., *Peasant Politics in Modern Egypt*, p. 211.
65 Moore, B., *Social Origins of Dictatorship and Democracy, Lord and Peasant in the Making of the Modern World*, Penguin Books, USA, 1966, p. 479.
66 Al-Menoufy, *Al Thaqafa Al Siyasiyya Lel falahin al-Masriyin*, pp. 120, 121.
67 Ramadan, A., *Sir'Al Tabaqat Fi Misr Or Class Struggle in Egypt 1837–1952*, al Mou'assa al-Arabia Lil Dirasat Wal Nashr, 1978, p. 182.
68 Ibid., p. 167.
69 Ibid., p. 166.
70 Al-Menoufy, *Al Thaqafa Al Siyasiyya Lel falahin al-Masriyin*, 123.
71 Brown, N., *Peasant Politics in Modern Egypt*, pp. 193, 194.
72 Al-Menoufy, *Al Thaqafa Al Siyasiyya Lel falahin al-Masriyyin*, p. 123.
73 Brown, N., *Peasant Politics in Modern Egypt*, p. 209.
74 Ibid., p. 212.
75 Davidheiser, Strong State, Weak States, p. 464.
76 Brown, N., *Peasant Politics in Modern Egypt*, p. 83.
77 Ibid., pp. 95, 96.
78 Ibid., p. 93.
79 Al-Menoufy, *Al-Thaqafa al-Siyasiyya Lelfalahin al-Masriyin*, p. 186.
80 Ibid., p. 179.
81 Ibid., p. 68.
82 Brown, N., *Peasant Politics in Modern Egypt*, p. 150.
83 Ibid., pp. 152, 153.
84 Ibid., p. 153.
85 Ibid., p. 154.
86 Ibid., p. 153.
87 Ibid., p. 171.
88 Almond, G. and Verba, S. *The Civic Culture*, Princeton University Press, 1963, p. 132.
89 Ibid., p. 482.

Notes to Chapter 3

1 Perlmutter A., *Egypt The Praetorian State*, Transaction Inc USA, 1974, p. 143.
2 Since 1952, seven were promulgated, including constitutional decrees and temporary and permanent constitutions.
3 Qandil A., *'Amaliyyat al-Tahawul al-Dimuqraty Fi Misr, 1981–1993* (The Process of Democratic Change in Egypt 1981–1993) Ibn Khaldoun Centre For Developmental Studies, 1995, p. 56.
4 *Constitution of the ARE*, p. 28.
5 Quoted in Al Shinnawy, M.A., *Community Development and Local Government in the Developing Nations: A Study based on the experience of the United Arab Republic [Egypt]*, unpublished Ph.D. thesis, New York University, 1964, p. 100.
6 Ayubi, N., "Government and State in Egypt Today" in Tripp, C. & Owen, R., (eds.) *Egypt under Mubarak*, Routledge, London 1989, pp. 5, 6.
7 *Constitution of the ARE*, p. 31.
8 *Constitution of the ARE*, p. 19.
9 Montesquieu, *The Spirit of the Laws*, Hafner Publishing Company, USA, 1949, pp. 151, 152.
10 Qandil, *'Amaliyyat al-Tahawul*, p. 63.
11 Ayubi, "Government and the State", p. 7.

12 *Constitution of the ARE*, p. 16.
13 Ibid., pp. 24–26.
14 Qandil, *'Amaliyyat al-Tahawul . . .*, p. 69.
15 Ibid., p. 71.
16 Al-Mikawy, N., "The Egyptian Parliament and Transition to Liberal Democracy", in *American-Arab Affairs*, No. 36 (1991), p. 20.
17 Qandil A., *'Amaliyyat al-Tahawul*, pp. 71, 72.
18 *The Constitution of the ARE*, p. 31.
19 *Al-Taqrir Al-Istratiji Al-Arabi* for the year 1997, 1998, p. 272.
20 Zahran G., "Al-dawr al-siyasi lil-qada' al-misri fi 'amaliyyat sana' al-qarar, diraset al hiqbat al ua lil ra'is Mubarak" or (The Political Role of the Egyptian Judiciary in the First Decade of Mubarak's rule) In Hilal A (ed.) *Al Nizam Al Siyasi Al Misri: Al Taghayyur Wa al-Istimrar* OR (The Egyptian Political System: Change and Continuity), The Centre for Political Research and Studies, Al Nahda Library, 1988, p. 280.
21 Hill E., "Laws and Courts in Egypt: Recent Issues and Events concerning Islamic Law", in Owesis I. (ed.) *The Political Economy of Contemporary Egypt*, Centre for Contemporary Arab Studies, Georgetown University, USA, 1990, p. 241.
22 Imam A., *Mazbahat al-Quda* or (The Massacre of Judges), Madbouli Bookshop, Cairo, pp. 68, 69.
23 Ibid., pp. 87, 88.
24 *The Constitution of the ARE*, p. 11.
25 *Al-Taqrir Al-Istratiji Al-Arabi* for the year 1988, 1989, p. 456.
26 Ibid., pp. 471, 472.
27 Ibid., pp. 472, 473.
28 *Al-Taqrir Al-Istratiji Al-Arabi* for the year 1984, 1985, p. 328.
29 Zahran, G., "al-dawr al-siyasi lil qada'a al-misri", p. 280.
30 *Al-Taqrir Al-Istratiji Al-Arabi* for the year 1988, 1989, pp. 472, 473.
31 Zahran G., "al-dawr al-siyasi lil qada'a almisri", p. 294.
32 A complete reference to the law is made in chapter four.
33 *Al-Taqrir Al-Istratiji Al-Arabi* for the year 1986, 1987, p. 368.
34 Ibid., p. 474.
35 The bill was presented by an NDP MP.
36 *Al-Taqrir Al-Istratiji Al-Arabi* for the year 1997, 1998, p. 274.
37 Zahran G., "al-dawr al-siyasi lil Qada'a almisri", pp. 297, 298.
38 *Al-Taqrir Al-Istratiji Al-Arabi* for the year 1996, 1997, pp. 291–294.
39 *Al-Taqrir Al-Istratiji Al-Arabi* for the year 1987, 1988, p. 329.
40 La Palombara, J., & Weiner, M., (ed.), "The Origin and Development of Political Parties", in *Political Parties and Political Development*, Princeton University Press, 1966, p. 4.
41 Waterbury, J., *The Egypt of Nasser and Sadat: The Political Economy of Two Regimes*, Princeton University Press, 1983, p. 313.
42 Mayfield, J., *Rural Politics in Nasser's Egypt*, pp. 104, 105.
43 Lacouture, J., and Lacouture, S., *Egypt in Transition*, Methuen & Co. Ltd., UK, 1958, p. 272.
44 Baker, R., *Egypt's Uncertain Revolution under Nasser and Sadat*, Harvard University Press, UK, 1978, p. 94.
45 Lacoutour, *Egypt in Transition*, p. 220.
46 Ansari, H., *Egypt, the Stalled Society*, State University of New York Press, USA, 1986, p. 85.
47 Vatikiotis, P.J., *The Egyptian Army in Politics, Pattern for New Nation?* Greenwood Press, USA, 1975, pp. 108, 109.
48 Harik, I., "The Single Party as a Subordinate Movement: The case of Egypt", *World Politics*, Vol. 26, No. 1, October 1973.

49 Harik, "The Single Party as a Subordinate Movement", p. 87.
50 Ibid., p. 87.
51 Waterbury, J., *The Egypt of Nasser and Sadat: The Political Economy of Two Regimes*, p. 317.
52 Mayfield, *Rural Politics in Nasser's Egypt*, p. 117.
53 Ibid., p. 117.
54 Ayubi, N., *Bureaucracy and Politics.*, p. 447.
55 Waterbury, *The Egypt of Nasser and Sadat: The Political Economy of Two Regimes*, p. 315.
56 Mayfield, *Rural Politics in Nasser's Egypt*, p. 118.
57 Binder, L., *In a Moment of Enthusiasm: Political Power and the Second Stratum in Egypt*, University of Chicago Press, USA, 1978, p. 305.
58 Alderfer, H. and El Khatib, M. and Fahmy, M., *Local Government in the United Arab Republic*, Institute of Public Administration, UAR, 1964, pp. 21, 22.
59 Harik, "The Single Party as a Subordinate Movement", p. 87.
60 Perlmutter, A., *Egypt: The Praetorian State*, Transaction Inc., USA, 1974, p. 160.
61 Dekemejian, R.H., *Egypt under Nasser: A study in Political Dynamics*, University of London Press Ltd., UK, 1972, pp. 192–199.
62 Moore, C., "Authoritarian Politics in Unincorporated Society, the case of Nasser's Egypt", *Comparative Politics*, Vol. 6, No. 2, January 1974, p. 197.
63 Harik, "The Single Party as a Subordinate Movement", p. 87.
64 Ibid., p. 87.
65 Perlmutter, A., *Egypt the Praetorian State*, p. 163.
66 Ayubi, *Bureaucracy and Politics*, p. 449.
67 Ibid., pp. 450, 451.
68 Hinnebusch, R., "Egypt under Sadat: Elite, Power Structure and Political Change in a Post-populist State", *Social Problems*, Vol. 28, No. 4, April 1982, p. 442.
69 Vatikiotis, P.J., *Nasser and his Generation*, Croom Helm, London, 1978, pp. 165, 166.
70 Ibid., p. 334.
71 Ansari, *Egypt, the Stalled Society*, p. 158.
72 Ino, T., "Democratisation and Local Government in Egypt," In *Local Relations in Egypt*, M&S Series, No. 25, 1989, p. 11.
73 Ansari, H., *Egypt, the Stalled Society*, p. 168.
74 Ibid., p. 164.
75 Baker, *Egypt's Uncertain Revolution under Nasser and Sadat*, p. 163.
76 Hinnebusch, J., *Egyptian Politics under Sadat: The Post-Populist Development of an Authoritarian Modernising State*, Cambridge University Press, Cambridge, 1985, p. 158.
77 Baker, *Egypt's Uncertain Revolution under Nasser and Sadat*, p. 163.
78 Ibid., p. 163.
79 Waterbury, *The Egypt of Nasser and Sadat: The Political Economy of Two Regimes*, p. 365.
80 Hinnebusch, *Egyptian Politics under Sadat: The Post-Populist Development of an Authoritarian Modernising State*, p. 159.
81 Ayubi, N., *The State and Public Policies in Egypt since Sadat*, Ithaca Press, UK, 1991, p. 96.
82 Vatikiotis, P.J., *The History of Egypt from Muhammad Ali to Sadat*, Weidenfeld & Nicolson, London, 1980, p. 418.
83 Nafaa, H., "Al-idara al-siyasiyya li-azmat al-tahawul min nizam al-hizb al-wahid ila nizam ta'addud al-ahzab" (The Political Management for the Crisis of Change from the One Party System to a Multiparty System. In Hilal, A. (ed.) *Al-nizam al-siyasi al-misri: al-taghayyur wa al-istimrar (The Egyptian Political System: change and continuity)*, The Centre for Political Research and Studies, El Nahda Library, 1988, p. 36.
84 Quoted in Rizk, Y., *Al-Ahzab Al-Siyasiya Fi Misr 1907–1984 OR (Political Parties in Egypt 1907–1984)*, Dar El Hilal, Cairo, 1984, p. 208.
85 Ibid., p. 208.

86 Hinnebusch, *Egyptian Politics under Sadat: The Post-Populist Development of an Authoritarian Modernising State*, p. 160.

87 Ibid., p. 160.

88 Hinnebusch, *Egyptian Politics under Sadat: The Post-Populist Development of an Authoritarian Modernising State*, pp. 162–164.

89 Springborg, *Mubarak's Egypt: Fragmentation of the Political Order*, Boulder Westview, 1989, p. 168.

90 Hinnebusch, *Egyptian Politics under Sadat: The Post-Populist Development of an Authoritarian Modernising State*, pp. 162–164.

91 Springborg, *Mubarak's Egypt: Fragmentation of the Political Order*, p. 169.

92 *Al-Taqrir A-Istratiji Al Arabi 1990, 1991*, p. 415.

93 Beattie, K., "Prospects for Democratisation in Egypt", *American Arab Affairs*, Vol. 36, 1991, p. 36.

94 Ansari, H., *"Mubarak's Egypt"*, *Current History*, January 1985, pp. 23, 24.

95 Springborg, Mubarak's Egypt, p. 169.

96 Ibid., p. 169.

Notes to Chapter 4

1 Almond, G., & Verba, S., *The Civic Culture*, Princeton University Press, p. 481.

2 Macridis, Roy, (ed.), *Political parties, Contemporary Trends and Ideas*, Harper Torchbooks, USA, 1967, p. 18.

3 Huntington, S., *Political Order in Changing Societies*, Yale University, USA, 1968, p. 24.

4 *Constitution of the ARE*, p. 106.

5 Ibid., p. 106.

6 Ibid., p. 109.

7 Ibid., p. 116.

8 Ibid., p. 124.

9 Ibid., p. 124.

10 Ibid., p. 107.

11 Ibid., p. 115.

12 Ibid., p. 115.

13 Ibid., p. 117.

14 Reference is made here to the performance of the MB as a political party through their alliance with other parties, although the constitution prohibits the formation of parties on religious grounds.

15 Al-Shurbaji, A., "Al-qadaya al-dusturiyya wa al-qanuniyya fi fatrat riyasat Mubarak al-thaniyya" or (The Constitutional and Legal Cases during Mubarak's Second Presidency) in Kharbousch, M. (ed.) *Al-tatawwur al-siyasi fi Misr 1982–1992* (Political Development in Egypt 1982–1992), Centre for Political Research and Studies, Cairo University, 1994, p. 43.

16 Najjar, F., "Elections and Democracy in Egypt", *American Arab Affairs*, Vol. 29, 1989, p. 98.

17 Ibid., p. 103.

18 Ibid., p. 103.

19 Ibid., p. 104.

20 Qandil, *'Amaliyyat al-Tahawul*, p. 66.

21 Najjar, "Elections and Democracy", p. 105.

22 Qandil, *'Amaliyyat al-Tahawul*, p. 66.

23 Hinnebusch, R.A., *Egyptian Politics under Sadat*, Cambridge University Press, UK, 1985, p. 165.

24 Ibid., p. 166.

25 Ibid., p. 166.
26 Younan, L., *Al-Ahzab al-Siyasiya Fi Misr 1907–1984.*, pp. 254–254.
27 Makram Ebeid, M., "The Role of the Official Opposition", in Tripp, C. & Owen, R. (eds.) *Egypt under Mubarak*, p. 38.
28 *Al-Shark al-Awsat*, 8/12/1995.
29 *Al-Ahram Weekly*, 23–29/11/2000.
30 An interview with Helmy Ahmad Salem 22/1/2000.
31 Hinnebusch, R., *Egyptian Politics under Sadat*, p. 187.
32 Makram Ebeid, M., The Role of the Opposition, p. 36.
33 Ibid., p. 36.
34 Hinnebusch, R., *Egyptian Politics under Sadat*, p. 192.
35 Ibid., p. 198.
36 Makram Ebeid, M., "The Role of the Official Opposition", p. 38.
37 Qandil, A., *'Amaliyyat al-Tahawul al-Dimuqraty*, p. 129.
38 Hassan, I., "Hizb El Tagammuu', al-binya wal-dawr al-Siyasi fi itar al-ta'addudiyya al-siyasiyya al-muqayyada" (The Tagammu Party: The Structure and Political Role in the Controlled Multiparty System) In Kharboush, M., (ed.) *Al-Tatawur al-Siyasi Fi Misr 1982–1992*, p. 338.
39 *Al-Shark al-Awsat*, 8/12/95.
40 *Al-Ahali*, 29/11/2000.
41 *Young Egypt* was one of the pre-1952 political parties.
42 Hinnebusch, R., *Egyptian Politics under Sadat*, pp. 167–170.
43 Makram Ebeid, M., "The Role of the Official Opposition", p. 33.
44 Nour al-Din, I., "Athar al-inshiqaq 'ala al-ada' al-siyasi li hizb al-'amal" (The Effect of the split on the performance of the Labour Party) in Kharboush (ed.) *Al-Tatawur Al-Siyasi Fi Misr 1982–1992.*, p. 352.
45 See the section which discusses the electoral law.
46 Nour al-Din, I., "Athar al-inshiqaq 'ala al-ada' al-siyasi li hizb al-'amal", p. 364.
47 Singer, H., "The Socialist Labour Party: A Case Study of a Contemporary Egyptian Opposition Party", *Cairo Papers in Social Science*, The American University in Cairo, Vol. 16, Spring 1993, p. 13.
48 Ibid., p. 25.
49 Ibid., p. 19.
50 Mainly by the distribution of a closed list which came to be known as Shoukry's list, containing all names of the Islamic members who were supported by Shoukry. The other secular candidates were identified as "undesired elements".
51 Ibid., p. 19.
52 Ibid., pp. 30, 31.
53 Makram Ebeid, M., "The Role of the Official Opposition", p. 35.
54 *Al-Shark al-Awsat*, 8/12/1995.
55 *Al-Ahram Daily*, 20/7/2000.
56 Hinnebusch, R., "The Reemergence of the Wafd Party: Glimpse of the Liberal Opposition in Egypt", *International Journal of Middle East Studies*, Vol. 16, 1984, p. 99.
57 Makram Ebeid, M., "dawr hizb al-wafd al-jadid fi itar al-muaarada al-siyasiyya" (The Role of the New Wafd Party as a Political Opposition). In Hilal, A. (ed.) *Al Nizam al-Siyasi al-Misri: Al Tagyyir Wa al-Istimrar*, p. 477.
58 Baker, R.W., *Sadat and After: Struggles for Egypt's Political Soul*, I.B. Tauris & Co. Ltd., 1990, p. 66.
59 Ansari, H., *Egypt, the Stalled Society*, p. 202.
60 Hinnebush, R., "The Reemergence of the Wafd Party", p. 116.
61 Ibid., p. 116.
62 Ibid., pp. 116, 117.

63 Younan, L., *Al-Ahzab al-Siyasiya Fi Misr 1907–1984*, p. 210.
64 Makram Ebeid, M., "dawr hizb al-wafd al-jadid fi itar al-muaarada al-siyasiyya", p. 479.
65 Hinnebusch, R., "The Reemergence of the New Wafd", p. 117.
66 Dorgham, A., "Hizb al-wafd wa fuqdan al-tawazun:dirasa tahliliyya li dawr al-wafd fi al-ma'araka al-intikhabiyya fi abril 1987" (The Wafd Party and the Imbalance, an analytical analysis for the role of the Wafd in 1987), in Hilal, A., (ed.) *Al-Nizam al-Siyasi al-Misri*, p. 403.
67 Ibid., p. 403.
68 Hinnebusch, R., 'The Reemergence of the New Wafd", p. 106.
69 Springborg, R., *Mubarak's Egypt*, pp. 202–207.
70 Ibid., p. 204.
71 Ibid., p. 205.
72 *Al-Shark al-Awsat*, 8/12/1995.
73 *Al-ahali*, 29/11/2000.
74 Siraj al-Din died on August 9th 2000.
75 *Cairo Times*, 9–15/11/2000
76 *Al-ahali*, 6/12/2000
77 Zubaida S: Islam: *The People & the State, Political Ideas & Movements In the Middle East*, I.B. Tauris & Co Ltd, London, 1989, p. 47.
78 Ibid, p. 47.
79 Mitchell, R., *The Society of the Muslim Brothers*, Oxford University Press, London, 1969, p. 9.
80 Ibid., p. 13.
81 Mustafa, H., *Al-Islam al-Siyasi fi Misr, min harakat al-Islah ila Jama' at al-unf*, al-Ahram Centre for Political And Strategic Studies, 1992, p. 75.
82 Mitchell, R., *The Society of the Muslim Bro*thers, p. 14.
83 Quoted in Ibid., p. 14.
84 In Ahmad, A., *Al-Harakat al-Islamia fi Misr wa kadayiat al-Tahawul al-dimoqraty*, Al Ahram Centre for translation & publication, Cairo, 1995, pp. 44, 45.
85 Ibid., p. 45.
86 Mitchell, R., *The Society of the Muslim Brothers*, p. 31.
87 Ibid., pp. 15, 16.
88 Ibid., pp. 17.
89 Ibid., pp. 16, 17.
90 Ibid., p. 17.
91 Zubaida, *Islam: The People & the State*, p. 48.
92 Ahmad, A., *Al-Harakat al-Islamia*, p. 47.
93 Zubaida, Islam: *The People & the State*, p. 49.
94 Mitchell, p. 32.
95 Zubaida, p. 48.
96 Ibid., p. 48.
97 *Al-Taqrir al-Istratiji al-Arabi li Sanat 1995* (The Arab Srategic Report for 1996) (Cairo; Al-Ahram Center for Political and Strategic studies, 1993), pp. 432–433.
98 Ahmad A., *Al Harakat al Islamia Fi Misr*, p. 246.
99 Mubarak, H., "What does the Gama' a Islamiya Wants? An interview with Tal'at Fu'ad Qasim, in Beinnin J. & Stork J. (eds.) *Political Islam, Essays from Middle East Report*, I.B. Taurus, 1997, p. 316.
100 Ibid., pp. 316, 317.
101 Ahmad A., *Al Harakat al Islamia Fi Misr*, p. 246.
102 *Al Intikhabat al-Barlamaniya fi Misr1995*, p. 45.
103 *Intikhabat Majlis Al Sha'b 1984: Dirasa Wa Tahlil*, p. 130.
104 *Intikhabat Majlis Al Sha'b 1990: Dirasa Wa Tahlil*, p. 50.

105 *Al-Taqrir Al-Istratiji Al-Arabi* for the year 1995, Al-Ahram Centre For Political & Strategic Studies, 1996, p. 385.
106 *Al-Ahram Weekly,* 23–29/11/2000.
107 Most of the major political parties, except for the NUPP, had decided to boycott the 1990 parliamentary elections for lack of sufficient guarantees on behalf of the government for running an honest election.
108 Qandil, A., *'Amaliyyat al-Tahawul al-Dimuqraty,* p. 130.
109 *Al-Taqrir Al-Istratiji Al-Arabi 1995,* 1996, p. 385.
110 *Al-Ahram Weekly* 23–29/11/2000.
111 Qandil, A., *'Amaliyyat al-Tahawul al-Dimuqraty,* p. 131.
112 *The Report of the Egyptian Committee for overseeing the elections,* p. 61.
113 *Al Hayat Arab Affair,* 4/12/1995.
114 *Al Ahram Weekly* 16–22/11/2000.
115 This unprecedented increase in the number of women contesting the 2000 elections is attributed to the institutional support provided by the newly formed National Council for Women (NCW).
116 *Al-Ahram Weekly,* 23–29/11/2000.
117 *Al Hayat Arab Affair,* 15/12/1995.
118 *Middle East Times,* 23/9/2000.
119 Zahran, G., " Al Mustaqillun", in *Intikhabat Majlis Al Sha'b 1990: Dirasa Wa Tahlil,* The Centre for Political and Strategic Studies, Cairo University, pp. 203, 204.
120 *Al-Ahram Weekly,* 23–29/11/2000.
121 *Ruz al-Yusuf Weekly Magazine,* 27/11/1995.
122 Zahran, G., "Al Mustaqillun", in *Intikhabat Majlis Al Sha'b 1990: Dirasa Wa Tahlil,* The Centre for Political and Strategic Studies, Cairo University, pp. 204.
123 As mentioned earlier, Egyptian politicians, whether independents or affiliated to political parties, depend on their popularity or on tribalism when they run for elections. As such they do not have any proper political manifesto or programmes which shape their stands and opinions on major policies. Once elected to the Peoples' Assembly, this lack of political outlook is mostly manifested in their inability to propose bills.
124 Al-Mikawy, N., "The Egyptian Parliament", p. 19.
125 The active role that the NDP MPs play in Parliament with regard to their legislative role proves that they are vehicles through which the government presents bills in the People's Assembly. Similarly; this activity in their scrutiny capacity helps the regime to maintain its democratic pretence.
126 Springborg, R., *Mubarak's Egypt: Fragmentation of the Political Order,* p. 189.
127 Ibid., p. 190.
128 *The Financial Times,* 24/11/1995.
129 *Al-Hayat Arab Affairs,* 15/12/1995.
130 *Cairo Times,* 26/10–1/11/200.
131 *Al-Ahram Weekly,* 16–22/11/2000.
132 *Al-Hayat Arab Affairs,* 15/12/1995.
133 *Ruz al-Yusuf Weekly Magazine,* 18/12/1995.
134 *Al-Ahram Weekly,* 16–22/11/2000.
135 *Middlle East Times,* 29/11/2000.
136 Springborg, R., *Mubarak's Egypt: Fragmentation of the Political Order,* p. 190.
137 *The Report of the Egyptian National Committee for Overseeing 1995 Parliamentary Elections,* p. 206.
138 Ibid., p. 204.
139 *Ruz al-Yusuf, Weekly Magazine,* 18/12/1995.
140 *Al-Ahali Daily Newspaper,* 13/12/2000.

141 *Cairo Times*, 16–22/11/2000.
142 *Akhbar Al Youm*, 9/12/1995.
143 Singr, H., "The Socialist Labour Party: A Case Study of a Contemporary Egyptian Opposition Party", p. 65.
144 Ibid., p. 65.
145 Springborg, R., *Mubarak's Egypt: Fragmentation of the Political Order*, p. 198.
146 Lapalombara, J., & Weiner, M., "The Origin and Development of Political Parties", p. 23.
147 Dorgham, A., "Hizb al-wafd wa fuqdan al-tawazun", p. 404.
148 *The Egyptian Committee for Overseeing the 1995 Elections*, p. 63.
149 Springborg, M., *Mubarak's Egypt: Fragmentation of the Political Order*, p. 188.

Notes to Chapter 5

1 Baer, G., "Social Change in Egypt 1800–1914" in Holt, P., (ed.), *Political and Social Change in Modern Egypt*, Oxford University Press, London 1968, pp. 142–144. For more information on the guild system in Egypt see Baer, G., Egyptian Guilds in Modern Times (Jerusalem, 1964).
2 Reid, D., "The Rise of Professions and Professional Organizations in Modern Egypt", *Comparative Studies in Society and History*, Vol. 16, 1974, p. 28.
3 Bianchi, R., "Interest Groups and Public Policy in Mubarak's Egypt" in Oweiss, I.M. (ed.) *The Political Economy of Contemporary Egypt*, Centre for Contemporary Arab Studies, Georgetown University, Washington, 1990, p. 211.
4 Bianchi, R., *Unruly Corporatism: Associational Life in Twentieth Century Egypt*, Oxford University Press, 1989, p. 62.
5 Bianchi, R., "Interest Groups and Public Policy in Mubarak's Egypt", p. 212.
6 Ibid., p. 93.
7 Ibid., pp. 93–98.
8 Schmitter, P., "Modes of Interest Intermediation and Models of Societal Change in Western Europe" in Schmitter, P., & Lehmbruch, G. (eds.) *Trends Towards Corporatist Intermediation*, Sage Publications, London, 1979, pp. 67, 68.
9 Lehmbruch, G., "Liberal Corporatism and Party Government", *Comparative Political Studies*, (10) April, 1977, p. 94.
10 Ibid., pp. 92, 93.
11 Jessop, B., "Corporatism, Parliamentarism, and Social Democracy", in Schmitter, P. & Lehmbruch, G., *Trends Towards Corporatist Intermediation*, pp. 185–196.
12 Cawson, A., *Corporatism and Political Theory*, Basil Blackwell, Oxford, 1986, p. 78.
13 Wiarda, H., "Corporatism and Development in the Iberic-Latin World: Persistent Strains and New Variations", Review of Politics, (36) 1974, p. 6.
14 Malloy, J., "Authoritarianism, Corporatism, and Mobilisation in Peru", Review of Politics, (36) 1974, p. 54.
15 Ibid., p. 84.
16 Ayubi, N., *Bureaucracy and Politics in Contemporary Egypt*, p. 395.
17 El-Shafee, O., *Workers' Struggle in Mubarak's Egypt*, Unpublished Master Thesis, AUC, 1993, p. 29.
18 Ayubi, N., *The State and Public Policies since Sadat*, Ithaca Press, Reading, 1991, pp. 74–78.
19 Ibid., p. 76.
20 Ibid., p. 82.
21 Bianchi, R., *Unruly Corporatism*, p. 91.
22 *Al-Ahram daily newspaper* on 17/2/1993.
23 *Al-Ahram daily newspaper* 13/2/1995.

24 *Al-Taqrir Al-Istratiji Al-Arabi 1993*, 1994, pp. 354–358.
25 *Al-Taqrir Al-Istratiji Al-Arabi 1992*, 1993, pp. 331–333.
26 Reid, D., "The Rise of Professions and Professional Organizations", pp. 37–41.
27 Reid, D., *Lawyers and Politics in the Arab World*, 1880–1960, Bibliotheca Islamica Inc, USA, 1981, pp. 46–48.
28 Reid, D., "The National Bar Association and the Egyptian Politics 1912–1954", *The International Journal of African Historical Studies*, Vol. 7 no.1, 1974, p. 610.
29 Reid, D., *Lawyers and Politics*, pp. 48–49.
30 Reid, D., "The National Bar Association", p. 615.
31 Ibid., p. 610.
32 Reid, D., *Lawyers and Politics*, p. 157.
33 Reid, D., The National Bar Association, p. 617.
34 Reid, D., *Lawyers and Politics*, p. 150.
35 Reid, D., The National Bar Association, p. 617.
36 Ibid., p. 608.
37 Al-Sayyed, M., "Professional Association and National Integration in the Arab World, with special reference to Lawyers Association", in Dawisha A. & Zartman I. (ed.) *Beyond Coercion, the Durability of the Arab State*, Croom Helm Ltd, USA, 1988, p. 100.
38 Reid, D., *Lawyers and Politics*, pp. 165, 166.
39 Springborg, R., "Professional Syndicates in Egyptian Politics, 1952–1970", *International Journal of Middle East Studies*, Vol. 9, 1978, p. 281.
40 Reid, D., Lawyers and Politics, p. 166.
41 Springborg, R., "Professional Syndicates", p. 281.
42 Baker, R., *Sadat and After: Struggles for Egypt's Political Soul*, I.B. Tauris & Co Ltd, 1990, p. 56.
43 Bianchi, R., *Unruly Corporatism*, p. 100.
44 Baker, R., *Sadat and After*, pp. 56–57.
45 For more information on this incident see chapter three.
46 Bianchi, R., *Unruly Corporatism*, pp. 100, 101.
47 Springborg, R., "Professional Syndicates", p. 288.
48 Ibid., p. 288.
49 Quoted in Reid, D., *Arab Lawyers and Politics*, p. 171.
50 The student strikes which took place in January 1972 reflected the anger of various sectors in the society concerning "the state of no peace no war" which had extended from the aftermath of the 1967 defeat war until 1973. Sadat's 'democratic' rule had reacted by imprisoning a large number of students and ordered the closure of all universities in Egypt.
51 Al-Sayyed, M., *Society and Politics in Egypt, The Role of Interest Groups in the Egyptian Political System (1952–1981)*, Dar Al Moustakbal Al Arabi, 1983, pp. 131, 132.
52 Ibid., p. 139.
53 Bianchi, R., *Unruly Corporatism*, p. 100.
54 Baker, R., *Sadat and After*, pp. 60, 61.
55 Al-Sayyed, M., *Society and Politics in Egypt*, pp. 140, 141.
56 Bianchi, R., *Unruly Corporatism*, pp. 101, 102.
57 For more details about this incident and the reaction of the oposition parties towards it see chapter four.
58 Al-Sayyed, M., *Society and Politics in Egypt*, p. 133.
59 Ibid., p. 145.
60 Bianchi, R., *Unruly Corporatism*, pp. 104–106.
61 *Al-Taqrir Al-Istratiji Al-Arabi 1986*, 1987, p. 387.
62 *Al-Taqrir Al-Istratiji Al-Arabi 1988*, 1989, p. 504.
63 *Al-Taqrir Al-Istratiji Al-Arabi 1989*, 1990, p. 465.

64 The information gained was given to the researcher in an interview held in April 1997 with Dr Osama Asfour, son of Dr Mohamed Asfour, a prominent Wafdist lawyer and the leader of the anti-government faction in the syndicate.
65 An interview with Dr Osama Asfour, in April 1997.
66 *Al-Taqrir Al-Istratiji Al-Arabi 1989*, 1990, p. 465.
67 Ibid., p. 465.
68 *Al-Taqrir Al-Istratiji Al-Arabi 1990*, 1991, p. 455.
69 *Al-Taqrir Al-Istratiji Al-Arabi 1991*, 1992, p. 415.
70 It has been revealed to the researcher that there was a sort of cooperation between al-Khawaja and the members who belong to the Muslim Brotherhood and Al-jihad in an attempt to preserve the formers leadership in the Syndicate in exchange for a predominantly Islamic council.
71 *Al-Taqrir Al-Istratiji Al-Arabi 1992*, 1993, p. 334.
72 *Al-Taqrir Al-Istratiji Al-Arabi 1994*, 1995, pp. 387, 388.
73 *Al-Taqrir Al-Istratiji Al-Arabi 1995*, 1996, pp. 430.
74 Reid, D., "The Rise of Professions and Professional", pp. 48–50.
75 Bianchi, R., *Unruly Corporatism*, pp. 107, 108.
76 Al-Sayed, M., *Society and Politics*, p. 108.
77 Springborg, R., "Professional Syndicates", p. 282.
78 Ibid., p. 282.
79 Bianchi, R., *Unruly Corporatism*, pp. 108–110.
80 Ibid., p. 110.
81 Ibid., p. 107.
82 Ibid., pp. 110–114.
83 *Al-Taqrir Al-Istratiji Al-Arabi 1988*, 1989, p. 506.
84 *Al-Taqrir Al-Istratiji Al-Arabi 1989*, 1990, p. 465.
85 By this law, journalists are liable to fines payable and imprisonment if they criticise any public service or government official touching his public or private life.
86 *Taqrir al Mougtamaa al Madani*, 1995, Ibn Khaldoun Center, 1996, p. 35.
87 Bianchi, R., *Unruly Corporatism*, p. 106.
88 Ibid., p. 114.
89 Moore, C., *Images Of Development, Egyptian Engineers in Search of Industry*, MIT Press, USA, 1980, p. 27.
90 Ibid., pp. 27–34.
91 Springborg, "Professional Syndicates", p. 281.
92 Al-Sayyed, M., *Politics and Society*, p. 93.
93 Moore, C., *Images of Development*, p. 50.
94 Dijani, N., *Corporatism within the Egyptian Context, a Profile of Business & Professional Politics in Egypt*, Master Thesis, AUC, 1982, p. 50.
95 Moore, C., *Images of Development*, p. 48.
96 AL-Sayyed, M., *Politics and Society*, p. 49.
97 Dijani, N., *Corporatism Within the Egyptian Context*, p. 50.
98 Moore, C., *Images of Development*, p. 48.
99 Ibid., p. 50.
100 These are second rate practitioners who lack proper technical training.
101 Moore, C., "Professional Syndicates in Contemporary Egypt", *American Journal of Arabic Studies*, Vol. 3, 1975, p. 73.
102 Bianchi, R., *Unruly Corporatism*, p. 115.
103 Moore, C., "Professional Syndicate", p. 78.
104 Ibid., p. 78.
105 Ibid., p. 79.
106 Bianchi, R., *Unruly Corporatism*, p. 115.

107 Al-Sayyed, M., *Politics and Society*, p. 98.
108 Moore, C., "Professional Syndicates", p. 74.
109 The acceptance of a huge project such as this clearly signifies the lack of any intention on behalf of the government to enter a war.
110 Ibid., p. 75.
111 Ibid., p. 81.
112 Bianchi, R., *Unruly Corporatism*, pp. 115, 116.
113 Ibid., p. 115.
114 Dijani, N., *Corporatism Within the Egyptian Context*, pp. 42, 43.
115 Qandil, A., *Al-Jara' im Al Iqtisadiya Al-Mustahdatha fi Al-Niqabaat Al-Mihaniya, A Case Study of the Engineers Association*, The National Centre for Social and Political studies, the18th International conference for analytical stastics and calculations and social and population research, Al-Shu'biya Al Ijtima'iya, 1992, pp. 19, 20.
116 Bianchi, R., *Unruly Corporatism*, p. 117.
117 Qandil, A., *Al-Jara 'im Al Iqtisadiya Al-Mustahdatha*, p. 21.
118 Ibid., pp. 23, 24.
119 Ibid., p. 25.
120 Ibid., p. 24.
121 Bianchi, *Unruly Corporatism*, p. 117.
122 Qandil, A., *Al-Jara 'im Al Iqtisadiya Al-Mustahdatha*, p. 28.
123 *Al-Taqrir Al-Istratiji Al-Arabi, 1988*, 1989, p. 499.
124 Ibid., p. 506.
125 *Al-Taqrir Al-Istratiji Al-Arab, 1991*, 1992, pp. 414, 415.
126 *Al-Taqrir Al-Istratiji Al-Arabi 1995*, 1996, pp. 431, 432.
127 Reid, D., "The Rise of Professions", pp. 46–48.
128 Ibid., p. 48.
129 Springborg, R., "Professional Syndicates", pp. 282, 283.
130 Moore, C., "Professional Syndicates", pp. 70, 71.
131 It should be recalled here that ASU membership was obligatory for any membership in any other organisation, including syndicates.
132 Moore, C., "Professional Syndicates", pp. 70, 71.
133 *Al-Taqrir Al-Istratiji Al-Arabi 1995*, 1996, pp. 432, 433.
134 Qandil, A., *Al-Jama' at Al-Mihaniya Wa Al-Musharaka Al-Siyasiya*, a report presented to the Symposium for Political Participation in Egypt, the Arab Centre for Research 1992, p. 25.
135 Ibid., p. 25.
136 These proportions has been compiled by the researcher based on the figures for the number of participants provided in Qandil, A., *Al-Jama' at Al Mihaniya Wa Al-Musharaka Al-Siyasiya*, p. 25.
137 *Al-Taqrir Al-Istratiji Al-Arabi 1989*, 1990, p. 465.
138 *Al-Taqrir Al-Istratiji Al-Arabi 1986*, 1987, p. 387.
139 *Al-Taqrir Al-Istratiji Al-Arabi 1989*, 1990, p. 465.
140 *Al-Taqrir Al-Istratiji Al-Arabi 1988*, 1989, p. 499.
141 *Al-Taqrir Al-Istratiji Al-Arabi 1988*, 1989, p. 493.
142 The information gained was given to the researcher in a special interview with Dr Osama Asfour, son of Dr Mohamed Asfour a prominent Wafdist lawyer and the leader of the anti-government faction in the Bar Syndicate.
143 Qandil, A., *Al-Jara' im Al Iqtisadiya Al-Mustahdatha fi Al-Niqabaat Al-Mihaniya, a case study of the Engineers Association*, 1992, pp. 19, 20.
144 *Al-Taqrir Al-Istratiji Al-Arabi 1988*, 1989, p. 499.
145 *Al-Taqrir Al-Istratiji Al-Arabi 1989*, 1990, p. 465.
146 *Al-Taqrir Al-Istratiji Al-Arabi 1992*, 1993, p. 413.

147 This information had been revealed to the researcher in an interview with Dr Osama Asfour.

148 *Al-Taqrir Al-Istratiji Al-Arabi 1989*, 1990, p. 467.

149 See for example Ahmad, A., *Al harakat al-islamia fi Misr*, p. 245.

150 Ibid., pp. 246.

151 Qandil, A., *Taqyim ada' al-islamiyin fi al-niqabat al-mihaniyya*, A report presented to the 5th Franco-Egyptian Symposium (The Phenomenon of Poltical Violence), Research Centre for Political Studies, University of Cairo, 1993, p. 26.

152 *Ruz al-Yusuf, weekly magazine*, 20/2/1995.

153 *Al-Ahali*, 22/12/1993.

154 Ahmad, A., *Al-harakat al-iIslamiyya fi Misr*, p. 264.

155 *Al-Ahali*, 15/3/1995.

156 Qandil, A., *Taqyim ada' al-islamiyyin*, p. 29.

157 *Al-Ahali*, 23/8/1995.

158 *Al-Wasat*, 26/12/1994.

159 *Ruz al-yusuf*, 27/2/1995.

160 *Al Musawer*, 17/3/1995.

161 *Al Musawer*, 3/3/1995.

Notes to Chapter 6

1 Posusney, M., "Collective Action and Workers' Consciousness in Contemporary Egypt", in Lockman Z. (ed.) *Workers and Working Classes in the Middle East*, State University of New York, 1994, pp. 213, 214.

2 Goldberg, E., "The Foundation of State-Labour Relations in Contemporary Egypt", *Comparative Politics*, Vol. 24, No. 2, 1992, p. 147.

3 Beinin, J. & Lockman, Z., *Workers on the Nile, Nationalism, Communism, Islam and the Egyptian Working Class, 1882–1954*, Princeton University Press, 1988, pp. 51, 52.

4 Ibid., pp. 57–61.

5 Ibid., p. 80.

6 Ibid., p. 450.

7 Quoted in Goldberg E., *Tinker, Tailor, and Textile Worker, Class and Politics in Egypt, 1930–1952*, University of California Press, 1986, p. 64.

8 Ibid., p. 64.

9 Quoted in Beinin, J., & Lockman, Z., *Workers on the Nile*, p. 104.

10 Goldberg, E., *Tinker, Tailor, and Textile Worker*, p. 66.

11 Saad Zaghlul was by then not only the Wafd leadership, but also Egypt's Prime Minister.

12 Quoted in Goldberg, E., *Tinker, Tailor, and Textile Worker*, p. 67.

13 Beinin, J., & Lockman, Z., *Workers on the Nile*, pp. 171–187.

14 This union was established in 1928 while Mustafa al-Nahhas, the leader of the Wafd after Zaghlul's death in 1927, was Egypt's Prime Minister presiding over a Wafd-Liberal coalition government.

15 Beinin, J., & Lockman, Z., *Workers on the Nile*, p. 187.

16 Ibid., p. 188.

17 Ibid., pp. 291–293.

18 Bianchi., *Unruly Corporatism*, p. 127.

19 These works can be easily controlled by the Wafd government, since they depend on the state for their livelihood.

20 Beinin, J., & Lockman, Z., *Workers on the Nile*, p. 293.

21 Ibid., p. 310.

22 Bianchi, *Unruly Corporatism*, p. 130.

23 Ibid., pp. 327–362.

24 Ibid., p. 452.

25 Ibid., p. 393.

26 Ibid., p. 383.

27 Ibid., p. 451.

28 An example given here is the refusal of workers on strike to return to work, despite the fact that they were offered higher wages and better working conditions, before their fired colleagues who were union leaders and strike organisers were also returned to work.

29 Davis, E., "History for the Many or History for the Few? The Historiography of the Iraqi Working Class", in Lockman, Z., (ed.) *Workers and Working Classes in the Middle East*, pp. 290–293.

30 Beinin, J., & Lockman, Z., *Workers on the Nile*, pp. 418–432.

31 Bianchi, *Unruly Corporatism*, p. 128.

32 Beinin, J., & Lockman, Z., *Workers on the Nile*, p. 432.

33 Bianchi, *Unruly Corporatism*, p. 128.

34 Major Tu'ayma was at that time the head of the Workers' Bureau of the Liberation Rally, and pro-Nasser.

35 Bianchi, *Unruly Corporatism*, pp. 135, 136.

36 Bianchi, *Unruly Corporatism*, pp. 128, 129.

37 Al-Shafie, O., *Workers' Struggle in Mubarak's Egypt*, Unpublished Master Thesis, AUC, 1993, pp. 29, 30.

38 Ayubi, N., *The State and Public Policies since Sadat*, p. 80.

39 Ibid., p. 81.

40 Bianchi, *Unruly Corporatism*, p. 129.

41 Ibid., p. 138.

42 Ibid., p. 129.

43 Ibid., p. 129.

44 Ibid, pp. 129, 130.

45 Bianchi, *Unruly Corporatism*, p. 131.

46 *Al-Taqrir Al-Istratiji Al-Arabi* for the year 1992, 1993, pp. 338, 339.

47 Bianchi, *Unruly Corporatism*, pp. 140, 141.

48 *Al-Taqrir Al-Istratiji Al-Arabi* for the year 1987, 1988, p. 351.

49 *Al-Taqrir Al-Istratiji Al-Arabi* for the year 1996, 1997, p. 322.

50 Bianchi, *Unruly Corporatism*, p. 141.

51 *Al-Taqrir Al-Istratiji Al-Arabi* for the year 1987, 1988, p. 351.

52 *Al-Taqrir Al-Istratiji Al-Arabi* for the year 1996, 1997, p. 320.

53 Ibid., p. 322.

54 Bianchi, *Unruly Corporatism*, p. 129.

55 *Al-Taqrir Al-Istratiji Al-Arabi* for the year 1995, 1996, p. 322.

56 *Al-Taqrir Al-Istratiji Al-Arabi* for the year 1986, 1987, p. 385.

57 Bianchi, *Unruly Corporatism*, p. 129.

58 *Al-Ahali*, 13/12/2000.

59 *Al-Taqrir Al-Istratiji Al-Arabi* for the year 1987, 1988, p. 350.

60 *Al-Taqrir Al-Istratiji Al-Arabi* for the year 1986, 1987, pp. 285, 287.

61 Posusney, M., "Collective Action and Workers' Consciousness in Contemporary Egypt", p. 232.

62 Goldberg, E., "The Foundation of State-Labour Relations in Contemporary Egypt", p. 147.

63 Ibid., pp. 155, 156.

64 Ibid., p. 157.

65 Ibid., p. 159.
66 Ibid., pp. 157, 158.
67 Posusney, M., "Collective Action and Workers' Consciousness", pp. 214, 215.
68 Ibid., p. 215.
69 Ibid., pp. 217–222.
70 Ibid., pp. 223–231.
71 Ibid., pp. 215, 216.
72 Ibid., p. 216.
73 Ibid., pp. 236–238.
74 Ibid., p. 238.
75 Beinin, J., "Will the Real Egyptian Working Class Please Stand Up?" in Lockman, Z. (ed.) *Workers and Working Classes in the Middle East*, p. 260.
76 Ibid., p. 261.
77 Al Sayyid, M., *Politics and Society*, pp. 54, 55.
78 Dijani, N., *Corporatism within the Egyptian Context*, p. 74.
79 Bianchi, *Unruly Corporatism*, p. 137.
80 Dijani, N., *Corporatism within the Egyptian Context*, p. 79.
81 Ibid., p. 73.
82 Al Sayyid, M., *Politics and Society*, p. 58.
83 *Al-Taqrir Al-Istratiji Al-Arabi* for the year 1987, 1988, p. 349.
84 Brackets added.
85 Dijani, N., *Corporatism within the Egyptian Context*, p. 84.
86 Ibid., p. 80.
87 *Al-Taqrir Al-Istratiji Al-Arabi* for the year 1986, 1987, p. 384.
88 Al Sayyid, M., *Politics and Society*, pp. 60–62.
89 Ibid., p. 62.
90 Ibid., p. 61.
91 Ibid., p. 58.
92 Ibid., pp. 56, 57.
93 Low turnover and longevity of leadership are one of the major characteristics that tend to weaken both the chambers and the confederation.
94 *Al-Taqrir Al-Istratiji Al-Arabi* for the year 1991, 1992, p. 411.
95 Dijani, N., *Corporatism within the Egyptian Context*, pp. 74, 75.
96 *Al-Taqrir Al-Istratiji Al-Arabi* for the year 1987, 1988, p. 348.
97 *Al-Taqrir Al-Istratiji Al-Arabi* for the year 1988, 1989, p. 503.
98 Al Sayyid, M., *Politics and Society*, pp. 60–62.
99 These small businesses are specialised among other things in leather, wood, and metal goods.
100 Many stories have been reported about the inability of these small businesses to achieve reasonable profits because of government intervention and some of them have been either bankrupted or driven out of the market by the larger tycoons.
101 Bianchi, *Unruly Corporatism*, pp. 168–171.
102 Brackets added.
103 Bianchi, *Unruly Corporatism*, p. 171.
104 Ibid., p. 172.
105 Bianchi, *Unruly Corporatism*, p. 173.
106 This figure was obtained from the Egyptian Businessmen's association.
107 *Al-Taqrir Al-Istratiji Al-Arabi* for the year 1985, 1986, p. 341.
108 Bianchi, *Unruly Corporatism*, pp. 175, 176.
109 The leftist NUPP was the only party, which supported the Minister's decrees and welcomed them as a step towards comprehensive economic reform. The decrees were also supported by some independent academics.

110 It was rumoured at the time that the NDP and governmental figures who opposed the decrees were either recieving commission from black marketeers or had joint ventures with them.
111 *Al-Taqrir Al-Istratiji Al-Arabi* for the year, 1985, 1986, pp. 340–342.
112 *Al-Taqrir Al-Istratiji Al-Arabi* for the year 1986, 1987, pp. 381, 382.
113 Bianchi, *Unruly Corporatism,* pp. 175, 176.
114 *Al-Taqrir Al-Istratiji Al-Arabi* for the year 1987, 1988, p. 346.
115 This figure was obtained from the Alexandria Businessmen's Association.
116 *Al-Taqrir Al-Istratiji Al-Arabi* for the year 1987, 1988, p. 346.
117 *Al-Intikhabat al-Barlamaniya Fi Misr 1995,* Centre for Political & Strategic Studies, pp. 83–86.
118 *Al-Ahram Weekly,* 16–22/11/2000.
119 *Al-Intikhabat al-Barlamaniya Fi Misr 1995,* pp. 83–86.
120 Quoted in Murphy, C., "The Business of Political Change in Egypt", *Current History,* January, 1995, p. 22.
121 Qandil, A., *Jama't al-masaleh wa al-siyasa al-kharijiya: dirasa li dawr rijal al a'amal fi Misr,* paper presented to the Second Conference on Political Research, Centre for Political Research and Studies, p. 8.
122 This took place despite the fact that the Egyptian law prohibits the formation of branches of foreign chambers in Egypt.
123 This figure was obtained from the American chamber of Commerce.
124 *Al-Taqrir Al-Istratiji Al-Arabi* for the year 1986, 1987, p. 383.
125 *Al-Taqrir Al-Istratiji Al-Arabi* for the year 1988, 1989, p. 494.
126 Lately Khamis had fell out of Mubarak's favour and been removed from both the Presidential council and from his position as head of the Egyptian Federation of Industries.
127 A lot of these subsidies have been eliminated anyway.
128 *Ruz al-Yusuf,* 17/3/1997.
129 Ibid., pp. 12–17.
130 Ibid., pp. 14–19.
131 Murphy, C., "The Business of Political Change in Egypt", p. 19.
132 Sadowsky, Y., *Political Vegetables, Businessman and Bureaucrat in the Development of Egyptian Agriculture,* The Brookings Institution, USA, 1991, p. 140.

Notes to Chapter 7

1 Rondinelli, D.A., "Government Decentralisation in Comparative Perspective: Theory and Practice in Developing Countries", *International Review of Administrative Science,* Vol. 47, No. 2, 1981, p. 137.
2 Hill, D.M., *Democratic Theory and Local Governments,* Allen & Unwin Ltd., UK, 1974, p. 19.
3 Stanyer, J., *Understanding Local Government,* Martin Robertson & Co. Ltd., 1976, pp. 30, 31.
4 Hicks, U.K., *Development from below: Local Government and Finance in Developing Countries of the Commonwealth,* Oxford University Press, 1961, p. 4.
5 Maddick, H., *Democracy, Decentralisation and Development,* Asia Publishing House, 1963, p. 54.
6 Al-Shinawy, M.A., *Community Development and Local Government in the Developing Nations: A Study Based on the Experience of the United Arab Republic (Egypt), India, and Pakistan,* Unpublished Ph.D. dissertation, New York University 1964, p. 137.
7 Nassouhy, M., *Local Autonomy under National Planning: The Egyptian Experience,* Unpublished Ph.D. dissertation, University of Southern California 1965, p. 45.

8 Al-Shinawy, M.A., *Community Development and Local Government in the Developing Nations,* p. 138.

9 Nassouhy, M., *Local Autonomy under National Planning,* pp. 67, 68.

10 Quoted in Al-Shinawy, M.A., *Community Development and Local Government in the Developing Nations,* p. 138.

11 Baer, G., *Fellah and Townsman in the Middle East,* Frank Cass & Co., UK, 1982, p. 113.

12 Al-Shinawy, M.A., *Community Development and Local Government in the Developing Nations,* p. 139.

13 Abu Fadl, M., *Achilles Heel in the Charybdis: A Treatise on Local Government in Egypt,* Anglo Egyptian Bookshop, Cairo, p. 24.

14 Ibid., p. 24.

15 Alderfer, H., Al-Khatib, M. & Fahmy, M., *Local Government in the United Arab Republic,* Institute of Public Administration, UAR & UN, 1964, p. 3.

16 Abu Fadl, M., *Achilles Heel in the Charybdis,* p. 26.

17 This exception was made for the Aswan province, because of its low standard of living and the fact that the agricultural land there, due to the geographic nature of the Nile, is limited.

18 Nassouhy, *Local Autonomy under National Planning,* pp. 74, 76.

19 Abu Fadl, M., *Achilles Heel in the Charybdis,* p. 55.

20 Nassouhy, *Local Autonomy under National Planning,* pp. 76–81.

21 Alderfer, *Local Government in the United Arab Republic,* p. 4.

22 Al-Shinawy, *Community Development and Local Government in the Developing Nations,* p. 142.

23 Alderfer, *Local Government in the United Arab Republic,* p. 4.

24 Abu Fadl, *Achilles Heel in the Charybdis,* p. 27.

25 Ibid., p. 27.

26 Alderfer, *Local Government in the United Arab Republic,* p. 4.

27 Ino, T., "Democratisation and Local Government in Egypt", in *Local Administration and Centre-Local Relations in Egypt,* MES Series, No. 25 1989, p. 23.

28 Abu Fadl, *Achilles Heel in the Charybdis,* p. 29.

29 Alderfer, *Local Government in the United Arab Republic,* p. 7.

30 Rashid, A., *Local Administration in Egypt,* Institute of Developing Economics, 1988, p. 9.

31 Alderfer, *Local Government in the United Arab Republic,* p. 9.

32 Auda, G., "Local Government/Administration and Development: political context and dynamics in the post Nasser era", in *Local Administration and Central-Local Relations in Egypt,* pp. 48, 49.

33 Alderfer, *Local Government in the United Arab Republic,* p. 8.

34 Auda, "Local Government/Administration and Development", p. 50.

35 Alderfer, *Local Government in the United Arab Republic,* p. 8.

36 Auda, "Local Government/Administration and Development", p. 50.

37 Heaphey, J., "The Organisation of Egypt", *World Politics,* Vol. 18 No. 2, 1966, p. 183.

38 Alderfer, *Local Government in the United Arab Republic,* pp. 8, 10.

39 Heaphey, "The Organisation of Egypt", p. 183.

40 Alderfer, *Local Government in the United Arab Republic,* pp. 9, 10.

41 Ibid., pp. 10, 11.

42 Heaphey, "The Organisation of Egypt", p. 183.

43 Abu Fadl, *Achilles Heel in the Charybdis,* p. 60.

44 Heaphey, "The Organisation of Egypt", pp. 186, 187.

45 Ibid., p. 187.

46 Nassouhy, *Local Autonomy under National Planning,* p. 130.

47 Auda, "Local Government/Administration and Development", pp. 50, 51.

48 Ibid., p. 55.

49 Abu Fadl, *Achilles Heel in the Charybdis,* pp. 41, 42.

50 Rashid, *Local Administration in Egypt,* p. 11.
51 Auda, Local Government/Administration and Development, p. 55.
52 Ayubi, N., "Local Government and Rural Development in Egypt in the 1970s", *African Administrative Sciences,* No. 23, 1984, p. 61.
53 Ibid., pp. 61, 62.
54 Ino, "Democratisation and Local Government in Egypt", pp. 23, 24.
55 Ayubi, N., "Local Government and Rural Development in Egypt in the 1970s", p. 162.
56 Ibid., p. 63.
57 Ino, "Democratisation and Local Government in Egypt", p. 25.
58 Ansari, H., *Egypt the Stalled Society,* p. 198.
59 Ino, "Democratisation and Local Government in Egypt", p. 14.
60 Ansary, *Egypt the Stalled Society,* p. 197.
61 Ayubi, "Local Government and Rural Development in Egypt in the 1970s", p. 67.
62 Ansari, *Egypt the Stalled Society,* pp. 211, 215.
63 Ino, "Democratisation and Local Government in Egypt", p. 18.
64 Ansari, *Egypt the Stalled Society,* pp. 202, 205.
65 Ayubi, "Local Government and Rural Development in Egypt in the 1970s", pp. 67, 68.
66 Ibid., p. 70.
67 Ibid., p. 70.
68 Ibid., p. 71.
69 Ibid., p. 71.
70 Abu Fadl, *Achilles Heel in the Charybdis,* p. 47.
71 *Kanoun Nizam al-Idara al-Mahalya Wa Laihatoho al-Tanfizia,* The Local Administration Law and its executive forum, 1989, Egypt, pp. 17, 18.
72 *The constitution of the Arab Republic of Egypt,* p. 212.
73 *Kanoun Nizam al-Idara al-Mahalya,* p. 19.
74 Qandil, A., *'Amalyyat Al-Tahawul Al Dimuqraty Fi Misr,* p. 204.
75 Ibid., p. 208.
76 *Al Ahaly daily Newspaper,* 7/2/1996.
77 *Al-Ahram daily Newspaper,* 20/4/1997.
78 *Al-Ahram daily Newspaper,* 20/4/1994.
79 De Tocqueville, A., *Democracy in America,* Translated by Lawrence, A., (ed.) Mayer, J.P., Doubleday & Company Inc., New York, 1969, p. 88.

Notes to Chapter 8

1 Quoted in Heady, F., *Public Administration, A comparative perspective,* Marcel Dekker, Inc. USA, 1991, p. 106.
2 Ibid., pp. 108, 109.
3 Quoted in Ayubi, N., *Bureaucracy and Politics in Contemporary Egypt,* p. 3.
4 Richards, A., "The Agricultural Crisis in Egypt", *The Journal of Development Studies,* Vol. 16, No. 3, 1980, p. 303.
5 Ibid., p. 303.
6 The feddan = twenty four karats.
7 Mayfield, J., *Local Institutions And Egyptian Rural Development,* Cornell University, New York, 1974, p. 1.
8 Hopkins, N.S., *Agrarian Transformation in Egypt,* Westview Press, USA, 1987, p. 7.
9 Sadowsky, Y., *Political, Vegetables? Buisnessman and Bureaucrat in the Development of Egyptian Agriculture,* The Brooking Institute, USA, 1991, p. 15.
10 Ibid., p. 19.

11 Ossama, H., "Egypt's Open Door Economic Policy: An attempt at Economic Integration in the Middle East", *The International Journal of Middle East Studies*, Vol. 13, 1981, p. 4.

12 Harrik, I., "Continuity and Change in Local Development Policies in Egypt: From Nasser to Sadat", *The International Journal of Middle East Studies*, Vol. 16, 1984, p. 52.

13 Waterbury, J., *Egypt: Burdens of the Past, Options for the future*, Indiana University Press, USA, 1978, p. 118.

14 Radwan, S., & Lee, E., *Agrarian change in Egypt: An Anatomy of Rural Poverty*, Groom Helm LTP, UK, 1986, p. 11.

15 Maddick, H., *Democracy, Decentralization and Development*, Asia Publishing House, 1963, p. 3.

16 Quoted in Ansari, H., *Egypt, The Stalled Society*, State University of New York Press, 1986, p. 189.

17 Abdalla, N., "Egypt's Absorptive Capacity During 1960 1972", *The International Journal of Middle East Studies*, Vol. 16, 1984, p. 191.

18 Ayubi, N., *The State and Public Policies in Egypt since Sadat*, p. 309.

19 The whole historical setting is based on Mabro's *The Egyptian Economy 1952–1972*, Clarendon Press, UK, 1974, p. 56–61.

20 Ibid., p. 61.

21 Radwan, *Agrarian change in Egypt*, p. 7.

22 Ibid., p. 7.

23 Richards, A., *Egypt's Agricultural Development 1800–1980: Technical and Social Changes*, Westwiew Press, USA, 1982, p. 177.

24 Ibid., p. 180.

25 Abdel Fadil, M., *Development, Income Distribution and Social Change in Rural Egypt (1952–1970)*, Cambridge University Press, 1975, p. 23.

26 Ansari, H., *Egypt, The Stalled Society*, p. 178.

27 Ibid., p. 178.

28 Ibid., pp. 179, 180.

29 Ibid., pp. 182, 183.

30 Gadalla, S., *Land Reform in Relation to Social Development: Egypt*, University of Missouri Press, USA, 1960, p. 16.

31 Mayfield, J., *Local Institutions and Egyptian Rural Development*, Cornell University, USA, 1974, p. 21.

32 Issawi, C., *Egypt in Revolution: An Economic Analysis*, Oxford University Press, UK, 1963, p. 158.

33 Gadalla, S., *Land Reform in Relation to Social Development*, p. 15.

34 Radwan, S., *Agrarian change in Egypt*, p. 8.

35 Mayfield, J., *Local Institutions and Egyptian Rural Development*, p. 21.

36 Richards, A., *Agricultural Crisis in Egypt*, p. 306.

37 Springborg, R., "State-Society Relations in Egypt: The Debate Over Owner-Tenant Relations", *Middle East Journal*, Vol. 45, No. 2, 1991, p. 235.

38 Ibid., p. 234.

39 Ibid., pp. 235, 236.

40 Ibid., p. 236.

41 Quoted in Ibid., p. 236.

42 Qandil, A., *'Amaliyyat Al-Tahawul Al Dimuqraty Fi Misr*, p. 100.

43 *Al-Ahaly daily Newspaper*, 16/2/2000.

44 El-Messiri, S., "Tarahil Laborers in Egypt", in Richards Alan & Martin Philip (eds.): *Migration, Mechanization and Agricultural Labor Markets in Egypt*, Westview Press, USA, 1983, pp. 80, 81.

45 Ibid., p. 81.

46 Mayfield, J., *Local Institutions And Egyptian Rural Development*, p. 14.
47 One Egyptian pounds = 100 piasters.
48 Radwan, S., *Agrarian Change in Egypt*, p. 8.
49 Mayfield, J., *Local Institutions And Egyptian Rural Development*, p. 14.
50 Issawi, C., *Egypt in Revolution:An Economic Analysis*, p. 162.
51 Warriner, D., *Land Reform and Development In The Middle East*, Greenwood Press, USA, 1962, p. 49.
52 El Messiri, S., "Tarahil Laborers in Egypt", p. 81.
53 Baker, R., *Egypt's Uncertain Revolution Under Nasser and Sadat*, Harvard University Press, UK, 1978, pp. 200, 201.
54 Bianchi, R., *Unrully Corporatism*, p. 148.
55 Baker, R., *Egypt's Uncertain Revolution*, pp. 200, 201.
56 Bianchi, R., *Unruly Corporatism*, p. 148.
57 Quoted in Ibid., p. 149.
58 Baker, R., *Egypt's Uncertain Revolution under Nasser and Sadat*, pp. 200, 201.
59 Harik, I. "Mobilization Policy and Political Change in Rural Egypt", in Antoun Richard & Harik Ilya (eds.): *Rural Politics and Social Change In The Middle East*, Indiana University Press, USA, 1972, pp. 295, 296.
60 Bianchi, R., *Unrully Corporatism*, p. 150.
61 Ibid., p. 150.
62 Ibid., p. 145.
63 Ibid., pp. 151, 152.
64 Ibid., p. 152.
65 Ibid., pp. 153, 154.
66 Ibid., p. 154.
67 Formerly such elections used to be under the supervision of the confederation.
68 Ibid., pp. 154, 155.
69 Sadowsky, Y., *Political Vegetables? Buisnessman and Bureaucrat in the Development of Egyptian Agriculture*, p. 12.
70 Springborg, R., "State-Society Relations in Egypt", p. 249.
71 Mayfield, J., *Local Institutions and Egyptian Rural Development*, p. 27.
72 Richards, A., *Egypt's Agricultural Development*, p. 181.
73 Warriner, D., *Land Reform and Development In The Middle East*, pp. 35, 36.
74 Sadowsky, Y., *Political Vegetables? Buisnessman and Bureaucrat in the Development of Egyptian Agriculture*, p. 67.
75 Von Brawn, J., & De Haen, H., "The Effect of Food Price And Subsidy Policies on Egyptian Agriculture", *International food Policy Research Institutes Research*, Report 42 November 1983 p. 22.
76 Richards, A., *Egypt's Agricultural Development*, p. 183.
77 Sadowsky Y., *Political Vegetables? Buisnessman and Bureaucrat in the Development of Egyptian Agriculture*, p. 80.
78 VonBrawn J. & De Haen H., "The Effect of Food Price and Subsidy Policies", p. 22.
79 Mabro, *The Egyptian Economy 1952–1972*, p. 75.
80 Richards, A., *Egypt's Agricultural Development*, pp. 184–200.
81 Mabro, *The Egyptian Economy 1952–1972*, p. 79.
82 Ibid., p. 79.
83 Sadowsky, Y., *Political Vegetables? Businessman and Bureaucrat in the Development of Egyptian Agriculture*, p. 75.
84 Mabro, *The Egyptian Economy 1952–1972*, p. 77.
85 Ibid., p. 77.
86 Bianchi, R., *Unrully Corporatism*, p. 149.

87 Sadowsky, Y., *Political Vegetables? Buisnessman and Bureaucrat in the Development of Egyptian Agriculture*, pp. 76, 77.

88 Ikram, K., *Egypt, Economic Management in Transition*, John Hopkins University, USA, 1980, pp. 205, 206.

89 Ibid., p. 208.

90 Ibid., p. 206.

91 Commander, S., *The State And Agricultural Development In Egypt Since 1973*, Ithaca Press, 1987, p. 34.

92 Sadowsky, Y., *Political Vegetables? Buisnessman and Bureaucrat in the Development of Egyptian Agriculture*, pp. 38, 39.

93 Hansen, B. & Nashashibi, K., *Foreign Trade Regimes and Economic Development*, Egypt, National Bureau of Economic Research, New York, 1975, p. 193.

94 Sadowsky, Y., *Political Vegetables? Buisnessman and Bureaucrat in the Development of Egyptian Agriculture*, p. 51.

95 Springborg, R., "State-Society Relations in Egypt", p. 246.

96 Ibid., pp. 242, 243.

97 Ibid., p. 245.

98 Ibid., p. 248.

99 Zahran, G., "Al Mustakiloun" or (The Independent Candidate), in *Intikhabat Majlis Al Shaab 1990: Dirasa Wa Tahlil* (The 1990 People's Assembly Election: Study and Analysis), The Centre for Political and Strategic Studies, Cairo University, pp. 203, 204.

100 *Ruz al Yusuf Weekly Magazine*, 27/11/1995.

101 Springborg, R., "State-Society Relations in Egypt", p. 248.

102 *Al-Intikhabat Al-Barlamaniiya Fi Misr 1995*, Centre for Political & Strategic Studies, 1997, p. 40.

Notes to Chapter 9

1 *The Information and Decision Making Centre*, al-Menia governorate.

2 'Izab: Sing 'Izba, is a populated area usually smaller than a village. A number of 'izab can form a village. Likewise a nag' (plural nugu') is smaller than a 'izba. A number of nugu' can form a 'izba.

3 The whole information on al-Menia governorate is extracted from *The Information and Decision Making Centre, the Periodic Bulletin* , No 2, October, 1993.

4 *The Statistical Directory for 1992*, the Central Statistical Department, al-Menia governorate p. 12.

5 *The Information and Decision Making Centre*, al-Menia Governorate.

6 *The Egyptian Village Directory*, the Information and Decision Making Centre, al-Menia Governorate, p. 4.

7 *The Information and Decision Making Centre*, al-Menia Governorate.

8 A. *The Egyptian Village Directory*, the Information and Decision Making Centre, p. 17, al-Menia Governorate. B. The feddan = twenty four qirrats and is equivalent to 4200 5/6 sq. meters.

9 *The Information and Decision Making Centre*, al-Menia Goverorate.

10 In Tihna it is believed that a girl who is unmarried by eighteen is not marriageable.

11 Although, officially, public education is free in Egypt, there is still some cost involved. This would include, for example, the cost of school uniform and shoes. With the swift rising prices in Egypt, such items are a real burden on most Egyptian families. Private tutoring is another example of the hidden costs of education, indispensable to most pupils because of the large numbers of pupils in each classroom which makes it difficult for teachers to work efficiently.

12 The 'Umda is the leader of the village. He is usually one of the village notables who is respected and obeyed by every one. The 'Umda used to be elected. Recently, and in a further blow to representation and democracy at the local level, the government issued the 'Umad law by virtue of which appointment replaced election in the selection of the 'Umda.

13 Samir never mentioned that he used to work in the Agricultural co-operative.

14 It has been rumoured that the corruption of the judges or their yielding to government instructions is becoming a widespread phenomenon. This, however, was not the case in the past, where Egypt's judges were known to be among the most honest and outspoken groups in society.

15 Note that he himself was among those corrupt people working in the agriculture co-operative and was the only one exposed and sentenced in court.

16 For more information on this topic see chapter three.

17 The 1995 elections came to verify Fayza's predictions not only at the local but also at the national level.

18 The garbage and the animals on the unused land surrounding the building is an illustration of the performance of the environmental health inspector.

19 The Egyptian Pound = 100 piasters.

20 The health Units are supposed to provide health services and medicine for the poor peasants, for minimal fees. This official fee is 25 piasters which includes both the medical examination and the medicine.

21 Dr Hany refused to name the village in which he previously used to work.

22 Notice the discrepancy between this and what members of the board of directors later said about these services.

23 Both are animal fodder.

24 Those that are not cash crops.

Notes to Chapter 10

1 Ayubi, N., *The State and Public Policies in Egypt since Sadat*, p. 263.

2 Ibid., p. 263.

3 Springborg, R., "The President and the Field Marshal: Civil-Military relations in Egypt Today", *Middle East Report*, N0147, July–August 1987, pp. 10–15.

4 Ayubi, *The State and Public Policies in Egypt since Sadat*, p. 255.

5 Ayubi, N., *Over-stating the Arab State: Politics and Society in the Middle East*, I.B., Taurus Publications, London, 1995, pp. 409, 410.

6 Ibid., p. 410.

7 Ibid., p. 410.

8 For more information on this type and other types of corruption prevailing in middle eastern countries see Waterbury, J., "Endemic and Planned Corruption in a Monarchical Regime", *World Politics*, Vol. 25, 1972–1973, pp. 533–555, and "Corruption, Political Stability and Development: Comparative Evidence from Egypt and Morocco", *Government and Opposition*, Vol. 11, 1976, pp. 426–445.

9 Cardoso, F., "On the Characterisation of Authoritarian Regimes in Latin America", in Collier D. (ed.) *The New Authoritarianism in Latin America*, Princeton University Press, 1979, p. 37.

10 This is particularly true, especially since the burden for the elimination of these economic benefits will naturally fall on the lower and middle working classes.

11 Ayubi, N., *Overstating the Arab State*, p. 26.

12 Sadowsky, Y., "The New Orientalism and the Democracy Debate", in Beinin, J. & Stork, J. (eds.) *Political Islam, Essays From Middle East Report*, p. 35.

13 Ibid., p. 35.
14 Ibid., p. 36.
15 Ibid., p. 36.
16 Hinnebusch, R.A., "The Formation of the Contemporary Egyptian State from Nasser and Sadat to Mubarak", in Oweiss, I.M. (ed.) *The Political Economy of Contemporary Egypt*, Centre for Contemporary Arab Studies, Georgetown University, Washington 1990, p. 189.
17 Ibid., p. 189.
18 Ibid., pp. 188, 195.
19 Sadowsky, Y., "The New Orientalism and the Democracy Debate", p. 37.
20 Migdal, J.S., *Strong Societies and Weak States: State-Society Relations and State Capabilities in the Third World*, Princeton University Press, New Jersey 1988, pp. 200–205.
21 Ibid., p. 185.
22 Ibid., p. 185.
23 Sadowsky, Y., *Political Vegetables? Businessman and Bureaucrat in the Development of Egyptian Agriculture*, p. 12.
24 Ibid., p. 90.
25 For more information on clientele network in Egypt see Springborg, R., "Sayed Bey Marei and Political Clientelism in Egypt", *Comparative Political Studies*, Vol. 12, No. 3, October, 1979, pp. 259–288, *Family, Power and Politics in Egypt, Sayed Bey Marei – His Clan, Clients and Cohorts*, University of Pennsylvania Press, USA, 1982 and *The Ties that Bind: Political Associations and Policy making in Egypt*, PhD dissertation, Stanford University, May, 1974. See also Moore, C., "Clientelist Ideology and Political Change: Fictitious Networks in Egypt and Tunisia," in Gellner, E., & Waterbury, J., *Patrons and Clients in Mediterranean Societies*, Duckworth, London, 1977.
26 Singerman, D., *Avenues of Participation: Family, Politics, and Networks in Urban Quarters of Cairo*, Princeton University Press, 1995, p. 39.
27 Ibid., p. 242.
28 Ibid., p. 270.
29 Richards, A., "The Political Economy of Dilatory Reform: Egypt in the 1980's", *World Development*, Vol. 19, No. 12, 1991, pp. 1726, 1727.
30 For more details on this distinction as is applied to the Middle East see Ayubi, N., *Overstating the Arab State*, Chapters 1 & 11.
31 Ibid., p. 411.
32 Ibid., p. 412.
33 Nordlinger, E., 'Taking the State Seriously', in Weiner, M. & Huntington, S., *Understanding Political Development*, Little Brown, Boston, 1987, p. 364.
34 Ibid., pp. 365–367.
35 Ibid., pp. 369–371.
36 Migdal, J., *Strong Societies and Weak States*, p. 4.
37 For more information on the different Islamic groups see Springborg, *Mubarak's Egypt: Fragmentation of the Political Order*, Westview Press, 1989.
38 For more information and critique of the views of those scholars see Toye, J., *Dilemmas of Development*, Oxford: Blackwell, 1987 & Lal, D., *The Poverty of 'Development Economics'*, Harvard University Press, 1985.
39 Sadowsky, Y., *Political Vegetables*, p. 314.
40 Ibid., p. 315.
41 A lecture given in the Middle East Forum in the Department of Politics at the University of Exeter on February 3, 1999.
42 Quoted in Sadowsky, Y., "The New Orientalism and the Democracy Debate", p. 33.

Bibliography

1. Books

A) Sources in English

Abdel Fadil, M., *Development, Income Distribution and Social Change in Rural Egypt (1952–1970)*, Cambridge University Press, 1975.

Abdel Malek, A., *Egypt, Military Society, the Army Regime, the Left and Social Change Under Nasser*, Random House, New York, 1962.

Abu Fadl, M., *Achilles Heel in the Charybdis: A Treatise on Local Government in Egypt*, Anglo Egyptian Bookshop, Cairo.

Adamson, W., *Hegemony and Revolution: A Study of Antonio Gramsci's Political and Cultural Theory*, California Press, 1980.

Alderfer, H., al-Khatib, M., & Fahmy, M., *Local Government in the United Arab Republic*, Institute of Public Administration, UAR & UN, 1964.

Alderfer, H., *Local Government in Developing Countries*, McGraw-Hill Inc, 1964.

Aliboni R., Dessouki, A., Ibrahim, S., Luciano, G., & Padoan, P. (eds.) *Egypt's Economic Potential*, Croom Helm, 1984.

Almond, G. and Powell, A., *Comparative Politics, A Developmental Approach*, Little, Brown & Company, 1966.

Almond, G. and Verba, S., *The Civic Culture*, Princeton University Press, 1963.

Amin, S., *Unequal development, An Essay on the Social Formations of the Peripheral Capitalism*, Harvester Press Limited, 1973.

Ammar, H., *Growing Up in an Egyptian Village, Silwa Province of Aswan*, Routledge & Kegan Paul, London 1966.

Ansari, H., *Egypt, The Stalled Society*, State University of New York Press, 1986.

Antoun, R., & Harik I., (eds.) *Rural Politics and Social Change in the Middle East*, Indiana University Press, 1972.

Aveniri, S., *Karl Marx on Colonialism & Modernisation*, Anchor books, 1968.

Ayrout, H., *The Egyptian Peasant*, Beacon Press, Boston, 1963.

Ayubi, N., *Bureaucracy and Politics in Contemporary Egypt*, Ithaca Press, London, 1980.

Ayubi, N., *Over-stating the Arab State: Politics and Society in the Middle East*, I.B., Taurus Publications, London, 1995.

Ayubi, N., *The State and Public Policies in Egypt Since Sadat*, Ithaca Press, London, 1991.

Baer, G., *Egyptian Guilds in Modern Times*, Jerusalem, 1964.

Baer, G., *Fellah and Townsman in the Middle East*, Frank Cass, 1982.

Baker, R., *Egypt's Uncertain Revolution Under Nasser and Sadat*, Harvard University Press, 1978.

Baker, R., *Sadat and After: Struggles for Egypt's Political Soul*, I.B. Tauris, 1990.

Baran, P., *The Political Economy of Growth*, Monthly Review Press, New York, 1957.

Barkey, H., (ed.) *The Politics of Economic Reform in the Middle East*, St Martin's Press, New York, 1992.

Baskin, D., *American Pluralist Democracy: A Critique*, Van Nostrand Reinhold, 1971.

Beinin J., & Lockman, Z., *Workers on the Nile, Nationalism, Communism, Islam and the Egyptian Working Class, 1882–1954*, Princeton University Press, 1988.

Beinin, J., & Stork, J., (eds.) *Political Islam, Essays from Middle East Report*, University of California Press, 1997.

Bentley, A., *The Process of Government: A Study of Social Pressure*, The Principia Press of Illinois, (1908) 1935.

Berque, J., *Egypt: Imperialism and Revolution*, Faber, London, 1972.

Bianchi, R., *Unruly Corporatism: Associational Life in Twentieth Century Egypt*, Oxford University Press, 1989.

Binder, L., *Islamic Liberalism, A Critique of Development Ideologies*, The University of Chicago Press, 1988.

Binder, L., *In a Moment of Enthusiasm Political Power and the Second Stratum in Egypt*, University of Chicago Press, 1978.

Blackman, W., *The Fallahin of Upper Egypt*, 1968.

Bowman, A., *Egypt after the Pharoahs: 332 BC–AD 642: From Alexander to the Arab Conquest*, British Muslim Publications, London, 1986.

Braun, J., & Haen, H., *The Effects of Food Price and Subsidy Policies on Egyptian Agriculture*, International Food policy Research Institute, Research Report 42, November, 1983.

Brown, N., *Peasant Politics in Modern Egypt, The Struggle Against the State*, Yale University Press, New Haven & London, 1990.

Callinicoz, A., *The Revolutionary Ideas of Marx*, Bookmark, 1983.

Cantori, Louis & Harik, I., *Local Politics and Development in the Middle East*, Westview Press, 1984.

Carnoy, M., *The State and Political Theory*, Princeton University Press, 1984.

Cawson, A., *Corporatism and Political Theory*, Basil Blackwell, Oxford, 1986.

Collier D. (ed.) *The New Authoritarianism in Latin America*, Princeton University Press, 1979.

Commander, S., *The State and Agricultural Development in Egypt Since 1973*, Ithaca Press, 1987.

Cooper, M., *The Transformation of Egypt*, Croom Helm, London, 1982.

Dahl, R., *Polyarchy; Participation and Opposition*, Yale University, 1971.

Dahl, R., *Dilemmas of Pluralist Democracy vs. Control* Yale University Press, 1982.

Dahl, R., *Who Governs? Democracy and Power in an American City*, Yale University Press, New Haven & London, 1961.

Dawisha, A., & Zartman, I., (eds.) *Beyond Coercion, the Durability of the Arab State*, Croom Helm, 1988.

De Tocqueville, A., *Democracy in America*, Translated by Lawrence, A., (ed.) Mayer, J.P., Doubleday & Company Inc., New York, 1969.

Dekemejian, R.H., *Egypt under Nasser: A study in Political Dynamics*, University of London Press, 1972.

Dekemejian, R.H., *Patterns of Political Leadership: Egypt, Israel, Lebanon*, State University of New York Press, 1975.

Draper, Hal, *Karl Marx's Theory of Revolution, Vol. 1: State and Bureaucracy*, Monthly Review Press, 1977.

Dunleavy, P. and O'Leary, B., *Theories of the State, the Politics of Liberal democracy*, Macmillan, 1987.

Duverger, *Political Parties: Their Organisation and Activity in the Modern State*, Methuen, 1954.

El-Messirie, S., *Ibn al-Balad, A Concept of Egyptian Identity*, E.B. Brill, Leiden, 1978.

Emmanuel, A., *Unequal exchange: A Study of the Imperialism of Trade*, Monthly Review Press, 1972.

Epstein, L., *Political Parties in Western Democracies*, Pall Mall Press, 1967.

Esman, M., & Uphoff, N., *Local Organisations, Intermediaries in Rural Development*, Cornell University Press, 1984.

Femia, J., *Gramsci's Political Thought*, Clarendon Press, Oxford 1981, p. 26.

Frank, A.G., *Capitalism and underdevelopment in Latin America, Historical Studies of Chile and Brazil*, Monthly Review press, New York, 1967.

Gadalla, S., *Land Reform in Relation to Social Development: Egypt*, University of Missouri Press, 1960.

Gellner, E., & Waterbury, J., *Patrons and Clients in Mediterranean Societies*, Duckworth, London, 1977.

Ghorbal, S., *The Beginnings of the Egyptian Question and the Rise of Mehemet Ali*, Routledge, London 1928.

Glanville, S., (ed.) *The Legacy of Egypt*, Oxford University Press, 1942.

Goldberg, E., *Tinker, Tailor, and Textile Worker, Class and Politics in Egypt, 1930–1952*, University of California Press, 1986.

Goldschmidt, A., *Modern Egypt, The Formation of a Nation-State*, Westview Press, USA, 1988.

Gordon, J., *Nasser's Blessed Movement: Egypt's free officers and the July revolution*, Oxford University Press, USA, 1992.

Gramsci, A., *Selections from the Prison Notebooks*, Hoare, Q. and Smith G. (eds.), Lawrence & Wishart, London 1971.

Hansen, B., & Marzouk, G., *Development and Economic Policy in the UAR (Egypt)*, North Holland Publishing Company, Amsterdam, 1965.

Hansen, B., & Nashashibi, K., *Foreign Trade Regimes and Economic Development*, Egypt, National Bureau of Economic Research, New York, 1975.

Harris, L. (ed.) *Egypt: Internal Challenges and Regional Stability*, Routledge & Kegan Paul, London 1988.

Heady, F., *Public Administration, A Comparative Perspective*, Marcel Dekker, 1991.

Heyworth-Dune, G., *Egypt: the Cooperative Movement*, The Muslim World Series, no.6, Cairo, 1952.

Hicks, U.K., *Development from below: Local Government and Finance in Developing Countries of the Commonwealth*, Oxford University Press, 1961.

Hill, D.M., *Democratic Theory and Local Governments*, Allen & Unwin, 1974.

Hillal, A., (ed.) *Democracy in Egypt*, AUC, 1978.

Hinnebusch, J., *Egyptian Politics under Sadat: The post-populist development of an authoritarian modernising State*, Cambridge University Press, 1985.

Holt, P., *Egypt and the Fertile Crescent 1516–1922*, Longman, 1966.

Holt, P., (ed.) *Political and Social Change in Modern Egypt*, Oxford University Press, 1968.

Hopkins, H., *Egypt the Crucible, The Unfinished Revolution of the Arab World*, Secker & Warburg, London, 1969.

Hopkins, N.S., *Agrarian Transformation in Egypt*, West View Press, 1987.

Hopwood, D., *Egypt, Politics and Society 1945–1984*, Unwin Hyman, 1989.

Hunter, F.R., *Egypt under the Khedives 1805–1879, From Household Government to Modern Bureaucracy*, University of Pittsburg Press, 1984.

Huntington, S., *Political Order in Changing Societies*, Yale University, USA, 1968.

Huntington, S., & Weiner, M., (eds.) *Understanding Political Development*, Little & Brown, Boston, 1987.

Hussein, M., *Class Conflict in Egypt 1945–1970*, Monthly Review Press, 1973.

Ikram, K., *Egypt Economic Management in a Period of Transition*, John Hopkins University Press, 1980.

Issawi, C., *Egypt in Revolution An Economic Analysis*, Oxford University Press, 1963.

Jessop, B., *The Capitalist State: Marxist Theories and Methods*, Martin Robertson, 1982.

Jessop, B., *Nicos Poulantzas: Marxist Theory and Political Strategy*, Macmillan, 1985.

292

Joesten, J., *Nasser, the Rise to Power*, Odhams, London, 1960.

La Palombara, J., & Weiner, M., (ed.), *Political Parties and Political Development*, Princeton University Press, 1966.

Lackey, P., *Invitation to Talcott Parson's Theory*, Cap and Gown Press, 1987.

Lacouture, J., and Lacouture, S., *Egypt in Transition*, Methuen, 1958.

Laqueur, W., (ed.) *The Middle East in Transition: Studies in Contemporary History*, Routledge & Kegan Paul, London, 1958.

Lippman, T., *Egypt after Nasser: Sadat, Peace and the Mirage of Prosperity*, Paragon House, 1989.

Lockman, Z., (ed.) *Workers and Working Classes in the Middle East*, State University of New York, 1994.

Lowi, T., *The End of Liberalism: The Second Republic of the United States*, W.W. Norton, 1979.

Mabro, R., *The Egyptian Economy 1952–1972*, Clarendon Press, Oxford, 1974.

Mabro, R., & Radwan, S., *The Industrialisation of Egypt (1939–1973), Policy and Performance*, Clarendon Press, Oxford, 1976.

Macdermott, A., *Egypt from Nasser to Mubarak, a Flawed Revolution*, Croom Helm, 1988.

Macridis, Roy, (ed.), *Political Parties: Contemporary Trends and Ideas*, Harper Torchbooks, 1967.

Maddick, H., *Democracy, Decentralization and Development*, Asia Publishing House, 1963.

Mahaffy, J., *A History of Egypt under the Ptolemaic Dynasty*, Methuen, London 1899.

Mansfield, P., *Nasser's Egypt*, Penguin Books, 1969.

March, D., & Stoker, G., (eds.) *Theory and Methods in Political Science*, Macmillan, 1995.

Marei, S., *Agrarian Reform in Egypt*, Cairo, 1957.

Mayfield, J., *Local Institutions and Egyptian Rural Development*, Cornell University, New York, 1974.

Mayfield, J., *Rural Politics in Nasser's Egypt, A Quest for Legitimacy*, University of Texas Press 1971, p. 61.

MES Series, *Local Administration and Centre-Local Relations in Egypt*, No. 25 1989.

Migdal, J., *Peasants, Politics and Revolution: Pressures towards Political and Social Change in the Third World*, Princeton University Press, 1974.

Migdal, J., *Strong Societies and Weak States: State-Society Relations and State Capabilities in the Third World*, Princeton University Press, New Jersey, 1988.

Miliband, R., *Marxism and Politics*, Oxford University Press, 1977.

Montesquieu, *The Spirit of the Laws*, Hafner Publishing Company, 1949.

Montet, P., *Eternal Egypt*, Weidenfeld & Nicolson, London, 1969.

Moore, B., *Social Origins of Dictatorship and Democracy, Lord and Peasant in the Making of the Modern World*, Penguin Books, 1966.

Moore, C., *Images Of Development, Egyptian Engineers in Search of Industry*, MIT Press, 1980.

Mosca, G., *The Ruling Class*, McGraw-Hill, 1939 (1896).

Mouffe, C. (ed.) *Gramsci and Marxist Theory*, Routledge & Kegan Paul., 1979.

Nakashima, Y., *The Political Understanding of Al-Infitah al-Iqtisadi: A Case Study of Economic Liberalisation in Egypt*, Institute of Middle Eastern Studies, 1987.

Nettl, J.P., *Political Mobilisation, A Sociological Analysis of Methods and Concepts*, Faber, London, 1967.

New Left Review, *Western Marxism, New Left Review*, 1977.

Nyrop, R., (ed.), *Egypt: A Country Study*, American University, Washington, DC, 1983.

O'Brian, P., *The Revolution in Egypt's Economic System From Private Enterprises to Socialism 1952–1965*, Oxford University Press, 1966.

Olson, M., *The Logic of Collective Action*, Harvard University Press, 1975.

Oweiss, I.M. (ed.) *The Political Economy of Contemporary Egypt*, Centre for Contemporary Arab Studies, Georgetown University, Washington, 1990.

Parsons, T., *The Structure of Social Action*, The Free Press of Glencoe, 1949.

Patai, R., *The Arab Mind*, Charles Scribner', New York, 1973.

Pelorynski, Z. (ed.) *The State and Civil Society: Studies in Hegel's Political Philosophy*, Cambridge University Press, 1984.

Perez-Diaz, V., *State, Bureaucracy and Civil Society: A Critical Discussion of the Political Theory of Karl Marx*, Macmillan, London, 1978.

Perlmutter A., *Egypt The Praetorian State*, Transaction, 1974.

Polk, W., *The Arab World Today*, Harvard University Press, 1991.

Poulantzas, N., *Political Power and Social Classes*, NLB, 1975.

Poulantzas, N., *State, Power and Socialism*, NLB, 1978.

Powell, I., *Disillusion by the Nile: What Nasser has done to Egypt*, Solstice, 1967.

Putnam, R., *Making Democracy Work, Civic Traditions in Modern Italy*, Princeton University Press, 1993.

Radwan, S., & Lee, E., *Agrarian change in Egypt: An Anatomy of Rural Poverty*, Croom Helm, 1986.

Rashid, A., *Local Administration in Egypt*, Institute of Developing Economics, 1988.

Reid, D., *Lawyers and Politics in the Arab World*, 1880–1960, Bibliotheca Islamica, 1981.

Richards Alan & Martin Philip (eds.) *Migration, Mechanization and Agricultural Labor Markets in Egypt*, Westview Press, 1983.

Richards, A., & Waterbury, J., *A Political Economy of the Middle East: State, Class and Economic Development*, Westview Press, 1990.

Richards, A., *Egypt's Agricultural Development 1800–1980: Technical and Social Changes*, Westview Press, 1982.

Rostow, W., *The Stages of Economic Growth: A Non-Communist Manifesto*, Cambridge University Press, 1960.

Rush, M., *Politics and Society: An Introduction to Political Sociology*, Harvester Wheatsheaf, 1992.

Sadowsky Y., *Political Vegetables, Businessman and Bureaucrat in the Development of Egyptian Agriculture*, The Brookings Institution, 1991.

Safran, N., *Egypt in Search of Political Community: An Analysis of the Intellectual and Political Evolution of Egypt 1804–1952*, Harvard University Press, 1961.

Salamé, G., *Democracy without Democrats? The Renewal of Politics in the Muslim World*, I.B. Tauris, 1994.

Sartori, G., *Parties and Party Systems*, Cambridge University Press, 1976.

Schmitter, P., & Lehmbruch, G. (eds.) *Trends Towards Corporatist Intermediation*, Sage Publications, London, 1979.

Schumacher, E., *Small is Beautiful: A Study of Economics as if People Mattered*, Sphere Books, 1974.

Shaw, S., *The Financial and Administrative Organisation and Development of Ottoman Egypt 1517–1798*, Princeton University Press, 1962.

Singerman, D., *Avenues of Participation: Family, Politics, and Networks in Urban Quarters of Cairo*, Princeton University Press, 1995.

Smith, B.C., *Decentralisation: The Territorial Dimension of the State*, Allen & Unwin, London, 1985.

Springborg, R., *Mubarak's Egypt: Fragmentation of the Political Order*, Westview Press, 1989.

Springborg, R., *Family, Power and Politics in Egypt, Sayed Bey Marei – His Clan, Clients and Cohorts*, University of Pennsylvania Press, 1982.

Stanyer, J., *Understanding Local Government*, Martin Robertson, 1976.

Thompson, H., *Studies in Egyptian Political Economy*, AUC, 1983.

Trip, C. and Owen, R. (eds.) *Egypt under Mubarak*, Routledge, 1989.

Truman, D., *The Governmental Process, Political Interests and Public Opinion*, A knopf, New York, 1951.

UNESCO, *Sociological Theories: Race and Colonialism*, New York, 1980.

Uphoff, N., Cohen, J., & Goldsmith, A. *Feasibility and Application of Rural Development Participation*, Cornell University, 1979.

294

Van Nieuwenhuijze, C., (ed.) *Commoners, Climbers and Notables*, Brill, Leiden, 1977.

Vatikiotis, P.J., *The Egyptian Army in Politics, Pattern for New Nation?* Greenwood Press, 1975.

Vatikiotis, P.J., *Nasser and his Generation*, Croom Helm, London, 1978.

Vatikiotis, P.J., *The History of Egypt from Muhammad Ali to Sadat*, Weidenfeld & Nicolson, London, 1980.

Von Brawn, J., & De Haen, H., *The Effect of Food Price And Subsidy Policies on Egyptian Agriculture, International food Policy Research Institutes Research*, Report 42, November 1983.

Wahba, M., *The Role of the State in the Egyptian Economy: 1945–1981*, Ithaca Press, 1994.

Warriner, D., *Land Reform and Development In The Middle East*, Greenwood Press, 1962.

Waterbury, J., *Egypt: Burdens of The Past, Options for the Future*, Indiana University Press, 1978.

Waterbury, J., *The Egypt of Nasser and Sadat: The Political Economy of Two Regimes*, Princeton University Press, 1983.

Weinbaum, M., *Food, Development and Politics in the Middle East*, Westview Press, 1982.

Wendell, C., *The Evolution of the Egyptian National Image: from the Origins to Ahmad Lutfi El-Sayyed*, University of California Press, 1972.

Wheelock, K., *Nasser's New Egypt*, Stevens, London, 1960.

Wilson, J., *The Burden of Egypt, an Interpretation of Ancient Egyptian Culture*, University of Chicago Press, 1951.

Wittfogel, K., *Oriental Despotism*, Yale University Press, 1957.

Woodward, P., *Profile in Power, Nasser*, Longman, 1992.

Zohny, A., *The Politics, Economics and Dynamics of Development Administration in Contemporary Egypt*, Jerry Bedu-Addo, 1988.

Zubaida, S., *Islam, the People and the State: Political Ideas & Movements in the Middle East*, I.B. Tauris, 1993.

B) Sources in Arabic

Ahmad, A., *Al-harakat al-iIslamiyya fi Misr, wa qadaya al tahawul al-dimoqraty*, or (*The Islamic movement in Egypt and issues of Democratic Change*), al-Ahram Centre for Translation & Publication, 1995.

Al-Intikhabat Al-Barlamaniiya Fi Misr 1995, or (*1995 Parliamentary Elections in Egypt*), Centre for Political & Strategic Studies, Cairo, 1997.

Al-Sayyed, M., *Al-mujtama'a wa al-Siyasa fi Misr: Dawr jam'at al masaleh fi al-hayat al-siyasiyya al-Misriya*, or (*Society and Politics in Egypt: The Role of Interest Groups in the Egyptian Political System: 1952–1981*), Dar Al Moustakbal al-Arabi, 1983.

Ayubi, N., *Al-Dawla al Markazia Fi Misr*, or (*The Centralised State in Egypt*), Centre for Arab Unity Studies, Beirut, 1989.

Hilal, A. (ed.) *Al-nizam al-siyasi al-misri: al-tagyyir wa al-istimrar (The Egyptian Political System: change and continuity)*, The Centre for Political Research and Studies, al Nahda Library, 1988.

Imam A., *Mazbahat al-Quda* or (The Massacre of Judges), Madbouli Bookshop, Cairo.

Intikhabat Majlis Al Sha'b 1990: Dirasa Wa Tahlil, or (*The 1990 elections for the People's Assembly: Study and Analysis*), The Centre for Political and Strategic Studies, Cairo University, 1991.

Intikhabat Majlis Al Sha'b 1984: Dirasa Wa Tahlil, or (*The 1984 elections for the People's Assembly: Study and Analysis*), The Centre for Political and Strategic Studies, Cairo University, 1985.

Kharbousch, M. (ed.) *Al-tatawwur al-siyasi fi Misr 1982–1992* (Political Development in Egypt 1982–1992), Centre for Political Research and Studies, Cairo University, 1994.

Qandil A., *'Amaliyyat Al-Tahawul Al Dimuqraty Fi Misr, 1981–1993* (The Process of Democratic Change in Egypt 1981–1993) Ibn Khaldoun Centre for Developmental Studies, 1995.

Qandil A. *'Al-dawr al-siyasi li jama'at al-masalih fi misr: dirasa li-halat niqabat al-atibaa'*, or (The Political Role of Interest groups in Egypt: A case study of the Doctors' Syndicate), Centre for Political & Strategic Studies, 1995.

Ramadan, A., *Sir'a al-Tabaqat Fi Misr* or *(Class Struggle in Egypt 1837–1952)*, al-Mou'asassa al-Arabia Lil Dirasat Wal Nashr, 1978.

Rizk, Y., *Al Ahzab Al Siyasiya Fi Misr 1907–1984 OR (Political Parties in Egypt 1907–1984)*, Dar al-Hilal, Cairo, 1984.

2. Articles and Unpublished Papers

A) Sources in English

Abdalla, N., 'Egypt's Absorptive Capacity During 1960–1972', *The International Journal of Middle East Studies*, 16, 1984, pp. 177–198.

Ajami, F., 'The Sorrows of Egypt', *Foreign Affairs*, 74, 1995, pp. 72–88.

Almond, G., 'A Developmental Approach to Political Systems', *World Politics*, 2, 1965, pp. 183–214.

Al-Sayyid, M., 'Professional Association and National Integration in the Arab World, with special reference to Lawyers Association', in Dawisha A., & Zartman I. (ed.) *Beyond Coercion, the Durability of the Arab State*, Croom Helm, 1988, pp. 88–115.

Ansari, H., 'Egypt: Repression and Liberalisation', *Current History*, 86, 1987, pp. 77–80 & 84.

Ansari, H., *'Mubarak's Egypt', Current History*, January 1985, pp. 21–24 & 39–40.

Auda, G., 'Local Government/Administration and Development: Political Context and Dynamics in the post-Nasser Era', in *Local Administration and Centre-Local Relations in Egypt*, MES Series, no.25, 1989, pp. 37–131.

Ayubi, N., 'Domestic Politics', in Harris, L. (ed.) *Egypt: Internal Challenges and Regional Stability*, Routledge & Kegan Paul, London, 1 988, pp. 49–78.

Ayubi, N., 'Local Government and Rural Development in Egypt in the 1970s', *African Administrative Sciences*, 23, 1984, pp. 61–74.

Ayubi, N., 'The Political Revival of Islam: The Case of Egypt', *International Journal of Middle East Studies*, 12, 1980, pp. 481–499.

Ayubi, N., 'Government and the State in Egypt Today', in Trip, C. and Owen, R. (eds.) *Egypt under Mubarak*, Routledge, 1989, pp. 1–20.

Baer, G., 'The Dissolution of the Egyptian Village Community', *The World of Islam*, 6, 1959, pp. 56–70.

Baer, G., 'Social Change in Egypt', in Holt, P., (ed.) *Political and Social Change in Modern Egypt*, Oxford University Press, London 1968, pp. 135–161.

Beattie, K., 'Prospects for Democratisation in Egypt', *American Arab Affairs*, 36, 1991, pp. 31–47.

Beinin, J., 'Will the Real Egyptian Working Class Please Stand Up?' in Lockman, Z. (ed.) *Workers and Working Classes in the Middle East*, State University of New York, 1994, pp. 247–270.

Bianchi, R., 'Egypt: Drift at Home, Passivity Abroad', *Current History*, February 1986, pp. 71–74 & 82–83.

Bianchi, R., 'Interest groups and public policy in Mubarak's Egypt' in Oweiss, I.M. (ed.) *The Political Economy of Contemporary Egypt*, Centre for Contemporary Arab Studies, Georgetown University, Washington 1990, pp. 210–221.

Bobbio, N., Gramsci and the Conception of Civil Society' in Mouffe, C. (ed.) *Gramsci and Marxist Theory*, Routledge and Kegan Paul Ltd., 1979, pp. 21–47.

Cardoso, F., 'On the Characterisation of Authoritarian Regimes in Latin America', in Collier D. (ed.) *The New Authoritarianism in Latin America*, Princeton University Press, 1979, pp. 33–57.

Chandra, B., 'Karl Marx, his Theories of Asian Societies and colonial rule' in *Sociological Theories: Race and Colonialism*, UNESCO publication, 1980, pp. 383–451.

Collier, D., 'Overview of the Bureaucratic-Authoritarian Model', in Collier (ed.) *The New Authoritarianism in Latin America*, Princeton University Press, USA, 1979, pp. 19–32.

Davidheiser, E., 'Strong State, Weak States, the role of the state in Revolution', *Comparative Politics*, 24, 1992, pp. 463–475.

Davis, E., 'History for the Many or History for the Few?' The Historiography of the Iraqi Working Class, in Lockman, Z., (ed.) *Workers and Working Classes in the Middle East*, State University of New York, 1994, pp. 271–301.

Deutsch, K., 'Social Mobilisation and Political Development', *The American Political Science Review*, 55, 3, September 1961, pp. 493–514.

Drower, M., 'The Political Approach to the Classical World', in Glanville, S. (ed.) *The Legacy of Egypt*, Oxford University Press, 1942, pp. 17–52.

Easton, D., 'An Approach to the Analysis of Political System', *World Politics*, 3, 1957, pp. 383–400.

Eilts, H., 'Egypt in 1986: Political Disappointments and Economic Dilemmas', *Washington Quarterly*, 10, pp. 113–128.

Eisenstadt, S., 'Modernisation and Conditions for Sustained Growth', *World Politics*, 4, pp. 576–594.

El-Messiri, S., 'Tarahil Laborers in Egypt', in Richards Alan & Martin Philip (eds.) *Migration, Mechanization and Agricultural Labor Markets in Egypt*, Westview Press, USA, 1983, pp. 79–100.

El-Mikawy, N., 'The Egyptian Parliament and Transition to Liberal Democracy', in *American-Arab Affairs*, 36, 1991, pp. 18–21.

Esposito, J., 'Islam in the Politics of the Middle East', *Current History*, February 1986, pp. 53–57 & 81.

Goldberg, E., 'The Foundation of State-Labour Relations in Contemporary Egypt', *Comparative Politics*, 24, 1992, pp. 147–161.

Gordon, J., 'Political Opposition in Egypt', Current History, February 1990, pp. 65–68 & 79–80.

Harik, I., 'Mobilisation Policy and Political Change in Rural Egypt', in Antoun Richard & Harik Ilya (eds.) *Rural Politics and Social Change In The Middle East*, Indiana University Press, 1972, pp. 287–314.

Harik, I., 'The Single Party as a Subordinate Movement. The case of Egypt', *World Politics*, 26, 1973, pp. 80–105.

Harik, I., 'Continuity and Change in Local Development Policies in Egypt from Nasser to Sadat', *The International Journal of Middle East Studies*, 16, 1984, pp. 43–66.

Heaphey, J., 'The Organisation of Egypt', *World Politics*, 18, 1966, pp. 177–193.

Hill, E., 'Laws and Courts in Egypt: Recent Issues and Events concerning Islamic Law', in Owesis I. (ed.) *The Political Economy of Contemporary Egypt*, Centre for Contemporary Arab Studies, Georgetown University, 1990, pp. 240–264.

Hinnebusch, R., 'Political Participation and the Authoritarian-Modernising State in the Middle East: Activists in Syria and Egypt', *Journal of Arab Affairs*, 3, pp. 131–155.

Hinnebusch, R., 'The Reemergence of the Wafd Party: Glimpse of the Liberal Opposition in Egypt', *International Journal of Middle East Studies*, 16, 1984 pp. 99–121.

Hinnebusch, R., 'Egypt under Sadat: Elite, Power Structure and Political Change in a Post-populist State', *Social Problems*, 28, 4, 1981, pp. 442–464.

Hinnebusch, R., 'The Formation of the Contemporary Egyptian State from Nasser and Sadat to Mubarak', in Oweiss, I.M. (ed.) *The Political Economy of Contemporary Egypt*, Centre for Contemporary Arab Studies, Georgetown University, Washington 1990, pp. 188–209.

Hirabayashi, G., & al-Khatib, M., 'Communication and Political Awareness in the Villages of Egypt', *Public Opinion Quarterly*, 12, 1958, pp. 357–363.

Huntington, S., 'Political Development and Political Decay', *World Politics*, 3, 1965, pp. 386–430.

Ino, T., 'Democratisation and Local Government in Egypt', in *Local Administration and Centre-Local Relations in Egypt*, MES Series, No. 25 1989, pp. 5–34.

Itling, K., 'Hegel's Concept of the State and Marx's early Critique', in Pelorynski, Z. (ed.) *The State and Civil Society: Studies in Hegel's Political Philosophy*, Cambridge University Press, 1984, pp. 93–113.

Jessop, B., 'Corporatism, Parliamentarism, and Social Democracy', in Schmitter, P., & Lehmbruch, G., *Trends Towards Corporatist Intermediation*, Sage Publications, London, 1979, pp. 185–212.

Johnston, M., 'The Political Consequences of Corruption', *Comparative Politics*, 18, 1986. pp. 459–477.

La Palombara, J., & Weiner, M., (ed.), 'The Origin and Development of Political Parties', in: *Political Parties and Political Development*, Princeton University Press, 1966, pp. 3–42.

Lehmbruch, G., 'Liberal Corporatism and Party Government', *Comparative Political Studies*, 10, April 1977, pp. 91–126.

Lindblom, C., 'The Market as Prison', *The Journal of Politics*, 44, 1982, pp. 324–336.

Makram-Ebeid, M., 'The Role of the Official Opposition', in Tripp, C., & Owen, R. (eds.) *Egypt under Mubarak*, Routledge, 1989, pp. 21–51.

Makram-Ebeid, M., 'Democratisation in Egypt: "The Algeria Complex"' *Middle East Policy*, 3, pp 119–124.

Malloy, J., 'Authoritarianism, Corporatism, and Mobilisation in Peru', *Review of Politics*, (36) 1974, pp. 52–84.

Marsot, A., 'Popular Attitudes toward Authority in Egypt', *Journal of Arab Affairs*, 7, pp. 174–198.

Marsot, A., 'Religion or Opposition? Urban Protest Movements in Egypt', International *Journal of Middle East Studies*, 16, 1984, pp. 541–552.

McFarland, A., 'Interest Groups and Theories of Power in America', in *British Journal of Political Science*, 17, 1987, pp. 129–147.

Merriam, J., 'Egypt Under Mubarak', *Current History*, January 1983, pp. 24–27 & 36–37.

Merrington, J., 'Theory and Practice in Gramsci's Marxism', in Western Marxism, *New Left Review*, 1977, p. 142.

Mitchell, T., 'The Invention and Reinvention of the Egyptian Peasant', *International Journal of Middle East Studies*, 22, 1990, pp. 129–150.

Moore, C., 'Clientelist Ideology and Political Change: Fictitious Networks in Egypt and Tunisia,' in Gellner, E.,& Waterbury, J., *Patrons and Clients in Mediterranean Societies*, Duckworth, London, 1977, pp. 255–273.

Moore, C., 'Authoritarian Politics in Unincorporated Society, the case of Nasser's Egypt', *Comparative Politics*, 6, 1974, pp. 193–218.

Moore, C. 'Professional Syndicates in Contemporary Egypt', *American Journal of Arabic Studies*, 3, 1975, pp. 72–95.

Moughrabi, F., 'The Arab Basic Personality: A Critical Survey of the Literature', *International Journal of Middle East Studies*, 9, 1978, pp. 99–112.

Mubarak, H., 'What does the Gama' a Islamiya Wants? An interview with Tal'at Fu'ad Qasim', in Beinnin J., & Stork J. (eds.) *Political Islam, Essays from Middle East Report*, I.B. Taurus, 1997, pp. 314–326.

298

Murphy, C., 'An Uneasy Potent of Change', *Current History*, February, 1994, pp. 78–82.
Murphy, C., 'The Business of Political Change in Egypt,' *Current History*, January, 1995, pp. 18–22.
Najjar, F., 'Elections and Democracy in Egypt', *American Arab Affairs*, 29, 1989, pp. 96–113.
Nordlinger, E., 'Taking the State Seriously', in Huntington, S., & Weiner, M. (eds.) *Understanding Political Development*, pp. 353–390.
Norton, A., 'The Future of Civil Society in the Middle East', *Middle East Journal*, 47, 1993, pp. 205–216.
O'Donnell G., 'Tensions in the Bureaucratic-Authoritarian State and the Question of Democracy', in Collier, D. (ed.) The New Authoritarianism in Latin America, pp. 285–318.
Ossama H., 'Egypt's Open Door Economic Policy: An attempt at Economic Integration in the Middle East', *The International Journal of Middle East Studies*, 13, 1981, pp. 1–9.
Posusney, M., 'Collective Action and Workers Consciousness in Contemporary Egypt', in Lockman, Z., (ed.) *Workers and Working Classes in the Middle East*, State University of New York 1994, pp. 211–246.
Reid, D., 'The National Bar Association and the Egyptian Politics 1912–1954', *The International Journal of African Historical Studies*, 7, 1974, pp. 608–643.
Reid, D., 'The Rise of Professions and Professional Organisations in Modern Egypt', *Comparative Studies in Society and History*, 16, 1974, pp. 24–57.
Rejwan, N., 'An Embattled Intelligentsia: The Case of Egypt 1962–1987', *Middle East Review*, 21, 1988, pp. 54–61.
Richards, A., 'The Agricultural Crisis in Egypt', *The Journal of Development Studies*, 16, 1980, pp. 303–321.
Richards, A., 'The Political Economy of Dilatory Reform: Egypt in the 1980's', *World Development*, 19, 1991, pp. 1724–1729.
Rodrik, D., 'Rural Transformation and Peasant Political Orientations in Egypt and Turkey', *Comparative Politics*, July, 1982, pp. 417–441.
Rondinelli, D.A., 'Government Decentralisation in Comparative Perspective: Theory and Practice in Developing Countries', *International Review of Administrative Science*, 47, 1981, pp. 134–145.
Roy, D., 'The Hidden Economy of Egypt', Middle Eastern Studies, 28, 1992, pp. 689–711.
Sadowsky, Y., 'The New Orientalism and the Democracy Debate', in Beinin, J., & Stork, J. (ed.) *Political Islam, Essays From Middle East Report*, pp. 33–50.
Schmitter, P., 'Modes of Interest Intermediation and Modes of Societal Changes in Western Europe' in Schmitter, P., & Lehmbruch, G. (eds.), *Trends Towards Corporatist Intermediation*, Sage Publications, London, 1979, pp. 63–94.
Shukrallah, H., 'The Impact of the Islamic Movement in Egypt', *Feminist Review*, 47, 1994, pp. 15–34.
Singer, H., 'The Socialist Labour Party: A Case Study of a Contemporary Egyptian Opposition Party', *Cairo Papers in Social Science*, The American University in Cairo, 16, 1993, pp. 1–69.
Smith M., 'Pluralism' in March, D., & Stoker, G. (eds.) *Theory and Methods in Political Science*, Macmillan Press, 1995, pp. 209–227.
Springborg, R., 'Sayed Bey Marei and Political Clientelism in Egypt', *Comparative Political Studies*, 12, 1979, pp. 259–288.
Springborg, R., 'Agrarian Bourgeoisie, Semiproletarians, and the Egyptian State: Lessons for Liberalization', *International Journal of Middle East Studies*, 22, 1990, pp. 447–472.
Springborg, R., 'Professional Syndicates in Egyptian Politics, 1952–1970', *International Journal of Middle East Studies*, 9, 1978, pp. 275–295.
Springborg, R., 'State-Society Relations in Egypt: The Debate Over Owner-Tenant Relations', *Middle East Journal*, 45, 1991, pp. 232–249.

Springborg, R., 'The President and the Field Marshal: Civil-Military Relations in Egypt Today', *Middle East Report*, 147, 1987, pp. 10–15.

Taylor, G., 'Marxism', in March, D., & Stoker, G., (eds.) *Theory and Methods in Political Science*, Macmillan Press, 1995, pp. 248–268.

Vatikiotis, P.J., 'Some Political Consequences of the 1952 Revolution in Egypt', in Holt, P.M. (ed.) *Political and Social Change in Modern Egypt*, Oxford University Press, London 1968, pp. 362–387.

Waterbury, J., 'Corruption, Political Stability and Development: Comparative Evidence from Egypt and Morocco', *Government and Opposition*, 11, 1976, pp. 426–445.

Waterbury, J., 'Endemic and Planned Corruption in a Monarchical Regime', *World Politics*, 25, 1972–1973, pp. 533–555.

Waterbury, J., 'The Soft State and the Open Door: Egypt's Experience with Economic Liberalisation', 1974–1984, *Comparative Politics*, 18, 1985, pp. 65–83.

Waterbury, J., 'Democracy without Democrats? The Potential for Political liberalisation in the Middle East', in Salamé, G., *Democracy without Democrats? The Renewal of Politics in the Muslim World*, I.B. Tauris, 1994, pp. 23–47.

Wiarda, H., 'Corporatism and Development in the Iberic-Latin World: Persistant Strains and New Variations', *Review of Politics*, (36), 1974, pp. 3–51.

B) Sources in Arabic

Al-Shurbaji, A., 'Al-qadaya al-Dusturiyya wa al-qanuniyya fi fatrat riyasat Mubarak al-thaniyya' or (The Constitutional and Legal Cases during Mubarak's Second Presidency) in Kharbousch, M. (ed.) *Al-tatawwur al-siyasi fi Misr 1982–1992*, Centre for Political Research and Studies, Cairo University, 1994, pp. 38–70.

Dorgham, A., 'Hizb al-wafd wa fuqdan al-tawazun:dirasa tahliliyya li dawr al-wafd fi al-ma'araka al-intikhabiyya fi abril 1987' or (The Wafd Party and the Imbalance, an analytical analysis for the role of the Wafd in 1987), in Hilal, A., (ed.) *Al-Nizam al-Siyasi al-Misri*, Centre for Political Research and Studies, El Nahda Library, 1988, pp. 393–430.

Hassan, I., 'Hizb El Tagammuu', al-binya wal-dawr al-Siyasi fi itar al-ta'addudiyya al-siyasiyya al-muqayyada' or (The Tagammu Party: The Structure and Political Role in the Controlled Multiparty System) In Kharboush, M., (ed.) *Al-Tatawur al-Siyasi Fi Misr 1982–1992*, Centre for Political Research and Studies, Cairo University, 1994, pp. 375–437.

Makram-Ebeid, M., 'Dawr hizb al-Wafd al-jadid fi itar al-mouarada al-siyasiyya' or (The Role of the New Wafd Party as a Political Opposition). In Hilal, A. (ed.) *Al Nizam al-Siyasi al-Misri: Al Tagyyir Wa al-Istimrar*, Centre for Political Research and Studies, El Nahda Library, 1988, pp. 467–496.

Nafaa, H., 'Al-idara al-siyasiyya li-azmat al-tahawul min nizam al-hizb al-wahid ila nizam ta'adod al-ahzab' or (The Political Management for the Crisis of Change from the One Party System to a Multiparty System. In Hilal, A. (ed.) *A-nizam al-siyas al-misri: al-tagyir wal-istimrar*, Centre for Political Research and Studies, El Nahda Library, 1988, pp. 29–70.

Nour al-Din, I., 'Athar al-inshiqaq 'ala al-ada' al-siyasi li hizb al-'amal' or (The Effect of the split on the performance of the Labour Party) in Kharboush (ed.). *Al-Tatawur Al-Siyasi Fi Misr 1982–1992*, Centre for Political Research and Studies, Cairo University, 1994, pp. 343–374.

Qandil, A., 'Al-Jara' im Al Iqtisadiya Al-Mustahdatha fi Al-Niqabaat Al-Mihaniya, Dirasa li halit niqabit al Muhandesiin', or (The Modern Crimes in Professional Syndicates: a case study of the Engineers Association), The National Centre for Social and Political studies, the 18th

International conference for analytical stastics and calculations and social and population research, Al-Shu biya Al Ijtima iya, 1992, pp. 1–31.

Qandil, A., '*Al-Jama' at al-mihaniya wa al-musharaka al-siyasiya*', or (*Professional Groups and Political Participation*), a report presented to the Symposium for Political Participation in Egypt, the Arab Centre for Research 1992, pp. 1–32.

Qandil, A., '*Jama't al Masaleh wa al Siyasa al Kharijiya: Dirasa li Dor Rijal al A'amal fi Misr*', or (*Interest Groups and Foreign Policy: A Case Study of the Role of Business Men in Egypt*) paper presented to the Second Conference on Political Research, Centre for Political Research and Studies, pp. 1–26.

Qandil, A., '*Taqyim ada al-islamiyin fi al-niqabat al-mihaniya,*' or (*An Evaluation of the Performance of the Islamists in Professional Syndicate*) A report presented to the 5th Franco-Egyptian Symposium (The Phenomenon of Political Violence), Research Centre for Political Studies, University of Cairo, 1993, pp. 1–36.

Zahran, G., 'Al-dawr al-siyasi lil-qada' al-misri fi 'amaliyyat sana' al-qarar, diraset al Hiqbat al ua lil ra'is Mubarak' or (The Political Role of the Egyptian Judiciary in the First Decade Of Mubarak's rule) In Hilal A. (ed.) *Al Nizam Al Siyasi Al Misri: Al Taghayyur Wa Al-Istimrar*), The Centre for Political Research and Studies, Al Nahda Library, 1988 pp. 277–314.

Zahran, G., 'Al Mustaqillun,' or (The Independents) In *Intikhabat Majlis Al Sha'b 1990: Dirasa Wa Tahlil*, The Centre for Political and Strategic Studies, Cairo University, pp. 198–207.

3. Unpublished Thesis & Dissertations

Al-Shinawy, M.A., *Community Development and Local Government in the Developing Nations: A Study Based on the Experience of the United Arab Republic (Egypt), India, and Pakistan*, Ph.D. dissertation, New York University 1964.

Al-Meehy, T., *The Relative Autonomy of the State*, Master dissertation, AUC, 1994.

Al-Menoufy, K., *Al Thaqafa Al Siyasiya Lelfalahin Al Masriyyin* or (*The Political Culture of the Egyptian Peasants*), Ph.D. thesis, Faculty of Economics and Political Science, Cairo University, 1978.

Al-Shafei, O., *Workers' Struggle in Mubarak's Egypt*, Master dissertation, AUC, 1993.

Dijani, N., *Corporatism within the Egyptian Context, a Profile of Business & Professional Politics in Egypt*, Master Thesis, AUC, 1982.

Fakhouri, H., *Kafr-El-Elow: An Egyptian Village in Transition*, Ph.D. dissertation, Michigan State University, 1969.

Nassouhy, M., *Local Autonomy under National Planning: The Egyptian Experience*, Ph.D. dissertation, University of Southern California, 1965.

Springborg, R., *The Ties that Bind: Political Associations and Policy making in Egypt*, Ph.D. dissertation, Stanford University, 1974.

4. Official Documents and Reports

Al-Intikhabat Al-Barlamaniiya Fi Misr 1995, al-Ahram Centre For Political & Strategic Studies, Cairo, 1997.

Al-Taqrir Al-Istratiji Al-Arabi for the years 1985–1997, al-Ahram Center for Political and Strategic Studies, Cairo.

Constitution of the ARE.

Kanoun al-'Umad wa al Mashaiek, (The Law of 'Umad and Shaiks, 1993).

Kanoun Nizam al-Idara al-Mahalya Wa Laihatoho al-Tanfizia, (The Local Administration Law and its executive forum, Egypt, 1989).

Taqrir al Mougtamaa al Madani, 1995, Ibn Khaldoun Centre, Cairo, 1996.

The Egyptian Village Directory, the Information and Decision Making Centre, al-Menia Governorate.

The Information and Decision Making Centre, the Periodic Bulletin, al-Menia Governorate, 1993.

The report of the Egyptian National Committee for overseeing the 1995 parliamentary elections.

The Statistical Directory for 1992, the Central Statistical Department, al-Menia governorate.

5. Newspapers

Akhbar Al Youm daily Newspaper.
Al-Ahaly daily Newspaper.
Al-Ahram daily Newspaper.
Al-Ahram Weekly.
Al-Hayat Arab Affairs.
Al-Shaab Newspaper.
Al-Wasat.
Cairo Times.
Middle East Times.
The financial Times.
Al-Shark al-Awsat daily Newspaper.

6. Magazines

Al Musawer.
Ruz al-Yusuf, Weekly Magazine.
Sabah al-kheir.

Index

Note: Page numbers in **bold** type refer to **figures**. Page numbers in *italic* type refer to *tables*.

303